FREDERICK LAW OLMSTED

The American Social Experience Series

GENERAL EDITOR: JAMES KIRBY MARTIN

EDITORS: PAULA S. FASS, STEVEN H. MINTZ,

CARL PRINCE, JAMES W. REED & PETER N. STEARNS

FREDERICK LAW OLMSTED

The Passion of a Public Artist

MELVIN KALFUS

NEW YORK UNIVERSITY PRESS

NEW YORK AND LONDON

1990

Library of Congress Cataloging-in-Publication Data
Kalfus, Melvin, 1931–
Frederick Law Olmsted : the passion of a public artist / Melvin
Kalfus.
p.   cm.—(The American social experience series : 18)
Derived from the author's dissertation (New York University).
Includes bibliographical references.
ISBN 0-8147-4606-3 (alk. paper)
1. Olmsted, Frederick Law, 1822–1903.   2. Landscape architects—
United States—Biography.   I. Title.   II. Series.
SB470.O5K35   1990
712'.092—dc20   89-13981
[B]   CIP

Book design by Ken Venezio

Frederick Law Olmsted

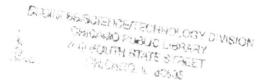

Contents

Illustrations

Acknowledgments

This book derives from my dissertation for the history department of New York University. Including the research and writing of the dissertation, my work on Frederick Law Olmsted has thus engaged me for more than twelve years. All during that period, I have been employed full-time at a New York City advertising agency. Under these circumstances, I have benefited from the encouragement, empathy, and active assistance of a great many people. Following are some of the individuals to whom I owe so much.

Carl E. Prince, former chairman of the history department, was my advisor when I enrolled in 1974. In the years since, he has become my steadfast friend, and his faith in me has helped me to keep going through the more difficult periods. As his student both inside and outside the classroom, I have learned most of what I know about the practical and the scholarly aspects of doing history. Thomas Bender is the present chairman of the history department, whom I first encountered as a teacher: my first work on Olmsted was written for his urban history seminar. Since he had already devoted considerable thought and writing both to Olmsted and to the nineteenth-century society in which Olmsted worked, Tom Bender has been the ideal critic for my own intellectual and psychological speculations. Tom served as director of my dissertation project, with Carl as codirector. Their detailed critiques of the dissertation manuscript—and their further encouragement—helped greatly in producing the book that has emerged from it.

Several others on the New York University faculty should also be mentioned. Patricia U. Bonomi was another who gave me enormous encouragement in the pursuit of my doctorate, and I learned a great deal about how to write history from her. Irwin Unger directed my first research on nineteenth-century gentry intellectuals as a group, and my later work has benefited from the hard questions he raised. The comments of Susan Ware, Paul Baker, and Lawrence Birken, who served on my dissertation review committee, were extremely helpful in visualizing the shape and substance of this book. The book itself owes much to the editorial skill and intellectual challenge provided by Kitty Moore of New York University Press.

My use of psychological and psychoanalytic theory in cultural and intellectual history has benefited from the strong interest and editorial scrutiny of David R. Beisel, former editor of the *Journal of Psychohistory*, who published two articles of mine in that journal—including my first paper on Olmsted (in vol. 7, no. 2, 1979). His friendship and good advice have been crucial all through the years. Edmund J. Wolf, Donna B. Bushnell, and Margot Tallmer went far beyond the call of friendship in the many ways in which they lent moral support, over the years, to me and to my scholarly efforts—listening, counseling, and encouraging.

Gail T. Guillet, whom I met when she was with the Landmarks Commission of New York City, showed a strong interest in my work on Olmsted and was instrumental in the reprinting of my Olmsted article in the book she coedited with Bruce Kelly and Mary Ellen Hern, *The Art of the Olmsted Landscape.* Alexander W. Allport, then executive director of the National Association for Olmsted Parks, also provided early interest in and encouragement for my efforts, as well as practical assistance. Also helpful at critical times were Shary Page Berg, Park Manager, National Park Service who shared her time and knowledge with me on a tour of Olmsted's home and office (now a National Historical Site), and Victoria Post Ranney, editor of volume 5 of *The Papers of Frederick Law Olmsted*, who provided me with important material from Olmsted's California years. And all through my work on the Olmsted dissertation, I depended enormously upon the assistance of the personnel and resources of the magnificent Bobst Library at New York University.

Segments of part 2 of this book were originally presented as papers at the International Psychohistorical Association and Psychohistory Forum.

The comments, critiques, and suggestions of my colleagues at these meetings were always useful and provocative—and I derived much inspiration from the friendship of Melvin Goldstein, Bernard Flicker, Jerry Atlas, Paul Elovitz, Henry Lawton, and Lloyd deMause.

My deepest debt, however, is to the best of my best friends—my wife, Alma. Only she can know how much I do owe her and in how many ways. To her, and to my patient and supportive children, Suzanne, Michael, and Joshua, this book is dedicated with my love and gratitude.

I call the old time back; I bring these lays
To thee, in memory of the summer days
When by our native streams and forest ways,

We dreamed them over; while the rivulets made
Songs of their own, and the great pine-trees laid
On warm noon-lights the masses of their shade.

And *she* was with us, living o'er again
Her life in ours, despite of years and pain,—
The autumn's brightness after latter rain.

. . . Her memory makes our common landscape seem
Fairer than any of which painters dream . . .

JOHN GREENLEAF WHITTIER,
I Call the Old Time Back

Introduction

In our time, the name of Frederick Law Olmsted is most often associated with the creation of the great urban parks: Central Park in Manhattan, Prospect Park in Brooklyn, Franklin Park in Boston. Secondarily, many consider him a pioneer in the profession of landscape architecture, an urban planner, and a social philosopher, one of the first theoreticians and activists behind the national park and conservation movements.

But most of this work took place after the Civil War, when Olmsted had passed his midforties. His involvement with Central Park had begun in 1857, at the age of thirty-five, when his literary and gentry friends had assisted him in securing an appointment as Superintendent of the new park. Prior to that, he had built a public reputation as a journalist (producing three historically important books on slavery and the antebellum South) and as General Secretary of the Sanitary Commission (the Civil War precursor to the Red Cross). He had also been an apprentice merchant, a seaman, a farmer, a publisher, and the manager of a mining plantation in California.

Olmsted had never graduated from a grammar school or high school and had only sat in on some classes for a few months at Yale. His real education derived from the family and friends of his youth, his varied experience and travels, his eclectic reading, and his openness to life. Lewis Mumford has called it "American education at its best," comparable "to the very best culture of the Renaissance."[1] But Olmsted's intellectual and occupational peregrinations were also remarkably similar to Erik

I

Erikson's concept of a *psychosocial moratorium*—a period, sometimes lasting many years, during which a young person seeks to find "a niche in some section of his society." For "very gifted people," Erikson adds, such psychosocial moratoria may be "especially pronounced."[2]

Olmsted *was* a gifted individual, blessed with "one of the best minds that the Brown Decades produced."[3] But Olmsted was also a psychologically troubled individual. He was a bachelor until he was thirty-seven, when he married the widow of the younger brother to whom he had been extremely close. Following the marriage, he immediately became ill and then traveled abroad alone in search of a cure. He returned as ill as when he had left, and the illness led directly to a terrible carriage accident that nearly killed him, an accident that he caused himself. Thereafter, he suffered recurring periods of illness, numerous accidents, and increasingly painful sieges of insomnia (during which he would write reams of notes on all sorts of matters, including memories of his earliest childhood). He practiced a smothering domination of his stepson (his brother's son), John Charles Olmsted, and of his own son, Frederick Law Olmsted, Jr. Finally, in his seventies, he gradually slipped into a complete mental breakdown (signaled initially by losses of memory and paranoid suspicions of his stepson). Olmsted died after a five-year confinement in an institution.

Most Olmsted biographers have dealt with Olmsted's varied occupations as discontinuities, as difficult to explain as the innumerable illnesses and accidents that occurred throughout his life or the contentiousness and obsessiveness that marked his personality. None has examined the impact upon his work and thinking of the tragic losses he endured as a child (his mother died when he was three) or of being sent away to rural boarding schools from boyhood through adolescence.

Working from Olmsted's own personal and professional writings, I seek in this study to establish the connections among these many facets of Olmsted's life and work. The study suggests that Olmsted's inner conflicts, founded in a troubled, sometimes tragic, childhood and adolescence, were bound up in his later intellectual development, including the mature philosophy of urban design that was the principal concern of his later years. It suggests that his childhood afflictions provided the inner sources of his creative imagination and of the linguistic and visual vocabulary employed in his creative work—and that these distressing early experiences were the source also of the painful narcissistic wounds that fired his ambition and led him so obsessively to seek the world's esteem through his works. Finally, it suggests that Olmsted's individual psychodynamics fitted him uniquely to the role of the creative professional in public life—to be the agent (or "delegate") for his society's needs, spoken and unspoken.

In seeking to understand the inner sources of Olmsted's lifework, I thus often focus upon Olmsted's psychological and emotional conflicts, his personal and public torments. But it must remembered that Olmsted was a strong, capable, functioning person, one who—as with so many creative people—put his own inner conflicts to constructive purpose and transformed his personal torments into works of great public good.

The following section of this introduction offers a brief, chronological sketch of the principal events and persons in Olmsted's life, focusing as much on his personal life as his professional history. The final section discusses the social and intellectual milieu in which Olmsted lived and worked.

I

Frederick Law Olmsted descended from Puritan stock, early arrivals in the New World during the seventeenth century. Numerous forebears fought in the Revolutionary War, and at least one was a hero of sorts— his father's uncle, the bachelor Gideon Olmsted.[4]

Frederick's father, John Olmsted (1791–1873), was a direct descendant of an early settler of Hartford, Connecticut. John Olmsted was one of the most admirable and likeable examples of the antebellum gentry. He was born and raised on a farm in East Hartford, but crossed the Connecticut River in 1807 to serve as an apprentice to a dry goods merchant, opening his own store in June 1815, at the age of twenty-four. His store prospered greatly, and in the 1840s he took on two of his former apprentices as partners, then sold the business to these two and another employee in 1851. The income from that sale, in addition to other successful investments, permitted him to live well, to travel, and to help support Frederick's various farming and business ventures. His journal and his letters reveal John Olmsted to have been a cultured and charitable man.

Charlotte Hull Olmsted (1800–1826) was John Olmsted's first wife, and the mother of Frederick and his younger brother, John Hull Olmsted. She was the daughter of a farmer and innkeeper, who was himself a direct descendant of an early Connecticut settler. Charlotte had apparently left her home in Cheshire while still quite young, coming to Hartford to live with her older sister, Stella, and Stella's husband, Jonathan Law.[5] Charlotte died six months after John Hull was born (when Frederick was three years, ten months old), reputedly of an overdose of laudanum taken while she was ill with influenza.

Fourteen months after Charlotte's death, John Olmsted married Mary Ann Bull (1801–1894), the daughter and sister of highly successful Hartford druggists. Mary Ann, one year younger than Charlotte, had been her friend. Her contemporaries described Mary Ann Olmsted as "a Puritan" who stressed order and system. She bore John Olmsted six children, only three of whom survived past early childhood.[6]

Just a few weeks after the first of these children, Charlotte, was christened (November 9, 1829), Frederick was sent away from home to a rural boarding school run by a minister. He was seven-and-a-half years old. Except for part of two school years, Frederick would continue to be sent to various, sometimes crude and cruel, rural boarding schools until his seventeenth year. Unlike Frederick, John Hull Olmsted—the second son of John Olmsted's first marriage—was kept at home during his childhood and attended the best schools Hartford had to offer.[7] He was a very bright student, tutored in languages and music, but was also quite a sickly child and would be subject to a variety of illnesses as he matured. At the age of fifteen, John Hull was sent to France in the company of a teacher. He was an honor student at Yale, from which he graduated in 1847, then went on to study medicine, becoming a doctor in 1851. It was while studying medicine that John Hull contracted the tuberculosis from which he would die in 1857.

While John Hull went off to Europe, Frederick—who had been studying engineering with the Reverend Frederick A. Barton—ended his school years by becoming apprenticed to a New York City dry goods importing firm, Benkard and Hutton, near Wall Street. After two unhappy years of long hours and dreary work, followed by a brief spell of idling at home in 1843, the twenty-year-old Frederick sailed to Canton as a cabinboy aboard the *Ronaldson*, passing part of the voyage below decks, suffering from recurring seasickness, paralysis of the arm, and typhoid fever.

The period between 1844 and 1850, while Frederick was still in his twenties, can be viewed as the first faltering steps at the beginning of his long search for a career—steps that were interspersed with several Eriksonian psychosocial moratoria. One of these occurred in the middle of 1844, as Frederick recovered from the ill effects of the China trip and before he was apprenticed at his uncle's farm in Cheshire. Others occurred during and after a brief career at Yale as a "special student" pursuing scientific farming, from mid-1845 to April 1846. (His few months at Yale came to an abrupt end when he suffered spells of something that seemed at the time like apoplexy.) His final moratorium period lasted until he was apprenticed to a gentleman farmer and politician, George Geddes, in Camillus, New York, an apprenticeship that also lasted but a few months. "I have looked on and talked more than I've worked," he told a friend.[8]

Joining John Hull at Yale was a crucial experience for Frederick. There he became part of his brother's New Haven circle of friends, forming a lifelong bond with Charles Loring Brace, who would become the driving force behind the Children's Aid Society in New York City, as well as a writer and civic leader. In those years—and with the inspiration of his New Haven friends—Frederick would also be aroused to furious intellectual and religious speculation and disputation. His was a generation influenced by Carlyle, Emerson, and Lowell and racked with the fever of public conversion experiences—its imagination fired both by Congregational fundamentalism and Romantic idealism. In those years, also, Frederick burned with idealistic love for a series of Connecticut belles—beginning with his hopeless yearning for Elizabeth Baldwin, the daughter of the Governor of Connecticut, and ending with a brief engagement to Emily Perkins, the niece of Harriet Beecher Stowe. And finally, in those years Frederick took up, rather fitfully, life as a farmer. His father was to purchase two different farms for him: the first in Sachem's Head, Connecticut (1847); the second at Southside, Staten Island (1848).

In 1850, two years after he moved to Staten Island, Frederick abandoned his farm during the planting season to undertake a walking trip through the British Isles and the Continent together with John Hull and Charley Brace. The English leg of this walking tour had enormous impact upon Frederick's search for a career. First, after his return to America, he produced a book—*Walks and Talks of an American Farmer in England*—

that would provide Frederick with the credentials for an attempt at a literary career in the mid-1850s and turn him finally away from farming. Second, there was the impact upon his creative imagination of the English pastoral countryside and of the great English public parks.

By the time *Walks and Talks* was published in 1852, the sectional storms of the 1850s—and the divisive political debate over slavery—were in full force. In the fall of 1852, Henry J. Raymond, editor of the *New York Daily Times*, wished to send a correspondent to the South who could objectively report on the slave states. Charley Brace proposed the recently published Olmsted as correspondent. Over the next two years, Frederick made two trips through the slave states, spending a total of some fourteen months on the road. He eventually published seventy-five dispatches in the *Times* between 1853 and 1854 and in the *New York Daily Tribune* in mid-1857.[9] These, in turn, formed the basis for three books: *A Journey in the Seaboard Slave States* (1856), *A Journey Through Texas* (1857), and *A Journey in the Back Country* (1860).

In 1855, Frederick went to his father for backing in a publishiing venture. He had been offered a junior partnership in the firm of Dix, Edwards and Company, which included the role of managing editor of its *Putnam's Monthly Magazine*. As always, John Olmsted agreed to put up the money. Frederick moved to Manhattan, while John Hull—married now and increasingly ill—took over the Staten Island farm.

Over the next two years, Frederick lived the life of a literary man and a Free-Soil activist. In 1856, he spent six months in London, representing his firm in seeking English literary works for American publication. But his publishing firm was ineptly managed and slowly declined into bank-ruptcy, failing in mid-1857, just as the great panic of that year erupted. The failure of this venture would prove to be an enduring humiliation to Frederick.

During the summer of 1857, Frederick was left alone in the depressed and at times chaotic city. John Hull had traveled with his wife and children to France, seeking a better climate for his deteriorating health. In August, while at a resort near New Haven, Connecticut, Frederick met an associate, a commissioner of Central Park, which was then under construction in Manhattan. This man told Frederick that a superinten-dent was being sought to head the labor force for that great public work, reporting to the Chief Engineer, Egbert Viele. Frederick spent the rest of the summer of 1857 canvassing votes for the job. Despite his marginal qualifications for the position, and with the support of the city's patrician and gentry leadership, he was elected to the position in September 1857.

Within two months, John Hull was dead at the age of thirty-two. "In his death I have lost not only a Son but a very good friend," John Olmsted wrote Frederick. "You, almost your only friend—."[10] But another young man came into Olmsted's life at this same time—one who would take on some of the diverse psychological roles that had been fulfilled by John Hull: friend, colleague, and rival. This man was Calvert Vaux. When the Central Park Commissioners announced a competition for a new design for the park, Vaux persuaded Olmsted to join him in submitting an entry. Their design, "Greensward," was selected over some three dozen others. The working partnership between Olmsted and Vaux would last until 1872, interrupted by the Civil War years. Their emotional attachment would last until Vaux died in the waters of Gravesend Bay in 1895, apparently a suicide.

In 1858, the selection of Olmsted and Vaux's Greensward plan meant far more for Frederick than simply a share of the prize money. He had won, for a span of time, complete control over Central Park, as Architect in Chief of Central Park, with Vaux as consulting architect. (Egbert Viele was dismissed from his office immediately after the competition was concluded.) The two shared the design responsibility for implementing their Greensward plan, while Frederick—in the superintendent function he very much coveted—was given almost complete autonomy in the direction of the work itself. In later years, Vaux stated that Olmsted had from the start seen Central Park as "a finished thing . . . as an oasis, an arcadia in the desert of brick & mortar vibrant with happy life from morning to night."[11]

In June 1859, at the height of his reign over the creation of Central Park, Frederick suddenly married his brother's widow, Mary Cleveland Olmsted, adopting the three children John Hull had left behind. (Frederick and Mary would have four children together, two of whom survived infancy.) He took his new family to live in the park, in apartments established in the Mount St. Vincent Convent. Several months later, Andrew Haswell Green (a Reform Democrat on the Park Board) was made Comptroller of the park and inexorably established his own dominion over Olmsted and the work force—putting an end to Olmsted's autonomy on the park.

In August 1860, while riding in a carriage through Central Park together with his wife and infant son, Olmsted—exhausted and in ill health —apparently dozed off, dropping the reigns. The horse bolted, and Olmsted was thrown from the carriage in a fall that smashed his left leg and very nearly killed him. Olmsted made an astonishingly quick recovery, though he was to walk with a noticeable limp and feel the pain of the once-shattered leg for the rest of his life.

By January of 1861, as another shattering was taking place—that of the Union—Olmsted made a desperate ploy to regain his lost autonomy at the park. He submitted his resignation to the Board of Commissioners, setting forth his grievances in a lengthy presentation. In the midst of this presentation, Olmsted—for the first time—asserted his ultimate contribution to the park as something stronger and more compelling than that of a superintendent of the work. "I shall venture to assume to myself the title of artist," he told the Board. He asserted that the final design—then being implemented day by day and acre by acre throughout the park— was one that existed almost exclusively in his own imagination. In emphasizing the need for a free hand in the future work, Olmsted claimed that the work done thus far was no more "than stretching the canvas & chalking a few outlines."[12]

In the event, his resignation ploy failed. That spring, he was granted more autonomy, but this only in a very limited sphere of "finishing work," while being removed altogether from any real executive control over the park itself. In June, Olmsted was invited by Henry W. Bellows, a leading Unitarian minister and a pillar of New York's cultural and philanthropic community, to become acting secretary of the Sanitary Commission. Olmsted received a leave of absence from his position at Central Park and moved to Washington in July, just a month before the Union defeat at Bull Run.

The Sanitary Commission was one of the most extraordinary bureaucratic and organizational achievements of the Civil War—an achievement that was, until that time, unique in philanthropic endeavors. Volunteer societies, composed mainly of women, and operating under the aegis of the Commission, contributed perhaps $15 million worth of medical supplies, clothing, blankets, and other materials. The massive organization created by Olmsted efficiently processed and distributed these contributions for the use of Union soldiers and the treatment of the wounded and sick throughout all the theaters of battle. Where the Army's Medical

Bureau could not handle the needs of the wounded alone, Olmsted's cadre of professionals shared the work. The most notable of these efforts took place during the Peninsula campaign in the spring of 1862, when Olmsted personally took command of a fleet of hospital ships that plied the Pamunkey River, carrying boatloads of sick, wounded, and dying Union soldiers from Fair Oaks and other battles back to base hospitals, treating them en route with a mixed crew of professional and volunteer workers.[13]

In mid-1863, Olmsted was once again exhausted and demoralized, worn out from increasing disagreements and quarrels with the Executive Committee of the Sanitary Commission—quarrels that were complicated by factional disputes within the Commission. As at Central Park, he began to see himself and his enterprise as doomed to failure. Frequently ill, Olmsted was ordered to make a tour of the Western theater, during which he began writing notes and essays for a proposed masterwork on the advance and decline of civilization in the United States. Upon his return, Olmsted spent his time partly in confrontations with Bellows and the Executive Committee and partly in promoting a proposed loyalist weekly newspaper, of which he hoped to become managing editor.

In mid-1863, Olmsted was suddenly offered the superintendence of the Mariposa (California) Mining Estate, an offer that included stock in the company. He resigned from the Sanitary Commission and sailed for California in September. There he found mines that were already largely played out and a rough, crude society: miners; vagabond adventurers; white, Mexican, and Chinese settlers; and local Indians. Olmsted brought his family out, managed the estate probably as well as it could be, and suffered continually from ailments of the head and eyes. The Mariposa stay was most notable for his involvement in a commission appointed for the preservation of the Yosemite valley and Mariposa Big Pines; his few independent assignments in landscape design; and his continued intensive and somewhat disorganized work on his "Civilization" masterwork, which he never finished. As the Civil War came to an end and the shocking news of Lincoln's assassination threw San Francisco into mourning, Olmsted seemed to reach a nadir of depletion and despair. Mariposa was in receivership and Olmsted was once again casting about for his place in life.

Throughout the spring of 1865, Calvert Vaux wrote a series of letters trying to persuade Olmsted to return to New York so that they might, in tandem, take control both of Central Park and the new Brooklyn Park, for which Vaux had already done the preliminary design. Vaux put before Olmsted a particularly ambitious vision—to undertake the "grand artwork of the Republic," a massive landscape design project that would establish a network of parks from the Atlantic shores of Brooklyn to Washington Heights along the Hudson River. After a good deal of hesitancy ("I don't consider myself an artist," Olmsted wrote Vaux), Olmsted resigned from Mariposa and returned with his family to New York in October 1865. Olmsted, Vaux, and Company was appointed landscape architect for both Central and Prospect parks.[14]

Olmsted's long-held literary ambitions sputtered to an end. He continued sporadically to accumulate notes for his "Civilization" masterwork and contributed occasionally to the *Nation*. But Olmsted, in 1866, had at last turned to the life's work for which we know him best today and to the role part 1 of this study will describe—the nineteenth century's premier landscape architect and theoretician of urban design. From this point forward, even his literary talents would be turned to these ends.

Between 1866 and 1868, a series of major proposals and plans, undertaken with Vaux, revealed the fusion that had taken place in Olmsted's mind between the principles of naturalistic landscape design and the psychological needs engendered by an increasingly urbanized society. In that period, Olmsted and Vaux issued reports and proposals for projects including: Prospect Park and Eastern Parkway in Brooklyn; a proposed urban park in San Francisco; a proposed campus at Berkeley, California; and a planned community at Riverside, Illinois, near Chicago. In these reports and proposals, Olmsted—as the spokesman for the partnership—was able to set forth basic design principles and planning objectives for urban parks, vehicular parkways, and suburban communities. In short, within the span of two or three years, he would set forth the vision of the great metropolitan centers that would arise all across America and propose the means of making them physically and psychologically healthier and more pleasing places in which to live and work.

In 1870, Olmsted gave an important address before a Boston meeting of the American Social Science Association, of which he had been a founder, an address that he later published as a pamphlet: *Public Parks and the Enlargement of Towns*.[15] Central Park was the great example that Olmsted set before this audience, and to them he admitted that most

New Yorkers had yet even to lay eyes on this great new urban park—for it was still four miles away from the center of population, and there was as yet no transit system to carry the general populace there for a convenient outing. "For practical everyday purposes to the great mass of people," Olmsted said, "the Park might as well be a hundred miles away." But Olmsted reminded his audience that Central Park had not been planned and built for the needs of their day alone, "but with regard to the future use, when it will be in the centre of a populatiion of two millions hemmed in by water at a short distance on all sides." It was for the sake of these great metropolises to come, and the people who would have to live and work in them, that Olmsted urged his urban design principles upon his gentry and patrician audience—in order to gain for this posterity "tranquility and rest to the mind."

Throughout the next dozen years, Olmsted's preeminence as a landscape architect, public and private, became solidified. He worked on the U.S. Capitol grounds, laid plans for the development of the North Bronx and Riverdale in New York, consulted on the preservation of the grounds surrounding Niagara Falls, helped to plan the completion of the New York State Capitol Building at Albany, and did landscape design for a score of private estates belonging to the barons of the Gilded Age (most notably in Newport, Rhode Island). By the end of his career, Olmsted would be the peer, and sometimes the working partner, of the leading architects of his age: H. H. Richardson, Leopold Eidlitz, D. H. Burnham, and Richard Morris Hunt.

In the first dozen years after his return from California, it was the New York parks—most especially Central Park—that commanded Olmsted's primary allegiance and his psychic energy. He battled continuously with colleagues and critics, commissioners, politicians, and journalists to assure that *his* vision of what an urban park should be would become reality. This "war," as Olmsted termed it, continued to take a terrible toll upon him, physically and mentally. He had a spell of temporary blindness in 1873, several months after the death of his father, John Olmsted. And by the end of 1877, he had to take a leave of absence from his position with the New York parks in order to travel abroad, in the hope of regaining his strength and a degree of psychological equilibrium. In the midst of this leave, the Board of Commissioners removed him from his post. His connection with Central Park had at last come to an end.

Brooding over this disaster, Olmsted poured out his bitterness in a pamphlet (published in 1882) he called—in words that would resonate in particular with the Mugwump intelligentsia of New York and New England—*Spoils of the Park: With a Few Leaves from the Deep-Laden Notebooks of "A Wholly Impractical Man."*[16] After two decades of struggle against a variety of political and mercantile figures who, at various times, held power over the creation and operation of Central Park, Olmsted had finally gone public with this anguished outcry against what he saw as the ruination of the park by these powerful, so-called practical men. These hack politicians, real estate developers, merchants, and bankers, Olmsted charged, had brought nothing to urban planning but a thirst for patronage, a hunger to extract some personal profit, or the chance to foist some pet projects or misguided "improvements" upon the public's parks.[17]

Removal from his position on the New York parks led Olmsted to remove himself altogether from the city with which he had had such an ambivalent relationship over the prior three decades. He relocated both his home and his office to Brookline, Massachusetts, where he would remain for the rest of his career. His office there became a training ground for talented young landscape architects, several of whom Olmsted made his partners—including his stepson, John Charles Olmsted, and his son, Frederick Law Olmsted, Jr., called Rick. The office would be responsible for the development of the Boston park system over the next two decades, including another of Olmsted's great urban parks, Franklin Park. That, the World Columbian Exposition in Chicago, and the Biltmore estate in Asheville, North Carolina (for George W. Vanderbilt) would be Olmsted's principal preoccupations for the last five years of his working life.

It was in the midst of an almost obsessive supervision of the work at the Biltmore estate that Olmsted began to slip into the final illness of his life—the mental illness that ended his career in 1895. In 1898, he was confined to the McLean Institute in Boston, where he died in 1903. Guided by John Charles and Rick, Olmsted Associates would continue to be an influential and successful landscape design firm for decades to come.

II

Olmsted's life spanned the greater part of the nineteenth century, encompassing decades of tremendous conflict and change both within the nation at large and within his own immediate social group, which Stow Persons has called the American gentry.[18] Even the statistical evidence supplies only a skeletal idea of the vast scope of the dramatic changes that took place in American life between 1840 and 1890—that is, between the time when most of these postwar gentry leaders had come to adulthood and the decade when most had retired from public life.

The country itself nearly doubled in territorial size, growing from a nation centered east of the Mississippi to a transcontinental colossus. The population nearly quadrupled in half a century, from some 17 million (smaller than New York or California today) to more than 63 million. The major reason, of course, was the floodtide of immigration that packed the eastern cities and swelled the internal migration to the open lands of the West. In the nation of Olmsted's youth, New York, Boston, and Philadelphia were still compact little cities whose length and breadth one could walk (George Templeton Strong, the Wall Street lawyer and diarist, frequently recorded such walks). By 1890, New York numbered more than a million people and was about to incorporate surrounding communities like Brooklyn into an even greater metropolis. Urban sprawl was under way in the major cities of the East, and all across the nation sturdy towns and cities now existed where there were, at best, villages fifty years before.

Linking together this still-burgeoning transcontinental giant were the telegraph and railroad—the mechanism of union in so large a nation. The telegraph was a quirky invention in the 1840s; by 1890, over 19,000 offices transmitted nearly 56 million messages annually, and there were already 234,000 telephones installed. There were but 2,800 miles of railroad in 1840, but by 1890, these had grown to some 167,000 miles. The young nation had required an energy production of 8.5 million horsepower in 1850 (the first year for which energy production is estimated); in 1890, that had grown to more than 44 million—this even before the age of electricity had arrived.

Of course the greatest impact upon the mentalities of those who lived through this period was in the almost revolutionary effect of these changes upon the way in which they conducted their lives. In the antebellum decades, John Olmsted regularly visited New York on behalf of his dry goods establishment; during three decades of business life recorded in his journals, his transportation changed from stagecoach, to steamboat, to "rail cars." After the Civil War, his son would later use the transcontinental railroads to engage in landscape architecture projects from coast to coast. And, toward the end of the century, his firm would also record its various projects with a Kodak camera.

Even in the 1840s, Americans had grown accustomed to rapid change: the materialists praised what had been accomplished; the idealists bemoaned the distance between American potential and American actuality. "Ah my country! In thee is the reasonable hope of mankind not fulfilled," Emerson complained in 1838. "It should be that when all the feudal straps & bandages were taken off an unfolding of the Titans had followed & and they had laughed & leaped young giants along the continent & ran up the mountains of the West with the errand of Genius & of love."[19] But idealists shared with the materialists a great optimism in the future: "Fear haunts the building of the railroad," Emerson wrote in 1843, "but it will be American power & beauty, when it is done." It was an optimism that allowed idealists like him to share in the ethnocultural sense of manifest destiny, even as they resisted it on political grounds. Thus, even though Emerson opposed the annexation of Texas in 1844, he could still write:

It is very certain that the strong British race which have now overrun so much of the Continent, must also overrun that tract & Mexico & Oregon also, and it will in the course of time be of small import by what particular occasions & methods it was done. It is a secular question.[20]

Robert Wiebe observes that despite this dynamic growth, America remained a nation of "island communities" for most of the nineteenth century. People, especially middle-class people, defined themselves by their roles and their status within the locality in which they lived. But as these island communities disintegrated, "certain Americans sought to transcend rather than preserve them." A new middle class began to form, whose members identified themselves "more by their tasks in the urban-industrial society than by their reputations in a town or a city neighborhood." Professionalization became the new pathway to middle-class status in "the rising scientific-industrial society."[21]

In fact, as early as midcentury, men like Olmsted, the art historian Charles Eliot Norton, and the journalist E. L. Godkin embraced this kind of professionalism. Thomas Bender refers to such men as "the metropoli-

tan gentry"—young gentry intellectuals who sought positions of leadership in their society by means of cultural activities, especially through the
sort of literary journalism offered by publications like *Putnam's Monthly*
and the *Nation*.[22] These cultivated professionals consciously sought to
foster a "translocal" outlook among an enlightened citizenry—a nationalism that would overcome the predominant American parochialism. In the
latter decades of the century, however, they and their peers would be
swept away by the processes they had helped to stimulate. They would
blame their painful loss of power and influence upon the selfish individualism and materialism of the American masses.[23]

By 1873, Norton was already looking back at early nineteenth-century
New England as a sort of Golden Age, "the pure and innocent" America
that existed "before 1830 . . . before General Jackson was chosen President and we had entered onto the new and less child-like epoch of our
modern democracy." And twenty-five years later, he recalled again, long-
ingly, "that very pleasantest little oasis of space and time," a time whose
spirit had been embodied "in Emerson, in Longfellow, in Holmes, in
Lowell."[24]

The world that Norton recalled was one in which his father, Andrews
Norton, had had a most secure and influential place. The elder Norton is
sometimes referred to as "the Unitarian pope of New England," a scholar
from the Harvard Divinity School who led the rationalist response to the
spiritual challenge of the Transcendentalists. His son, Charles, who had
admired his father tremendously, would never know nearly as much
security or influence in American life.[25] Norton characterized the America in which he lived and worked after the Civil War as a nation in which
spiritual and intellectual enterprises were starving "in the midst of the
barbaric wealth of the richest millions of people in the world." As the
Gilded Age flowered, Norton found that there was "less civic patriotism,
less sense of spiritual and moral community," due mainly, he said, "to
the selfishness of individualism in a well-to-do democracy."[26]

Others in gentry society condemned the dominant materialism of
American society in similar terms even before the Civil War. George
Templeton Strong was only nineteen when he noted his detestation of "a
rich commercial city." And he was twenty-four when he complained
about the barren political choice that had been put before the country:
the Democrats, who fostered "the jacobinical spirit and the antipathy to

law and order and the overthrow of everything worth preserving," or the
Whigs, a "money-worshipping" party that would create "a commercial
aristocracy" meaner than "the world has seen yet."[27]

In 1856, Julia Ward Howe begged her brother (the future lobbyist Sam
Ward) to give up the "enemy country" of business for "the old Puritan
morals, the only ones for the Anglo-Saxon race." In place of "the acquisition of wealth," she urged upon him the "simple life," the "sweet
touches of Nature," Beethoven and Emerson and "the good and beautiful
things." Nor was this an idiosyncracy of New Englanders. Even earlier,
in 1843, Sam Ward had heard a similar lecture from the patrician New
Yorker, Washington Irving, who noted that the pursuit of wealth "rapidly
demoralizes the community," sweeping away "all moral restraints . . . all
generous sentiments and all rules of justice." In a fine Romantic attack
upon the realities of commercial utilitarianism, Irving charged that the
money-making passion "dissolves societies into individualities, each man
becomes avaricious and insatiable, distrustful and selfish."[28]

Henry Adams, in his *Education of Henry Adams*, lamented the state of
Gilded Age America as strongly as Norton had. The main difference
between the two was that Adams recognized that the tension between
idealism and materialism had been there at the founding: it was a tension
he had come to personalize within himself, the "inherited quarrel" between the Quincy statesmen of the Adams family and the Boston bankers
and merchants of the Brooks family. He himself could never be convinced
"that moral standards had nothing to do with it, and that utilitarian
morality was good enough for him." But after 1865, he admitted, materialism had triumphed and American society had become "a banker's world"—
moral law had expired in the age of Grant. "The system of 1789 had
broken down," Adams wrote, "and with it the eighteenth-century fabric
of *a priori*, or moral principles." He could only bemoan, in *Education* and
(even more) in his private letters, the uninhibited growth of America's
capitalistic system—a system that "ruthlessly stamped out the life" of the
class into which he had been born, creating the monopolies that alone
seemed able to control "the new energies that America adored."[29]

In his notes for a projected masterwork on civilization in the United
States, Olmsted also saw the divergent forces of idealism and materialism
as contending for the ultimate character of the American nation, although
he cast the struggle more in terms of the two "strains" he saw in the
American democracy—a strain toward civilization and a strain toward

barbarism. The problems in American democracy lay not with its common men and women, whose vices foreign travelers so loved to enumerate, Olmsted wrote. Their barbarous behavior was to be expected, for "the fountain head of the stream of American civilization . . . was not in the civilization of Europe, but in the uncivilization of Europe." But the common people were educable; they could be taught to exercise self-restraint and to pursue cooperative efforts for the common good—so long as the communities in which they lived provided civilizing institutions and associations. The great problem for Olmsted, as for Henry Adams, lay with the actions of "practical men"—selfish individualists who "have been in the habit of considering every public question with regard to its relations direct or remote upon their own business."[30]

But unlike Norton and Adams, Olmsted was never to turn his back on the process of modernization and the society it had created. When in his later years he looked back to the decades of his youth, he saw no golden age to lament. Writing to Brace in 1887, Olmsted saw all about him signs of the "amazing progress" New England had made since his youth. In spite of the growth of "a wretched leisure class" and a consequent "spread of anarchism," Olmsted added, "I can't think that in any half century before the [world] has advanced nearly as far as in the last." He thought of himself and his friends as "exceedingly blessed."[31]

Gentry intellectuals took from the great English Romantics and Victorians—Coleridge, Wordsworth, Carlyle, and Ruskin—an idealist vocabulary and perhaps even a bill of particulars, for both their reform movements and their later dissent from rampant materialism.[32] The idealism of these English thinkers served the American gentry intellectuals as a rebuke to the values and the behavior of the mercantile-industrial society for which they shared such a great distaste. And this idealism reinforced the need, felt by most, to distance themselves from that society—to serve, if not as its reformers, then as its most trenchant critics.

But the most powerful English influence upon gentry intellectuals like Olmsted and Norton was surely John Stuart Mill.[33] Mill's idealism was a modification, an enlargement, of Utilitarianism—a wedding of the Romantic dissent from capitalistic materialism with the practical spirit of Utilitarianism. Thus, Mill's writings provided gentry intellectuals with a rationale for participating in a materialistic society even while they sought to serve as its critics and reformers.[34]

Mill's argument in *On Liberty*, inspiring in its generality, was essentially elitist in its particularity, greatly concerned, as it was, with the preservation of individual liberty for "the best men" (his term), to whom would fall the responsibility of social reform and cultural leadership. "The initiation of all wise or noble things comes and must come from individuals; generally at first from some one individual," Mill wrote. "The honor and glory of the average man is that he is capable of following that initiative, that he can respond to wise and noble things, and be led to them with his eyes open." In modern society, where "the opinions of masses of merely average men are everywhere become or becoming the dominant power," Mill added, the only corrective was in the example set by "exceptional individuals," "those who stand on the higher eminences of thought."[35]

The *idealism* of Millite Utilitarianism lay in the concept that protection of individual liberty must not be seen as a license for the few to obtain their own well-being, or profit, at the expense of the many, and the talented elite received no sanction, from Utilitarian philosophy, to exploit the common weaknesses of human nature. Everyone who receives "the protection of society owes a return for the benefit, and the fact of living in society renders it indispensable that each should be bound to observe a certain line of conduct towards the rest."[36]

Olmsted himelf would evolve his own Millite enlargement of Utilitarianism, made evident during his stay in California, when, as Laura Wood Roper reports, he argued that a democratic government had a right, even a duty, to preserve Yosemite Valley and Mariposa Big Pines from "private preemption" at the expense of public enjoyment. Certainly the argument could be made in a Utilitarian balance-sheet fashion, he said—for example, in the financial benefit that the commonwealth might derive from tourism. But there was a fundamentally more important consideration: "It is the main duty of government, if it is not the sole duty, to provide the means of protection for all its citizens in the pursuit of happiness against the obstacles, otherwise insurmountable, which the selfishness of individuals or combinations of individuals is liable to interpose to that pursuit."[37]

Despite the influence of the English Romantic and Victorian writers and of Mill, Olmsted and his peers all framed their struggle for identity in uniquely American terms, seeking to define not only their own identity but also a national identity. J. G. A. Pocock regards the fact that there *was* such a struggle for national self-definition as demonstrating in itself that "American culture is haunted by myths." One of these myths—politically, the chief of them—is "the republican commitment to the renovation of virtue" (the "system of 1789," in Henry Adams' words: the eighteenth-century fabric of "moral principles"). Thus, Pocock adds, the "curious extent to which the most post-modern and post-industrial of societies continues to venerate pre-modern and anti-industrial values, symbols and constitutional forms and to suffer from its awareness of the tension between practice and morality."[38]

When we consider the later careers of Olmsted and his peers—and the ideologies through which they defined themselves—we must remember that they were born during a period close to the formation of these myths and that they came to manhood during the Emersonian elaboration and exaltation of these same myths.[39] The notion that each citizen had a responsibility for the creation and maintenance of a virtuous republic had a very particular appeal to the sons of the New England antebellum gentry, as one can see from Adams' ruminations on "the system of 1789." It was a notion that gave purpose to their own ambitions—a purpose appropriate to the late Puritan milieu in which they had been born and raised. Theirs had been a religiously impelled culture that provided the terms under which its young men might properly find a place for themselves in the adult world of antebellum America. As Stow Persons observes, "the obligation to serve and elevate humanity . . . was an integral part of the gentry tradition." And Martin Duberman comments that even though the "stark theology" of Calvinism was then giving way among the gentry youth of New England, "there remained the strong moral purpose, the insistence that life was serious business, that men had the obligation to devote themselves to active usefulness."[40]

Thus, from their childhood on, young gentry intellectuals ingested two powerful, conjoining beliefs: that the useful life was one with strong moral purpose and that the arena for the creation of a useful life was within a republic of virtue. One result of these twin beliefs was that these young men were led to identify their own individual futures with that of their young country. Nevertheless, it proved extremely difficult for such men to find their appropriate roles of "active usefulness"—at least in ways that also satisfied their own inner needs. Daniel Wilson has theorized that a major problem for these men was that they were "out of joint with the larger world."[41] These sons of the antebellum gentry had reached the years of their "identity crisis" just at the point when their society was itself undergoing rapid change—at a time when the young nation was still defining itself, a time when the outlines of an unrestrained, aggressive, and enormously energetic capitalistic society were just beginning to emerge.

Olmsted's difficult struggle to find a meaningful life's work was, therefore, not an unusual one among his more gifted peers. Charles Eliot Norton had tried and failed at the importing business before fleeing the commercial world for a sort of Grand Tour abroad ("for his health"); he had never contemplated following his father, Andrews Norton, into the ministry, although he spent two years editing his father's papers after the latter's death. By the end of the Civil War, he would be a published writer and coeditor of the *North American Review*. Returning home from a long stay in Europe in 1873, Norton became professor of fine arts at Harvard, where he served till 1893. William Wentworth Story gave up his seat as a judge to pursue a career abroad as a sculptor and writer. Like Norton, he made good his escape only after the death of his father (Supreme Court Justice Joseph Story) in 1845—and only after "incessant labor" had brought on "a severe attack of brain and typhoid fever." "My mother thought me mad," he later said, "and urged me to pursue my legal career, in which everything was open to me, rather than to take such a leap in the dark." George William Curtis had tasted business as a clerk before joining the Transcendentalist utopian community at Brook Farm for two years. His four years of travel abroad afterward furnished material for several books. In 1856 he became Olmsted's partner in a publishing firm, having already taken on the editorial duties for its well-regarded magazine, *Putnam's Monthly*. After that publication failed, Curtis went on to a long career as a writer, editor, and orator. Henry Lee Higginson (later to be a financier, philanthropist, and founder of the Boston Symphony) escaped his father's business in the 1850s to study music abroad. Like Olmsted, he had abandoned academic studies (at Harvard) because of "eye trouble." Urged by his father to "come back and *earn*," he responded: "What can you offer at home? Nothing tempting." George Templeton Strong had been somewhat coerced into a law career by *his* father, but Strong's inner identity remained bound to a life of the mind, his inner self realized through the incredible diaries he kept up for forty years—diaries that, in addition to their literary, social, and historical worth, offer remarkable insight into the world of music and letters in the years surrounding the Civil War. Though he knew his career as a Wall Street lawyer and a civic leader had made him "estimable," there were times when he found his life a "dreary succession of listless, unsatisfying days, varied now and then by intense and bitter disgust at myself and everything about me."[42]

Adding to the difficulties of these gentry men was the fact that finding an appropriate career was not in itself a source of satisfaction, a reason for content. For the very notion of a career carried with it an extraordinary sense of burden—a sense that taking up *any* sort of career meant also taking up unending duties and responsibilities. Consider the implications of Olmsted's rather cool assessment of his father, John Olmsted, made shortly after the latter's death in 1873:

My father was well-fitted to live only in a highly organized community in which each man's stint is measured out to him according to his strength. As the world is going he was perhaps as fortunately placed in this regard as he well could be. Yet the world was driving along so fast that a man of any spirit could not but feel himself cruelly prodded up to take more upon himself than he was equal to.[43]

This passage is as much about Frederick as it is about John Olmsted, for clearly it was Frederick who felt *himself* "cruelly prodded up" to take on grandiose projects and numerous responsibilities—tasks that at the same time he must have feared were more than "he was equal to." Even as late as 1894, when he was almost seventy-two, Olmsted was to complain to a young associate: "I feel I have been taking on rather appalling loads," adding, however, that he could not "convict" himself of having undertaken more than was his "professional responsibilities." And to an old friend, Olmsted wrote two months later that he was "always taking on loads heavier than I can carry."[44]

On one occasion Olmsted *did* seek to avoid what promised to be a most troublesome duty. In 1883, Olmsted sought to remove himself from the committee appointed for the creation of a national park at Niagara Falls —having learned that his old nemesis from the New York parks, Andrew H. Green, was also to be involved in the effort. Olmsted told his friends that he had to "decline any responsibility that I might have . . . and to escape my interest in it as fast and as far as I can." But Charles Eliot Norton immediately chastised Olmsted, telling Olmsted that although he might well decline any responsibility for Niagara Falls, he could *not* escape his interest in the matter. Olmsted stayed on. As it happened, Norton had held himself to this same call of duty only a few years earlier, when he commented to a friend: "My life would doubtless be better in many ways in Europe; but I should be of less service than here."[45] And their friend, the editor E. L. Godkin, suggested that the essence of being truly cultivated lay in "doing easily what you don't like to do at all."[46]

A feeling of being imprisoned by their responsibilities was thus shared by many, if not most, of Olmsted's contemporaries. Near the end of his rather short life, George Templeton Strong was named the comptroller of the Trinity Church, and he retired from his Wall Street law firm in order to accept. On the first day of his new life, Strong noted in his diary: "It seems like a dream that I should be free to keep away from Wall Street without an uneasy conscience and a feeling that someone should consider me a malingerer or a shirk. I hardly recognize myself."[47]

After service in the Union Army, Henry Lee Higginson, together with his wife, bought a plantation in the South, where he intended to employ and educate freed blacks. (Mills *Essays* was one of the books he and his wife read at night.) After the plantation failed, he finally entered his father's business—later telling a relative that "he never walked into 44 State Street without wanting to sit down on the doorstep and cry." Henry Adams would recall, forty years later, how "Henry Higginson, after a desperate struggle, was forced into State Street."[48]

These issues—of identity, of finding a place for oneself, of duty and responsibility—can also be seen as aspects of the search for authenticity in life. Raymond Williams describes the various conformist and nonconformist roles that can be adopted by an individual in defining his existential place in society, whether it be society at large or some particular segment of society.[49] Authenticity can be found in either role—can be achieved, for example, either by being a member of or by becoming a rebel against one's society. For Williams, membership means that a person

feels himself to belong to [his society], in an essential way. . . . [He] looks upon it as the natural means by which his own purposes will be forwarded . . . he is confident of the values, attitudes and institutions of the society, accepts the ways in which its life is conducted.

It is clear from Olmsted's correspondence that he more often saw himself—correctly, I think—as either a rebel or a servant. Williams defines the *rebel* as one who "fights the way of life of his society because it is wrong." The new reality that the rebel proposes—whether it be in art, religion, or politics—"is more than personal; he is offering it as a new way of life." The *servant*, on the other hand, is one who has "the illusion of choice, and is invited to identify himself with the way of life in which his place is defined." His choice is illusory, because he has no way of maintaining himself if he refuses to identify himself with (in Olmsted's case) those who employ him.[50]

The noted humanistic psychoanalyst D. W. Winnicott speaks of a *true self*, which is the seat of a person's human potential—a most sensitive part of a person's being, which, if exposed to others, could be annihilated. It is protected by a *false self*, which develops in compliance with the social demands of the person's environment. In mental health, the false self is mere facade, and the true self can assert itself if need be. At the other extreme, the false self is taken to be real, and the true self, hidden from the world, perhaps even hidden from consciousness, is allowed at best a secret life. "Only the True Self can be creative and only the True Self can feel real," Winnicott writes. For him, a person who feels dominated by the false self may achieve an enviable worldly success (particularly in the intellectual sphere), yet derive no satisfaction from his or her accomplishments or personal relationships.[51]

In this manner, contemporary psychoanalytic theory seems to furnish a corollary to existential philosophy, in that sought-after existential authenticity *cannot* be achieved unless one's earliest childhood relationships have provided the basis for the development of a mature and whole ego. Erik Erikson's holistic psychosocial viewpoint serves well to link the interior and exterior significance of this coupling: "Somatic tension, individual anxiety, and group panic are . . . only different ways in which human anxiety presents itself to investigation."[52] Psychodynamically, existentially, we confront the three important aspects of a central inner conflict—felt in one's *self*, analogized within one's *body* and projected upon one's *society*. Proceeding from sociological rather than psychoanalytic premises, Raymond Williams makes a similar point in his description of the hazards of leading an inauthentic life:

It is clearly possible for an individual to acquiesce in a way of living which in fact fails to correspond with or satisfy his own personal organization. He will obey authorities he does not personally accept, carry out social functions that have no personal meaning to him, even feel and think in ways so foreign to his actual

desires that damage will be done to his own being—often deep emotional disor-
ders, often physical damage to his own organic processes.[53]

It is perhaps then understandable that Olmsted and his peers were
continually subjected to a great variety of illnesses—many of which we
would today think of as psychosomatic and most of which were then
covered by a blanket diagnosis of "neurasthenia." The term was coined
by George M. Beard, a New York physician and neurologist, and it
included a very large number of complaints: insomnia, eye problems,
dyspepsia, vertigo, headache, depression, heart palpitations, and so forth.
Beard thought that neurasthenia was unique to the new, intense competitive pressures generated by nineteenth-century American society—striking down especially those with "a frail, fine constitution . . . superior
intellect and a strong emotional nature."[54] Olmsted—who suffered greatly
from such illnesses himself—made much the same diagnosis of his society
as did Beard, and he prescribed his own treatment for it: escape to
pastoral scenery. In the Olmsted and Vaux proposal for a Brooklyn
parkway (1868), Olmsted wrote: "Civilized men . . . are growing more
and more subject to other and more insidious enemies to their health and
happiness and against these the remedy and preventive can not be found
in medicine or in athletic recreations but only in sunlight and such forms
of gentle exercise as are calculated to equalize the circulation and relieve
the brain."[55]

John Stuart Mill's belief in the social obligations—and the moral authority—of "the best men" could be, and was, both an inspiration to
public service and a source of the sense of burden that made gentry men
so susceptible to neurasthenic illness. But Mill's philosophy was also a
source for the belief that there exists a "natural aristocracy," an elite
meant by birth or education or talent to lead the masses. And, indeed,
the charge of elitism has been laid upon men such as Olmsted, Norton,
and their gentry peers by many contemporary historians.

George Frederickson has taken issue with patrician and gentry elitism
as embodied in the powerful Civil War relief organization, the U.S.
Sanitary Commission. For Frederickson, the authoritarian, bureaucrati-
cally organized endeavors of the Commission left much to be desired—
especially when compared with the more spontaneous, amateur, and
humanitarian efforts of other organizations such as the Christian Commis-

sion (which used unpaid volunteers) and of individuals such as Dorothea Dix and Walt Whitman.

Frederickson agrees that the Sanitary Commission "undeniably performed valuable work" and that a nation "engaged in total war cannot afford the luxury of too much democracy or humanitarianism; military efficiency must be the paramount consideration." But he suggests that "the motives of the elite that ruled the [Sanitary Commission] were more complicated" than the "legend" of simple benevolence it created for itself. The Commission, he states, "was a predominantly upper-class organization, representing those patrician elements which had been vainly seeking a function in American society." He argues that the Sanitary Commission was ruled in "supremely authoritarian manner" by a "small but increasingly confident coterie who favored a much more conservative idea of government and society." What these patricians hoped to gain, Frederickson speculates, was to educate the nation for disciplined leadership by such elites, a leadership exercised via the country's *nonelective* institutions. In the hands of these "conservative activists," such institutions were thus intended to become instruments for "social control," the means for instilling "principles of order and stability . . . in the popular mind."[56] One presumes, therefore, that both Brace's Children's Aid Society and Olmsted's urban parks were created to be such instruments.

As convincing as Frederickson's argument is in the main, there are nevertheless problems with some aspects of it. In structuring these gentry intellectuals as an identifiable group, Frederickson makes representative such men as Commissioners Henry W. Bellows, George Templeton Strong, and Charles Eliot Norton, and he presents them as far more organized, single-minded, efficient, and conspiratorial than they actually were.[57] Moreover, Frederickson, who seems to admire "the hardheaded Olmsted," tends by implication to exempt him from the more elitist and antidemocratic behaviors and attitudes of this group. Yet Olmsted often provides the strongest example of such behaviors and attitudes.

For example, Frederickson has much to say about the "twilight of humanitarianism" and the new reverence for science and scientific methods among this gentry elite. But it was Olmsted who, within this group, most embodied the distrust of humanitarian enthusiasm and the elevation of rational methodology—probably because he had been led to mistrust the enthusiast and to project the pragmatist in himself.

Embroiled in a series of administrative disputes with the patrician members of the Executive Committee, Olmsted appealed to a friend: "Are there not authorities on the abstract science of administration?" He wondered if there was "a Euclid of Administrative Science," who might set forth "established axiomatic truths" on the order of: "As the measure of free-will so is the measure of responsibility."[58] Olmsted's point was that if he was to be burdened with the professional responsibility for running the Sanitary Commission, he must be relatively autonomous from the patrician amateurs of the board. In this area, as in so many others, Olmsted had anticipated the operating philosophy of modern professional managers.

But even more, one can argue that what motivated *all* the gentry activists—Olmsted, Norton, Strong, and Bellows—was their moral earnestness and their sense of mission, a belief that their talents and their positions in life *demanded* they make a contribution to the war effort. It was in fact Olmsted—whose creative imagination ran to grandiose enterprises—who alone foresaw the eventual scope of the organization's activities. The others were much more swept along by events, responding to the logic of the military need and their own fear of failing to meet that need.[59] Bellows would comment to Olmsted (as the latter prepared to leave the Commission in 1863) that the Commission had accomplished "ten times more" than he had hoped when the work had begun: "The war has been vaster, the army ten times larger, the whole field immensely broader than I contemplated."[60]

Taken at their own word, it is possible to see these gentry activists as liberals, whose fundamental impulse was always the betterment of society, the improvement of the common welfare. Indeed, this point of view has provided the operative approach for important assessments of Olmsted by such historians as Albert Fein and Laura Wood Roper.

Fein discerns a "creative unity" throughout the various stages of Olmsted's career, which he ascribes to Olmsted's impulses as a Jeffersonian democrat, to "his constant search for means by which to translate human ideals into environmental forms" and to "retain the basic elements of Jeffersonian ideology within the new forms required for urban living."[61] Roper—though more mindful of Olmsted's essentially conservative nature—also tends to see Olmsted as a latter-day Jeffersonian, "democratic to the marrow," whose works expressed "a life-long concern for the character and condition of the masses of his countrymen."[62]

Nevertheless, it is also true that the gentry activists saw themselves as the natural creators of a new nationalist culture and as the natural leaders of the social reforms that would flow from it. John G. Sproat refers to those of Olmsted's gentry circle by Mill's term as "the best men," "men of breeding and intelligence, taste and substance." Advocates of "liberal reform," they actually occupied the Center and the Right in the politics of the Gilded Age, according to Sproat, and he notes:

They had little sympathy with labor's grievances, or the farmers' predicament. Their special fears concerned corruption in politics and business, extravagant government, excessive taxation, and the general breakdown of order and morality in society.

Such men, he adds, were Jeffersonians mainly insofar as they believed in "limited government" and were religious mainly insofar as they assumed that "tested Christian moral precepts" would preserve social order. Their concept of governmental reform was based upon putting "good men" (men much like themselves) into office and opposing the malignancy of party politics.[63] Taking a similar tack, Gilman Ostrander has seen the gentry's self-proclaimed struggle against rising materialism as more truly the conflict between "patrician stewardship" and "plutocratic steward- ship"—the latter embodied in the growing political power of late–nine- teenth century tycoons.[64] In fact, when Olmsted worked with his Sani- tary Commission colleague, Wolcott Gibbs, to help establish an elite Loyalists' Club (which would become the Union League Club of New York), Olmsted argued that they and their peers represented a "heredi- tary, natural aristocracy"—an elite group that would offer an alternative, in social leadership, to the "other sort," the wealthy New York bankers and merchants who would "if they could, have a privileged class in our society, a legal aristocracy."[65]

For Geoffrey Blodgett, Olmsted was representative of "an aspiring American elite," possessed of "a common urge to focus professional intel- ligence on goals of social order and cohesion." "Olmsted's parks," he argues, "are among the most durable relics of this urge."[66] The central belief of Olmsted and his colleagues, Blodgett states, "was a stubborn faith in political and social democrary—provided that democracy re- mained responsive to the cues of trained and cultivated leadership. It was a benign elitism with a functional bent." If that is so, what is Olmsted's relevance for us today?

Albert Fein argues that Olmsted's "renaissance" in our own time has resulted from "the extent to which he adapted a Jeffersonian rural-born ideology to the requirements of the modern American city." When, in the 1960s, Fein writes, "there developed almost simultaneously national reform movements concerned with civil rights, urban needs and environmental quality, Olmsted was recognized as one of the few Americans—perhaps the only one—whose career addressed all three issues in ways meaningful to the second half of the twentieth century."[67]

But Blodgett counters that the efforts of writers like Fein, amidst this Olmsted renaissance, resulted in "a certain historical deracination of the man." Rather than seeing Olmsted's social philosophy as having particular relevance for twentieth-century America, Blodgett observes:

> Olmsted's way of life, together with many of the values he shared with the genteel reformers of the Gilded Age, disappeared before the nineteenth century was out. His hopes for a measure of social amelioration through projects in landscape architecture . . . depended upon an all-but-forgotten social vision. Its believers thought that adequate structures of social and political intercourse could be defined for the popular mass by a cultured elite hovering above. . . . Few of them ever wholly dropped their faith in gradual human improvement under the stewardship of trained talent. But their chosen tactics of improvement—even Olmsted's—only dimly anticipated the wrenching demands of the century ahead.[68]

The urban historian Jon Teaford argues that "Olmsted's vision has not stood the test of time," that there is little room in our time for the "pseudo-rural meadow" of Olmsted's pastoral parks. He also feels that Olmsted's "suburban schemes for upper-middle-class enclaves . . . purposely laid the foundations for the class-segregated city of the twentieth century." And Teaford adds that New York's grid system of street layout, which Olmsted detested, is actually an "egalitarian" plan—"giving preference to no area and creating no preconceived bastions for an urban aristocracy." Another historian, Edward Orser, asks: "Isn't it necessary to question the extent to which Olmsted and the urban landscape reformers were sufficiently attentive to the needs of the urban masses?" Orser suggests that their preference for " 'pastoral serenity' over active recreation and social congregation" was more indicative "of a middle class rather than a 'republican' vision."[69]

I disagree with such historians regarding Olmsted's contemporary relevance—the applicability of his ideas (elitist though they may have been) to our own times. Indeed, the overbuilding of our American cities leads us to cry out more than ever for a return to the principals of urban design that Olmsted laid down a century ago. A case in point is the recent controversy over the proposed construction of a mammoth, twin-towered skyscraper at Columbus Circle in New York City. Much of the debate over this colossus has called attention to the huge shadow it would cast "all the way across Central Park in late afternoon." Writing in the *New York Times*, Paul Goldberger condemned this proposal with truly Olmstedian indignation: "The open space and sky of the southwest corner of Central Park can never be replaced; if they are sold off to Boston Properties, the city will have truly sold its soul for a mess of pottage."[70]

On a more positive note, a $58.7 million restoration of Eastern Parkway in Brooklyn was also recently reported.[71] Of particular importance to the project, the article commented, was the fact that Eastern Parkway had been designed in 1870 by Olmsted and his partner, Calvert Vaux, thus introducing to the United States "the concept of parkways, or broad, pastoral stretches of road." The restoration would reintroduce this Victorian vision as a form of uplift or inspiration for neighborhoods that had become blighted and depressed—a fulfillment of the kind of social improvement Olmsted and his peers had sought from their public works.

Olmstedian ideas are today part of an even larger struggle than simply that of preserving our nineteenth-century heritage as embodied in a given park or parkway. This larger struggle has to do with the need to combat modern urban sprawl through regional planning. "At a time when much of the remaining landscape of New York, New Jersey and Connecticut is being rapidly plotted for development," another recent article stated, "government agencies and urban planners have undertaken a broad new campaign to preserve open space." These efforts, it was reported, will include acquiring more parks and linking together various scenic areas with "corridors of undeveloped land."[72] This notion of comprehensive metropolitan planning, as David Schuyler points out, was in fact pioneered by Olmsted and Vaux in the decade following the Civil War, and it was central to the design work Olmsted and his associates later performed in cities such as Buffalo and Boston.[73]

In an important, retrospective letter of 1890 to Elizabeth Baldwin Whitney, Olmsted expressed his basic existential dilemma in words that recalled the earnest philosophical discussions of their antebellum New

Haven circle of friends: "I have been selling being for doing."[74] This almost despairing apposition of "doing" and "being" was a paradigm for an array of related ideological and psychodynamic conflicts central to Olmsted's struggle for identity: the forward thrust of competitive striving and practical achievement versus the yearning for passive, blissful psychological retreat; masculinity versus femininity; rationality versus transcendentalism; head versus heart. Moreover, all of these were aspects of the existential conflict that Olmsted shared with his peers—the conflict between idealism and materialism, between Romanticism and Utilitarianism.

It is my belief that Olmsted was a psychological "delegate" for his society—especially for the gentry circles in which he moved.[75] The delegate and his society exist in a reciprocal arrangement. The delegate has an inner need to define his identity, in part at least, through the work that his society needs done for its own group psychological needs. And his identity (as well as his self-esteem) comes to rest upon society's recognition of his importance in fulfilling those needs. Only the delegate can sense if the role for which he is selected and for which he selects himself is the manifestation of his true self or of his false self. That individual who feels himself an impostor and a failure despite (or because of) his worldly achievements, who feels all the more empty inside himself for the honors heaped upon him, is a person who feels himself a servant rather than a member of society, who feels that his triumphs are, at the same time, victories for his false self and defeats for his true self. He is a person, that is, who, no matter how much success he achieves in his role as delegate, must ultimately feel himself a failure—a position in which Olmsted was to find himself during the final years of his career.

Gentry leaders had seen in Olmsted someone who could bridge the gap between their Romantic idealism and the increasingly materialistic Utilitarian society around them. It was a task for which Olmsted was peculiarly well fitted, because his own inner psychological conflicts demanded integration of similar opposing forces within himself—the forces he had envisioned as *being* versus *doing*. In tracing the roots of Olmsted's identity and the work that flowed from it, we must attend to his role as a delegate for his peers and to the inevitable heartbreak (not to say physical and mental breakdown) that followed from the impossible task he had been assigned and to which he had assigned himself.

With Utilitarian individualism triumphant in the latter part of the nineteenth century, as Raymond Williams demonstrates, the Romantic movement gave way to a separation of "high culture" from the rest of society.[76] In fact, for many American Romantics, such as Olmsted's friend and colleague, Charles Eliot Norton, culture also became a realm of exile *from* society, a refuge from crass commercialism and democratic excess; it fostered an "us against them" mentality. Thus, Norton wrote to James Russell Lowell: "in this flourishing land of ours, you and I and the few men like us who care for the ideal side of life, are left from year to year in a smaller and smaller minority." And while allied with Olmsted in the fight the save Niagara Falls as a public parkland, Norton wrote a friend that their work was "not so much to save the Falls, but to save our own souls."[77]

Olmsted, as a landscape architect and as a delegate for his gentry peers, practiced a public art. And through his art, Olmsted remained committed to this existential and social struggle far longer than Norton—until 1895, when he was seventy-three years old. Then he, too, went into exile, the only form of exile he could then permit himself—the mental illness that enfolded him in his last eight years of life.

PART I

Cruel Burdens

Earth gets the price for what Earth gives us, and the truth is that, regarding the price I have paid, I need all the esteem I have earned from you to sustain my self-esteem. I have been selling being for doing.

FREDERICK LAW OLMSTED, 1890

CHAPTER I

The Olmsted Legend

Frederick Law Olmsted was one of those men—precious few in any age —who were "honored in their generations . . . the glory of their times."[1] Indeed, Olmsted's tragic decline into mental illness—a decline that was coupled with and perhaps related to his growing anxiety about his stature and his worth—followed almost immediately upon a series of remarkable tributes that were bestowed upon him in 1893, tributes that indicated his unique standing among his peers.

Harvard and Yale conferred honorary degrees upon him on the same day.[2] A few months prior to that, at a dinner honoring the architect D. H. Burnham, Charles Eliot Norton of Harvard said: "of all American artists, Frederick Law Olmsted . . . stands first in the production of great works which answer the needs and give expression to the life of our immense and miscellaneous democracy." In his own speech, Burnham cited Olmsted's "genius," and he added that it was Olmsted who should have been honored that night, "not for his deeds of later years alone, but for what his brain has wrought and his pen has taught for half a century."[3] And it was in October of that same year (1893) that the influential *Century* magazine published the first full-scale appreciation of Olmsted and his work, written by Mariana Van Rensselaer, a distinguished critic of art and architecture.[4] Frederick J. Kingsbury, by then a friend of some fifty years' standing, one who had long ago recognized both Olmsted's worth and his driving ambition, wrote: "Well, you have earned your honors and you have them and I congratulate you."[5]

Ironically, the twilight Olmsted soon entered upon in his own mind
was a harbinger of the eclipse of his reputation that would take place over
the next half-century. There seemed little place for the pastoral tranquility revered by Olmsted and his peers in the America that the Progressive
Era had ushered in—when the definition of civilization and progress
included immense steel-girdered skyscrapers, asphalt highways and cement playgrounds, cubist abstraction and Art Deco restlessness. Even
within the related fields of urban planning and architecture, S. B. Sutton
has observed, the man who had been celebrated as the dean of American
landscape architecture "subsided into near obscurity," as the practitioners
in these fields "fought to shed the burden of the historic past and fixed
their attention upon the International School and other modern movements." "The greatest irony occurred during the 1920s," Thomas Bender
adds, "when Olmsted's son, himself a leading planner, used the overpass
invented by his father to preserve the natural landscape at Central Park,
to begin the obliteration of the landscape at Los Angeles."[6]

As recently as twenty years ago, few people other than historians could
identify Frederick Law Olmsted. Since then, however, his name has
become omnipresent in discussions of cities and their public spaces.
When his name comes up, it usually has something to do with a debate
over one of the parks associated with him—most often Central Park.
Indeed, it is in terms of park design that the most avid efforts are made to
keep his name alive, and—as he had in his own lifetime—he becomes
the rallying point of those who would defend what they perceive to have
been Olmsted's intent against the encroachments of political and commercial interests, as well as against the proposals of other, perhaps misguided,
park aesthetes. There is even an organization called the National Association for Olmsted Parks, dedicated to sustaining Olmsted's legacy.

The effort to preserve Olmsted's legacy was begun by the same son
who, as a planner, had already given himself over to the new age. The
first volume of the work published by Frederick Law Olmsted, Jr., (Rick)
and Theodora Kimball is devoted to the elder Olmsted's formative years
and includes a frequently unreliable biographical sketch, composed primarily of a highly selective offering of Olmsted's early recollections and
letters.[7] Until the advent of Laura Wood Roper's massively researched
and superbly written biography, this earlier "official" biography had
served as the basis of later sketches by cultural and urban historians.

More recently historians have made use of Roper's work, as well as the work of other excellent Olmsted scholars: Albert Fein, Charles Capen McLaughlin, and Charles Beveridge.

But as rich and perceptive as most of these works have been, the net effect has been essentially celebratory, emphasizing the best of Olmsted and sliding past, or even omitting, that which is problematical in both the man and his work. And it is the most celebratory aspects of this collective body of work that the organized Olmstedians prefer to focus upon. Indeed, the fine biography by Elizabeth Stevenson—one which, though equally admiring, tries to some degree to come to grips with "the raging ego" within Olmsted—is seldom mentioned when works on Olmsted are discussed in Olmstedian organs.[8]

Some of the effects of the collective celebration of Olmsted are almost inescapable: that Olmsted's accounts of his many public and private controversies have become the accepted versions; that many of the reports and proposals that Olmsted produced in tandem with his various partners and associates have come to be identified, simply, as Olmsted papers;[9] and, finally, that the public works with which the average person is most familiar today—Central Park and the other great urban parks—have become, collectively, the "Olmsted parks."

Some signs of backlash are naturally to be expected. One such erupted in the press when M. M. Graff, a park historian who would deflate Olmsted's reputation as *the* architect of this great enterprise, assailed the Olmstedians as exploiters who have "a vested interest" in his reputation. "They run an annual Olmsted convention and they don't want the name Olmsted sullied," Graff stated.[10] In her book about the creation of Central Park and Prospect Park, Graff deplores the fact that the publicity devoted to Olmsted's career as a landscape architect has "overshadowed the gifted men who taught Olmsted his craft." Such men as Vaux, Jacob Wrey Mould, Ignaz Pilat, Andrew Haswell Green, and Samuel Parsons, Jr., have thus been "denied due credit" for their "major contributions" to the creation of Central Park. Nor has Graff been content only to give these men their due credit; she has called into question Olmsted's credentials for an important aspect of the work: "Horticulture is a profession in which no unqualified person ever hesitates to meddle. Olmsted was no exception. Central Park still suffers from the effects of his ignorance of the nature and habits of plant materials."[11]

1. Frederick Law Olmsted in the final years of his career—c. late 1880s. About sixty-five here, Olmsted nevertheless remained heavily involved in his firm's work. Now established in Brookline, Massachusetts, he was already at work on the Boston park system and would soon begin work on the Columbian Exposition and the Biltmore estate. It was in the midst of the latter work, in 1895, that Olmsted, beset by fears of failure, slipped into the mental illness that would enshroud the last eight years of his life. (National Park Service, Frederick Law Olmsted National Historical Site.)

And the urban historian Jon C. Teaford was moved to complain about one writer's "genuflecting before the achievements of Frederick Law Olmsted," a practice Teaford found all too commonplace among "students of nineteenth-century urban planning." Olmsted, Teaford observed, is put forth as the "authoritative teacher laying down the law," while such notable figures as the architect Richard Morris Hunt are presented as "philistines at best and more likely dullards" for daring to challenge Olmsted's vision, a vision that Teaford claims "has not stood the test of time."[12]

But—as Richard Hofstadter has said of Lincoln—the first author of the Olmsted legend was Olmsted himself.[13] Olmsted's interrelated concerns for his own reputation and that of his profession led him to attempt numerous essays and books in his later years—the subject matter covering autobiography, various aspects of landscape architecture, the philosophy of design and the graphic arts, and so forth.[14] Usually he got no further than innumerable drafts of the opening sections, or dozens of pages of notes, toward such a work. "I do my duty in writing but nobody can imagine how hard it is . . . how much it costs me to write respectably," he told Mariana Van Rensselaer in 1887.[15] At the time, he was seeking to enlist her as a propagandist for *his* aesthetic of landscape design, noting that it was a comfort to find what he "would like to say written by someone else."

One of Olmsted's concerns was to lay out an official—and rather romanticized—account of his early preparation for his profession. This he did in his embittered pamphlet of 1882, *Spoils of the Park*.[16] According to this account, Olmsted had begun the "study of the art of parks" in his childhood, and he had read "the great works upon the art" before he was fifteen. Between his adolescence and his employment on Central Park in 1857, he states, not a year passed in which he "had not pursued the study with ardor, affection, and industry." His two trips to Europe, he writes, were for the express purpose of studying the parks of England and the Continent, while his travels across America were devoted to the "study of natural scenery." And he adds:

I had been three years the pupil of a topographical engineer, and had studied in what were then the best schools, and under the best masters in the country, of agricultural science and practice. I had planted with my own hands five thousand trees, and, on my own farms and in my own groves had practised for ten years every essential horticultural operation of a park. I had made management of labor in rural works a special study, and had written upon it acceptably to the public.

The Van Rensselaer article, published a decade later, presented Olmsted's early years in far greater detail, but still held to the tenor of this "official" version of Olmsted's youth and training—hardly a surprising fact, since the biographical aspects of the article were so heavily based upon Olmsted's own testimony.[17] Echoes of this version can be found as late as 1931, in Lewis Mumford's appreciation of Olmsted. Mumford rhapsodized Olmsted's preparation for his career as a "combination of wide travelling, shrewd observation, intelligent reading, and practical farming"—just as Olmsted had claimed for himself in *Spoils*—and Mumford called it an example of "American education at its best."[18]

After Roper's exhaustive study of Olmsted's life and after the efforts of Roper, Fein, McLaughlin, and others to make Olmsted's papers accessible, historians have come to see Olmsted's career as something other than inherently disciplined or even charmingly eclectic. They have come to see it as serendipitous, if not actually haphazard.

Such a view, in fact, was one that Olmsted, near the end of his career, presented to his son, Rick, when Olmsted made use of his own early misadventures as a cautionary tale for his son. This version was set forth in one of Olmsted's most revealing letters—written, appropriately enough, on New Year's Day, 1895.[19] This was a letter that cast a far different light on Olmsted's earlier years than did the official version he had put forth in *Spoils* or had fed to Van Rensselaer for the *Century* article:

> I was younger than you now are when my father, wishing to make me a merchant, secured me a situation in what he thought a very notable and promising place to learn the business. After trying it a year and a half, I threw it up, and with his consent . . . went to sea. Then I threw that up, and after wasting a year, wandered from farm to farm thinking that I was learning the business and so on.

At thirty, he wrote, he had finally entered the business world, as a publisher, and five years later this enterprise was bankrupt.[20] It was only then that he had begun upon "the business" (landscape architecture) in which—except for the Civil War years—he worked ever since.

All that period of backing and filling between the point in which, nominally a farmer, I really acquired my profession, was a sad matter. If my father had not been comparatively (to his wants) rich, and generous and indulgent—over-much indulgent and easy-going with me—it would not have occurred. I have been successful but I should have been far more successful . . . if at your period, I would have given myself to methodological study of the profession I have since followed, or probably of any profession or calling.

Olmsted's official version of his youth (in *Spoils* and elsewhere) often took liberties with objective truth—a truth that, in his anxiety over Rick's future, he had presented here. Yet passages such as the one quoted from *Spoils* usually had a poetic truth about them. As noted in the introduction, Olmsted's young manhood provides an excellent example of an Eriksonian "psychosocial moratorium"—that delay in the acceptance of adult commitments during which the young person experiments with various roles in life. Lucian Pye comments that one can see a common pattern in the lives that Erikson has studied: a pattern of the "ideological innovator . . . coming upon his life work without prior planning or design."[21] When the right opportunity presents itself, the skills such a gifted person has acquired almost by accident are fused together through his creative imagination into a work that, in retrospect, seems to have been inevitable. Van Rensselaer makes this point about Olmsted in her *Century* article, writing with her great good sense:

It may almost seem as if mere chance had determined that Mr. Olmsted should be an artist. But the best chance can profit no man who is not prepared to turn it into opportunity. If, at the age of thirty-four, Mr. Olmsted had not been fitted for a landscape gardener's task, the chance which made him superintendent of the workmen in Central park could not have led him on to the designing of parks; while, on the other hand, knowing how well fitted for such tasks he was, we feel that if just this opportunity had not offered, another would somehow have presented itself.[22]

Olmsted's claim that from adolescence onward he had been engaged in the constant study of parks is utter nonsense. And one may credit him with at best only a sporadically intense interest in what he called "scientific farming." Whenever he was actually confronted with the lonely hard work this occupation entailed, however, he would develop a burning desire to be elsewhere: back in his father's Hartford home; attending lectures at Yale, where his brother was enrolled; off on a walking tour of Europe; reporting on the South for the *New York Daily Times*.

That walking tour—the first of the two trips to Europe Olmsted mentions in the *Spoils* passage cited earlier—was clearly a classic Erikson-

ian *Wanderschaft*, a bit of a romantic lark. At the time, 1850, Olmsted had
put in nearly a year on his Staten Island farm, the second of two his
father had purchased for him. Learning that his brother, John Hull, and
their friend, Charles Loring Brace, were to ship off on this walking tour
of England and the Continent, Olmsted begged his father to be allowed
to go along (he was almost *twenty-eight*), writing that "it tries my whole
manliness to have such a trip as this brought so close to me." Almost
desperately, he added: "I hope you won't consider my opinions as if they
were those of a mere child, nor my desires as senseless romantic impulses
only." To sell his practical father upon the idea, Olmsted had to make
practical arguments: such a trip would allow him to obtain *"useful, profitable* information" for his farming venture; it would increase his "vigor of
constitution;" and he could "enjoy and use the advantage of travelling
vastly more than John."[23]

As S. B. Sutton, an Olmsted partisan, drily observes: "a dedicated
farmer would not usually leave his land during planting, growing, and
harvesting seasons." Yet, as she adds, the trip resulted in Olmsted's first
book: *Walks and Talks of an American Farmer in England*.[24] The trip also
produced an article for the May 1851 *Horticulturist*, entitled "The People's
Park at Birkenhead, Near Liverpool."[25] If not for that book and for his
articles in such magazines, there is no way Olmsted could have obtained
the position of Superintendent of Central Park in 1857. And that is the
poetic truth the *Spoils* passage contains. His search for a career was far
more erratic than the aging Olmsted cared to admit in public, but it *did*
prepare him unusually well for the pioneering of landscape architecture
in America.

That Olmsted did the things he did, learned the lessons he learned,
responded to certain opportunities rather than others, and forged out of
all these a singular career was the result of his unique psychodynamics as
well as of his unique genius. That essential intellectual strength must not
be obscured in the course of exploring his psyche. In this regard, I agree
with Lewis Mumford's observation that Olmsted had "one of the best
minds that the Brown Decades produced."[26]

In any event, it would be unfair to Mariana Van Rensselaer to suggest
that she had permitted herself to be exploited by Olmsted, that she
was no more than Olmsted's propagandist, or that she had been totally
influenced by Olmsted's more romantic musings about his youth. Her

article does indeed propagate some of the Olmstedian myths, yet she was also capable of criticizing Olmsted's work with great intellectual rigor.

Van Rensselaer recognized how irregular had been Olmsted's formal preparation for his ultimate career, but she also understood how his "creative power" had worked together with an "unconscious receptivity" to make the most of such training as he had had. She called attention to his deficiencies in architecture, engineering, and draftsmanship, and she felt that a "lack of practical knowledge"—in dealing with plants, for example—had "limited his imagination somewhat" and had "forced him to depend upon others, in the execution of his works." She added, however, that any defects in Olmsted's work tended to be "mistakes or short-comings in the elaboration of his scheme, not in the scheme itself, not in the fundamental artistic conception." A more thorough "technical training," she wrote, would have put the mark of his "great intelligence and good taste" and his "remarkable originality" upon all the details of his work. Addressing Olmsted's "peculiar education, so deep and rich in some directions, so scanty in others," Van Rensselaer warned would-be landscape architects that they were not likely to profit from such "a passive course of education." These persons must remember that "genius can learn much where talent or mere intelligence would gather sparse instruction."[27]

The question of Olmsted's strengths and weaknesses as a landscape architect almost inevitably raises the question of the respective roles of Olmsted and his associate, Calvert Vaux, in the design of Central Park. That question was addressed, at Olmsted's death, by Fred Kingsbury, an old friend, but a shrewd and discerning one.[28] Working from almost exactly the same premises as Van Rensselaer, Kingsbury commented that the fact that Olmsted had had no technical education was one of his "greatest glories," for what Olmsted nevertheless accomplished "has been the result of fine genius laboring under the greatest difficulties."[29] Kingsbury then made the case for Olmsted's preeminence in the strongest possible terms:

If he had been an engineer or draftsman when he first conceived Central Park he would not have needed, and probably would not have employed, Mr Vaux to put his ideas on paper. Of course, in time, he acquired a good deal of this sort of technical knowledge and he had the artistic instinct which enabled him to sketch plans of what he saw so clearly in his mind. . . . His power was as an idealist and he looked to others to give his ideas visible forms.

A very different point of view is offered by M. M. Graff in her book on "the men who made Central Park." She cites the testimony of Samuel Parsons, Jr., superintendent of Planting for the New York parks in the 1880s. Parsons stated that it likely had been Vaux, more than Olmsted, who had created Central Park. "Mr. Olmsted was a leader of men, a man of magnetism and charm, a literary genius," Parsons stated, "but hardly the creative artist that Vaux was."[30]

Charles Beveridge, a shrewd judge of Olmsted's abilities, has discussed the respective contributions of Olmsted and Vaux during the first years at Central Park.[31] Beveridge notes that during the 1857–1861 period, Olmsted "viewed himself as primarily an administrator—a person capable of realizing on the land, efficiently and effectively, a park design of which he happened to have become co-author." "Not until 1865," Beveridge adds, "did Calvert Vaux convince Olmsted to consider himself as much an artist as an administrator." Even then, Beveridge believes, it was Olmsted the administrator rather than Olmsted the artist whose help Vaux sought on Prospect Park.

The most extreme presentation of precisely the opposite view was that offered by Lewis Mumford. It is to Olmsted alone that Mumford ascribed credit for the heroic effort that went into the early designing and construction of the park. Olmsted had done more than just "design a park" and fight off politicians, "rascally city appointees," and vandals, Mumford wrote: "he had introduced an idea—the idea of using the landscape creatively." Calvert Vaux received credit merely for having "the intelligence to see Olmsted's possibilities."[32]

Insofar as their respective technical and design capabilities are concerned, it is virtually impossible today to make a definitive judgment as to whether or not Olmsted could have done his great work on Central Park without the aid of Calvert Vaux under any circumstances or as to what precisely each contributed to it. One *can* demonstrate, however, that these two men often served each other's psychological and emotional needs; that nowhere is this more evident than in their early work on the New York parks; and that, from the psychodynamic point of view at least, neither one could have accomplished this great work without the other. This certainly was Olmsted's final, and most deeply felt, view of their great partnership. In an important 1893 letter to Van Rensselaer, Olmsted wrote of the Central Park work: "I hope you will not fail to do justice to Vaux and to consider that *he and I were one.* I should have been nowhere but for his professional training."[33]

The subject of credit for the creation of Central Park was one that troubled Calvert Vaux for three decades. In October 1863—just as Olmsted settled in California as Superintendent of the Mariposa Mining Estate— Vaux complained bitterly to Olmsted that the press had virtually ignored his (Vaux's) role in the park project. "The public has been led to believe from the commencement of the Central Park work to the present time that you are pre-eminently the author of the executed design," Vaux wrote, "and such we all know is the general impression to day."[34] Vaux argued that this impression had been fostered by Olmsted's assumption of the Architect-in-Chief title, a title Vaux had never felt was appropriate, and he suggested now that they should have governed the implementation of the park plan together, in a "simple partnership on equal terms." He had always supposed, Vaux added, that Olmsted would one day take steps "to restore the balance thus disturbed to my disadvantage." Instead, he observed, Olmsted seemed to have exhibited an "absence of any apparent desire . . . to alter the existing state of things" or to "give up the name of A. in C."

In a second letter, Vaux stated that he himself had "sacrificed" his own "professional rights for the good of the common cause . . . of the park."[35] But he did so, Vaux added, only because of his "absolute trust" in Olmsted's "purity of aim and intention." And he had continued to believe that their relationship "meant equality in your eyes as absolutely as it did in mine." That belief had later been undermined, however, by articles about the park that had appeared in the press. These had convinced Vaux that Olmsted had "conveyed to everyone" that their positions "were not nearly as equal" in Olmsted's mind as Vaux had thought them. Vaux added that he knew Olmsted had tried to defend his (Vaux's) rights to such journalist friends as E. L. Godkin and Parke Godwin. But the net result was totally inadequate, Vaux charged: "you had not convinced the men, not as I should have convinced them speaking of you and therefore you were not convinced yourself, never would be to all appearances. We had a joint title you did not believe in."

But no matter how great his bitterness, Vaux still felt a great dependency upon Olmsted and still yearned to renew their partnership. In the spring of 1865, Olmsted was facing bankruptcy at Mariposa. Vaux was in the process, without Olmsted's help, of getting their firm reappointed as the landscape architects for Central Park; and, alone, he had prepared a proposal for the Brooklyn Park Commission that was to be the guiding plan for the creation of Prospect Park. It was at this point that Vaux initiated a correspondence with Olmsted filled with complaints and accusations about the way in which Olmsted had behaved as Architect in Chief of Central Park between 1858 and 1861. Notwithstanding those complaints and accusations, however, Vaux's letter-writing campaign was designed primarily to get Olmsted to give up his California venture and to return to work together with Vaux on the creation of the Brooklyn park and on renewed work for Central Park.[36] Yet, since Vaux seems to have managed fairly well on his own, why the great need for Olmsted's return?

Both Vaux's complaints about Olmsted and the reasons for his so ardently seeking Olmsted's return will be explored in part 3 (chapter 10). But it is worth noting here that a major reason was Vaux's own pervasive insecurities, those that had led him to subordinate himself to Olmsted from the beginning.[37] He seemed to sense in Olmsted some power that was lacking in himself and saw any hope of fulfillment only in a psychological bondage to Olmsted. "After the first seven years you gave me Leah," he wrote; "after seven [more] will you give me Rachel." He had also told Olmsted plaintively: "alone I am a very incomplete Landscape Architect and you are off at the other end of the world." He needed Olmsted at his side in order to overcome this feeling of incompleteness, noting a few weeks later that "temperamentally" they complemented one another. Vaux felt himself "wholly incompetent" to do the job alone. But Olmsted's implacable drive for individual recognition, his insatiable ambition, continued to trouble Vaux. He thought it due to immaturity and that Olmsted would grow out of it, though he added that Olmsted was "a damned long while about it."[38]

Vaux's psychic dependency upon Olmsted fed an inner feeling that they shared a common destiny, but a destiny achievable only in tandem. "To me [the work on the New York parks] seems & always has seemed a magnificent opening," Vaux wrote, "possible together, impossible to either alone." Several weeks later, he returned to the theme, but on a loftier plane. He held that the two of them were "better fitted" than anyone else to the work ahead. What they, and they alone, could accomplish together would be "of vital importance to the progress of the Republic."[39]

By December, Olmsted had returned to New York, leaving yet another bankruptcy behind him, and restored the firm of Olmsted and Vaux. Seven years later (1872), the two men would dissolve their partnership, Vaux still hoping some day to wrest his "Rachel" away from Olmsted.

It would never cease to trouble Vaux that Olmsted was routinely given all the credit for Central Park and that Olmsted, from Vaux's point of view, did not do enough to change that perception. On at least one occasion, Vaux made public his displeasure with Olmsted. In 1878— after Olmsted had been dismissed as Landscape Architect for the New York parks—the leading gentry figures of the day addressed letters of protest to the New York press, letters that tended, once again, to assign to Olmsted the sole credit for Central park. Vaux was particularly out-raged by a letter Olmsted's friend Godkin had written to the *Tribune*. Vaux published a follow-up letter himself, condemning Olmsted for his failure to disavow "the greedy misrepresentations made in his behalf" by Godkin. Actually, Olmsted had been out of the country at the time. Vaux was moved to make a public apology after the *Tribune* printed a letter from Olmsted's stepson, Owen, a letter that was probably written by Olmsted's wife, Mary. The letter stated the family's official position: "no one has or can have the smallest authority for claiming for Mr. Olmsted either more or less than an equal share with Mr. Calvert Vaux in the design of the Central and Brooklyn Parks."[40]

Both the family's "party line" and its real attitude on the subject of Calvert Vaux would later be well expressed by John Charles Olmsted during an upsetting period in 1887. This was an occasion when Olmsted —who had left New York City five years earlier—was being drawn in a prospective consultancy for the New York parks over the vehement objections of Vaux, who was then in contention to become architectural superintendent of the parks. The New York Park Board, John explained to his associate, Charles Eliot, had simply assumed that his stepfather "had a greater genius for original design or planning great undertakings" than did Vaux. However, John added, this must never be stated publicly, since to do so would "only give rise to jealousy and ill-feelings between the friends of both."[41] It is quite evident that the assumption John ascribed to the Park Board was that of the Olmsted family itself (and of many Olmstedians today).

The fact is that Olmsted *did* tend to get the credit, while Vaux tended to be forgotten. But the question raised by Vaux was: what role had Olmsted played in all of this? Vaux's answer was that Olmsted would make polite protestations on Vaux's behalf, but never go far enough to convince people of Vaux's equal role in design matters. When one examines Olmsted's participation in the preparation of Van Rensselaer's *Century* magazine article in 1893, Vaux appears to have been substantially right, despite Olmsted's firm belief that he and Vaux "were one" on Central Park and that he had tried to make the public realize it. It is worth noting that six years earlier—about the time of the furor over the prospective New York parks consultancy—Olmsted had written disarmingly to Van Rensselaer: "I am sorry that you did not know that Vaux was equally with me the designer of the Central and Brooklyn Parks but it is one of those mistakes that one has always to be contending with hopelessly."[42] He had, at this point, known Van Rensselaer for three years. Moreover, many today would question whether *Olmsted* was "equally" the designer of Prospect Park.[43]

In July 1893, after reading the published version of Van Rensselaer's *Century* magazine article, Olmsted expressed his regret that Vaux had not been given "full justice" for his role in the design of the sunken transverse roads in Central Park, which Van Rensselaer had hailed as one of the Park's most remarkable innovations.[44] I suspect that there was more than a little conscience-salving by Olmsted in this remark. The fact is that by the time Van Rensselaer had completed her article, she had of course had extensive communications with Olmsted, both in person and in writing, as well as having been given complete access to his office files. In addition (as has been noted) Olmsted had been shown, several months prior to its publication, at least half the article in its earlier typewritten version. With this in mind, it is instructive to compare the two versions with regard to the major design innovation in the Greensward plan for Central Park: the sunken transverse roadways that shield those who stroll or ride through the park from the sights, and much of the clamor, of the busy, mostly commercial crosstown traffic that cuts through the park at four separate latitudes.[45]

2. Central Park under construction: the view west from Vista Rock, showing one of the transverse roads at center. The *1866 Guide to New York City* describes these "sub-ways" as "of infinite importance to the beauty and convenience" of the park—allowing traffic to cross through the park without disturbing the "pleasure-seekers" strolling or lounging in the wooded areas above. (The New-York Historical Society.)

In the earlier (manuscript) version, Van Rensselaer wrote: "From the beginning he [Olmsted] felt that the chief problem was to secure transit across the park for utilitarian purposes in such a way that pleasure-driving would not be interfered with." One day, Olmsted chanced to see fire-engines "rushing across the park," and he realized the deleterious effect such happenings would have upon the mood of the park-goer. With this in mind, Olmsted and Vaux "began to reorganize the plan" for their Greensward concept so as to make possible sunken transverse roads.[46] "Mr. Olmsted says he could not have done it without Mr. Vaux," Van

Rensselaer comments, "as he was not a draftsman and Mr. Vaux's architectural training made him invaluable for consultation." Having read this
version well in advance of publication of the article, Olmsted surely
should have realized that he was being given credit for the basic idea,
while Vaux was being made to appear as no more than a technical
consultant. Olmsted had clearly had the opportunity to advise Van Rensselaer that her final draft should give Vaux far more credit, if the principle
of their equality in the park design was to be upheld.

As it happens, the text of the printed version telescopes the discussion
of the transverse roads concept into a single reference, contained within
Van Rensselaer's general review of how Olmsted and Vaux had prepared
their Greensward proposal. She writes: "The main ideas for the [Greens-
ward] scheme then worked out by the two young men were Mr. Olmsted's, including the one which probably did more than anything else to
determine its success—the idea of conducting traffic across the park by
means of sunken transverse roads." Van Rensselaer then adds that Vaux's
role ("equally essential") in the Greensward design was to do the "actual
work of draftsmanship," to design structural features and to make work-
able Olmsted's various schemes and ideas.

It will be noted that where the earlier version slighted Vaux's contribution to the sunken transverse roads, the printed version diminishes
Vaux's contribution to the *entire* Greensward design proposal. Whatever
the comments Olmsted may have made to Van Rensselaer after reading
her earlier draft, the result was that he got even more of the credit for
Central Park, not less, and got *all* of the credit for the sunken transverse
roads concept.

Here again, we cannot know today the precise roles played by Olmsted
and Vaux, respectively, in the design of the sunken transverse roads. The
extreme example of crediting Olmsted is, once again, Lewis Mumford.
His observation, cited earlier, that Olmsted had "one of the best minds
the Brown Decades produced" followed upon assignment of sole credit
to Olmsted for this major innovation in the design of Central Park.
Charles Beveridge, always fair to Vaux, states in his description of the
Greensward plan: "Olmsted and Vaux went on to devise a unique solution to the problem of transverse roads."[47] On the other hand, even Bruce
Kelly, a strong Vaux partisan, describes the sunken transverse roads as
one of "Olmsted's innovations."[48] Julian Fabos, Gordon Milne, and V.
Michael Weinmayr twice ascribe this concept to Olmsted alone, stating

in one place: "Olmsted used underpasses and depressed roadways to preserve the harmony of nature."[49] Indeed, the latter mention Vaux's name only three times, and then only in the most general way, in their appreciation of the Central Park design. Finally, Stephen Rettig has pointed to the possible English origins of this concept—particularly the pedestrian underpass in the Regents Park Zoo, constructed in 1829, with which both Vaux and Olmsted would have been familiar.[50]

Olmsted chose to complain—after the publication of Van Rensselaer's article—that Vaux had not been given "full justice" for his part in the sunken roadways design; but he might equally have complained about Vaux not receiving "full justice" for *any* part of Greensward. Van Rensselaer's account may well have been a fully accurate description of the respective roles played by Olmsted and Vaux. But it hardly fits within the stated family policy of not "claiming for Mr. Olmsted either more or less than an equal share with Mr. Calvert Vaux in the design of the Central and Brooklyn Parks." And it seems quite likely that Olmsted bore a great responsibility for whatever opinion Van Rensselaer had of Vaux's role.

The question of credit for a joint venture was not a new one for Olmsted. The second of his three books about the South, *A Journey Through Texas*, was a joint project with his brother, John Hull Olmsted, who had made the trip with him. The book was published under Frederick's authorship, though he noted in the preface: "Owing to the pressure of other occupations, the preparation of the volume from the author's journal has been committed, with free scope of expression and personality, to his brother, Dr. J. H. Olmsted, his companion upon the trip."[51] In his own introduction to the book, John Hull referred to himself as the editor of the book and stated that his duty had been "simply that of connecting, by a slender thread of reminiscence, the copious notes of facts placed in his own hands," adding that there was a little unavoidable "alter-egoism" in the book. Larry McMurtry agrees that John Hull's contribution was greater than the latter claimed in his introductory note, yet argues that the book is "clearly Frederick's work," though McMurtry also refers to the "light, humorous, and fanciful hand of John Hull Olmsted." The reportage in *Texas* is certainly akin to that of the other two books on the South produced by Frederick alone, but stylistically it is by far the best-written book of the three.

John Hull's real opinion of his own role was more clearly expressed in a letter to Frederick about the sharing of possible profits. Late in 1856, with a year of life left to him, John Hull wrote: "My work seems to have been the hardest part by the good deal & my ideas to have added a share. But the plan & the notes etc yours & it will sell for your name." John went on to propose that he should get two-thirds of any profit "or *loss*," or else be paid a salary "for having written it" for Frederick. His brother chose the two-thirds option.[52]

Both the early draft of Van Rensselaer's article and the published version refer to the brothers' collaboration on *Texas*.[53] In the draft version, Van Rensselaer reports that Olmsted considered *Texas* the best of his three books on the South "because his brother largely wrote it from Olmsted's notes." In the printed article, this rather generous comment was reduced to: "the one on Texas [was] put into shape by his brother from his notes." As with the case of Vaux and Central Park, Olmsted's opportunity to review Van Rensselaer's draft version had somehow resulted only in the diminution of his collaborator's role.

In the correspondence in which Vaux tried to cajole Frederick into returning to New York, he referred to Frederick as both the "head artist" and the "representative man" of their joint project on Central Park. John Hull seems to have had similar feelings about *Texas*, yet, like Vaux, he clearly felt the need to assert his own rights. Vaux was but a year older than John Hull and had come into Frederick's life just as John Hull had left it. As we have seen, Vaux became as dependent upon Frederick as John Hull had been and as vulnerable to hurt by Frederick.

It is clear from the early family letters that the Olmsteds thought of John Hull as the talented member of the family. He was given the finest possible education in childhood, was tutored in the arts, and later became an honor student at Yale. His teenaged half sister, Mary, had once told John Hull to consider using "your talents in writing treatises on fruits and fruit trees, for the Horticulturist, & perhaps you would turn out another Downing, and have your books translated into German & French, and read all over Europe."[54] It turned out, however, that it was Frederick who was published in the *Horticulturist*, whose books received wide readership, and who was to be considered by many as "another Downing."

CHAPTER 2

"The Price I Have Paid"

After Olmsted had had the chance to read the early draft of Van Rensselaer's biographical sketch, he wrote her: "I am proud of the elevation in which its places me, but must say it makes me feel a little giddy and unsafe to stand in such a position." The word *unsafe* is one clue to Olmsted's inner fears as he contemplated his achievements and his fame. But there was an even stronger clue in the manuscript of the letter. Olmsted had originally written "it makes me feel a little *guilty*," but struck out *guilty* and wrote *giddy* above it.[1] When it is remembered that this was a period in which academic honors and public acclaim were being heaped on Olmsted, the profound unease with which he bore his public reputation—as if it had not been deserved, as if he had been sure to fall from such an eminence—becomes more apparent. A few years earlier, he had written to the sweetheart of his youth: "Earth gets the price for what Earth gives us, and the truth is that, regarding the price I have paid, I need all the esteem I have earned from you to sustain my self-esteem. I have been selling being for doing."[2] The words "from you" were added as an afterthought; his real need was far more all-encompassing. The original statement demonstrates vividly Olmsted's long struggle to achieve and to preserve a great reputation—his deep-rooted need for a general "esteem" to set against his inner fears, all the while anticipating that "earth" would "get its price" in the end. Moreover, the transition from this thought to the last—"selling being for doing"—reveals that this hunger for esteem was linked to his fundamental identity conflict, the conflict between authenticity (associated here with a feminine idealism) and the inauthentic (masculine, achieving) life.

This passage convincingly reveals the trap within which Olmsted lived out his life—the trap of the gifted but wounded person who needs ever-increasing "fixes" of adulation and admiration to sustain his grandiose defenses against inner feelings of failure and worthlessness. Olmsted felt, apparently, that he had to purchase esteem through "doing"—through practical, utilitarian material success. Yet there was within Olmsted another self, a dreaming, idealistic self that yearned for blissful retreat from this worldly struggle.

Earth, of course, did get its price from Olmsted, and not just in his last years of terrible mental illness, when his mind slipped away from the present into nightmare fantasies of his past.[3] Olmsted had actually been paying that price for the greater part of his life, and he seemed to have a need for—a pleasure in—paying that price. It was a phenomenon that had not escaped his wife's notice. Olmsted was in his sixties when she wrote Fred Kingsbury that her husband was "off in pursuit of more accidents," and, she added, "He has accidents at irregular intervals to be sure but four or five a year. How he does enjoy these! As you may perhaps remember at the [Staten Island] farm."[4]

The price Olmsted continued to pay throughout his life came to be inextricably linked to the career that had become the public expression of his inner self. The profession he had created for himself required him to travel extensively well into his later years. In 1893, Olmsted told Kingsbury that he had come to "greatly dread traveling, being pretty sure to break down somewhere on every journey and have to lie about a few days under care of a strange physician."[5]

Of course there was no exterior power forcing this man, then in his seventies, to undertake such arduous trips. His young associates stood ready to take over his duties. But turning those duties over to them would not have offered a real escape from his inner urgencies and the price they extracted. That much was implicit in his admission to Kingsbury (in the letter above) that, being unable to "meet the demands" placed upon him, he had run away to England. "The attempt was a failure," Olmsted wrote. "More than a failure. I was more disabled when I returned than when I left."

The list of crises and accidents Olmsted suffered, particularly in the pursuit of a vocation, is remarkably long: chronic eye problems troubled his adolescence; extreme seasickness, typhus, and various accidents marked his brief attempt to be a sailor; headaches and fainting spells ended his semester at Yale and hampered his attempts to work the Sachem's Head farm his father had bought him. "Is it from Mental Causes that he is subject to this tendency of blood to the head?" his father, John Olmsted, was led to wonder.[6]

Olmsted was to suffer at least three major periods of serious physical and mental collapse during his two-decade connection with Central Park. The first was between 1859 and 1860, at the height of his first round of administrative and political conflicts over the direction of the park and culminated in a carriage accident that nearly killed him. The second was in 1873, after the breakup of his partnership with Vaux and his father's death, during which he had a protracted temporary blindness, probably hysterical. The third occurred as a result of a painful dispute over the management of the New York parks (described in *Spoils of the Park*) and ended in his final dismissal as Landscape Architect for the park system.[7]

The first breakdown period began only a few months after Olmsted's marriage to his brother's widow, John Hull having died of tuberculosis some eighteen months earlier. According to Roper, the precipitating cause of the illness was the exasperating financial supervision of Park Commissioner Andrew Haswell Green, who had been appointed Comptroller of Central Park several months earlier and who continually extended his dominion over Olmsted and the park construction. "Olmsted strove to behave toward Green with scrupulous subordination," Roper writes, "and paid for his smothered exasperation in sleeplessness, digestive upsets, and headaches," soon to be followed by total exhaustion. Other causes, she adds, were a "vexatious" political inquiry into his administration and his own personal money troubles. A trip to Saratoga with his wife shortly after their marriage and a trip alone to England in the middle of this period had brought him only a little relief.[8]

These problems were real enough. On April 14, 1860, Olmsted had been subpeonaed to appear at the Astor House for a State Legislature investigation of "the affairs, condition and progress of the New York Central Park." And the humiliations he was to endure at the hands of Andrew Green chafed him endlessly, though far more in the year *following* the accident than the year prior. But the sources of Frederick's exhaustion and mental breakdown in this period seem to have been essentially self-generated—especially in the way that he had been driving himself in his multiple duties on the park. Long before the legislative inquiry and the worst of the Green torments, Olmsted had written to his father: "I feel just thoroughly worn-out, used up, fatigued beyond recovery, an older man than you, and am determined to let the park take care of itself for a while at whatever cost."[9]

On August 6, 1860, while riding in a carriage through Central Park together with his wife and infant son, a horrendous accident occurred. The accident, Roper claims, was caused by a new mare that Olmsted was trying out. The mare was "tormented by flies" and bolted, one rein caught beneath her tail. "Olmsted stood up to free it" and was "flung out against a rock," shattering his left thigh bone. Mary and the child were "tossed out," uninjured. For her version of the accident, Roper cites only her own interview with Olmsted's then elderly son, Rick, who had not been born until ten years after the accident took place. Nevertheless, this version is virtually identical to the account that appeared in the *Tribune* three days after the accident: "The calamity appears to have been caused by the reins getting caught in the horse's tail; in the effort to dislodge them, the animal, which Mr. Olmsted was driving for the first time, took flight and ran away."[10]

There is, as it happens, another version of the accident—a version that also sheds further light on the illness that had preceded it. This version is recorded in a memorandum made by Theodora Kimball, based upon an interview of her own conducted with Olmsted's widow, who had of course been in the carriage with Olmsted. It is worth citing in full:

> Mr. Olmsted was in very poor health, very weak, in 1859 (after his marriage) —he went to Saratoga to recuperate,—returning was so weak he couldn't sit up alone in the carriage. Dropped reins when driving which was cause of accident, pitched out of carriage, broke leg. So weak, his life was dispaired of—leg couldn't be set immediately.
>
> After a few days and careful feeding to give him more strength he was on the road to recovery.
>
> In 2 days after the accident he had men from the park up to his room & was going over things with them on a map spread out on the floor.[11]

Clearly, the version given to the press shortly after the accident makes Olmsted appear as a somewhat heroic figure—injured in a desperate attempt to save his wife and child from the effect of a frightened, runaway horse. This is a far more appealing portrait than that of an enfeebled man who had put his wife and child in jeopardy by dropping the reins of the carriage in which they had been riding. As with the published versions of Olmsted's youth and education, as with the press accounts of the roles played by Olmsted and Vaux in the design of Central Park, this official version of the accident serves Olmsted's reputation. Thus, it was this official version that Olmsted's son still purveyed some ninety years later.

Olmsted himself contradicted this official version of his illness and accident in a letter of resignation written to the Central Park Board of Commissioners in 1861.[12] In this letter, Olmsted described the physical and mental exhaustion that overwhelmed him in 1859 and 1860, an exhaustion that brought him "close on the edge of a brain-fever" and that "once or twice" caused him to faint and be "carried to my bed." His difficulties, he stated, were "normal & constant" and existed from "the beginning of the work." Finally, he wrote, it was from this weakness and exhaustion "that I fainted in my carriage & was run away with last summer [1860], & so damaged as you know."

The Kimball version makes it clear that the immediate cause of the accident was Olmsted's physical and mental condition, not a new mare "tormented by flies." Further, it implies that there had been other occasions when he had dropped the reins, occasions that were, perhaps, dress rehearsals for this accident. It also makes a direct connection between Olmsted's illness and his marriage, while making no reference to Andrew Green or to Olmsted's troubles with the park. Finally, it suggests that the tonic he had needed for the cure of his long, debilitating illness was the accident itself, not a trip to Saratoga with his wife and not a trip to England by himself.

All sources agree that the accident inflicted terrible damage upon Olmsted's thigh and threatened his life. Moreover, within a few days of his accident, his infant son died suddenly and tragically, apparently of cholera. "Bereaved and crippled," Roper says, "Olmsted yet presented a stoic face to the world," recovering his strength and "his passion for his work" within two months. With this, all sources agree.[13]

It is as if this accident itself was an expiation for whatever he might have done to bring on his physical and mental breakdown. Even the tragic death of his infant son seems only to have spurred on Olmsted's recovery and the restoration of "his passion for his work"—as if the son's death was some sort of puritanical punishment (and thus further expiation) for the father's sin. What deed could Olmsted have committed that would seem so terrible to his psychic self? In the context of the Kimball memo, might it not have been to marry his brother's wife? Was this not, to his unconscious self, yet another usurpation of that which had been rightfully John Hull's?

Olmsted, riding alone, had suffered a similar accident some six years previous to this one, in November 1854. That accident occurred on Staten Island, a few months after his return from his last trip through Texas and the South and several months before he abandoned the Staten Island farm to his brother in order to take up a literary career. He was, at the time, already committed to these literary ventures, and John Hull—married, ill, the father of one child and his wife pregnant with a second—had begun to take responsibility for running the farm.[14]

Olmsted's wagon was being drawn by Bell, a horse he had purchased in Texas and had ridden, apparently without accident, throughout the latter half of his journey. It was a "cold, damp & windy" evening, and Olmsted's horse was startled by another wagon attempting to pass. Olmsted stated that his horse "jumped" and was struck by the other wagon, which "terrified him" and caused him to bolt. "I . . . was trying to get myself loose of my wrapping when he kicked in the dash board and jerked the reins out of my hands," Olmsted wrote. "They are short reins, but I am much ashamed of it." In the wild ride that followed, the horse ran into the fields and headed for "a large old apple tree" with low branches. Olmsted "threw up the front seat and lay . . . down in the bottom as the safest position." The branches tore "every thing higher than the dash board" off the carriage. After bouncing and bucking across the fields, the carriage was righted as the horse regained the road and headed for a toll gate. Olmsted kicked out the rear seat and threw himself over the back, holding on with one hand as he tried to lower himself as close to the ground as possible before letting go. In the aftermath, though the wagon had been badly damaged, he found that his horse had suffered only a cut shoulder, while he himself was "stiff & sore," with a slightly sprained right knee.

As with the later Central Park incident, this narration (made by Olmsted to his father), placed the immediate cause of the runaway with an outside force—a passing wagon here, tormenting flies in the Central Park accident. In both cases, Olmsted's efforts to bring the horse under control seem rather heroic. But what if there was another factor involved in the triggering of the Staten Island runaway? What if Olmsted, wrapped like "a mummy" in his "blankets & buffalos," had dozed off as his horse trotted along on the road from town? Could he have dropped the reins *before* the passing wagon startled Bell and sent the horse galloping? Would not that have been even greater cause for Olmsted to be "ashamed" before his father? And would that not have made the Staten Island incident an even stronger precursor to the Central Park accident?

The year-long illness that had struck Olmsted in 1859–1860 and culminated in that horrendous accident clearly was the worst and most significant of the three periods of physical and mental collapse referred to earlier. The second, in sequence and in degree of severity, was his temporary blindness in 1873. This attack seems to have been blamed on overwork, but the timing suggests deeper, psychic causes.

During the previous year, his relationship with Calvert Vaux had taken some odd twists. As that year (1872) had begun, the firm of Olmsted and Vaux was once again serving as landscape architects for the New York parks (their third tour of duty since 1858). In May, Olmsted was appointed a commissioner and elected President and the Treasurer of the Board, with Vaux becoming Landscape Architect. In October 1872, Olmsted resigned from the Board and was once more reappointed Landscape Architect, with Vaux now a consultant. The week prior to this, the firm of Olmsted and Vaux was dissolved (although the two men continued to be associated on the New York parks and other projects).[15]

On January 21, 1873, Olmsted's father—eighty-one years of age—fell on some ice and broke his hip; he died on the 25th. During that time, Olmsted made two trips to Hartford to be with his father and was with him at his death. Only a month earlier, he had summoned Frederick to Hartford to discuss "a matter of business."[16] He wanted Frederick to become a trustee of his estate, along with Frederick's half brother, Albert Henry, now a Hartford banker. The latter had been appointed a trustee for the estate when John Olmsted's will was created in 1863.

During Frederick's first trip to Hartford, after his father's accident, it was thought that the injury was not dangerous, and his father seemed quite cheerful; so Frederick returned to New York. Summoned back to

Hartford the next day, he found that his father had declined considerably
and "appeared dreadfully older than the day before." His father was in a
great deal of pain, "moaning and tossing like one in typhoid fever,"
getting very little relief from opiates. Nevertheless, he was pleased to see
Frederick, who gave him a "punch of sherry, brandy & lemon." Frederick
later wet his father's lips as the old man cried: "air—give me all the air
you can." Frederick gathered other members of the family, and then his
father "breathed his last without a struggle, apparently unconscious &
with his perfect senses until the very end of life."[17]

The loss of his father was a tremendous blow to Frederick, who was
still dependent upon him to a remarkable degree and who still suffered
from any sign of his father's lack of respect for him. Only a few years
before, John Olmsted had once again come to the rescue of his hard-
pressed son with a "loan," raising money on his own collateral to give to
Olmsted and Vaux, telling Frederick it was clear that *he* could not raise
the money "since your firm is not known." Thus, it was with acute self-
knowledge that Frederick now told Kingsbury: "He was a very good man
and a kinder father never lived. It is strange how much of the world I feel
has gone from me with him. The value of any success in the future is
gone for me."[18] In this the son's desperate hope to have yet impressed his
father, somehow, in some way is apparent. Frederick must have been
gratified to find among his father's papers "a number of scraps of newspapers running back 20 years," referring to Frederick's books and his
parks and other works.

But this aside, Olmsted was scarred by both the loss and the ordeal. In
the Kingsbury letter, he recorded a conversation in which John Olmsted
had expressed some feeling of guilt toward his own father (Frederick's
grandfather). John Olmsted (Frederick reported) said he had done what
he could in his younger days to make life comfortable for his father, but
added that what he gave "was nothing to what he had."[19]

It is likely that, in reporting his father's guilt feelings, Frederick was
expressing feelings he himself felt, having received so much from his
father, but seldom seeming to think of what his father might have needed
from *him*. "The weight of my father's death is very heavy upon me," he
told another friend.[20] And he added: "I can not but wonder that I should
have known so little how large a part of all I cared for in life was with my
father."

Olmsted also reported to Kingsbury another incident that took place as his father was dying—one that cast a poignant shadow over the events of the next few months. On the morning before his death, John Olmsted had received a letter from an old friend, recalling some joke he and another young man had played upon John "on the day of his wedding with Miss Hull, more than half a century ago." Frederick added: "Father was much gratified, and . . . he said to my [step]mother, 'It is very pleasant that an old man like me should be so much thought of.' " This charming incident, a light moment in Frederick's long ordeal, had its more somber aspect, contrasting, as it did, the memory of the lost mother of his childhood (Charlotte Law Hull) with the reality of the woman who had become his mother (Mary Ann Bull).

Mary Ann Olmsted was "the only mother the boys ever knew," Fred Kingsbury later recalled, adding that she was "a woman of high character, very religious, with the puritan theology of her youth and endeavored to bring the children up in accordance with its precepts." In time, however, Kingsbury added, they had reacted strongly against "her stern theological views."[21] The events of the next several months after John Olmsted's death were to produce an even greater estrangement between Frederick and his stepmother, for Mary Ann Olmsted hired a lawyer and hotly contested her late husband's will, directing her efforts, in particular, to getting Frederick removed as a trustee.[22]

In late August 1873, Olmsted set off on a trip to Canada, sailing to Newfoundland, then travelling to the Gaspè Peninsula and Quebec. Olmsted was accompanied by his stepdaughter Charlotte, who had been ill, and he seemed in very good spirits, writing a quite charming and playful letter about the stormy passage northward.[23] His return home, however, brought him back to both political and family strife. Albert wrote to say that Mary Ann Olmsted had insinuated that the two sons had bribed the probate judge and that Albert had perjured himself. Within days of receiving this letter, Olmsted drafted a letter to the President of the Department of Public Parks, S. H. Wales, asking to be "relieved of responsibilities which under present circumstances" (his continuing disagreements with the Commissioners) he could not satisfactorily meet.[24] The commissioners with whom Olmsted had been squabbling at this time were actually men of his own gentry circle who had come to power with the ouster of the Tweed Ring in 1871. But Olmsted's antagonist, Andrew H. Green, had returned along with this group—all of them in Samuel Tilden's coterie of Democratic reformers. Immediately after his letter to Wales, however, Olmsted received a telegram stating that the Board had nevertheless voted to continue his employment.

It was shortly afterward that Olmsted was suddenly afflicted with a temporary blindness, which apparently was treated by having him confined to a darkened room. "I cannot express the regret I feel that both your great Parks are to lose your guidance and controlling influence," one associate wrote during this siege. [25]

By mid-December, Olmsted was again writing long and impassioned letters to his closest friends. As Stevenson notes, the diatribe he directed toward Charles Loring Brace was "compulsively personal" and reveals Olmsted to have been "not entirely well in his nerves." In one place, he wrote:

Suppose a man who sees things so far differently than the mass of ordinarily healthy men is thereby classified as of defective vision, as of diseased brain. Thus I have not a doubt that I was born with a defect of the eye, with a defect of the brain.

This passage suggests that Olmsted clearly saw the hysterical nature of his eye ailment—that he understood the connection between the defective vision of one's eyes and the defective vision of one's psyche, both of them products of a "diseased brain." But a later passage reveals even more strongly the morbid frame of mind afflicting Olmsted during this period. "Did you ever hear of a case," Olmsted asked Brace, "in which the son of a Christian mother was oppressed with melancholy and reflected on suicide as he began to face his great work in the world." [26]

As Olmsted was recovering in December, he seems also to have written a similar, very long, impassioned letter to another of his most intimate correspondents, Katharine Prescott Wormeley, a woman who had shared with him a great crisis of the Civil War. Wormeley, like Brace, was a person of considerable intellectual accomplishment and, also like Brace, she was someone with whom Olmsted had long had a close emotional attachment. After Olmsted's death, Wormeley would state to Brace's daughter that Olmsted was one of "the two men I had loved best in life out of my own family" and that his death would leave "a great void" in her life. [27]

In her reply to Olmsted's letter (which has not survived), Wormeley noted that Olmsted had spoken "of not having much self-possession within one's brain—of feeling so nearly frantic with mortification, perplexity, disappointment, & deeply wounded feeling." She suggested that his depression had resulted from "purposes thwarted, worthy *useful* beautiful objects miscarried—high aims misunderstood."[28]

One can believe that Olmsted had been truly "frantic with mortification, perplexity, disappointment, & deeply wounded feeling" during these months of sequestration. His sudden eye affliction had caused an abrupt hiatus in his obsessive work habits—habits that could so easily be used as a shield against unwanted self-examination. After the year had begun with brief but intense mourning for his father, absorption in his work had seen him, rather cheerfully, through bitter contention both with his stepmother and with his peers in the park system. Now he was prevented not only from working, but even from reading and writing, confined day after day in a darkened room, alone with his thoughts and his memories.

The timing of his illness, coming as it did toward the end of September, should be especially noted. In that month were the birthdays of John Hull (September 2), Frederick's mother, Charlotte (September 9), and his father (September 27). Anniversaries of this sort—events that are inescapable reminders of the past—can serve as "triggers" for the development of neurotic symptoms that are themselves linked to the past.[29] The original trauma, seemingly silent in the unconscious, only awaits, or perhaps even seeks, its cue to come on stage. That it was *this* set of birthdays, and not a previous September's, which touched off such a powerful reaction was surely due to the fact that this set was the first after his father's death—so that the birthdays only served to remind him that he had now lost all those who had meant the most to him in his childhood and who were most closely connected to the earliest, most formative years, and to whatever wounds these years might have left. It was also particularly meaningful that Olmsted's *eyes* were affected, whatever the source and the nature of the original psychological wound (or wounds).

As with the accident in Central Park, Olmsted's temporary blindness of 1873 also had a precursor in the severe eye trouble he had developed as an adolescent. The most extensive evidence for the nature and effect of this earlier problem is found in one of a series of fragments written by

Olmsted in the mid-1890s (probably 1893), material he was apparently
considering as an autobiographical preface to an intended work on landscape architecture.[30] Much of this material clearly was written under an
elderly man's inner compulsion to understand those factors, including the
experiences of early childhood, that had prepared him for his life's work.

The published version of these fragments contains this passage:

When fourteen I was laid up by an extremely virulent sumach poisoning, making
me for some time partially blind, after which, *and possibly as a result*, I was troubled
for several years with a disorder of the eyes and the oculists advised that I should
be kept from study.

It followed that at the time my schoolmates were entering college I was
nominally the pupil of a topographical engineer [Frederick A. Barton, in Andover, Massachusetts] but really for the most part given over to a decently
restrained vagabond life, generally pursued under the guise of an angler, a fowler
or a dabbler on the shallowest shores of the deep sea of the natural sciences.
(Emphasis added.)

Olmsted himself referred to such an accident in two other documents,
in each case without labeling it as "sumach poisoning." These documents
also date from the 1890s: a letter to Elizabeth Baldwin Whitney of December 16, 1890, and a letter to Mariana G. Van Rensselaer of June 11,
1893.[31]

In the former, complaining that he had been "uneducated—miseedu-
cated," Olmsted wrote: "Because of an accident putting my eyes in some
peril, I was at the most important age left to 'run wild' and when at
school, mostly as a private pupil in the families of country parsons of
small poor parishes, it seems to me I was chiefly taught how not to study.
. . . While my mates were fitting for college I was allowed to indulge my
strong natural propensity for roaming afield and day-dreaming under a
tree." The Van Rensselaer letter covered similar ground, but added that
it was due to "medical advice" that he was "allowed and encouraged to
spend a great deal of time riding and walking upon rural roads and across
country," and so on, rather than fitting himself for college.

In all of these reflections upon the pacific outdoor life of his youth,
there is a sort of pride in his rustic woodsmanship; a sly admission that
when he was at "the most important age," he had led an idling life; and
an enduring shame over his lack of formal education, which required that
it be explained by an accident—nameless at first, then sumac poisoning

—lest he otherwise be thought to have been intellectually inferior or simply lazy. Indeed, in a follow-up letter to Van Rensselaer, he speaks of his possible laziness, then writes: "Laziness? No, hardly; but a wandering, contemplative, day-dreaming, and in that respect self-indulgent habit —sympathetic with those moods of men which are best satisfied in listening to music and gazing upon scenery."[32] Evidently, these years of seemingly aimless drift had remained a sticking point with Olmsted, had left an inner conflict that required him both to condemn himself and to excuse himself and that had prompted him to project the image of an artlessly self-educated person as a kind of intellectual superiority.

In another memoir—written in 1860, in almost a stream-of-consciousness fashion, more than thirty years before the "sumach poisoning" story was recorded—Olmsted also referred to his eye problems, embedding them in a recital of his early schooling:

From seven to thirteen private pupil with country clergymen—experienced religion 72 times, but cream constantly rising and froth overflowing—nature pretty strong—*at 13 eyes gave out*—at home a year and got a gun—not much at ball or marbles but good swimmer & skater & fond of rabbits & Midshipman Easy. At 14 a year on sea shore & episcopal training [with Reverend Eastman at Saybrook]—Boats & deep sea fishing—feat with a [. . .] & flounder—15 & 16 nominally a pupil to an Engineer [Barton], *but weak eyes favored natural disposition*, copied maps & planned ideal towns, but most of the time in the mountains. Then a year in New York, French importing house didn't suit a good deal—Went to sea for a year & had a tough time—. (Emphases added.)[33]

In detail, timing, and sequence, this passage closely follows the events of Olmsted's boyhood and youth as given in John Olmsted's journal.[34] The tenor of it is that Olmsted had begun to suffer recurring eye problems with the onset of puberty and adolescence. (The vivid psychic imagery from his 1860 memoir will be discussed in part 2.) The eye weakness he developed continued to bother him throughout adolescence and interfered with his engineering studies at Barton's, to which he was not disposed anyway, his natural inclination seeming to be indolence.[35] Nowhere is there a mention of sumac poisoning or any other accident endangering his eyesight, nor of the eye problems interfering with plans to attend college.

Another piece of evidence is to be found in Fred Kingsbury's remembrance of Olmsted, written after the latter's death. Kingsbury recalls Olmsted's adolescence in this manner:

The two boys were educated in the schools of the town and entered the Hartford Hopkins Grammar School to prepare for college.

About this time, however, Fred had trouble with his eyes which interfered with his studies and, perhaps being tired of routine, he persuaded his father to prepare him for a business life.[36]

Clearly, Kingsbury had his information from Frederick himself when first John Hull and then Frederick were together with him at Yale in the mid-1840s. All mention of boarding with country ministers is missing; Frederick supposedly had been given the same education that John Hull had. It seems that only a few years after these events, Olmsted had totally suppressed his educational misadventures.

Further, Kingsbury makes no mention of sumac poisoning or an accident of any sort; he notes only Olmsted's "trouble with his eyes." Finally, Kingsbury indicates that the apprenticeship at Benkard and Hutton was Frederick's idea, not his father's. This is contrary to the accepted version, but Kingsbury is probably right.[37]

It happens that three letters are extant, written by John Olmsted to Frederick during the fall of 1838, when Frederick was at Barton's.[38] The latter two, of September and October 1838, plainly reveal John Olmsted's attitude toward Frederick's education and choice of career:

Yours of 24th at hand this morning—If you will not go back in your surveying by giving it up this term & pursuing other studies . . . I have *no objection.*

It will be an excellent chance for you to study Rhetoric etc & it may be desirable to pursue it another term before returning to Surveying. I am sorry however to have your mind unsettled on the subject of your studies, while the mind is vacelating [sic] & unsettled you will pursue neither with ardour—I hope if this change is made you will get so interested in yr new Studies as to prefer to go on with them another term rather than go to Collinsville [with Barton]. . . .

I have no recollection of ever saying I wishd you to go into a store—if you did you would want no other rules than you practice in Mathematics.

I should regret to have you study a great deal evenings unless your Eyes are strong. . . .

Be desirous of pursuing such studies as will most tend to your intellectual and moral improvement & to fit you for usefulness & employment when you take your place in the great theatre of life & throw everything from you that tends to distract your from this pursuit.

In the letter of October 10, two weeks later, John Olmsted added these remarks:

3. Frederick's father, John Olmsted, c. 1860. A successful businessman and investor, he was also a cultured man with a great love of nature. Though reserved, he was devoted to all his children, especially the sons of his first marriage: Frederick and John Hull. (Society for the Preservation of New England Antiquities.)

I am very pleased with the account of your studies . . . & very glad to learn
that you are now getting so much interested in them—I thought it could not be
otherwise—At 16 or 17, if ever, we begin to feel that the time is come for us to
throw off boyish notions & habits . . . without these literary & scientific attainments, in this age of the world, we cannot expect to be respected or to respect
ourselves.

What these letters suggest is a loving and concerned father who at times
grew exasperated by his son's inability to focus on his studies or to choose
a path in life but was ready to support his son in whatever he chose—
just so long as he chose something, *anything*. There is no sign in these
letters of what Olmsted was later to imply: that his father had acquiesced
in Frederick's leading a "decently restrained vagabond life." Certainly, he
was concerned with Frederick's eye problems, but he well knew his son's
propensity for wandering afield, daydreaming, and the like, and he longed
to see these "boyish habits and notions" come to an end. Further, he
clearly had not forced a merchant's life on his son; the Benkard and
Hutton apprenticeship was likely Frederick's idea, as Kingsbury states.[39]

In regard to the chronic eye weakness, it should also be noted that
Olmsted often claimed for himself a prodigious amount of reading while
a youth, and he continued to be both a heavy reader and a voluminous
writer throughout his life, despite recurrent complaints about his eyes.
The only major surcease from this intense use of his eyes occurred late in
1873, in his attack of hysterical blindness several months after his father's
death. It is hard to understand how the study of engineering, let alone
rhetoric and other classic studies, could have been considered a lesser use
of his eyes than would have been involved in a college career. John
Olmsted suggests only that night-reading would be bad for Olmsted's
troubled eye-sight—true wherever he might have pursued the academic
life.

Late in 1845, Frederick finally did become a student at Yale, where
John Hull had been enrolled since 1842. Frederick was categorized as a
"special student," studying chemistry with Professor Benjamin Silliman,
ostensibly to assist in the pursuit of "scientific farming."[40] But after a few
months of Yale, Frederick experienced several "alarming" attacks, which
apparently were fainting spells serious enough to raise some concern of
apoplexy.[41] Frederick's college career came to an end within a few weeks.
Several months later, Frederick was to write to Kingsbury:

In study I am wonderfully lazy or weak and very soon get tired out. I am romantic—fanciful—jump at conclusions and yet always find headaches or convenient excuses when I want them. I have a smattering of education—a little sum, from most everything useful to such a man as I—learned as I took a fancy to it.[42]

Frederick's chronic eye problems—like his fainting spells at Yale and the blindness that afflicted him in 1873—were thus psychosomatic. What Frederick likely had been resisting as an adolescent was hard study of any kind, especially if it involved a structured, supervised routine.

The great variety of physical afflictions that Olmsted suffered over the years—eye troubles, fainting spells, palpitations of the heart, frequent mental and physical exhaustion, insomnia—were hardly unique to him, but rather were epidemic among his gentry peers. Many historians have focused upon the work of George M. Beard, a New York physician and neurologist who, in the post–Civil War decades, pioneered the study of nervous illnesses.[43] As I mentioned in the introduction, Beard coined the term *neurasthenia* for what we would today consider the physical effects of neurosis: a "grab bag" of complaints that included insomnia, dyspepsia, vertigo, headache, depression, heart palpitations, and so forth.[44] Beard thought neurasthenia unique to nineteenth-century America, caused by the pressures a newly industrial, competitively materialistic society brought to bear on the individual. Moreover, this was a society, Stow Persons adds, in which new forms of communication brought "all the woes of the world to each man's doorstep with the morning paper." Neurasthenia afflicted a definite physiological type, Beard thought: "small in size, with a frail, fine constitution, frequently of superior intellect and a strong emotional nature."[45]

Howard Feinstein reports Beard's observation that these invalided patients usually were in their teens to midforties. A variant of the disease "affected the eyes, causing weakness and difficulty reading"—a chronic affliction of William James (and of Frederick Law Olmsted). Beard further observed that this problem had spread throughout "many of the colleges and seminaries of the country—in some instances compelling young men to abandon their plans of a liberal education."[46]

Among the gentry figures suffering from "more or less incapacitating nervous illness," according to Persons, were: Horace Bushnell (the famed Hartford minister who was the Olmsteds' neighbor and an inspiration for

Frederick's own social thought), William Graham Sumner, Charles Eliot
Norton (Olmsted's friend and associate), Edmund J. Stedman, and George
William Curtis. Persons cites the frequent references to ill health and
travel "in search of health" encountered in the records of that era—to
which again I might add the example of John Olmsted and his children.
Persons reports that one gentry leader thought his generation burdened
by a "dreadful, nervous, hurried feeling," while another "doubted that
anyone ever reached the age of thirty-five in New England without
wanting to kill himself."[47]

For Persons, the "traditional gentry emphasis on obligation and personal responsibility"—often identified with "manliness"—accentuated
other environmental and constitutional tendencies toward nervousness.
Daniel Wilson comments (in reviewing Beard's work) that neurasthenic
symptoms "allowed the individual to opt out of the pressures of seeking a
career, of finding a spouse, or dealing with rapid [social] changes." They
were, in fact, one solution to the conflict that arose in such individuals
when these critical stages of the life cycle were "out of joint with the
larger world," a situation that occurred in ninetheenth-century America:

Men coming of age in the Civil War years and after and seeking professional
careers were caught in the transition from the patterns of antebellum America to
the newer professional and academic patterns that would be established by the
late 1880s. They sought careers which did not yet fully exist and the disjunction
between their life-cycle and the world of work caused the [neurasthenic] problems
so evident in this generation.

For such men, neurasthenia was one answer, often temporary, to the
psychic tension and disequilibrium that arose when they seemed unable
to identify or to achieve personal objectives that would be meaningful to
them.[48]

The social role of invalidism in mid–nineteenth-century New England,
Howard Feinstein observes, is to be found in the Romantic and Puritan
roots of the gentry intellectuals who suffered so markedly from neurasthenia. "Salvation through work, condemnation of idleness, suspicion of
pleasure, and the belief that suffering leads to grace flowed from the
Puritan source," he writes; "Insistence upon self-expression, a high val-
uation of leisure, and the admiration of delicacy and acute sensibility
from the Romantic." In such a social setting, Feinstein concludes, "illness
had considerable utility."[49]

Olmsted's chronic sufferings throughout his life, his tendency to respond to personal and social pressures with illness, accidents, and physical and mental exhaustion (as in 1859–1860, 1873, and 1877–1878), and the specific symptoms he developed were at once unique to his own individual psychological development and widely shared among his gentry peers. It is precisely such an intensely personal realization of the same inner conflicts that afflict their peers that allows creative artists to become the "delegates" of their peers—to produce works that evoke such enthusiastic response and approval from these peers.

Olmsted continued year after year to pursue the public and private career of a landscape architect while the disjunction became ever greater (in his mind) between his own inner needs and the work he was able to accomplish in what he regarded as a hostile environment. This was the disjunction Olmsted so poignantly acknowledged in his 1890 letter to Elizabeth Baldwin Whitney, when he said he had been "selling being for doing."

The last of the three major breakdowns that marked Olmsted's twenty-year association with Central Park was the breakdown of which he writes in *Spoils of the Park*, when he suffered a mental and physical exhaustion (1877–1878) that preceded his final dismissal from work on the New York parks. The onset of his decline seems to have become apparent to his friend Katharine Wormeley through his unwonted bitterness toward the Tilden Democrats in the disputed election of 1876. "I cannot help thinking," she wrote him at the beginning of 1877, "that your life in NY where the democrats are rampant, odious, & corrupt, darkens your mind—& even narrows it." By November, he had been ill for several months, and Wormeley was once again urging him to get away from his life in New York: "You *are* overworked—You are not really a *well* man . . . with worry of mind;—and your way of life is not good for you." [50]

Olmsted's correspondence with Katharine Wormeley came to an end shortly after this, apparently at Mary Olmsted's behest. [51] Charles Loring Brace was now the last of those few intimate friends to whom Olmsted could still write from the heart, as he had in his youth. It was in a letter to Brace, after suffering a railroad accident in 1887, that Olmsted recalled the agonies of his youthful religious fervor and his preoccupation with theological speculation—"all that used to be such a terrifically cruel burden upon me." Olmsted noted that he had long since freed his mind from such religiosity. "What a different, happier and better life I should have had, had it always been so," he added, thus acknowledging that this "cruel burden" had been one of the sources of his own psychic torment. [52]

Brace died in 1890, and a few years later, Olmsted, seventy-one years old, seems to have made one final attempt to renew his friendship with Katharine Wormeley, composing a draft letter—perhaps never sent— late in 1893. [53] This was, of course, the period when the first intimations of his final mental breakdown arose. It was a period during which, in his letters and his nocturnal jottings, he seemed to be searching for his true self, for whatever would give his life a meaning that could not be satisfied by honorary degrees and published appreciations. The period in which Olmsted was once again moved to reach out to Katharine Wormeley was the same one in which he was turning almost totally toward his son, Rick, in a last desperate attempt to connect with at least one other human being.

CHAPTER 3

A Sense of Failure

Toward the end of 1884, two years after his move to Brookline and the severing of his ties with New York, Olmsted took the measure of his own career as against that of Charles Loring Brace. [1] "You decidedly have had the best & most worthy successful career of all whom I have known," he wrote to Brace. He himself had done "a good deal of work" in his own way, Olmsted noted; but it was "constantly & everywhere arrested, wrecked, mangled and misused" and it was not easy for him "to get above intense disappointment & mortification." Later on, Olmsted added:

> I keep working as close to my possibilities as ever, my possibilities, never large, growing perceptively smaller with every year. John [his stepson] takes more & more off and I have two good young men as "pupils," but the character of my business becomes smaller & brings a greater multitude of diverse concerns to me & I get very weary of turning so often from one thing to another and of so many long & short expeditions.

Roper considers that the second use of *smaller* in the above passage was a slip on Olmsted's part, that he actually meant to write *larger*, for he was then carrying "a heavy burden of professional works, some of staggering complexity." And she adds that there was "a curious disparity between his passion for the contemplative enjoyment of scenery and his compulsion to work to his utmost limit." [2] But it is clear from Olmsted's usage here and from his measuring of himself against Brace that his reference both to the possibilities and to the "character" of his work reflected precisely its *inner* meaning—that with the ending of his ties to the New York parks, his work had, to him, become much less significant. [3]

It is important to remember that Olmsted's dissatisfaction was a function both of his own tormented psyche and of his sense of his place in his society. The perceptive Fred Kingsbury, commenting on Olmsted's letter to Brace, wrote Brace:

> It is a pity that he [Olmsted] should attach so little importance to the much he has accomplished and so much to the little he has not succeeded in doing in his mind. No man ever comes up to his ideals who has any. And for reputation there are few men who have a more enviable one than Fred. Well known and highly regarded in two hemispheres and in three departments of human effort, Literature, Philanthropy and Art. Most men would be fairly satisfied (if men are ever satisfied) with his position in either.
> He ought to be able to thoroughly enjoy the fruits of his labor. [4]

Unfortunately, enjoying the fruits of his labor was something that Olmsted would not, could not, do. As Roper pointed out, Olmsted had a "compulsion to work to his utmost limit." Let us recall that cool assessment Olmsted had made of his father's life's work, shortly after John Olmsted's death:

> My father was well-fitted to live only in a highly organized community in which each man's stint is measured out to him according to his strength. As the world is going he was perhaps as fortunately placed in this regard as he well could be. Yet the world was driving along so fast that a man of any spirit could not but feel himself cruelly prodded up to take more upon himself than he was equal to. [5]

As I noted in the introduction, it was Olmsted himself who had felt so "cruelly prodded up" to take upon himself so many burdens—burdens that at the same time he must have feared were more than "he was equal to." Not even age and infirmities could free him from these self-imposed burdens. "I feel I have been taking on rather appalling loads for the warm weather," he wrote to his young associate, Charles Eliot, in 1894; "Yet I can't convict myself of having undertaken more than was [my] professional duty."[6] And two months later, Olmsted complained to Fred Kingsbury of "always taking on loads heavier than I can carry."[7]

The Central Park accident had left him with a noticeable limp, and the railroad accident of 1887 had aggravated that injury, so that in his later years he usually walked with a cane. Nevertheless, now in his late sixties, he continued to drive himself forward in his obsessive work habits, and he experienced even more illnesses and accidents. He was to continue paying the "price" of "doing."

Despite the scope of his undertakings in the decade after his dismissal (which included the U.S. Capitol grounds, the Niagara Falls park grounds, and the Boston park system), Olmsted never freed himself from the hold the New York parks, especially Central Park, had upon his professional pride and upon his psyche. By 1887, he found himself once more embroiled in the endless public squabbles over the fate of the New York parks.[8] In the process, he stumbled into a painful epistolary argument with his quondam colleague, Calvert Vaux, who clearly feared that Olmsted would overshadow him in the reformist efforts to set the park aright, refusing to accept Olmsted's repeated assurances to the contrary. "I have not, so far as I am aware of yet taken a step in the matter without more regard for you than for myself," Olmsted wrote Vaux in midsummer, earnestly but with a perhaps unconsciously motivated escape clause ("so far as I am aware of").[9] Both his embittered pamphlet of 1882, *Spoils of the Park*, and his emotion-laden letters to Vaux were written out of the same deep need, a need that came from the core of his being and had driven him forward with manic intensity time and again during his long association with the New York parks—and had driven him, too, into his repeated breakdowns. In both the 1882 pamphlet and the 1887 Vaux letters, there is to be found the same *cri di coeur*. After reciting, in *Spoils of the Park*, the events which had led up to his dismissal, Olmsted wrote:

> Let it be understood what this meant to me,—the *frustration* of purposes to which I had for years given *all my heart*, to which I had *devoted my life;* the *degradation* of works in which *my pride was centered;* the *breaking of promises to the future* which had been to me as *churchly vows.* However I was able to carry myself by day, it will not be thought surprising that I should have had *sleepless nights*, or that at last I could not keep myself from *over-wearing irritation and worry.* . . . It has taken me *four years to recover* the strength which I then lost within a week.[10]

In one of his letters to Vaux, written from Boston several years later, Olmsted protested that he had no further ambitions relative to New York.[11] "After coming here I diligently cut myself away from New York and all its associations," he wrote. But that there was something that could never be cut away he revealed in a heated outburst later on in the same letter:

I don't want to have to come back to New York but I am not sure that I should not even do that rather than lose all chance of bringing the parks back to original principles so far as that is now possible. To that end, with you or without you, I shall always do what seems to me best. *There is nothing else I care so much for.*

The words and phrases that I have emphasized in these two passages indicate the depths of Olmsted's psychic commitment to the New York parks. This commitment was revealed not only in Olmsted's later years. In September 1859, after returning from a sorely needed vacation in Saratoga—one from which he had been summoned home by his nemesis, Andrew Haswell Green—Olmsted was "besieged by fevers" and took to his bed, saturated by pills, tonics, and quinine prescribed by his doctors.[12] Sick, troubled, and exhausted, he wrote the letter to his father referred to in the preceding chapter, a letter that reveals once again the depth and nature of his commitment to a certain vision of Central Park:

I feel just thoroughly worn-out, used up, fatigued beyond recovery, an older man than you, and as determined to let the Park take care of itself for a while at whatever cost. I have been growing weaker & more deeply fatigued since I began with it. . . . I have fixed what I most cared for on the park beyond reconsideration & shall not be so zealous probably in [the] future.[13]

He would, in fact, leave Central Park altogether, between 1861 and 1865, first to direct the United States Sanitary Commission and then to manage the Mariposa mining plantation in California. While still in California, however, he wrote to Vaux about Central Park: "There is no other place in the world that is as much as home to me. I love it all through and all the more for the trials it has cost me."[14]

There was a second, and related, psychic need of Olmsted's that was connected to the great New York park: the fostering and protection of his professional reputation. A career ardently pursued is obviously an expression of one's selfhood, a means for defining one's personhood and for validating one's worth. For Olmsted, the profession of landscape architecture, his public reputation, and Central Park were all inextricably bound up together.

In 1893, Olmsted wrote to his young partners that their work on the Boston park system would be as historically important to American landscape architecture as Central Park itself: "Twenty years hence you will be looking back on Muddy River as I do Central Park." Olmsted was, at the time, at Biltmore, the estate of George W. Vanderbilt, for which he had been engaged to design and implement the landscaping.

Biltmore, too, was critical, he told them: *"critical* for you—for our 'school,' for our profession." It was critical, that is, for establishing the reputation of Olmsted Associates for "private places" as well as for public projects. [15] Biltmore represented, also, Olmsted's own, almost desperate, efforts to "marry" the increasingly popular neoclassical architectural style into his own system of "natural or naturalistic landscape work." It was an attempt he had already made, with some misgivings, at the World Columbian Exposition in Chicago, which is considered the beginning of the "City Beautiful" movement. But Biltmore, he told an associate, represented "heavier risks in this respect." [16]

The expositors of the City Beautiful movement, as David Schuyler observes, were evolving a very different scheme of urban design than Olmsted's naturalistic city. In place of Olmsted's "nostalgic pastoralism" —his vision of "a more openly built urban environment"—D. H. Burnham and his associates would introduce a new vision. Schuyler calls this alternative vision "the neoclassical cityscape," an application of the Beaux Arts school to America's cities in order to create a more formal and imposing urban environment "characterized by ensembles of neoclassical monuments." [17]

As it happened, it was Calvert Vaux's struggles against the intrusion of the neoclassic movement into the New York parks that thrust them back into Olmsted's consciousness during this period. Vaux was enduring almost continuous harassment from the New York park commissioners, who were now intent upon bringing "conspicuous classicism and imposing monumentality" to the city's park system. [18] Dragged into the controversy, albeit at a distance, Olmsted, now in his seventies and quite depressed, wrote:

It is an official condemnation of Central Park. It is a verdict from the most important tribunal in the country against that which I have stood for and most cared for in all my life. It is a verdict in favor of that with which I have been most in contention and of which contention I am wearied almost to death. . . . It all makes me shrink at the last moment from carrying out my plans for advancing my son Rick's education for my profession. It is very difficult for me to avoid thinking that the profession as a profession and the art as an art is [*sic*] ruined. [19]

The extremity of Olmsted's reaction to this "contention" reveals once again his deep psychic commitment to, and the interconnections among, Central Park, his profession, and his selfhood.

It is to be expected that a man would see his only natural son, and the one who bears that man's name, as an extension of his own self. So Olmsted saw his son, Rick (Frederick Law Olmsted, Jr.). In this period of increasing self-torment, Olmsted had come to feel that he had failed in his life's mission. This pervasive anxiety seemed to spur the aged Olmsted into pouring out his feelings and fears and hopes in a virtual torrent of lengthy letters to his twenty-four-year-old son. "You must, with the aid of such inheritance as I can give you, make good my failings," he told Rick, in the midst of an impassioned twenty-one-page letter. [20]

Several months later, increasingly hampered by his infirmities and approaching his final breakdown, Olmsted begged his son to be his "eyes" at Biltmore. The old man added that he was passing his night in worries of which Rick alone could relieve him, though he thought his sleeplessness might also be due to his "morbid puritanic conscience." Two weeks later, Olmsted pressed Rick to make the most of his opportunities, adding, in the words he had once used about Central Park, "really there is little else in the world that I care so much for." [21]

As he began sinking into his final mental breakdown, Olmsted feared that his stepson, John Charles, had executed a "coup" and would freeze both him and Rick out of the firm. His last letters were filled with advice to Rick on how to first make himself indispensable to the others and then to become their superior in the profession. Surely he was concerned for Rick's future, but it is clear that Olmsted's desire for Rick to outmaneuver his half brother was also linked to the role he intended for Rick to play as his alterego. What he wanted, Olmsted wrote, was "the assurance that you are taking up what I am dropping." [22]

John Charles Olmsted had by this time been working with his stepfather in the latter's landscape architecture office for nearly two decades, in New York City as well as in Brookline. In the summer of 1876, he had stayed on in New York with his stepfather while the rest of the family vacationed in Plymouth. Mary Olmsted had remanded her husband to her son's care. She feared for Olmsted's health, she had written John Charles, and she urged him to do all he could to make things "cheerful" for his stepfather, favoring the young man with these astonishing and provocative observations:

you do not seem to recognize that there is a natural difference in men's capacities, brain powers, that no amount of industry and reasoning will equalize—Some men are born to see into things and to give orders and other men to take orders,

4. John Charles Olmsted, the oldest son of John Hull and Mary Cleveland Olmsted, who was later adopted by his stepfather. John Charles entered his stepfather's business a few years after the senior Olmsted and Calvert Vaux dissolved their partnership (1872). By the time Olmsted moved his family to Brookline, John Charles carried a great deal of responsibility for the firm's operations—particularly for the creation of the Boston park system. (National Park Service, Frederick Law Olmsted National Historical Site.)

though the love of power is unfortunately sweet to all. Just so with the desire for money. [I]t is just as well to make up your mind early that you are not likely to gratify that desire *neither* [*sic*]. There is a certain heroism in accepting circumstance and *leading a life of somber devotion to a stronger nature*—At any rate you seem to have a clearer idea of this than your sister has and are gaining in subordination— Go on improving and be a comfort to your father and to your affectionate mother.

Three summers later, Mary had cause to admonish her twenty-seven-year-old son: "Take good care of your father and don't contradict him— He is not such a fool as you think him!"[23] John Charles surely had gone on "gaining in subordination" for nearly two decades, until the nature of Olmsted's final illness had, in Stevenson's words, "made John cruel to his father."[24]

What is most significant about Olmsted's fantasy of John Charles' "coup"—even assuming that it *was* only a fantasy—is that it pitted the son and namesake of Olmsted's brother against Olmsted's own son and namesake. What Olmsted was imagining at the onset of this terrible illness, then, was a reenactment of the sibling rivalries of his earlier years. And if Olmsted had been the dominant figure, perhaps even the exploitive one, in these earlier sibling encounters (which included those with Calvert Vaux), then the situation had now become reversed. John Charles was now seen as the dominator, a sinister figure who would redress the balance of the past by "taking back" all that Olmsted had "usurped," not the least of which was the fair share of credit that had belonged to John Hull and to Calvert Vaux.

If this was Olmsted's fantasy, John Charles had probably given him grounds for it, judging by one of the letters that had passed between them during this bitter period. Impatiently answering his stepfather's questions about Biltmore, John Charles told the older man: "When the time comes for you to look into it we will let you know." He told Olmsted that his "failing memory" would eventually "necessitate some slight adjustment" in the conduct of their business affairs; and John Charles reminded his stepfather that the latter had already agreed to a reduction in his share of the firm's earnings. Finally John Charles told the ailing old man:

It would help us very much if you would constantly bear in mind that your memory for current events is no longer working basis for your thoughts. Until you do so realize you will give us no end of trouble and worry. I fully sympathize with your condition of mind but until you "give in" about your memory ailment there seems to be nothing I can do to make life easier for you.[25]

Perhaps it was necessary for John Charles to be so harsh in order to make an impression upon an increasingly befuddled mind. Perhaps this was just the natural reaction of a harassed businessman, irritated by an old man's reluctance to step aside. No matter, for the important point is that it is at just such times that one gives vent to the passions that lie deep in the unconscious and are ordinarily repressed. It can be fairly surmised, therefore, that John Charles had played an active role in the genesis of Olmsted's fearful fantasy. There is, in fact, one fascinating piece of evidence of a hidden, unconscious scenario that lay behind the family drama being enacted in those years. The harsh letter John Charles sent to his stepfather was written on September 2, 1895, on what would have been the seventieth birthday of his real father, John Hull Olmsted.

Olmsted *did* have serious "defects" in his professional abilities. He often relied upon others to help make his grandiose ideas a reality. And he quite likely had a general and haunting fear of his own inadequacy. How would a moral and decent man, which Olmsted was, react in contemplation of these facts (and contemplate them he did)? How would he have reacted, within his inner self, to the thought that he might well have exploited John Hull, Vaux, and his stepson—that the reputation he had achieved might have come in part at the expense of these men and many others? I believe that his reaction would have been one of a pervasive sense of guilt and fear of retribution, much in keeping with the "coup" fantasy discussed above.

By this time, all of Olmsted's hopes had been placed in his only surviving natural son, who had originally been named Henry Perkins Olmsted, after Mary's father. As a toddler, he had been called Boy, but letters of 1875 and 1876 called him Henry. In the summer of 1877, the boy was suddenly referred to as Fred, and by 1879 he had become Rick. The name-change to Frederick Law Olmsted, Jr., seems to have taken place in mid-1877. It is hard to know what decided Olmsted at that time to give his only natural son his own name. Perhaps his rapidly deteriorating position with Central Park (which was terminated once and for all the following year) and his associated physical troubles had provided the psychological necessity, an inner need to make concrete his identification with the boy who had now come to represent the future to him. [26]

In his long New Year's Day (1895) letter to Rick, Olmsted made very clear that an intergenerational dynamic was at work. He wrote that he had no intention of being as indulgent with Rick as his own father had been with him. Here again, he revealed his identification with Rick: "You seem to me to have very much my character; you are weak where I am weak, you are strong where I am strong." Any differences between them were only those of environment and education. Thus, to determine what would be best for Rick, Olmsted had only to think: "What would have been the best course for me under similar circumstances?" The answer was clear:

I think that my father might rightly have exercised his own judgment and not let me follow what—really I must say it—what I persuaded myself and persuaded

5. Frederick Law Olmsted, Jr., called "Rick"—originally named Henry Perkins Olmsted and renamed when he was seven or eight years old. His father closely supervised his education and his apprenticeship at the Biltmore estate. Rick took over the supervision of the Biltmore work when his father's deteriorating condition forced the latter to retire by the beginning of 1896. (National Park Service, Frederick Law Olmsted National Historical Site.)

him was my own judgment—much more than he did. I think he was really overindulgent to my inclinations disguised as I now see they were as reasonable forecast and judgment. It is this reflection, and I know myself, this reflection only, that deters me now from saying that I want you to give up the business and chose [sic] for yourself how you can best serve the world and get your living. [27]

With all his candor, with all his insight into himself, Olmsted seems oblivious here to the full import of what he is saying. He had written his former sweetheart, Elizabeth Baldwin Whitney, that he had sacrificed "being for doing." Yet is that not precisely what he is here asking Rick to do? Even more, Olmsted acknowledged that *his* father had fully supported his own youthful efforts at finding his rightful place in the world, offering Olmsted the kind of patient support Olmsted now refused to give Rick. Why did Olmsted now deny *his* son the "moratorium" his own father had once granted to him? Because—as this letter so clearly shows —he saw Rick mainly as an extension of himself.

It is this blindness to Rick's individuality that led Olmsted into depriving Rick of autonomy. But Rick was not just to be *him*; Rick was to be a *better* him. Olmsted's inner fears about his own self-worth were pronounced in this period, as shown in a letter written to Rick little more than a week earlier. [28] Olmsted had urged Rick not to be "backward" in confessing to his father all aspects of his life and thoughts, so that his father might help him in his mental and moral growth. To encourage Rick in such an introspective effort, Olmsted burst out: "I also am a *sinner* and after a long and hard discipline am still awfully neglectful of my duty to myself and to you and others. *Do I not hate myself for it* & keep striving to do better? I hope so." The morbid language suggests a pervasive sense of guilt—a guilt so profound that it might be necessary to once more sacrifice "being for doing." Perhaps one lifetime was not enough to expiate the inner guilts that demanded such a "sacrifice," that demanded that Earth be paid its "price." Perhaps Olmsted was now prepared to offer up a second life, Rick's life, all the while insisting that Rick be better at it.

However, the fundamental theme of Olmsted's letters to Rick during these years of decline was that it was Rick's duty to make good his father's failures. Ironically, the areas of failure Olmsted chose to focus upon were precisely the ones Graff and Van Rensselaer would point to as his principal weaknesses: horticulture and the usage of plants. "Let everything else go if necessary," but master botanical and horticultural knowledge, Olmsted advised Rick in mid-1895. He himself had failed in these areas "for want of zeal," Olmsted said, adding: "There is nothing in which I feel my incompetence to advise you more." Two weeks later, Olmsted wrote that Rick's main purpose at Biltmore was to acquire the "knowledge of trees and plants and horticultural operations which will make you a master, and eventually a public authority on these subjects."[29]

This was the theme that Olmsted was to work at throughout that summer and fall. And as he did so, what began to emerge was the reason for Rick's having to become "a master"—and, by implication, the reason for Olmsted's having had to drive himself toward a mastery he could never achieve to his own satisfaction. Late that year, he drove the point home forcefully:

John and Eliot are so qualified and so situated that you can make yourself *indispensable* to them, and, in a few years, be able to command your terms of them, *only by having qualified yourself in a much greater degree than any other man that they can get*, to design, planting and horticultural works. . . . I assure you that it is perfectly possible for you, in a few years, to be *the best man in the world* for landscape planting. And, of course, a much better man than Olmsted and Eliot can obtain except by employing you on your own terms.[30]

The mastery, the supremacy, Olmsted continually urged upon Rick in these letters was something more than a means by which his son was to gain financial independence, for that might well have been achieved by Rick's turning his talent and such enormous effort to another field altogether. The *psychic* factors involved here were far more important to Olmsted. First and foremost of these was his desire that Rick should *regain* Olmsted's position of *sibling supremacy*, by demonstrating Rick's superiority to both his half brother and to Charles Eliot (and thus, symbolically, Olmsted's to John Hull and to Calvert Vaux).

But even sibling supremacy was not an end in itself. Rick's mastery of these professional arts was also to be devoted to securing the eventual triumph of Olmsted's principles—which is to say, to validate the very core of Olmsted's existential being. Later on in this same letter, there occurred a striking example of this second factor, the need to see Rick dedicate himself to the achievement of Olmstedian principles. Thus, Olmsted implored Rick to take up the decades-long struggle from which he himself had now been removed. Decorative planting, Olmsted told Rick, is "at war with simple, real landscape *scenery* planting."

Let it be your work, your mission, to stand for real landscape work; for effects of scenery; for the reconciliation of convenience with scenery; for the making of gardens when gardens are wanted *as gardens*, and making scenery where scenery is wanted; gardens being exceptional and episodic passages of scenery.

Olmsted closed this letter by urging Rick once again "to be *master*, working out your own [Olmsted's] art." And he then urged upon Rick the very situation that had caused so many of his own conflicts as a landscape architect in private practice. "You must be loyal to those for whom you work," Olmsted said, adding that Rick must also think for himself and prepare himself "for original work." That is, he urged upon Rick the conflict between being a servant and being a rebel.

Rick was not only to be the champion of Olmstedian principles in practice, according to yet another long letter from this period; he was also to be theorist and propagandist in his father's stead. Olmsted told Rick that there should be a demand for "a *really good work* on the planting of shrubbery," written from the point of view of a "landscape artist" rather than a botanist. "I had a notion of undertaking such a book . . . when I was on the Brooklyn Park," Olmsted wrote, noting that he had given up the idea when he moved to Brookline. Olmsted then suggested that Rick might wish to write such a book himself, and he advised that Central Park and the Brooklyn Park (that is, the works most associated with Olmsted's career) would furnish Rick with the examples he needed. A page later he once more revealed how crucial this was to the surrogate identity Rick had to bear: "Your life is turning upon it," Olmsted stated. "It is too late to turn back."

In the closing months of 1895, with Olmsted's final breakdown becoming ever more evident, a sea change was prescribed by his doctors. In something of a panic, Olmsted wrote: "It seems I *am* going to England with Marion and your Mother. I can not quite believe it. . . . And I do so want you. I try every night to find some excuse that will serve to insist upon your being with us." Olmsted found it hard to understand why the doctors should propose a "tempestuous winter trip," and he suggested that "fully half" the purpose of it was to get him away from the office. Now he could only hope that he could persuade "them" to permit Rick to go along, musing on how nice it would be if he could travel with Rick "in Italy or anywhere in the South of Europe." "I do so want to educate you," he added. Olmsted then turned again to his darker theme, stressing that Rick must keep him informed about Biltmore. "Don't assume 'the office' tells me anything," he wrote. "You understand this sets me out of the office."[31]

And in another letter from this time, he summed up his fears and the desperate hopes he had fastened upon Rick:

> My doctors wish me to think that I am to be cured. All this that I ask will help to that end. I need hardly say that the worst thing that could happen with reference to any gain that may be hoped is the impression that my influence at Biltmore is at [an] end; that what I had hoped to accomplish will fail. [32]

Almost to the end, Olmsted was thus struggling with his twin fears: the fears of usurpation and failure.

As it happened, Rick *did* join his father, mother, and sister on the trip to England—and perhaps this recalled to Olmsted's troubled memory the season in 1850 when he had made the walking tour with John Hull and Charley Brace. While Olmsted and Rick were visiting in different parts of England, the old man wrote his son one last letter in regard to the Biltmore project, a letter that revealed yet another facet of its psychic importance to Olmsted. [33]

A major feature of the plan for Biltmore was an arboretum, which Olmsted described as being "on a very large scale" and designed to display "the ultimate in *landscape value* of the trees." He urged Rick to visit the Kew Arboretum in England, suggesting he tell those in charge about the Olmsteds' plans for Biltmore and of "our docility . . . and our humble desire to make use of the opportunity" that George W. Vanderbilt was providing upon his enormous estate near Asheville, North Carolina. "You know what my motives are," Olmsted told Rick: to create "not only an arboretum but a Museum of Economic Botany, and a school of Science." In this way, he said, Vanderbilt's wealth would be used to accomplish in America "the same public purpose" served by the Kew Arboretum in England.

Julius Fabos and his colleagues have taken note of Olmsted's dedication at Biltmore "to results that might not be achieved for generations," foreseeing that "such private work might still realize public good." And they note that what Olmsted had hoped to achieve eventually came to pass. "Today, 12,000 acres of the original 100,000 in the estate, including the mansion, have become a school of forestry and the core of North Carolina's Pisquah State Forest."[34]

In Olmsted's final years, therefore, Biltmore had come to assume the psychological burden Central Park had borne for so much of his life. Indeed, it was this psychic connection between the two that made Rick's involvement in Biltmore all the more important to Olmsted. Biltmore was to be a second chance at achieving all that Olmsted had sought to accomplish with Central Park. The private uses of Biltmore, such as may have motivated his client, George Vanderbilt, were to Olmsted merely the means of finally realizing *his* own ends. The facets of Biltmore that Fabos, Milne, and Weinmayr have commented upon—serving the public good and planning for the needs of generations ahead—are precisely those that had marked Olmsted's obsession with Central Park.

From its inception, Central Park seems to have been the work most deeply connected to Olmsted's future-mindedness. While in California in 1864, he had told Vaux that people should be made to realize "that the Park has been constituted not nearly so much for the present day as for the future." The result their design had "aimed at," he added, would not become apparent in less than twenty years, "while its perfection must not be expected in less than fifty."[35] And even earlier, during that bitter period when he had suffered from the "humiliations" imposed upon him by Andrew Green, Olmsted protested to the Central Park commissioners: "I don't care a copper for myself, Sir, or for what becomes of me, but I do care for the park, which will last after I'm dead and gone, years & years, I hope."[36] To secure at Biltmore a second chance for accomplishing the same great artistic and social purposes, Olmsted was even willing to show his employer "docility . . . and [a] humble desire to make use of the opportunity," to be servant rather than rebel.

As I have noted in the introduction, the British psychoanalyst Donald Winnicott has written of a true self, which is the essence of a person's human potential, and a false self, which mediates between the true self and the social demands of the person's environment. In extreme cases, the false self may "take over" the personality, the true self thereby being deeply suppressed. Winnicott offers this stunning image of such an extreme case: it is as if the true self had been " 'put into cold storage with a secret hope of rebirth' into a better environment later on."[37]

Winnicott's image of "rebirth" in a more favorable environment is suggestive of Olmsted's pervasive future-mindedness and his long-held insistence that artistic goals, the results of true creativity, could be achieved only after generations had passed. By the end of 1895, Olmsted had become convinced that in Biltmore lay his last chance for eventually realizing the success of his principles. This, in turn, would validate his true self, establish that he had been not merely a servant after all—but rather the artistic rebel who had proposed a "new reality" to his society, "a new way of life."[38] Fittingly, it would be an existential and psychological triumph he did not expect to live to see—a triumph that could be achieved only by his reborn self, his namesake, his son Rick.

In the middle of that last productive year before his final breakdown, an incident occurred that epitomized the role Rick had come to play in Olmsted's psyche. The eminent painter John Singer Sargent had been engaged by Vanderbilt to paint the portraits of Olmsted and Richard Morris Hunt to be hung in Biltmore's chateaulike mansion. By the time Sargent had completed Olmsted's head to his own satisfaction, his subject had become very restless and anxious to leave Biltmore. Roper notes that "with no doubt unconscious symbolism he [Olmsted] left his clothes and his son, the young Frederick Law Olmsted, to wear them and pose in his place."[39]

Olmsted's letters of 1895 reveal the urgency with which he sought to bring Rick along as his surrogate. Surely he understood the nature of the confusion then descending upon him. It would enshroud the last eight years of his life—five of them to be spent at the McLean Hospital in Massachusetts, whose grounds he had helped to select the year of his father's death. The terrible fate overtaking him in 1895 was one he had long feared. Thirty years earlier, while still Superintendent of Mariposa, Olmsted had been seized with a fit of melancholy while watching the frantic mourning with which the city of San Francisco had marked the assassination of Abraham Lincoln. "All I ask of fortune is to be saved from growing weak & incapable before my time," he wrote to Mary. "My brain and nerves tire so easily & I am so incapable without excitement & excitement is so destructive to me."[40]

Olmsted declined as the nineteenth century declined, worn down by his need to defend a Romantic vision of the century's youth, and his. And in his decline, he attempted to bind over his own child to that Romantic vision and to a psychic and existential struggle that was his, not Rick's.

PART II

Childhood and Youth

Send one of your boys to school far away for a long time, when he comes home if he is a stout-hearted boy does he not love home more than the one you have kept by you, and do you not love him the more for the absence and make more of him[?]

FREDERICK LAW OLMSTED, CA. 1863

CHAPTER 4

The Wounds of Childhood

When Olmsted was a child, Hartford was a town of some seven thousand people nestled in a long strip of thirty-odd streets stretched out in the rolling meadows alongside the Connecticut River. Surrounded by beautiful, sparsely populated hills, Hartford was a booming, bustling commercial town. The 1825 directory lists twenty-six pages of businesses, and John Olmsted's dry goods store had over twenty competitors.[1]

Before Frederick was born, John Olmsted had rented a house on College Street, just off Main Street, in a relatively undeveloped area of Hartford several blocks south of his store at the corner of Main and Pearl. The Dodd House, as it was called, was near the Hartford Grammar School and a few blocks to the east of a large tract of land upon which Washington College (now Trinity College) was established in 1825. Professor Frederick Hall, who would teach chemistry and mineralogy at the college, came with his wife to board with the Olmsteds early in March 1825, a few weeks before Frederick's third birthday.[2] The household also contained a cook, a handyman, one or two live-in maids (teenage girls), and occasionally an apprentice from the store.

The entries in John Olmsted's journal for 1825–1826 show that while their needs were basic, the Olmsteds lived well enough. There were regular expenditures for calico, gingham, and cambric, but also for silk, boots, and a mantuamaker for Charlotte Olmsted and a new frock coat and pantaloons for John Olmsted. In the fall and winter of 1825, they bought chocolate as well as turkey, goose, steak, and veal. There was a

6. View of Hartford from Asylum Hill, 1847. At this time, the Olmsted family lived in their own home on Ann Street, near the upper left of this view of the city. As a child, Frederick lived in the Dodd House on College Street, at the right of center in this view. (The Connecticut Historical Society.)

drum for Frederick, bought for twenty-five cents. John Olmsted also kept an abundance of spirits in his home, including wine, gin, brandy, and cider.

Descriptions of John Olmsted as he had been in later life were recorded decades afterward in memoirs written by Mary Cleveland Olmsted (widow of Frederick and John Hull) and by Fred Kingsbury.[3] Mary remembered her father-in-law as "the kindest and most indulgent of fathers—a man with a sense of justice and duty exacting to himself rather than to others." This impression is certainly borne out in John Olmsted's letters, written throughout the years to the oldest two of his sons. He was the kind of father who carefully recorded the age his children began to walk, their first teeth, their most minor illnesses. The early deaths of his first wife and three of the children of his second marriage left him distraught.

But it should also be noted that John Olmsted had another side to his personality. There is evidence of cutting sarcasm as a form of remonstrance, especially with his oldest son. When Frederick was fourteen, boarding at a school near the Connecticut shore, his father wrote: "We received your letter but could make very little head or tail of it." And a decade later, when Frederick was a young man and had suffered several misadventures on an ill-fated trip through Connecticut, his father remarked to John Hull that Frederick "ought to have a conservator put over him if he ever attempts that journey again."[4]

The Kingsbury memoir recalled John Olmsted as "a tall, broad-shoul-

dered man, dignified, rather reserved in manner but kindly and cour-
teous, and highly respected." The obituary published in the *Courant* after
John Olmsted's death described him as one of Hartford's "best citizens,"
"a cultivated gentleman, of large and varied reading."[5] It noted that the
store he had established at the beginning of the War of 1812 (at the age of
twenty-one) "had become, at the close of his connection with it, the most
select and approved place of the kind in Hartford."

Frederick himself drew a curious picture of his father in his 1873
memoir, "Passages in the Life of an Unpractical Man," written after his
father's death earlier that year.[6] He too described a reserved man, but his
description is of a man whose reserve seemed to arise from inner conflicts
—particularly from a tension, as Frederick put it, between "self distrust
and indisposition to acquit himself fully in his proper part, and the
confused and conflicting demands which he supposed were made upon
him . . . in the name and with the authority of Society, Religion and
Commerce." Because of this reserve, and because his "real qualities had
so little of brilliancy," Frederick added, his father "passed with others,
even with many of his friends, for a man of much less worth, ability and
attainments than he was." We should also recall again here Frederick's
comment that his father had been "well-fitted to live in a highly organized
community in which each man's stint is measured out to him according
to his strength."

Frederick also implied that both his father's reserve and his sensitivity
to the demands of "Society" could lead him to act hypocritically at times.
If someone were to compliment his father on his love of beauty, Frederick
said, he would probably "try to justify the compliment by referring
admiringly to something which he thought had the world's stamp of
beauty upon it, quite possibly something which, but for the stamp,
would be odious to him." Frederick noted that his father's reserve was
such that he "rarely talked even [with] his family at all out of the range of
direct and material domestic interests." In company, even during "lively
and pleasant conversation," his father would "sit silent and even answer
questions unfrankly and with evident discomfort." Yet, Frederick added,
"a decided companionship was always necessary to his comfort."

The veiled charge of inauthenticity suggested in these remarks should
also put us in mind of Frederick's unending battles with "practical men"
during his public career. John Olmsted was preeminently a practical man

—practicality being one of the virtues he constantly urged upon his oldest son during the latter's various farming, business, and public enterprises. Nevertheless, what Frederick seemed to see in his father, with justice, was another, "truer" self, one that Frederick preferred to emphasize in his written recollections, in which he spoke rarely of his father's business or civic achievements, but rather of his love of nature.

Charlotte Hull Olmsted has been described by one Olmsted biographer as "a shadow,"[7] but she is more than that. Charlotte left behind a travel journal, written when she was twenty, that reveals a vibrant young woman. It describes a trip she made through Rhode Island and Massachusetts in 1820, the year before she married John Olmsted (who was nine years older than she). Charlotte made the journey with a group of people that included her sister, Stella; Stella's husband, the Hartford postmaster Jonathan Law; and her friend, Mary Ann Bull, who would become John Olmsted's second wife.[8] Jonathan Law, from whom Frederick got his middle name, supposedly had adopted Charlotte, although her own parents, who lived in Cheshire, would survive her.[9] We may suppose, at the very least, that Charlotte had gone to live with Jonathan and Stella Law—a childless couple—while still quite young and may indeed have gotten most of her mothering from this married sister, fourteen years older than she.

The travel journal reveals Charlotte to have been an intelligent, lively, sharp-eyed young woman. It is anecdotal and attentive to detail, whether discussing nature or visits to such cities and towns as Providence, Newport, Quincy, and Boston. Interestingly, Frederick's own travel journals bear a strong resemblance to his mother's journal. The following vignette from Charlotte's journal, for example, is one that might have appeared in Frederick's chronicles of his southern trips:

we saw a great number of habitations of colored people many of them hideous— some of the buildings quite smart looking—But . . . far away from any dwelling a miserable hut presented itself out of which issued three children in almost a perfect state of nudity: before however we came past a woman that I presume must have been the mother of these pitiful objects, who appeared like a lunatic.

Yet a curious sense of emotional detachment is also evident in this journal. For the most part, Charlotte commented upon the *things* she saw rather than people, and when she commented upon people, it was usually at a remove and without any sense of personal involvement. In the anecdote above, there is no indication that the deranged mother and naked children may have aroused some emotion in her—pity, shame, fear. Elsewhere she wrote, "Child fell in the water," then moved immediately to the tavern her party stopped at the next day. Her only comment on the populace of Boston, the largest city she had ever seen, was that in the Mall, "all sorts of people crowded thick as flies." Indeed, the emotional detachment Charlotte displayed as an observer is another way in which her journal seems similar to Frederick's later books. In fact, since she was rather a more graceful writer than her older son, it is John Hull's writing (as in *Texas*) which seems most similar to Charlotte's journal.

The journal reveals Charlotte to be a woman who would rise early and walk far to take in as much of her travel surroundings as possible, who was fond of food and quick to be critical of poor fare, and who could enjoy a glass of wine and an evening of music. From these pages Charlotte appears bright, cheerful, and filled with curiosity. Though she seems emotionally somewhat detached from the world around her, the journal also suggests considerable warmth and playfulness in the company of the family and friends making the journey with her. She certainly seems well-equipped, at the least, to have been an attentive and conscientious mother to her little boy, Frederick, though one imagines that she could have been as brisk and no-nonsense in her demands on the child as she was in her requirements for her food and drink.

For the first three years of his life, then, this was Frederick's home: an ambitious, preoccupied, reserved but caring father; a lively, intelligent mother who was probably both firm and affectionate; a crowded, bustling, prosperous household. For that time, he was an only child, very likely sharing his parents' bedroom, as was the practice of the time (even more so because of the crowded nature of the Dodd House). He would have been the sole object for his parents' attention, admiration, and love.

Thus, Frederick seems to have been given a good start in life—good enough, at least, to provide a fundamental strength for his later psychic functioning. [10] Frederick was in the midst of the critical stage of childhood development Mahlerian psychologists refer to as the *rapprochement crisis*. At this age, the little child seems to be looking in two directions at once: forward to growth and independence; backward toward the security, warmth, and love it knew while it was totally dependent upon its mother. [11]

During this sensitive stage of development, a child—especially when he has thus far been the *only* child—is quite susceptible to blows to his still fragile self-esteem.

Those blows were to come with a terrible regularity over the next several years. They can be easily enumerated—perhaps too easily to allow us to fully empathize with the cumulative emotional damage, the grief and terror and rage, that the small child experienced in a world so much beyond his control.[12]

The summer after his third birthday, Frederick's problems began routinely enough. His father was busy and distracted, preoccupied by a flood of business troubles; his mother was pregnant, now in her last trimester.[13] When John Hull was born on September 2, Frederick had a rival for his parents' affection. Before the household could return to normal, Frederick's mother, Charlotte, got caught up in one of those periods of intense religious revival that swept Connecticut in the antebellum years. Conversion, at Hartford's First Congregational Church, involved an extended inner ordeal of painful self-scrutiny, an ordeal that, for Charlotte Olmsted, could only have heightened and been heightened by any lingering postpartum depression.[14] Only a few weeks after that ordeal had ended in a public profession of faith—when Charlotte could have turned her full attention back to her little boy, Frederick, and her infant son—the two boys suffered the most devastating loss possible. Charlotte Hull Olmsted died on February 28, 1826.[15] Frederick was three years, ten months old; John Hull was six months old.

A note by Frederick's widow, filed with the Olmsted papers, states that Charlotte died "from an overdose of laudanum while ill from influenza" and adds "Miss Sheldon nurse," thus subtly implicating Miss Sheldon in the tragedy.[16] But it seems clear from John Olmsted's journal that Miss Sheldon was hired to take care of the children, either in Charlotte's final hours or shortly after her death. It is possible that John Olmsted or a friend taking care of Charlotte accidentally administered the overdose. Indeed, Mary Ann Bull Olmsted, recalling her presence at Charlotte's deathbed, seemed to feel a lingering guilt almost three decades later, although she ascribed her "pain" to her failure to pray publicly with Charlotte as Charlotte had requested.[17] It is also possible that Charlotte took the overdose herself, thus consciously or unconsciously committing a tragic act of self-destruction.

Frederick was old enough to respond with increasing anxiety to the mood of the household during Charlotte's illness, as the adults' concern gave way to despair. When his mother died, Frederick's world was shattered; his most frightening fears had come to pass.[18] How Frederick would eventually deal with his mother's death was, in part, shaped by how John Olmsted mourned for his wife and how Frederick's father had helped him to cope with the tragedy.[19]

John Olmsted may have been regarded by those who knew him as a reserved man, but he was also a man who loved his family deeply, and there were times, particularly times of tragedy, in which those feelings showed through the reserve to at least some degree. During the period of his wife's illness, death, and burial, his journal falls silent, after which there is the simple entry: "Tuesday, Feb. 28th at 1/2 past 5 P.M. my dr wife died & was buried on Sunday following." However, when his three-year old daughter (named for Charlotte) died of measles in 1832, he described the entire course of the illness and treatment in agonizing detail. In his later years, John Olmsted seemed taken with Thackeray's observation (one of a number by various authors copied into his journal in 1869) that the death of a small child "which scarce knew you" will occasion "a passion of grief and frantic tears," while the death of an adult, even intimately connected to you, may be stoically borne.[20]

The best evidence available for how John Olmsted handled the situation is contained in a letter he wrote to Frederick in 1838, when Frederick's two-year-old half brother, Owen, died after a short illness.[21] John had sat beside the remains of the little boy as he wrote to his eldest son, three hours after the child died at seven in the evening. Owen was now "in truth an angell of light in heaven his home," John wrote. After describing Owen's illness, the anguished father mused: "How inexplicable are the ways of God. We cannot fathom them. Our house is suddenly a house of mourning. Everything is bright without, the world goes on as before, but we are in darkness, unexpectedly cut to the ground." John told his eldest son to "take this affliction to heart & improve upon it, & God grant if called thus suddenly, you may be prepared to join yr dear departed brother in a better world."

Since John Olmsted's letter seems consistent with the attitudes of his society,[22] it is reasonable to assume that he had given Frederick similar instruction when the boy was less than four and had to assimilate the death of his mother. And it should be noted that behind the promise of "a better world," there lurked the implicit Puritan threat of eternal damnation should the child falter morally ("God grant . . . you may be prepared"). Both images would create emotional problems for the small child struggling to grasp the reality of death. The thought of his mother departing for a "heavenly home" would strengthen his feelings of abandonment and, thus, anger; the threat of God's punishment for his sins would terrify him and add to his natural fear of death.

A crucial task of mourning, according to D. W. Winnicott, is to permit the individual to work though "the feeling of responsibility for the death because of the destructive ideas and impulses that accompany loving." Guilt feelings over these "destructive ideas and impulses" become almost unbearable after the death of a loved one, such as a parent. [23] In healthy mourning, the image of the deceased (with all its complex associations) is gradually taken into the mourner's own psyche, where it can become a source of inner strength and comfort. But it is difficult enough for any human being to experience "healthy mourning," let alone a toddler. The death of a mother will not necessarily cripple the personality of the small child who suffers such a loss, John Bowlby observes. But the result is much the same as with a physical trauma, such as rheumatic fever: "scar tissue is all too often formed that in later life leads to more or less severe dysfunction." [24]

Remember that Charlotte Olmsted's pregnancy, delivery, conversion experience, and death had all followed one upon the other at a time when Frederick's inner self was still quite fragile and immature. Frederick was largely dependent upon the nature of the environment created around him and the circumstances of life beyond his control to help him overcome this difficult period. For the year following his mother's death, he seems to have received the love and security of a nurturing environment provided by John Olmsted and Nurse Sheldon, the woman hired to care for the children. [25] But what Frederick was to experience next and in subsequent years was further trauma of a kind that could only rub raw the "scar tissue" that had already been formed.

Some fourteen months after his wife's death—around Frederick's fifth birthday—John Olmsted moved his children to a new home, dismissed Nurse Sheldon, and married the twenty-six-year-old Mary Ann Bull. [26]

Mary Ann Bull came from a prosperous Hartford family: her grandfather, Dr. Isaac D. Bull, was a druggist, apothecary, and deacon; her father, also named Isaac D. Bull, was a wholesale druggist; her oldest brother, E. W. Bull, operated a retail drug store "under the sign of the 'Good Samaritan.' " All three had real estate holdings. When Harriet Beecher Stowe was twelve years old, studying at her sister's Female Seminary in Hartford, she was sent to live in the well-to-do Bull household. This home, Harriet noted, was pervaded by the "very soul of neatness and order." She further recalled Mary Ann as "a celebrated beauty of the day," with "long raven curls falling from the comb that held them up on the top of her head." Mary Ann had "a rich soprano voice, and was the leading singer in the Centre Church choir."[27] Mary Ann must have seemed a fine choice for John Olmsted's second wife, an attractive, cultivated, religious woman. However, the marriage seems to have been more a useful one for John Olmsted than an affair of the heart, for his heart seems to have remained with Charlotte.

For Frederick and his brother, John Hull, a warm and sympathetic stepmother, with a great capacity for giving and receiving love, might have facilitated their mourning process. While the stepmother's role is a difficult one at best, both Mary Ann and Frederick could have benefited from the fact the child had known her all his life. But the descriptions we have of Mary Ann Olmsted do not suggest a person who was emotionally adequate to care for an energetic five-year-old boy.[28] She had been in fact a reserved and puritanical woman who insisted upon order and system.

One indication of Mary Ann's influence on the household was the quickly dwindling expenditures in John Olmsted's journal for alcoholic spirits, to be replaced finally by contributions to the Temperance Society.[29] We know of her strong-mindedness from the dispute with Frederick and Albert Henry over John Olmsted's estate (described in part 1), when she insisted that, with her husband's death, *she* had become the head of the family—not the typical response of a Victorian woman.[30]

Six weeks after John Olmsted married Mary Ann Bull, Frederick and John Hull were baptized, and the week following they both contracted whooping cough. On April 20, 1828, a year after the marriage and two days before his sixth birthday, Frederick was sent 350 miles away from home to spend four months with an uncle he scarcely knew.[31] This was but the first of many times Frederick would be sent away from home in the next twelve years.

Two weeks after returning from his uncle's home in upstate New York, Frederick returned to the school he had attended before going away, that of Miss Naomi Rockwell, who had undergone public conversion during that same revival season when his mother and stepmother had. [32] During this period, his stepmother became pregnant with her first child. As Mary Ann became preoccupied by the late stages of her pregnancy, Frederick may well have sought an emotional attachment to his teacher, Miss Rockwell. But on a Friday evening, February 8, 1829—in his stepmother's eighth month and very nearly the third anniversary of Charlotte Olmsted's death—Naomi Rockwell burned to death when her clothes caught fire. [33]

Six weeks later, on March 18 (several weeks before Frederick's seventh birthday), Mary Ann Olmsted gave birth to her first child, a girl who was given the name of Frederick's mother, Charlotte. A month later, John Olmsted noted, the boy was bitten by a dog, seriously enough to have a doctor tend to him. That summer, in July, after all the children had been taken ill, the entire family went to Sachem's Head on the Connecticut seashore for several days. But not Frederick, who either stayed home with the housekeeper, or went to the home of John Olmsted's parents in East Hartford.

A month later, Frederick changed schools again, returning to his very first school, Miss Jeffrey's. A month after that, on October 11, the family celebrated Charlotte's christening. And a few weeks later, on November 9, Frederick was sent away from home to board with the Reverend Zolva Whitmore, a Congregationalist minister in North Guilford, a rural village not far from Sachem's Head, where he would remain for the next ten months.

During the next eleven years of Frederick's life—from ages seven to eighteen, from a little boy to a young man—he spent only two extended periods at home with his family: the fall of 1830 through the spring of 1831, when he attended the Hartford Grammar School; and September through November of 1836, when he was at that school once again. [34]

To be sure, there were a number of brief visits home; several vacations of a few weeks duration; and a few pleasant trips with the family, especially the memorable carriage tour of the White Mountains in August 1838 with his father, stepmother, and John Hull. But Frederick spent fifteen of the most formative years of his life in virtual exile from his family. In his adolescent years, he was deprived of a relationship with his father, who could have acted as his mentor—a role for which John Olmsted, apart from his business cares, was particularly well suited and which he would later on try so hard to fill during Frederick's adult years.

In early nineteenth-century New England, it was hardly unusual for "the sons of prosperous fathers" to be sent away to boarding "academies" in order to receive a more rigorous scholastic and religious upbringing. [35] But the emotional and intellectual care Frederick received from his "deputy fathers" [36] ranged from benign neglect at best to ignorant cruelty at worst. Indeed, his schoolmaster for most of these years, the Reverend Joab Brace, was more Frederick's tormentor than mentor.

Roper sums up well the results of Frederick's childhood and academic schooling under various clergymen:

> It neither taught him to think nor encouraged him to learn; it permanently incensed him against particular ministers; and it may well have been the fount of his profound distaste as an adult for organized religion and its practitioners, lay and clerical. On the other hand, it allowed him considerable liberty to roam the countryside in idle and contemplative enjoyment, and it permitted, mostly by default, his natural curiosity to flourish. If it failed to encourage his tastes, which were intellectual and creative, at least it did not stultify them, and the influence that developed them was steadily at work independently of it. [37]

The essential question here is *why* the child was sent away from home in the first place, especially to live and learn in such clearly inadequate environments. The answer given by Olmsted himself is that his father had a "superstitious faith in the value of preaching and didactic instruction" and little faith in his own capacity to "do for me in that way." He further added, "my father's affection and desire to 'do right by the boy' made him always eager to devolve as much as practicable of my education upon ministers." [38] I cannot accept Olmsted's theory that his father had thought to improve upon his education in this way. After all, John Hull received an excellent education and had prepared for Yale almost entirely in Hartford area schools. (He spent two terms at Joab Brace's during Frederick's last year there).

Charles Beveridge hints at another, and perhaps more important, factor, when he discusses the early start Frederick had been given at Hartford's dame schools: "his attendance at school relieved his step-mother of many supervisory chores." [39] In 1830, the puritanical Mary Ann Olmsted, who so prized order, had on her hands a sickly toddler (John Hull) and an infant (Charlotte). She may well have had little patience for a boisterous and perhaps precocious older boy. Indeed, Frederick's report card from the Hartford Grammar School, at age eight-and-a-half, describes a bright little boy who was too fond of play for Puritan tastes. And Olmsted offers this description of himself, as shaped by the schoolmasters and other adults of his childhood world:

> I was active, imaginative, impulsive, enterprising trustful and heedless. This made what is generally called a troublesome and mischievous boy. Some thought me a bad boy and this view was taken at Boggs's. I had never cared much that I was called so before but here my exceeding badness [in a world of total badness] was so constantly [screwed down upon] driven in upon me that it had a strong effect upon a disposition not wholly shy—not that I thought so very badly of myself but that I got a habit strongly fixed [of expecting] of considering the favorable regard of others as something not to be expected and when obtained as evincing a character to be admired and gratefully looked up to. [40]

As Joseph Kett notes, it was not unusual to send young boys away from home, and to schools no better than Frederick attended before adolescence, in large part to have them disciplined. In such schools, prior to 1840, he writes, "brutality and burlesque mixed with slackness and informality."[41]

Graff, alone of the leading biographers of Olmsted, seems to have grasped the hurt and resentment that such a prolonged exile from his home would arouse in a little boy. She writes that with all the admirable schools available in Hartford, it seemed "irresponsible to the point of cruelty to have banished Fred at the impressionable age of seven" to live in the miserable conditions of poor country parishes. And she notes that Olmsted would recall, "with unfaded bitterness more than sixty years later," the awful schooling to which he had been subjected as a boy.[42] Most often, Olmsted chose either to pretend that his education as a "private student" of rural ministers was far more thorough than it was or else to argue the superiority of self-education to formal education.

In assessing the impact made upon Frederick by his schooling and by his exile from home, I would suggest that he had been one of those wounded, but gifted, narcissistic children of whom Emanuel Klein has written, "children to whom fate has been very harsh."[43] For such a child, the inner sense of being different from others, superior to others, becomes his major defense against the lack of esteem he perceives from those around him. Thus could Frederick write that he had never been led to think badly of himself, but that he "got a habit . . . of considering the favorable regard of others as something not to be expected."

Thinking back to Olmsted's adolescent problems, we can reflect on what a perfect excuse "weak eyes" would be for a boy who had been a wounded, narcissistic child, one who needed some explanation for the fact that he could not do as well in school as his friends or, more particularly, as his bright, achieving, younger brother, John Hull.

The poignant traces of his exile from home continued to linger in Frederick's unconscious self all though his adulthood. It led him, in "Passages," to insist that his father had exiled him from home out of "affection and desire to 'do right by the boy.' " And it led him, in the 1860s, to construct the following curious argument (in a piece claiming that there was a special relationship between England and those Americans who were of English descent):

> Send one of your boys to school far away for a long time, when he comes home if he is a stout-hearted boy does he not love home more than the one you have kept by you, and do you not love him the more for the absence and make more of him[?][44]

This seems like the rationalization of one whose unconscious still sought to deny the massive hurt done him as a child by those whom he had loved and depended upon.

Olmsted also denied this massive hurt by concealing it within a child-like pride, a pride in the independence that, he insisted, his father and stepmother had purposely instilled in him. Some sixty years after these events, near the end of his life, he would write that when he had been "yet a half grown lad," his parents had let him "wander as few parents are willing their children should."

> If in my rambling habits I did not come home at night it was supposed that I had strayed to some other homes where I would be well taken care of, *and little concern was felt at my absence;* but it several times occurred before I was twelve years old that I had been *lost in the woods* and finding my way out after sunset had passed the night with strangers and had been encouraged by my father rather than checked in the adventurousness that led me to do so. [45] (Emphasis added.)

Based upon these passages, it seems to me that Frederick believed his parents, especially his father, had not cared enough about him to make sure that he was safe and secure. Following the passage cited above came an unfinished sentence: "His motive might have been . . ." In truth, Olmsted never found a valid motive for the lack of caring he imputed to his father.

Such a *laissez-faire* attitude is hard to imagine in a father who had so carefully recorded the doings of his two oldest children in his journals— journals that show no sign of such childhood "rambles" by Frederick. Even harder to imagine is an escapade such as Olmsted described to Mariana Van Rensselaer in a letter of 1893. He claimed that when he "was but nine," he had walked "sixteen miles over a strange county with my brother who was but six" to reach the home of his aunt, Linda Brooks, in Cheshire. They were on the road for two days, he stated, and had spent the night at a rural inn. After reaching their aunt's house, he wrote, they had sat in front of the "great fire place being feasted," so exhausted that they had to be carried off to bed. [46]

Such an episode would surely have been noted in John Olmsted's journal, particularly since the sickly John Hull Olmsted, only six years old, was supposed to have accompanied Frederick on this very long trip, covering on foot a distance that was actually some twenty-seven miles by stage. But the journal contains no reference to such an expedition during Frederick's childhood. However, John Olmsted did note that Frederick had spent two days walking to Cheshire in 1842, when Frederick was *twenty*. [47] Further, while Frederick was in Hartford in 1846, a nine-year-old boy, who had been feared drowned, was discovered to have skated the frozen Connecticut River all the way to Windsor (about eight miles), staying the night at a hotel there. "Quite a feat for one of his age," a young Olmsted cousin commented. [48]

Olmsted's recollections and his correspondence both suggest that he had been emotionally closer to his mother's family—to Jonathan and Stella Law and to David and Linda Brooks—than to his stepmother's family. The act of recalling, in this letter to Van Rensselaer, his mother and her family seems to have stirred memories of his many happy visits to Cheshire and to have prompted Olmsted's unconscious to combine the walking trip of his own young manhood with the never-forgotten skating feat of the Hartford boy.

Earlier that year, before his banishment to Brace's, Frederick had had to undergo the extraction of two teeth, immediately followed by a short, brutal stay at Ellington High School, an experience Olmsted recalled with particular pain. "Here I suffered in many cruel ways," he wrote some four decades later, "and I still carry the scars of more than one kind of the wounds I received." One kind of wound was surely in being "again the smallest boy among sixty."[49] Another kind of wound came from the school's brutal corporal punishment. John Olmsted fetched the boy home after being informed (by a classmate's father) that a teacher had hoisted Frederick up by his ears "and had so pinched one of them that it had bled." Olmsted wrote that he was "glad to remember" telling his father that "the teacher had told me that he did not mean to do it and that I liked pinching better than ferruling."[50]

The wounds bitterly remembered by a man in his fifties do not seem to fit with a rather foolish pride in his juvenile stoicism. What had made Frederick believe having his ear pulled till it bled was better than receiving a caning? Was the latter a more humiliating form of punishment, a more humiliating form of submittal to adult authority?[51] I suggest that through his Ellington brutalization and his subsequent seven-year repression under the tutelage of the puritanical Joab Brace, Frederick formed a particular horror of submission to oppressive, authoritarian father figures.

Ellington, incidentally, was sixteen miles from Hartford by stage—precisely the distance that Olmsted claimed he had walked at age nine. At Joab Brace's, Frederick would entertain his schoolmates with tales of "runaways." The story of the walk to Cheshire may well have memorialized his wish as a nine-year-old boy to run away from Ellington High School, the sixteen miles to his home. Altogether, the year that Frederick was nine had been a year of terrible assaults upon his selfhood and his body—but one that had been defensively enshrined in Olmsted's memory as the year in which he had accomplished a heroic feat.[52]

As previously noted, Frederick's exile from home had continued long into his adolescence, but the harshness of life at Joab Brace's eventually gave way to what Olmsted called "a decently restrained vagabond life" while he was ostensibly studying engineering with the Reverend Frederick A. Barton. In his old age, Olmsted would claim that at age fourteen he had had an accident ("sumach poisoning," he said in one version) that had left him with chronic "weakness" of the eyes. For this reason, he would claim, the agreeable fiction of engineering studies had been decided upon, in order to permit him to pursue an idling, restful outdoor life while his "mates were fitting for college." As was demonstrated earlier, I believe the accident itself is a fiction and that Olmsted's father had meant Frederick's education at Barton's to be taken quite seriously. The chronic eye trouble was real enough but, I believe, was of psychosomatic origin —Olmsted's way of avoiding the structured school life that had become so hateful to him.[53]

One important result of Frederick's last year at Joab Brace's was the cementing of a close relationship between himself and his younger brother, John Hull Olmsted. Indeed, the "walk to Cheshire" story memorializes John Hull's later role as his brother's sidekick, sailing on the Connecticut River, touring England and the Continent, tending the farm in Staten Island, traveling to Texas and writing a book about the trip, and so forth. As Charles McLaughlin observes: "John Hull Olmsted came to share more and more in his life."[54] John Hull, he adds, must have provided "the sympathy and ready ear that Olmsted's busy father and stepmother apparently could not give this energetic, independent, and perhaps somewhat obstreperous young man."

During Frederick's long years of exile, a "second family" was growing in his father's house—four half sisters and two half brothers were born in those years. Elizabeth Stevenson writes: "The tie between Fred and John Hull on the one hand and the second and growing family on the other was warm and friendly, but cousinly rather than brotherly."[55] This is an accurate description, but neglects Frederick's heightened feelings of rejection and envy caused by the appearance upon the scene of such "interlopers"—the *real* children of Mary Ann Olmsted—while he was so far from home. In the household also lived the teenage boys who worked in the family store. E. T. Goodrich came in 1831, when Frederick was almost nine (the age of his supposed walk to Cheshire), and S. P. Thacher came in 1834, when Frederick was almost twelve. Both boys were to become John Olmsted's partners.

Frederick had first tasted sibling rivalry with the birth of his brother, John Hull. This would have been the natural, unavoidable emotion of the small child, but almost as inevitably such feelings of sibling rivalry would have been greatly intensified when he was exiled to boarding school while John Hull and his infant half sister, Charlotte, were kept at home. And it was a bitter emotion that he would experience again and again as this second family grew and as young apprentices came to stay and to prosper in their close relationship with his own father.

The legacy of childhood for Frederick was that of painful loss, of the inexplicable and bitter experience of being exiled from home, of searing envy of those who remained behind, of maltreatment and humiliation in the crude and cruel schools to which he had been sent. The loss of his mother had created the first, the cruelest scar upon his psyche; the succeeding trauma rubbed raw the wound. Yet withal, Frederick not only survived, but survived with extraordinary strength and determination.

There has been a great deal of psychological speculation on the nature of "survivors"—those children who manage to rise above even the most awful tragedies (though never, it would seem, without some inner psychic cost), to which most others succumb in one way or another. Certainly John Hull, who was kept at home while Frederick was sent away, seems to have had little of Frederick's strength and determination. The difference was surely, in part, inherent in their natures. But it must also be remembered that Frederick had had three years of Charlotte Olmsted's mothering, while John Hull had had several months at best. Contemporary psychoanalysts such as Winnicott and Mahler have placed great stress on the importance, for psychic strength, of the first three years of a child's development. While the loss of his mother at a critical age surely left its mark upon his psychic functioning, it may also be true that Frederick's fundamental inner strength was Charlotte's most lasting legacy to her first-born child. [56]

In their young manhood, the prescient Kingsbury would write of Frederick:

He is an Enthusiast by Nature. . . . Well the world needs such men—and one thing is curious—disappointments never seem to trouble them—. They must in the Nature of things meet with them often and yet they go right on in the same old way just as if it had not happened. They never get disheartened. I think Fred will be one of that sort. Many of his favorite schemes will go to naught—but he'll throw it aside and try another and spoil that and forget them both while you or I might have been blubbering over the ruins of the first. [57]

A year earlier, Frederick had expressed what must have been his own view of himself at the time in describing to Kingsbury the kind of person the latter both was and (more importantly) was *not:* "[you are] a *long-headed genius* bound to rise, if the wind's fair—but you are not a steamboat to go in spite of weather—to make circumstances favorable whether they will or not." [58] Olmsted clearly saw himself as a "steamboat"—and that was true enough, for the steam that drove him did come boiling up from inside him. But it was also true that he often needed a "fair wind" to keep him going. Pulled toward and yet resisting the religious conversions that had swept his New Haven circle of friends in mid-1846, Olmsted wrote to John Hull: "Next to the bread of Life, I live by Sympathy. How much I have needed advice! How much I have needed encouragement!"[59]

Olmsted was, in fact, both steamboat and sailboat, torn between the different life urges these symbols represented: on the one hand, autonomy, expressing his selfhood as self-sufficient, inner-directed, totally in control; on the other, merger, being one with some other (the wind), some thing or some group. One aspect of such wishes is the childlike desire for another to know one's mind without needing to speak it. Thus Frederick wrote to Kingsbury of his need for "such folks" as he and Elizabeth Baldwin, "who can & will guess and know what a fellow thinks & feels & *wants*, and sympathize with him so easily."[60]

But the steamboat remains a vivid and useful image for the powerful forces within Olmsted that would drive him forward again and again throughout his life in search of autonomy and self-realization. "I certainly have been declaring Independence this summer, and cutting myself loose from the common rafts of men," he wrote to Kingsbury in the summer of 1846, during a burst of manic optimism, adding: "I don't give my helm to Father, Mother, Schoolmaster, editor or minister, again."[61] But throughout the next few decades of his life, Olmsted would find that someone else's hand was on the helm he sought to control: his father, who purchased his farms for him and kept hard watch on his finances; Andrew Haswell Green, who usurped his Central Park domain; the Executive Committee of the Sanitary Commission, which wrested control of that bureaucracy away from him in the middle of the Civil War. And he chafed and fumed and struggled to regain control of his helm all the while.

Henry Bellows, President of the Sanitary Commission, saw through to the heart of Olmsted's situation and wrote in an exasperated letter to Olmsted in 1863:

I have long felt that your constitutional qualities, both bodily, mental and moral, made you a most difficult subordinate. You ought not to work *under* any body. I think you the most singular compound of the practical philosopher and the impracticable man-of-business I have ever encountered. I don't believe any

Board of Directors could get along two years with you. And this because your own notions are so dominant and imperative.

Bellows advised that Olmsted should work "in some independent position," where his temperament and organizational abilities would have free play to accomplish "unalloyed" good work. "With *subordinates*, you have, and would have, no difficulties," Bellows added. "It is only with *peers* or *superiors* (official) that you cannot serve." He concluded that Olmsted's "imperfect health, irritable nerves and . . . fastidious character," his "ever-teeming and brooding brains," all combined to make "practical men" doubt his "qualification for affairs."[62]

To realize his ambitions and to achieve a unique identity, Olmsted had to overcome the temptation of retreat from the competitive world, rife with rivalries and struggles for dominance and control. Any kind of submission to male figures—superiors or peers—would always be problematic for Olmsted. To him, such submission represented a loss of selfhood, a loss of control over his life and his destiny. Of course, this is a problem for many men, to at least some degree. But I believe that such fears were particularly strong in Olmsted as a result of his childhood abandonment by his father; of the brutal treatment he received at Ellington High School, along with the humiliations inherent in being "the smallest boy among sixty"; and of the cold and dreary repression he endured under Joab Brace.

Standing behind these later wounds and hurts was the fundamental trauma—the loss of his mother when he was less than four. This tragic loss took place at an age at when, according to Mahlerian psychologists, the child is beginning to solidify its sense of selfhood.[63] Thus it seems to me that fragility of selfhood and, correspondingly, of self-esteem (so much a function of the mother's continuing esteem for the child) would be a particular problem for Olmsted, a problem further exacerbated by his later exile from home. Indeed, this fragility of selfhood would be so severe a problem for Olmsted that, in his adult life, submission to the will of others would often be interpreted by him as a betrayal of his "true self" and therefore especially humiliating and intolerable.

CHAPTER 5

Memories and Symbols

In his later years, Olmsted sometimes sought to identify the sources of his own creativity, which he held to be "a matter of . . . involuntary and unconscious growth."[1] In notes for a book he hoped to write during these latter years, Olmsted added: "It is difficult to realize how largely we owe most of our cherished opinions to circumstances of our personal history of the action in [which] respect we have been unconscious."[2] And indeed, Olmsted tried, at various times, to locate the origins of his later career in memories of his childhood.

The most numerous and most detailed recollections by Olmsted of his early childhood are to be found in the autobiographical fragments of the 1893 period. The obsessive introspection and physical distress of that period and the very early events with which Olmsted dealt suggest that these recollections have fundamental significance.[3]

They begin with Olmsted recalling that when he was three, he "chanced to stray into a room at the crisis of a tragedy therein occurring."[4] He fled from the room, "screaming in a manner adding to the horror of the household." The adults who, with difficulty, had soothed him, commented that Frederick would never forget what he had seen. Several years later (probably when he was eight), he was asked by various people if he recalled that scene. To their surprise, he did not. Instead he remembered three "trivial experiences" from a period when he was less than three years old. These were:

First, that I had once stood upon a table with my hands upon the glass of a window, out of which I looked. Second, that I had once been lifted through a trap door into the cockloft of an outhouse, through the dimness of which darts of sunlight half disclosed various objects hanging from the rafters overhead. . . . Third, that while in the arms of a woman I had looked up and reaching out my hand (probably saying "pretty"), that which I saw being bits of blue sky through the leaves of a fine spreading tree.

It seems clear that these three recollections are "screen memories," somehow connected to the repressed central material of the indirectly recalled "tragedy." Their content fits the general description of screen memories given in psychoanalytic literature.[5] Formation of a screen memory is a creative act, which seeks in the memory created to suppress an experience that could be deeply troubling, too painful to recall in its actuality. One can think of screen memories as the person's present defending itself against the past.

My first impulse is to suppose that the partially recalled tragic scene was of Charlotte Hull Olmsted upon her deathbed. However, Olmsted himself does not even suggest the possibility, even though he had mentioned his mother's death to Mariana Van Rensselaer during this same period.[6] Moreover, it is not credible that people would later ask the young boy if he could recall screaming and running from the room in which his mother lay dying. Though deaths in the family may have been rather commonplace in that era, the subject would be more likely used for moral instruction than to satisfy idle curiosity.

But the hidden source of this memory becomes more clear when we recall that another crucial event occurred when Frederick was three. As the little boy "strolled" into that dimly remembered room, what probably was taking place—the event that inquisitive adults later asked him to recall—was his mother giving birth to John Hull. Such a scene is powerfully described in Freud's "Little Hans" case. A little boy of three-and-a-half is called into the room in which his mother has just given birth to his sister, only to stare—not at his mother—but at "the basins and other vessels, filled with blood and water, that were still standing about the room."[7] Understandably, Frederick would regard the birth scene with horror, believing that something terrible had been done to his mother.[8] Almost seventy years later, Olmsted would still find it difficult to deal with what he had observed in that room. Further, the fact that there was now a rival for his parents' affection and attention would certainly be regarded by the small child as a tragedy—and would continue to be so regarded in the unconscious of an adult who had been that wounded, narcissistic child.

But the tone and content of the "tragic scene" memory also tells us that it is greatly colored by the later death of his mother. It is likely, in fact, that this memory has been made to carry the entire emotional weight of Frederick's fourth year, with *all* of its losses and rejections. Thus, it is significant that the three "trivial" memories date, not from the time of the "tragic scene," but from an earlier age—"certainly not yet three," in Olmsted's words. This fact (and the content of the "trivial" recollections) suggests that the substitution of the three "trivial" memories for the "tragic scene" memory, in the boy's mind, represented an emotional retreat from a period of tremendous pain, of psychic damage and blows to his self-esteem, to that more blissful time of his "love affair with the world"—very likely to the peak period of the separation-individuation process, when the child, according to Phyllis Greenacre, is "exhilarated by his own abilities, continually delighted with the discoveries he makes in his expanding world."[9] And that is what makes these three idyllic recollections such a good antidote for the pain and damaged self-esteem associated with Frederick's fourth year.

This assumption is supported by the uncanny emphasis Olmsted himself had given to the concepts of perception and separation when he reflected upon why his mind should have retained these three "trivial" incidents:

May it have been that the mind was pleasantly exercised, first to *separate* from the substance of the glass that seen through it and beyond it, second to *separate* from the rafters and roof boards that hanging from them; third to *separate* that which at first seemed a plane of figured material into the two matters of the foliage and the sky.[10]

This emphasis upon separation of objects certainly puts us in mind of the fundamental task of the separation-individuation process, the psychic separation of the self from all other persons and objects.

Referring to the window memory, Olmsted wrote of "separating from the substance of the glass that seen through and beyond it." Thus, the window may be understood as the boundary both of Frederick's physical self and of his inner self. It is the boundary of the physical self because the child is touching that which separates him from the surrounding world. In the second memory, the child is taken into the outside world—lifted into the loft of an outhouse. It is in image of adventure and discovery, but one also that suggests a more anxious experience for a child, an experience associated with the more familiar usage of "outhouse" —that is, the child's anxieties over toilet-training.

Another association can be made to this outhouse memory. On Sunday, August 27, 1826, at 8:30 in the evening, there was a fire in the outhouse in which John Olmsted stored his wood and coal.[11] This took place during what must have been a period of considerable anxiety for Frederick. His mother had died recently; his father had been away on a trip to Geneseo for nine days (and would be away for seventeen days more); and the adults still present were likely to be much more concerned with John Hull, seriously ill from dysentery, than with the four-year-old Frederick. It may be that Olmsted's "outhouse memory," with its shafts of sunlight illuminating the dimness, also commemorates this fire late on a summer evening, when the bright flames lit up the dim twilight. A fire, to a little boy, is exciting as well as dangerous; it is suggestive of the excitement and dangers of his growing sense of autonomy, of moving beyond the security he has known at his mother's side.

It is interesting that the first two memories, clearly from the toddler stage, make no mention of his mother or a woman (we do not know who lifts him to the loft in the outhouse). The third, however, specifically recalls being "in the arms of a woman," looking at "bits of blue sky" through the leaves of a low-spreading tree. The importance of this memory is emphasized by the fact that he reported a similar memory in his 1860 autobiographical notes: "first recollection, a grassed slope thro a cherry tree—." In referring to the third trivial memory, Olmsted himself recalled that the vision "at first seemed a plane of figured material"—a very good symbolization of the toddler's focus upon his mother's skirt, to which he clings as he first begins to explore the world.

The 1860 recollection specifies a cherry tree—that is, a fruit-bearing tree. The 1893 recollection does not specify the type, but seems to describe a shade tree. Together, the two recollections suggest the feminine attributes of a woman (or more specifically of the child's mother): child-bearing in the 1860 instance; providing shelter, protection, and comfort in the 1893 memory. It is to be expected that the leafy boughs of a tree would always represent these qualities to Olmsted during his later career.

In so many ways, then, the retreat from the terrible memories of the "tragic scene" to the more delightful memories of the three "trivial" incidents is a retreat into the comfort and joys of the little universe consisting of a small child and its mother. [12] But there is a danger in the lingering temptation to make a retreat, in one's inner self, to this idealized maternal environment—a danger Robert Stoller has conceptualized as *symbiosis anxiety:* "The ubiquitous fear . . . that one's sense of maleness and masculinity are in danger and that one must build . . . ever vigilant [inner] watchguards against succumbing to the pull [of] merging again with mother." What Stoller is suggesting is that there is a fundamental conflict in the psyche of a male child, one that can also be put in terms of the Mahlerian rapprochement crisis: it is the struggle between the polar opposites of his psychic needs, wherein the wish for growth and autonomy embodied in his emerging sense of masculine identity is opposed by the deep yearning to retreat into blissful merger with his mother and her femininity. [13]

Olmsted was in his seventies when he first set down (after considerable struggle) his "tragic memory" and then immediately retreated to the far more blissful screen memories of his toddler years, memories that suppressed the natural anxieties of the young child. In so doing, he was reenacting the pervasive psychic defense he had engaged in throughout his life: whenever the hard realities of "Oedipal striving" brought him into periods or situations of extreme stress—burdens "more than he could bear"—Frederick would yield to "psychic retreat" to a misremembered time of paradisiacal bliss, of oneness with the idealized mother of early childhood.

What is central to all of these memories is the importance of vision— for they all recall the act of seeing. The centrality of vision to these and so many other recollections in Olmsted's various autobiographical notes suggests an identity constructed upon vision as the organizing experience. But these recollections, as screen memories, are notable not only for what has been recalled as having been seen, but also for what, having been seen, had then been repressed. The "tragic scene" itself is incomplete (what did he *see* in the room?) and is only a recollection of a recollection, defended against by the substitution of three "trivial memories." Olmsted first repressed what he had seen in that room and then repressed the entire memory altogether. Thus, an identity constructed upon vision as the organizing experience is also one that could achieve a retreat from a striving life through a *refusal* to see—hence the weak eyes resulting, allegedly, from "sumach poisoning" and the hysterical blindness following his father's death.

This linkage between psychic retreat and Oedipal striving is also clearly discernible in another autobiographical fragment, recorded in the same period that Olmsted wrote down the "tragic scene" and three "trivial memories." This recollection deals with an event that happened much later in his life, but under circumstances that revived the original childhood perceptual and psychic disturbances marked by the "tragic scene" and "trivial memories."

In this recollection, Olmsted puzzled over an experience of "double consciousness." While under the influence of opium administered by a surgeon, Olmsted wrote, he had visualized himself undergoing two distinct "happenings" simultaneously, "passing rapidly from one to the other." One "happening" was the operation itself (which I assume was in the aftermath of the Central Park accident). The other was a strange, "trivial" experience that Olmsted took to be as real as the operation then taking place, although clearly it was an opium dream or a hallucination:

I was in the hold of a great ship looking with the second mate at the manner in which she had been stowed and her freight consisted wholly of small, old and dull tin bake pans, set in tiers separated by boards. I was watching the passage of an endless strip of coarse manilla paper carrying at regular intervals of eighteen inches a pint measure of freshly picked strawberries dumped upon it and lying loosely in a heap. [14]

The first, striking, image of this "opium dream" is that of being inside "the hold of a great ship." The image itself strongly suggests a mother figure, a notion supported by the fact that his mother's name was Charlotte *Hull* Olmsted. But the dream image suggests more than just his mother alone; it suggests also his early family environment, an environment created by his real mother. She was a "hull" literally and figuratively, the hull of the family, who had carried him and his brother in her belly as in the hull of a ship. The younger brother, John Hull, was also Frederick's second mate—often sharing a bedroom, in the home of their boyhood and youth, at the Sachem's Head farm, aboard ship to England; sharing a last year at Joab Brace's; sharing sailing trips on Long Island Sound; sharing the walking trip in Europe and the saddle trip in Texas. John Hull was his junior partner, and, like the second mate in the dream, he was the faceless and anonymous sidekick in Frederick's schemes.

The "great ship-as-mother" image suggests also the providing/protecting role of the mother figures in Frederick's life—Charlotte Hull Olmsted, Mary Ann Olmsted (who was literally John Olmsted's second mate), and, of course, nature itself. The "ship-mother" provides the bounty of freshly picked strawberries (which seem to come out of her own body). The bakepans are symbols of domesticity, as well as of the womb (a womb— "small, old and dull"—no longer used).

Another set of images is suggested by the most likely occasion for this "opium dream"—during the surgery that followed Olmsted's 1860 carriage accident. This accident took place in Central Park, midst all the symbols of what can be considered Olmsted's Oedipal striving, the forward thrust of autonomous achieving. Central Park was an empire Olmsted had won in competition, of which he was Superintendent and Architect in Chief. By 1860, he also lived there with the wife and family he had taken over from his brother, John Hull. In this case, it was *Frederick* who was literally the second mate to his brother's wife. In the carriage with Olmsted were this wife and his own natural, newly born son—the carriage being another womb symbol, like the ship's hold. Oedipal striving, in Olmsted's case, resulted in serious damage to his body and the threat of amputation (castration).

The "opium dream" is a retreat from Oedipal striving and competition to a more peaceful and restful place, like the mother's body. But Olmsted did not retreat to a mother symbol such as "nature in the raw," to strawberry fields, for example. He retreated to an artificial place, a man-made refuge, a safe place within the engulfing sea, as Central Park itself was a man-made refuge within the engulfing city. In this dream, the beauties of nature (strawberries) had to be conveyed into the ship through a mechanical contrivance, such as Olmsted had used on Central Park to bring in earth and trees and shrubs. Further, the mechanical contrivance itself was made of coarse manilla paper, like that which Olmsted often used for his initial designs or sketches. The paper represents his diagram out of which "nature" will be created (in conjunction with Mother Nature). There are two observers of this process, himself and the second mate. The latter is anonymous, faceless. This was precisely the position of Calvert Vaux in relation to Central park, the second mate to Olmsted and all too often faceless and anonymous.

This dream seems to me a metaphor for the same "rapprochement crisis" concerns that are suggested by the "tragic scene" and three "trivial memories." On the one hand, Olmsted wants to stay in the painful, autonomous, striving present—for this is the way to selfhood, to a sense of identity. Yet it is pleasant to retreat to the other refuge. It is calm and peaceful. There is no responsibility on this ship; all is being taken care of. But the retreat is disturbing to him: remerging with the great mother is disturbing; he is losing his selfhood, his identity. The great anxiety aroused by these interwoven images, with all their echoes of childhood trauma, is reflected in the language Olmsted used in his effort to accurately record the comment he made to the surgeon after relating the "opium dream." He stated that he had told the surgeon to give him no more opium. He would rather die, Olmsted added, "than be as uncertain of myself" or "as embarrassed about my identity" as he had been during this experience of "double consciousness."[15]

Falling between, and connecting, the memories of early childhood and this "double consciousness" in these 1893 autobiographical notes, there are several fragments describing a peculiar object associated with his infancy—a description Olmsted took great pains to record. This was of an "imaginary and impossible plaything" of which he had "dreamed recurrently" as a child. Olmsted could still recall "the experience of manipulating a substance" that he could now only compare, inadequately, to "soft putty or white wax"—a substance that, from time to time, would be brought to mind, "dimly and evasively, by old ivory." Olmsted also recalled that he had been accustomed to "draw it apart and join it together," and as he did so, "it seemed to go before the movement of my hands as if it were a living thing acting sympathetically."

The texture, the appearance, and the malleability of the object Olmsted tried so painstakingly to evoke, as well as the hallucinatory quality of the memory of this "impossible plaything," suggest what Donald Winnicott refers to as a "transitional object," or what is today more commonly called the "security blanket."[16] Whether actually a blanket or a toy or something else, the transitional object "is usually soft, malleable, and has been an integral part of the child's life since birth." It is the soothing representation of the child's symbiotic tie to the mother, helping the child to separate from its mother by providing another source for the tactile comforting and reassurance first supplied by the mother—evoking unconscious memories of its mother and the security she provided. So powerful a symbol is such an object to a child, Winnicott notes, that the memory of it alone has the ability to comfort. The child Frederick after the loss of his mother is evoked in Phyllis Greenacre's poignant words: "Such illusory memory feelings . . . tend to reassure the child 'You are not alone.' "[17]

What seems most important in Olmsted's recollection of this "ivory object" is the process of destruction and reintegration that is central to Frederick's use of it (drawing it apart and joining it together again). The symbolic power contained within the "ivory object" recollection lies in the fact that what Frederick's own impulses would destroy, in his mother and in himself, could be restored through his reparative urges. That, I might add, is a most positive and creative use of the transitional object, and it is just such a use that Frederick seems to have made of his "impossible plaything." Indeed, in a striking reminder of Olmsted's actions with the "ivory object," William Niederland writes: "Artistic imagination bespeaks the capacity to take apart and put together—that is, to break established patterns of relationships and to replace them with new ones."[18] I see the "ivory object" as a prototypal symbol of Olmsted's life and his identity, as the symbol for achieving reintegration through the creative act.[19]

This persistence in advancing again after retreat, in rebuilding after loss, in making reparation after giving into destructive urges also requires a high degree of psychic courage. This was a courage Olmsted would demonstrate to the end of his life. It suggests, once again, not only his own constitutional qualities, but also that, for all the trauma of his early life, he had also been given enough love and nurturance to serve as the basic foundation for his psychic strength.

There are men whose inner anxieties are so great, so threatening to their selfhood, that they must adopt a fetish object, or fetishistic behavior, to defend against their fears.[20] Most often the notion of a fetish is associated with sexual behavior, but in popular vernacular we often speak of a person "making a fetish" of some thing or some activity—meaning that the person has invested it with an unusual degree of significance or reverence. We can think of such an object as a *psychosocial* fetish—that is, an object that offers comfort and reassurance, restitution and integration, affirmation of identity. It is my belief that Frederick, quite early in life, invested *trees* (particularly elm trees) with precisely that type of psychic significance.[21] Such a symbolic investment is suggested by his usage of the tree in the third of his three "trivial memories." But it is even more evident in the fact that trees, both as subject matter and as symbol, are central to so many of Olmsted's later attempts at autobiography, both in his own notes and writings and in his letters to Mariana Van Rensselaer.

In several such recollections, Olmsted related the following incident about his Grandfather Olmsted, who was a Revolutionary War veteran —an incident that happened when Frederick "could not have been over five years old."[22] Frederick was lying with his head "between the roots of a lofty elm, looking up at its swaying boughs and leafage" when his grandfather "hobbled" out of the house, dressed in the holiday finery of the previous generation. His grandfather supported his weight upon "a long silver headed Malacca cane used as a walking stick"—a walking stick that was now in Olmsted's possession. Olmsted noted that his grandfather claimed to have planted that elm tree all by himself when *he* was a boy, digging it up in "the Swamp" and dragging it home. Olmsted added:

It came to me after a time as he went on talking about it that there had been nothing in all his long [and strange] life of which he was frankly so proud and in which he took such complete pleasure as the planting and beautiful growth of this tree [and I did not wonder for before I had had no idea that a tree could grow to be so great in a man's life].[23]

Thereupon Frederick, having heard about locust trees, decided to plant the seeds of such a tree. Before long, he found a twig sprouting "among the weeds there growing," and that twig turned out to be a honey locust tree that he was proud to call his own. When he was twelve, Frederick transplanted the tree to a place with more suitable soil, and it flourished there. "Forty years afterwards I went to look at it and thought it the finest honey locust I ever saw." But when he returned "lately," "it had been felled." Olmsted first noted, and then struck out, the fact that he "knew enough to bless the man who felled it." He left standing the comment that he "was glad of it, for its individual beauty was out of key with the surrounding circumstances and its time had fully come."

This anecdote about his grandfather begins with Frederick's lying beneath an elm tree, passively contemplating its swaying, leafy boughs (its most feminine aspect). The incident took place when Frederick was five, the period of intense Oedipal striving in a little boy and of identification with various father figures, so that the scene itself suggests a peaceful moment of psychic retreat into the maternal environment, a moment that ends when his aged grandfather, whose dress recalls the heroic Revolutionary generation, summons the little boy back to Oedipal concerns. The grandfather has brought with him a valuable walking stick —a symbol of established masculinity—which Frederick would come to possess in due course.

Bruno Bettelheim's analysis of a certain type of fairy tale, in which the aging king holds out the scepter of the kingdom to his heir, speaks to this reading of the incident. According to Bettelheim, "Never in a fairy tale does a son take his father's kingdom away from him. If a father gives it up, it always because of old age. Even then the son has to earn it."[24] The tasks set for the young heir are those that prove his fitness to rule, for "gaining the kingdom is tantamount to having reached moral and sexual maturity." Thus, there was an implied task involved when the grandfather pointed out the elm tree (here the symbol both of essential selfhood and of achievement) that he had brought back, as if a trophy, from his venture into "the Swamp"—the latter being a graphic representation of sexual activity. The tree trophy also symbolized what was best, most permanent in his grandfather's life. Until then, Frederick had had no idea "that a tree could grow to be so great in a man's life." But thereafter the task, his goal in life, was set before him, in the symbolism of the elm tree.

Olmsted's repeated references to this anecdote over the years suggests that it had great meaning for him. To plant his own tree was not only to embark upon the tasks Bettelheim refers to (gaining his inheritance and achieving masculinity); it was also a way to identify with this idealized father figure (the Revolutionary War hero), an Oedipal task. Among the "weeds" of Frederick's troubled boyhood, the seeds of his creativity had taken root, perhaps symbolized by the honey locust he had planted.

Powerful imagery for Olmsted's life was vested in that honey locust: planting it at the Oedipal age (five); transplanting it to more favorable soil at the dawn of his puberty (twelve); its full flourishing during his middle years, to be a thing of pride at the time of his father's death, when his own career was in full flower; its being cut down during his final years, because it was unsuitably placed and "its time had fully come" (for which Olmsted blessed the axeman). It is the last image that is perhaps most striking and poignant about the honey locust anecdote. For one recalls the losing struggle of Olmsted's last years to defend the concept of "natural scenery" in an era given over to monumentalism and the celebration of buildings rather than landscape.

While trees generically were an identity symbol for Olmsted, and the honey locust in this last anecdote seems an appropriate symbol for his creative energies, it was the elm tree that held the greatest significance for Olmsted over the years. The most suggestive evidence for the way in which the elm tree symbolized Olmsted's selfhood is contained within his 1860 autobiographical notes.[25] This document is divided into two major sections: first, a seriocomic treatment of his genealogy, written in stream-of-consciousness fashion; second, a series of terse and, with some exceptions, accurate references to his life between his birth and the time of writing (mid-1860). The genealogical section is bracketed by a clever pun. This section begins with the words "E Pluribus," and it ends several paragraphs later with the word "Unum"—a rather grandiose reference to the individual as a culmination of the preceding generations. The sequence of words that form the transition between the first (genealogical) and second (personal) sections are of particular interest. These words are: "Elm trees. Unum—Born April 1822." But in order to measure the significance of these words, they must be seen in the context of the preceding material—material that is also of interest for demonstrating the connection between Olmsted's genealogy and his psychic identity.

This association between his selfhood and his ancestory is strongly suggested in the following passage:

Two brothers etc. Essex & Heligolandish waits—shrink from public, but one Lieut Olmsted pops out in the King Philip War—probably motive not military ardor [or] fear of Indians but desire to explore the Thames & see the riches of the neighboring swamps. Fine effect of setting sun on tussock of Calamus in the dry season—Night attack with flames—Deacons etc.—discipline.

The "two brothers etc." reference seems nominally to refer to Nicholas and Nehemiah Olmsted, the second generation of Olmsted's forebears in the New World.[26] "Essex & Heligoland" could be references to his

Anglo-Saxon heritage, since Essex is the county in England from which the Olmsted family derived, and *Heligoland* is the English spelling of a small German island in the North Sea. The two also have a connection to significant variations on the Olmsted name. *Elmsted* is a variation that derived from a place name, a parish in Essex meaning "the place of Elms, as being remarkable for the growth of trees of that kind." *Heligoland* seems related to that variation known as *Holmsted*, in which *holm* is defined as a "small island."[27]

The sense of this reference is that the emigrant brothers lived in obscurity until Lieutenant Nicholas Olmsted served in the King Philip War. The latter was indeed called to arms in 1675, marching along the Thames River to New London in response to an Indian alarm, but it is not clear that he saw any action on that occasion. He did, however, participate in a *morning* attack on a Pequot Indian fort in 1637, for which service he was rewarded with land. The house he built on that land was still standing when Frederick was a boy, being torn down about 1835.[28]

What led Olmsted to record these references to that second Olmsted generation in Hartford, especially with the addition of material that was clearly invented? As it happens, this little vignette seems to be rich in allusions to Olmsted's own life, and it suggests a great many unconscious associations.[29] For example, the two brothers referred to can be seen as stand-ins for Frederick and John Hull, who had lived in obscurity during their young manhood. Among the highlights of those early years are two that Olmsted referred to later on in these same 1860 notes: first, when he spent time with his brother, who was attending Yale, in New Haven— the "Elm City," or place of elms; second, when the brothers lived in Staten *Island* (Heligoland), on the farm possessed first by Frederick, then his brother.

It is certainly possible that Frederick here identified himself with Lieutenant Olmsted, the elder of the two brothers. The desire "to explore the Thames & see the riches of the neighboring swamps" is probably related to Olmsted's actual visit to the Great Dismal Swamp of Virginia and North Carolina during his first trip to the South—a trip he made at the behest of Harriet Beecher Stowe, to whom he reported his findings in two long letters.[30] Like his forebear Lieutenant Olmsted, Frederick did indeed break out of what he considered the obscurity of Staten Island when he set out on this journey through the Slave States.[31] It was

Frederick's first real adventure on his own, and it resulted in his dispatches to the *Times* and in the first of his books about the South—both of which were to lift him out of obscurity and establish him in the "Literary Republic." But the anecdote also serves as a reminder of his grandfather going into "the Swamp" to obtain the elm tree he was to plant and which was to "grow to be so great" in his life. Thus, this reference to Lieutenant Olmsted's trip of exploration—one that began as a desire to see "the riches of the neighboring swamps" and ended in military glory—is rich in intergenerational associations, both conscious and unconscious, of self-assertion, of masculine adventure and achievement.[32] Further, as Melanie Klein has observed, the new territory sought out in such explorations "stands for a new mother, one that will replace the loss of the real mother," a view suggesting that this genealogical anecdote may also be a metaphor for the wanderlust that was to afflict Olmsted all his life.[33]

This same passage also contains some very striking images embedded within the genealogical vignette. First, there is the reference to his ancestor marching off to an Indian war; then we are assured that this was a sight-seeing adventure (to "see the riches of the neighboring swamps") rather than a martial or an anti-Indian exercise; then we are told that the principal sight beheld was the "Fine effect of setting sun on tussock of Calamus in the dry season"; and then there is a resurgence of militaristic imagery ("Night attack with flames"). The lovely, picturesque image of the "tussock of Calamus" illuminated by the sunset provides a peaceful retreat between the aggressive image of marching to war and the fury of the night attack. Whatever the historical basis for this anecdote, it is clear that both the "tussock of Calamus" and the "Night attack with flames" are visual images from Olmsted's imagination and thus enrich this vignette with unconscious symbolism.

The "Night attack with flames," which is the last of Olmsted's references to the King Philip War, calls to mind the evening one of outbuildings in the Olmsted home on College Street was destroyed by fire.[34] That, in turn, suggests the second of Frederick's three "trivial memories": being lifted into the cockloft of an outhouse, a sort of aboriginal adventure in exploration, perhaps in his mother's arms. And the "shafts of sunlight" filtering through the dim outhouse, in that memory, recall the rays of the setting sun that illuminate the tussock of calamus.

Are these images, then, all related? Discussing his "outhouse" memory (in the 1893 fragments), Olmsted stated: "Even now something occasionally comes to my nose that leads me to think of the air in that loft, possibly reviving a memory of it but more likely only a memory of past memories of it."[35] It is possible that the original odor was some scent or fragrance peculiar to his mother or some other woman who was with him in the outhouse. Such a scent would relate to one of the several meanings of *calamus*—as an aromatic plant also called *sweet flag*. A second possible meaning of *calamus* derives from both the plant's "blade-like leaves" and its "floral spike," which thrusts forth between these leaves—phallic imagery that contrasts strongly with the feminine associations of both the tussock ("a tuft of grass") and its scent.[36]

Thus the calamus reference seems to be filled with ambivalent and provocative associations. The superphallic associations of calamus seem very appropriate to the militaristic aggressiveness of the passage itself. Moreover, the "tussock" allusion can also suggest a phallic grouping, as in men marching off to war, men attacking, the explosive destructiveness of males together. The calamus reference, in this sense, symbolizes a potential for destruction that belies the passive, peaceful imagery inherent in a femininely aromatic plant, nesting at the edge of swamps, looking pretty in the sunset.

These contrasting and powerful masculine and feminine associations are consonant with the psychoanalytic notion of a fetish object as a bisexual symbol—that is, a symbol meant to allay the male's anxieties over the female's anatomical difference by denying that such a difference exists.[37] In the situation suggested by Olmsted's genealogical narrative, the unconscious anxiety seems to be what Robert Stoller calls *symbiosis anxiety:* the fear of loss of masculine identity, which is aroused by the desire to retreat to the maternal environment. The frightening imagery of the harsh masculine life—life as warfare and achievement as victory through armed struggle — is here offset by the pacific imagery of a retreat to tranquil nature, an immersion in the soft, feminine "riches" of the quiet swamp.

But the loss of masculine identity implicit in such a retreat must itself then be defended against, perhaps by clinging to the notion that this retreat need not mean such a loss, that masculinity can be found even within the feminine environment. The tussock of calamus is proof that this is so, for its quiet, aromatic beauty coexists with the "blade-like leaves" and the thrusting "floral spike" of the individual plants. The tussock of calamus, then, can be seen as another bisexual symbol of selfhood, of the sense of integration that can be maintained even when one wants to retreat from the masculine world of competition to the feminine world of beauty and tranquility. And it would be an especially apt symbol for Olmsted to employ at the time he probably wrote these 1860 notes—the time of the Central Park accident, with its overtones of an enforced retreat from Oedipal striving to a more passive, and thus more "feminine," self.

The reference to calamus, especially in a writing of 1860, cannot be read without thinking of Walt Whitman's "Calamus" poems, written about 1856 and printed as a part of *Leaves of Grass* in 1860.[38] It is generally acknowledged that these poems offer the first, and most powerful, evidence of Whitman's homosexual impulses, and biographers and critics have tended to see such imagery behind Whitman's use of the phallic calamus plant in his title for the poems he wrote in this period.[39]

More to the point, however, is the notion that both Whitman and Olmsted, as Romantic lovers of nature, may have perceived quite similar imagery in the calamus. David Cavitch describes the calamus as "a type of grass that does not grow everywhere alike but only by quiet ponds and marshes." As such, it symbolizes for him the choice of "a secret life" far removed from the main byways of society: in Whitman's case, the private and personal pursuit of homosexual love rather than his former public role as the celebrator of heterosexual love. Cavitch cites Whitman's lines:[40]

> In paths untrodden
> In the growth by margins of pond-waters.
> Escaped from the life that exhibits itself
> From all the standards hitherto publish'd, from
>   the pleasures, profits, conformities,
> Which too long I was offering to feed my soul . . .

In this usage, the calamus can stand for the kind of psychic retreat ("Escaped from the life that exhibits itself") that Whitman sought at this point in his life and that Olmsted sought (mostly through accidents and illness) at various points in *his* life—as in the Central Park accident.

For me, *Leaves of Grass* presents a powerful, devastating example of the struggle between the true self and the false self. "As I Ebbed with the

Ocean of Life," a poem first written in 1860, contains these moving, tragic lines: "amid all that blab whose echoes recoil upon me I have not once had the least idea of who or what I am . . ./Before all my arrogant poems the *real Me* stands yet untouch'd, untold, altogether unreach'd" (emphasis added). This is a poetic rendering of Winnicott's description of deep psychic disturbance, when the true self is hidden even from the person's own consciousness. And I believe that the "two brothers" passage from Olmsted's 1860 notes is very much *his* poem upon the same theme, the search for true selfhood—a poem that is in its way as much a parable for *his* inner life as one finds in Whitman's poetry.

Even Olmsted's reference (in this genealogical passage) to "Deacons etc.—discipline" makes sense as a symbol of selfhood contained within the imaginative history of his ancestry. The phrase is, genealogically, an allusion to Nicholas Olmsted's son and grandson, both named Joseph and both of them deacons.[41] But we recall that Frederick, as a young boy, had been sent away from home to board with rural ministers ("Deacons"). And the schoolmasters at Ellington High School and Joab Brace had not been loathe to use brutal punishment in the handling of their charges; hence the link between "Deacons etc." and "discipline."

The final paragraph of the genealogical section leads directly to the elm tree reference and closes the "E pluribus unum" pun:

The Maine expedition & old shoe leather stewed in Snow water—Arnold crossed in love. The Marquis & village green dances. Elm trees. Unum.

The paragraph recalls the adventures and hardships connected with his paternal grandfather's participation in Benedict Arnold's Quebec campaign, as well as his grandmother's tales of having danced with Lafayette's officers "as they passed thro' Hartford, moving from Newport to join Washington."[42]

The Arnold reference may, like the Lieutenant Olmsted usage, involve another case of identification, for Olmsted himself had been "crossed in love" a decade before this was written. And Benedict Arnold lost his leg in that failed attack upon Quebec, a fact that can be associated with Olmsted's own near loss of his leg in the Central Park accident. In classic psychoanalytic theory, castration (symbolized by the loss of a leg) is the feared punishment for Oedipal "betrayal" of the father. The paragraph thus offers both a positive and a negative identification for Olmsted. The positive image is, of course, the Revolutionary grandfather who serves as an exemplar for masculine striving—the heroic, achieving, idealized self. The negative identification is of the sinister, betraying, castrated "shadow" self represented by Benedict Arnold. Any existential fears raised in Olmsted through the contemplation of such possible negative aspects of his selfhood would surely have been allayed by the comforting symbol of selfhood and integration with which the paragraph ends: "Elm trees. Unum."

Indeed, it is important to note that it is the symbol of the elm tree toward which the whole of the genealogical section inevitably flows. However, before examining the significance of the elm tree within the transitional sequence of words between the genealogical and personal section of these 1860 notes, it would be useful to examine what imagery elm trees would communicate to someone with Olmsted's background in the mid-nineteenth century. For this purpose, Andrew Jackson Downing's great work on landscape gardening is useful.[43] Olmsted not only considered himself (and was considered by others) to be Downing's successor, but he also mentions this specific work a few sentences later in these same 1860 autobiographical notes.

Downing's treatise contains a lengthy discourse on elm trees.[44] In particular, he calls attention to the nobility of the size of its trunk, as contrasted with its branches—the latter being "comparatively tapering and slender, forming themselves . . . into long and graceful curves." Downing's description, then, with its contrasting masculine and feminine qualities makes the elm an exemplar of trees as a bisexual symbol of selfhood—a symbol, that is, which is meant to alleviate anxiety by integrating a lingering identification with the mother's feminine qualities and a later identification with the father's masculine qualities. I have already suggested that the leafy boughs of the tree represented to Olmsted the essentially feminine attributes of beauty and nurturance—here embodied in the "graceful curves" of the elm. The trunk of the tree personifies the nineteenth-century masculine virtues of solidity, stability, and (from Downing) nobility. Thus, the elm tree here serves as an integrating and restorative symbol—a bisexual symbol (similar to the "tussock of Calamus") and a symbol of self-acceptance in a society that vigorously differentiated between and stereotyped masculine and feminine qualities. But in suggesting a unique role for the elm tree, I should also note that almost every kind of tree shares to some extent its symbolic quality of integrating contrasting masculine and feminine attributes into an aesthetically pleasing whole of great social utility.

Two especially significant associations come to mind concerning the importance of elm trees in Olmsted's later life. One is the double row of elm trees set in long straight lines along each border of the Mall (originally called the Promenade) in Central Park—several hundred elms in all. This elm-lined mall was designed and constructed to serve as the "vestibule" of the park, carrying the visitor from the artificial, masculine beauty of urban architecture into the natural, feminine beauty of the park. The Mall runs on a straight line from the original divide of the Fifth Avenue entrance-drive northwest to the Terrace and offers the single most important sight line in the Greensward plan: across the eastern section of the lake and the Ramble toward Vista Rock, crowned with Belvedere Castle.[45]

The American elm, an addendum to the Greensward plan states, was particularly well suited to its use on the Mall, in part because it retained the "vigor and vitality of a young tree" long after achieving full maturity and therefore would bear up well under transplanting to the park. Use of the elm would thus more quickly make the Promenade an "avenue of considerable dignity."[46] This suggests Calvert Vaux's comment to Olmsted that the latter had "come into the business at 40 with the spirit of a boy of 20."[47] Certainly, Olmsted's own "transplanting" into the park had taken well and was largely responsible for the quick results achieved in construction.

The second association referred to above deals with Olmsted's "psychic retreat" from New York City (and his association with the New York parks) to his new home and office in Brookline, Massachusetts, in 1882–1883. Roper tells us that his friend H. H. Richardson, one of the most successful architects in post–Civil War America, had invited Olmsted to build on property close to his. But Olmsted fell in love with the Boylston homestead on Warren Avenue, and it took patient and imaginative negotiating on the part of John Charles to obtain it for his stepfather.[48] What is distinctly noticeable about the plan view of Fairsted, as Olmsted called his estate, are two very large elm trees—the two largest trees on the property and both visible from the main house. The one off Warren Street has since fallen in a storm. But the second is a magnificent elm that still stands at Fairsted today, close to the main wing of the house, near

7. The Central Park mall, c. 1894, designed to serve as the formal "vestibule" for the natural beauty of the park—especially the Ramble just beyond it. It is lined on both sides with rows of elm trees, three hundred elms in all. (The New-York Historical Society.)

the conservatory on the first floor and the bedrooms on the second.[49] It must have provided Olmsted with much-needed restorative comfort in his later years.

Finally, in a section devoted to trees as a symbol of selfhood, it is worth noting that Olmsted was devoted to the creation of arboretums throughout his career as a landscape architect.[50] Such an arboretum had been planned for Central park, where the East Meadow is located now. It was to include "one to three examples of each species of tree" found in the northeastern United States, but it seems never to have been completed in a formal way, though plantings to that end may have taken place.[51] A proposal to include an arboretum of California trees on the Stanford University campus was rejected, but the Arnold Arboretum is one of the glories of the Boston Park system. And, as was noted in part

1, the arboretum at Biltmore became the justifying passion of Olmsted's last years of work. "The arboretum had come to be to him, of all Biltmore projects, the most cherished," Roper writes. "It loomed in his mind as one of great national importance."[52]

Returning to the elm tree in particular, it is clear that in Olmsted's 1860 notes, at least, the elm stood as a metaphor both for his genealogy and for his identity. The two were interrelated, as we have seen, through the imaginative way in which Olmsted had assimilated his ancestry into his inner life. This relationship between ancestry and selfhood becomes dramatically symbolized in another fact revealed by Downing—that the elm tree produces a flower that appears "in the month of April." This provides the key to understanding the transitional sequence of words: "Elm trees. Unum—Born April 1822." In this case, elm trees represent the Olmsteds: out of these many (E pluribus) came the one (Unum) whose flowering was in April 1822—Frederick himself.

CHAPTER 6

Images of Mother

Frederick was scarcely six years old when he was sent away from home for the first time, on the 350-mile trip, by stage or carriage, to Geneseo in upper New York State.[1] Clearly, the trip had left its psychic impact, for Olmsted writes of it both in his 1860 notes and in "Passages" (1873), using in part identical imagery. The "great trees & river banks" recalled in the 1860 notes are to be found again in "Passages," in which Olmsted writes of being driven "rapidly and silently over the turf of the bottom lands among great trees." In the latter instance, the "great trees" seem to provide a masculine image to set against the sensual feminine imagery of "river banks" and "bottom lands." In classical psychoanalytic theory, trees are generally seen as phallic symbols, while rivers are considered to be symbols for the mother figure. I have stressed, however, that trees were bisexual symbols for Olmsted. This bisexual emphasis can be seen in the fact that in all of the memories where trees are described, their leafy boughs are a crucial element, either overtly or implied.

In "Passages," Olmsted prefaces the "bottom lands and great trees" imagery with two other Geneseo recollections:

I remember being taken to see Indians making baskets, to visit a house in the dooryard of which there was a fawn; and at which a beautiful woman gave me some sweet meats.

The lone fawn in the dooryard is quite representative of Frederick in that same situation—a six-year-old far from home. The fawn is a most appealing, if ungainly, young animal, notable for its curiosity and its timidity. Similarly, the circumstances of this visit could have stimulated in Frederick a feeling of both adventurous exploration and frightened loneliness. It is the kind of situation that seems to be a reenactment of the rapprochement stage of a child's individuation, during which the child experiences both the exhilaration and the fears associated with autonomy with a concomitant need for the psychic comfort of his mother, a mother whom Frederick had lost two years earlier. And that comfort is found here in the guise of the "beautiful woman" who offers him some sweet meats—a confection that is a most apt symbol for the mother's love that both nourishes and delights.

The warmth and nurturance implicit in the imagery of the fawn and the beautiful woman offer a curious counterpoint to Olmsted's only substantive recollection of Charlotte Hull Olmsted, given earlier in the same 1873 memoir, in this passage:

> My mother died while I was so young that I have but a tradition of memory rather than the faintest recollection of her. While I was a small school boy if I was asked if I remembered her I could say "Yes; I remember playing on the grass and looking up at her while she sat sewing under a tree." I now only remember that I did so remember her, but it has always been a delight to me to see a woman sitting under a tree, sewing and minding a child.[2]

One of the most striking things about this screen memory is the care that Olmsted's unconscious has taken to distance him from the actuality of his mother. This can be seen in two aspects of the passage: first, she has been reduced to "a tradition of a memory"; second, the child's relationship to his mother is visual only—that is, at a physical distance from her.

The scene itself seems like a sentimental Victorian painting of an idealized domestic tableau, especially as it is placed in the ubiquitous pastoral setting of such paintings. While Olmsted focuses attention upon his pleasure in the mother caring for her child, it is the pastoral setting that was actually the major preoccupation of Olmsted's creative imagination. Indeed, precisely this pastoral theme was noted in 1903 by Arthur Spencer, one of his most perceptive critics: "Olmsted loved the broad meadow, richly carpeted with turf, and the great tree standing in stately solitude in the midst of the gently undulating, wood-bordered field."[3]

It is significant that this pastoral theme, which was to be so important to Olmsted's life and work, forms the setting for this sole recollection of

8. The Long Meadow in Prospect Park. Many critics believe that Prospect Park was Olmsted and Vaux's finest collaboration—the perfect realization of a Romantic, naturalistic landscape. The park was first laid out by Vaux while Olmsted was in California. Olmsted's contributions came in the implementing of Vaux's plan on the ground. (National Park Service, Frederick Law Olmsted National Historical Site.)

his mother. It implies that certain connections exist between the pastoral theme and the way in which Olmsted chose to remember her.

One connection is the *visual* quality associated both with the pastoral setting and with the relationship of Frederick to his mother in this recollection. Just as an observer "takes in" the pastoral setting, so does Frederick maintain his relationship with his mother here by "taking her in" visually.[4] This is also a reminder of Frederick lying on his back and looking up at the leafy boughs of the elm tree (in his "grandfather" memory). This screen memory, then, provides a powerful suggestion of how important visual contemplation—"taking in" with his eyes—would be to Olmsted throughout his life. And it offers further evidence for the psychosomatic origins of his later eye problems (the so-called "sumach poisoning" of his adolescence and the attack of blindness in 1873). If vision was his preferred means of relating to the world, then loss or impairment of vision would have been an appropriate form of psychic retreat.

As in the "trivial memories," it is Frederick as an early toddler who is recalled here, an infant still developing a sense of himself as distinct from his mother, still displaying the "visual pattern of 'checking back to mother,' " which is a part of individuation.[5] And there is an important, positive aspect to the "together but separate" quality of individuation in the manner suggested here. For, as D. W. Winnicott points out, the child's capacity for "being alone in the presence of the mother" is the basis for the sharing of solitude that is an essential aspect of a loving adult relationship.[6] Unfortunately, it is the *only* aspect that Olmsted demonstrated here —suggesting that it represented his chosen method of relating to others. Indeed, his park design philosophy would stress the passive sharing of solitude rather than dynamic forms of human interaction. Parks were to be a place of psychic retreat to the feminine sphere, a palliative for the effects of masculine Oedipal striving and competition, not a place for that competition to be practiced in another form—as "manly sport."[7]

The second connection between the pastoral theme and the way in which Olmsted chose to remember his mother is represented in the qualities of nurturance, shelter, and protection suggested by this scene. In this way, the "sewing memory" connects the idealized pastoral setting to only one of the two aspects of the mother as the little child experiences her—aspects that can be referred to as the *environment mother* and the *sensual mother*.[8]

The *environment mother* represents the protective and nurturing aspects of the woman with respect to her child. In this role, she provides a sense of security and an affectionate aura within which the child develops, and she shares in his growing awareness and enjoyment of the world at large. In fact, she encourages her child's response to the world by providing sights and sounds for her child to delight in.

The *sensual mother* is that aspect in which a woman meets her child's most urgent physical needs—feeding him, bathing him, and so on. By virtue of her intimate contact with her child, she becomes the target of all its passions (including resentment and destructive thoughts, when the child is frustrated). It is the sensual mother who introduces each human being to physical gratification. In Freud's words, the child's mother "regards him with feelings that are derived from her own sexual life: she strokes him, kisses him, rocks him." In so doing, she "is only fulfilling her task in teaching the child to love."[9]

The woman in Olmsted's screen memory, like the pastoral setting itself, represents the environment mother. There is no touching, no form of sensual contact or physical intimacy between Frederick and his mother in this recollection. There is no passionate feeling here; indeed, there is no emotion at all. What the memory enshrines is not a dynamic exchange between mother and child, but rather the child existing within the maternal environment, secure in the knowledge that his mother is close by, quietly protective of his serenity. Olmsted's psychic use of this memory associates the passive enjoyment of pastoral scenery with the passive quality of a child secure within the sheltering care of the environment mother.

The ubiquitous tree—which figures so prominently both in the screen memory itself and in Spencer's thematic summation of Olmsted's art— calls to mind Olmsted's use of trees as a symbol of idealized selfhood, from which he could draw reassurance, a sense of being whole and undamaged. Its presence here adds another measure of psychic comfort to the tranquil scene, a comfort deriving from the feminine aspect of trees —the leafy boughs that shelter and protect. John Olmsted's journal shows that while Olmsted was a boy, Connecticut often experienced severe and lengthy winters. And Olmsted's youthful letters show that he enjoyed the winter season. Further, Connecticut, like all of New England, is particularly beautiful in the fall, when the leaves turn colors. Yet Olmsted's recollections are always of the trees of summer and almost always of shade trees—that is, trees in their most feminine aspect.

In an article printed in 1882, Olmsted considered the beauty to be found even in maltreated, stunted trees:

looking down upon [a row of such trees] I say it is not beautiful. But looking up at the continuous green canopy which these trunks support, swaying in the light summer breeze against the serene blue beyond—swaying not only with the utmost grace of motion but with the utmost stately majesty—. . . if the result is not to be called beautiful it is only because it has more of sublimity than beauty.[10]

The passage suggests that the sublime beauty of a tree is to be found in its green canopy of foliage (which can be seen only part of the year) and thus is intrinsic to all leafy boughs by their very nature. And that beauty is essentially feminine—the feminine ideal of Victorian America, combining "grace of motion" with "stately majesty."

I have suggested that trees were a bisexual symbol for Olmsted, an integration of the masculine and feminine aspects of himself. But the feminine aspect of this bisexual symbol of selfhood is primarily that of the sheltering environment mother, and it is romantic in its essence—as in the image of the swaying, leafy boughs against the serene blue sky. The masculine aspect (as in this passage) exists to support the feminine, beautiful aspect—that is, the masculine aspect is utilitarian. "And, I ask," Olmsted wrote at the end of this passage, "if man does not live by bread alone, what is better doing than the planting of trees?" This suggests to me that Olmsted's false self (the utilitarian, "doing" self) could be justified only so long as it served to nurture and support his true self (the romantic, "being" self of the artist).

The greatest danger to a creative person like Olmsted was for him to feel that he had lost touch with his true-self's purposes. An example of this can be seen in a letter Olmsted wrote to Charley Brace, after returning to Staten Island from their walking tour in Europe in 1850.[11] Clearly suffering a letdown after the exhilaration of foreign travel, Olmsted wrote as one totally out of touch with his real purposes, imprisoned within the society in which he now found himself:

Daylight has walked into my theatre. A half crazy Philosopher, I am woke up, my feet shackled and my hands tied, a mask on my face, carried downstairs with the rest of the crowd. The sun shines, ice is cold, fire is hot, punch is both sweet and sour. Fred Olmsted is alone, is stupid, is crazy and is unalterably a weak sinner and unhappy and happy.

No matter how flippantly Olmsted had intended it, this passage offers Olmsted's unconscious vision of himself: an ego-split truth seeker, his true self shackled and tied, wearing the mask of his false self, forced into a conscious life in which his real self has no interest, swept along with the crowd.

Olmsted's true self's purpose as an artist, his usage of the trees of summer as a symbol of selfhood, and the pastoral theme that dominated his life's work seem to be linked together by his devotion to the idealized mother of infancy who lived on in his psyche—the lost mother whom he could recover only in his life's work and to whom he could make reparation only through that work. Charlotte Hull Olmsted's death had removed from the scene, in the most painful way imaginable, the real and loving woman who had been the natural object of his devotion as a child. What was left of her was an unconscious image of the idealized environment mother, memorialized in the "sewing memory." Indeed, the same idealized presence, in symbolic form, is to be found in another of the important recollections in "Passages"—one that seems at first glance to concern only Frederick's relationship to his father.

The remembered incident occurred on "a [lovely] Sunday evening," when he and his father were crossing a meadow, alone with each other:

I was tired and he had taken me in his arms. I soon noticed that he was inattentive to my prattle and looking in his face saw in it something unusual. Following the direction in his eyes: I said "Oh! there's a star." Then [in the lowest tone/in the low voice of the deepest reverence/a hushed voice/but in simple and child like words he spoke of infinite Being] he said something of Infinite Love [with a tone and expression which showed subdued exaltation] with a tone and manner which really moved me, chick that I was, so much that it has ever since remained in my heart.[12]

Olmsted speaks of his father and himself as being *alone* in the meadow. Yet they are not alone: the intruding star is the crucial centerpiece in this incident. In Olmsted's Victorian era, a star would be a most appropriate symbol for that culture's ideal qualities of womanhood: beautiful, pure, inspiring, and remote.[13] For Olmsted, the star represents the idealized aspects of the mother he'd lost when he was less than four—the maternal image of the "sewing memory," the environment mother who was loved visually, at a distance. The symbol of the star also has a most appropriate vernacular association, for Charlotte Hull Olmsted was surely the "star" both of this memory and of Olmsted's imaginative, creative internal psychodrama.

The symbolism employed here is reinforced by the two phrases Olmsted gave, alternatively, as his father's description of the star. The phrase in the final draft is "Infinite Love," representing John Olmsted's undying love for the wife of his youth. The phrase in the original draft is "Infinite Being," or that in Charlotte which had not died and could not die. Indeed, the star as Infinite Being recalls the description John Olmsted had employed when writing of the death of his little boy, Owen: "now in truth an *angell of light* in heaven his home." The meadow, domesticity in Olmsted's idiom, here symbolizes the romanticized home of his infancy, *before* his brother's birth. *This* triad—father, son, and star-mother, alone in the meadow—is an image that memorializes the family at a time when Frederick was his parents' only child; it is an image of paradise lost. It was perhaps this association that had kept this particular image alive "in his heart" and had so moved him that, after his father's death, he formed out of it his most intimate memory of him.

I argued earlier that Mary Ann Olmsted had not provided a satisfactory replacement for the mother he had lost. As Winnicott notes, the child needs a mother "who can be loved as a person and to whom reparation can be made" (for the many angry, hurtful feelings he harbors towards her). If the child does not obtain a "reliable mother-figure," Winnicott writes, then "guilt becomes intolerable," and the child's capacity to express concern in his relationships with living people will be blunted.[14] Thus, if Mary Ann Olmsted failed to become the mother "who can be loved," then Frederick's gestures of reparation could not be made to her as a person, nor even to her inner representation within his psyche. I would suggest that his reparative gestures were, in fact, directed toward his symbolic mother—nature. According to Melanie Klein, nature is a common symbolic replacement for the lost mother. More specifically, she has stated that those who refuse to sever their ties with nature "keep alive the image of the mother of the early days."[15] The aptness of this observation for Olmsted's later creative direction is obvious, but I must stress the potential that exists for severe emotional problems when one devotes more of one's energies to such a symbolic attachment than to satisfying human relationships.

Winnicott writes: "we often forgive a man or woman for mental ill-health or for some kind of immaturity because that person has so rich a personality that society may gain through the exceptional contribution he or she can make."[16] Olmsted's attachment to the symbolic mother, nature, clearly added to the richness of *his* personality (even while it expressed a developmental flaw) and facilitated his later "exceptional contribution" to society. Moreover, Frederick's adoption of the symbol of nature as an inner "replacement mother" not only impacted upon his later creative work, but also surely helped him to survive, psychically, the many separations from home during his boyhood and adolescence.

When Olmsted was nineteen and suffering through his unhappy apprenticeship at Benkard and Hutton's "counting-house," he wrote to his stepmother: "Oh, how I long to be where I was a year ago: *midst two lofty mountains, pursuing the uneven course of the purling brook*, gliding among the fair granite rocks, & lisping over the pebbles, meandering through the lowly valley, *under the sweeping willows, & the waving elms.*"[17] Aside from the psychosexual implications of his imagery, what seems obvious here is Frederick's desire to make a psychic retreat from the masculine Oedipal world of commerce to the symbolic breasts and flowing milk of the lost mother as found within the feminine world of nature. Not only is the "sweeping willow" another very feminine tree, but Olmsted has also chosen to emphasize the feminine aspect of his "identity tree"—the "waving elms." Once again, the image is of being "under" the trees, with its association of being sheltered within the maternal environment.

Finally, note that he did not write to his stepmother of his desire to be home with her at the Ann Street house in Hartford. He preferred to be where he was "a year ago"—which, as the editors of *The Papers* point out, was in the countryside near the second of Reverend Barton's two academies, in rural Collinsville.[18] It was perhaps Olmsted's way of informing his stepmother of his rejection of her in favor of his symbolic mother, nature—a subtle response to her own earlier rejection of him when he was a child.

If any single *person* took over the role of "environment mother" (the warm nurturing mother figure) from Charlotte Hull Olmsted, it was surely John Olmsted's sister—Frederick's maiden aunt, Maria Olmsted. "Aunty" Maria was two years older than Frederick's mother, three years older than his stepmother, and thus of the right age to be their surrogate. She has been described as "plain as a pikestaff," a kindly person, devoted to her brother's family. Maria was especially protective of and caring for Frederick, acting as his housekeeper the seven years he owned the Staten Island farm, helping him to furnish his rooms in Manhattan, and generally fretting about him.[19]

Stricken with typhoid fever while aboard the *Ronaldson*, it was to Maria, not his stepmother, that Frederick's most anguished cry was directed: "Oh! Aunt Maria, to be sick in a ship's forecastle is the extent of human misery."[20] I think it likely that the death of Maria Olmsted—for most of his life a nurturing mother figure to him—was a strong contributing factor in Frederick's decision to marry his brother's widow.

A bachelor of thirty-seven, Olmsted was married, quite suddenly, to Mary Cleveland Olmsted on June 13, 1859, in a civil ceremony performed in Central park by the mayor of New York. Ten days earlier, on June 3, 1859, Olmsted's Aunt Maria had died after a short illness.[21]

It must be stressed that the real mother-of-infancy contains within herself all possibilities: she is *both* the nurturing environment mother and the tempting sensual mother. As a male matures, he ought to be able to see these simply as two of the attributes he attaches first to his mother and then to other women—the very real human beings who may be both lovingly protective and physically affectionate. But many men (especially those, I think, who remain caught up in an inner rapprochement crisis) tend to "split" womankind into the overly idealized pure saintly woman and the dangerous sexual women (the "madonna" and the "whore").

Clearly, it was the nurturing environment mother that predominated in Olmsted's usage of nature as a symbol for his lost mother—as is made most evident in a rumination that appears in Olmsted's first book, *Walks and Talks*, written during 1851–1852. It begins with this passage:

> Dame Nature is a gentlewoman. No guide's fee will obtain you her favour, no abrupt demand; hardly will she bear questioning, or *direct, curious gazing at her beauty;* least of all will she reveal it truly to the hurried glance of the traveller . . . always we must quietly and unimpatiently wait upon it.[22]

Olmsted suggests that "Dame Nature" distances herself from the observer (that is, the one who loves her), that she permits no intimacy, and that she plays "hard to get." Interestingly, most of the action words suggest ways in which a little child might interrelate with its mother: "demand," "questioning," "curious gazing," "hurried glance." But such behavior would lead *this* mother to withhold herself.[23] A child who grows up in a relationship like this soon learns that a response from his mother will only come if he waits "quietly and unimpatiently," whereupon he will be rewarded with "a tender filial-like joy."

Further, there is the image of nature as a "gentlewoman" rather than a sexual object who can be bought for a fee or who would submit to a peremptory demand. The position of nature Olmsted describes here is akin to the position in which his psyche had placed the belles of Hartford and New Haven whom he had courted so vigorously during his twenties —the young women whom he insisted upon referring to as "angels," too good for "a mere man" like him.[24] Angels can have no aspect of sensuality about them. The sensual woman is dangerously close to being a whore, who submits for a fee.

This passage memorializes the splitting of the maternal image—it is a celebration of the environment mother and a repression of the sensual Oedipal mother. The splitting would leave its impact upon Olmsted's creative imagination. His preference for quiet, even demure, rural scenery was quite emphatic, for only such scenery could be restorative. In 1886, he told a park commissioner that the "irritating effect of confinement overlong to urban scenery" could not be corrected through "such gorgeous floral displays" as many had urged for Central Park. And in 1889, disputing proposals for a "conspicuous display" of "showy blooms" in the Boston park system, Olmsted wrote that one may often see ladies "very splendidly dressed with jewels and bright ribbons and flowers" and think them to be in good taste, while other ladies may appear in equal good taste although "dressed quietly without jewelry or any finery of color or material." It was the latter that *he* preferred.[25] "Showy" floral scenery recalled too much the dangerous sexual woman, was too alluring to that young man who, as Olmsted later said of himself, found the "cream constantly rising . . . nature pretty strong."[26] Quiet, modest, "natural" scenery was far more in keeping with his ideal of womanhood, such as the "angels" who had been the earthly representatives of that revered, lost environment mother whose realm was more domestic than worldly.

But "Dame Nature" is far too complex a symbolic figure to remain encompassed within imagery of quiet, sedate scenery. For a man of Olmsted's intrinsically passionate sensibility, other aspects of nature must, and did, impinge themselves upon his creative imagination. Early in his work on Central Park (as Charles Beveridge points out), he had sought to recreate in the Ramble "the special lushness of vegetation in the tropics" as he recalled it from his voyage in the South Seas and his trips to the southern states of America.[27] Like a minister losing his head over a streetwalker, Olmsted was later to become totally enthralled by the exotic scenery he encountered in Panama in 1863, as he was crossing the Isthmus by train, on his way to take over the Mariposa mining estate in California. "I don't know when I ever have had such a day of delight," he wrote to his wife. The vegetation he had encountered was "superb and glorious," making North America's "beauty of foliage" seem "very tame & quakerish." It produced for him "a very strong moral impression through an enlarged sense of the bounteousness of Nature." But the language of his arousal was strongly sensual. The play of "sun-shafts" among the "dizzy gorgeousness of the foliage," he told his wife, "has excited me very much."[28]

To Ignaz Pilat, chief Landscape Gardener of Central Park, Olmsted wrote that this scenery had "excited a wholly a different emotion from that produced by any of our temperate zone scenery."[29] Olmsted felt that he had been reaching "instinctively and blindly" for such an effect in his "luxuriant jungled" plantings around the Lake and the Ramble, an effect that would be "the very reverse of the emotion sought to be produced in the Mall and playgrounds region—rest, tranquility, deliberation and maturity."[30] He thought that the tropics-induced emotion rested upon "a sense of the superabundant creative power, infinite resource and liberality of nature—the childish playfulness and profuse careless utterance of Nature." This is not only an excellent description of the power of one aspect of nature (an aspect very different from that of the nurturing environment mother); it is also an effective description of the power men ascribe to sexual woman.

So much was Olmsted under the spell of this sensual aspect of nature ("a wild aberration," Graff calls it) that he instructed Pilat to attempt to reproduce this Panamanian scenery in the Ramble of Central Park, al- though—since he had previously resigned from his position in the park —he had no authority to do so.[31] Of course, his self-assumed right to order such a major planting project reflects the degree to which Central park remained, in Olmsted's psyche, *his* property—an intensely personal, rather than a public, work.

In the main, however, Olmsted seems to have used nature to memor- ialize his idealized, lost environment mother in an attempt to repress the conflicted, ambivalent feelings associated with the actuality of his mother. The Panamanian adventure demonstrates how complex a symbol nature truly was and how difficult repression must have been for him. Conflict and ambivalence will always find a way to make themselves felt, as can be seen in the deeply felt (perhaps even anguished) puzzlement also found in the material Olmsted later excised from *Walks and Talks*. Referring back to the reflections on "Dame Nature" cited above, Olmsted asks:

Does this seem nonsense to you? Very likely, for I am talking of what I don't understand. Nature treats me so strangely; it's past my speaking sensibly of, and yet, as a part of my travelling experience, I would speak of it. At times I seem to be her favourite, and she brings me to my knees in deep feeling, such as she blesses no other with; oftener I see others in ecstasies, while I am left to sentimentalize and mourn, or to be critical and sneering, and infidel. Nonsense still.[32]

Inner conflict begins and ends the passage. Olmsted can make *no sense* of his strange relationship with nature (his lost mother). Yet, though he doesn't understand it, he feels compelled to speak of it—as everyone is compelled to deal with their repressed conflicts in one way or another.[33] In the central part of this passage, the nature of Olmsted's repressed conflicts become more clear. Here we can see Frederick, the first-born child, who once was his mother's favorite, having to learn to share her favor with the new-born infant, John Hull, who was to be his rival. To be the favorite for the little child is to receive from the mother that which is bestowed upon no one else. To see another "oftener" experience the "ecstasies" one has considered exclusively one's own is to know jealousy and resentment—jealousy of the invading other, resentment against both the interloper and the betraying mother. Smoldering resentment then can turn one against the person loved, cause one to be "critical and sneering" toward the person one most desires.

Finally, I must take note of the telling use of "sentimentalize and mourn" in this passage. It is the evidence not only that mourning, for Olmsted, would always include the enormous anguish connected with his mother's death, but also that his defense against that pain was to create an idealized, "sentimentalized" mother figure (nature) to take her place.

Far into his adulthood, Olmsted harbored within himself the hurt and angry child, the child who was abandoned time and again, who saw others favored over himself, and who longed to regain the unique position and undivided attention that an adoring mother might give her first-born child. There was a child in his psyche who needed to achieve, but hated to compete; who needed to be *in* control, but hated to *be* controlled; who needed to create, but feared the process of creativity; who needed undemanding love, but who feared he was unworthy of being loved. And all of these needs and limitations were anchored in a fragile self-esteem and consequent need (which could never be satisfied) for the world's esteem.

I think of this child in Olmsted's psyche as the *rapprochement child* who forever strives to press forward into the competitive mode of the Oedipal years, yet longs to turn backward to the absolute bliss of remerger with the mother-of-infancy—the paradisiacal relief from mortal anxieties, which, ultimately, can only be achieved through a state of not-knowing, of loss of self, of obliteration. "I do detest life and fear death and would gladly purchase annihilation as the end and reward of an age in Hell," Olmsted would write, at twenty-six, in a lonely, despairing, undefended moment.[34]

Olmsted would search throughout his middle years to find himself and his place in life—every man's Oedipal struggle. He was searching for that unique identity in which he could try to resolve what was unresolvable in himself—the opposing demands of the rapprochement crisis. So unrelenting and conflicting were these demands that Olmsted would try several times to flee from this unique identify even after he had found it.

Olmsted had written his own identity statement several years before he was to find his place in Central Park. It was set forth in a passage in *Walks and Talks*, and Olmsted would repeat it again and again over the years, citing it both in his letter of acceptance on being appointed Architect in Chief of Central Park and in *Spoils of the Park*, his bitter farewell to New York more than three decades later:

What artist so noble . . . as he who, with far-reaching conception of beauty and designing power, sketches the outline, writes the colors, and directs the shadows of a picture so great that Nature shall be employed upon it for generations, before the work he has arranged for her shall realize his intentions.[35]

Here Olmsted has defined his own identity even before he had known, consciously, that it was himself he was talking about. It was a definition that offered not only the possibility of union with the idealized mother-of-infancy (nature), but also the means of making reparation to that lost mother. Furthermore, both this (re)union and this act of reparation, each in its own way, promised fulfillment of the ultimate narcissistic wish: the wish for immortality.

In his appreciation of Olmsted, Arthur Spencer saw through the apparent narcissism of his oft-stated artistic wish to its real goal—the ultimate self-annihilating hope of merger with the longed-for mother-of-infancy. Olmsted's wish as a designer, Spencer noted, was "*to obliterate himself utterly*, that the art which he loved might be glorified."[36] This might be amended to say that even more than glorifying his art, Olmsted joined with nature to glorify nature—that he had sought to obliterate all traces both of himself and his art in order to realize more perfectly his image of his idealized, lost mother.

Olmsted's identity statement, first enunciated in *Walks and Talks*, was thus also a statement of his true self's purposes, the only purposes that could authenticate his life and his work. Throughout the 1850s and 1860s —Olmsted's middle years—he would be caught up in the demands of Oedipal striving, the false self's ambitions for practical success and the world's esteem. He could never shed these ambitions, but he could validate them by making them serve his true self's purposes—his artistic purposes of merger with and reparation to the idealized environment mother, Dame Nature.

PART III

Identity and Career

I never before had the question so clearly before me, how such a loitering, self-indulgent, dilletante sort of man as I was . . . could, at middle age, have turned into such a hard-worker and *doer* as I then suddenly became and have been ever since?

FREDERICK LAW OLMSTED, 1890

CHAPTER 7

The Making of a Free-Soil Journalist

In his 1890 "being and doing" letter to the sweetheart of his New Haven days, Elizabeth Baldwin Whitney, Olmsted reflected upon his long life, his many achievements, and the honors he had received. "I never before had the question so clearly before me," he wrote, "how such a loitering, self-indulgent, dilletante sort of man as I was when you knew me and for ten years afterwards, could, at middle age, have turned into such a hard-worker and *doer* as I then suddenly became and have been ever since?"[1]

At the time that the twenty-four-old Frederick had fallen in love with "Miss B."—the New Haven days of 1846—he had embarked, rather half-heartedly, on the career of a farmer; eleven years later, he was appointed the Superintendent of Central Park. By then, he had published four books, and he was on the verge of two enormous achievements: the creation of the park and the organization and supervision of the Sanitary Commission, the largest and perhaps most complex civilian bureaucratic structure of the Civil War years. During that period, the nation itself had to come to the edge of a fundamental transformation. The period had begun with the nation engaged in the Mexican War, and the acquisition of New Mexico and California and had been marked by an outburst of communitarian and utopian movements (along with the socialistic revolutions of 1848 in Europe). It had then seen the nation stumble into the turmoil of sectional violence, spurred by abolition and Free-Soil passions in the North, by defiance and slavery-driven expansionism in the South. The period ended with the nation embroiled in an embryonic civil war in Kansas and in a financial panic at large. And Olmsted had got himself caught up in almost all of it, one way or another, looking for a place in the new society that was developing before his eyes.

Farming had been Frederick's first attempt at asserting his identity, in a career far removed from the center of action in his turbulent society. Whatever else may have motivated that choice of life's work, it was surely also a rather deliberate rejection of his father's life of commerce. The twenty-three-year-old Frederick (then apprenticing with the farmer Joseph Welton in Waterbury) had given Charley Brace his view of business life: "which I suppose amounts to writing at a desk all day & half the night, or practicing assumed politeness or eulogizing a piece of silk or barrel of lamp oil—I would sooner recommend to study the profession of butcher and learn to stick a hog with accuracy and dispatch, or something as manly and refined." [2] It is not too hard to see in these comments—and in Frederick's repression, throughout his autobiographical writings, of the commercial John Olmsted—a son's disapproval of the obsequiousness, the trivial concerns of a dry goods merchant ("practicing assumed politeness or eulogizing a piece of silk"), a disapproval that had surely been reinforced by the hard grind of his own apprenticeship with the mercantile firm of Benkard and Hutton.

When Frederick had faced his first choice of a career, presumably between farming and a merchant's life, it must surely have seemed to him that there was little else open to him. After all, what were the choices then available to the sons of the antebellum gentry? Among the respectable professions, there was law, medicine, and the ministry. Ironically, all three of his closest associates would chose one of these for his intended life's work: his brother, John Hull, would decide upon a medical career; Charley Brace, the son of an acamedician who would become the editor of the Hartford *Courant*, was studying for the ministry; and Fred Kingsbury had selected law. None of them was to end up practicing the profession of his choice. John Hull, who contracted tuberculosis while at medical school, later replaced Frederick on the Staten Island farm; Brace took up both writing and philanthropy; and Kingsbury moved from law to banking to industry (as President of Scovill Manufacturing). Frederick also had other examples before him besides his father's dry goods busi-

9. Looking south on Main Street, Hartford, c. 1857. John Olmsted's dry goods store (sold a few years previously) was at the corner of Main and Pearl, where the white awning reaches out over the sidewalk, right center. While Frederick was beginning his work at Central Park in New York, Hartford still maintained a sedate, small town look. (The Connecticut Historical Society.)

ness: his uncle, Jonathan Law, had been a lawyer and the Hartford postmaster, until the Jackson administration removed him from his long-held office; and his father's cousin, Denison Olmsted, was a professor at Yale. Even if any of these professions had held some interest for Frederick, it would have required an intensive academic preparation—something of which Frederick, in personality and intellectual style, seemed incapable (though he was capable of intensive, if eclectic, self-education and wide reading, when his interest was aroused).

But I believe, also, that the life of a farmer represented for Frederick a form of retreat from the hard world of competition and rivalry—something that he had made most clear to John Hull at just about the same time he had written the above-quoted letter to Brace. While Frederick was farming with Joseph Welton, John Hull was still at Yale, driving himself to academic honors (seemingly at the expense of his health), honors that had thus far eluded Frederick.[3] Not yet decided upon his own future, the younger brother had asked Frederick's advice about a career choice: whether Frederick thought that John Hull would be more contented as a farmer or a merchant. Frederick replied that no man "of respectable mind" could be content to be a merchant.[4] And he added: "The best of them are either half engaged with other things, or are looking forward with impatience to the time when they shall be." On the other hand, Frederick wrote:

The objects of a farmer . . . are such as to relieve him from the annoyances which the *envy and opposition of rivals* constantly inflict on most other occupations. And the higher *you* rise in distinction, the more are you marked with the *shafts of malice.* (Emphases added.)

The dire warnings of the dangers of the competitive commercial world were also, surely, a projection of Frederick's own unconscious envy of and rivalry toward his brother—a warning that the more *John Hull* rose in distinction, the more likely *he* was to excite the "envy and opposition" of Frederick himself and to become the target of Frederick's aggression and destructiveness ("shafts of malice"). In the meantime, it was, of course, Frederick who would attempt to retreat from the dangerous life of competitive striving by his exile on an isolated farm on the rocky coast of Sachem's Head, Connecticut.

Actually, Frederick's first attempt at a career (as noted in part 2), *had* been in the commercial world, when he had been apprenticed as a merchant in the New York City import firm of Benkard and Hutton, a position he took after John Hull had been sent to study in Paris with a tutor. When Frederick came to Manhattan as an eighteen-year-old apprentice in 1840, it was still a rather compact place, containing more than a quarter of a million people. Olmsted worked at 53 Beaver Street, less than two blocks below Wall Street. The commercial structures of this neighborhood were not unlike those of Hartford, though the density was far greater.[5] Moreover, Frederick lived across the East River in Brooklyn Heights, where he boarded at 120 Henry Street, an area of Brooklyn that was exceedingly open and sparsely settled in the early 1840s, rural in every aspect except for the magnificent vista it offered of lower Manhattan. Frederick's daily commute to and from work was the pleasant ferry ride across the East River immortalized by Walt Whitman, with its panorama of "mast-hemmed Manhattan," of "River and sunset and scallop-edg'd waves of flood-tide."[6] But the position Frederick's father had secured for him had probably left him with little time either for poetic reflection or for walking the streets of Broadway like the peripatetic young George Templeton Strong. "The business is such that I am engaged from morning to night without ceasing," he wrote John Hull.[7]

After two unhappy years in the counting house, Frederick returned home for a spell of the kind of youthful enjoyments he had missed during his boarding-school years—socials, music and dance lessons, riding and sailing and a brief immersion in the study of natural history under the tutelage of his father's cousin.[8] During these several months of idling, Frederick convinced his father to send him to sea. At twenty, he sailed to Canton as a cabinboy aboard the *Ronaldson*, passing part of the voyage belowdecks, suffering from recurring seasickness, paralysis of the arm, and typhoid fever. Though the captain seems to have been relatively kind to Frederick, he was to the other seamen more demanding and cruel than even the most brutal of the schoolmasters Frederick had boarded with.[9] Thereafter, puritanical schoolmasters and sadistic ships' masters stood together in Frederick's mind for the worst kind of tyranny, more cruel than any slave overseer he encountered in his later trips through the slave states.

Frederick's first attempt at the farmer's life had taken place in the fall of 1844 (after he had recovered from the ill effects of his voyage to China), when he apprenticed at the Cheshire farm of his uncle, David Brooks. In mid-1846, after a brief career at Yale as a "special student" pursuing "scientific farming," he apprenticed at George Geddes's farm in Camillus, New York. This apprenticeship lasted a few months, and by summer he was back in Hartford, joining his father and John Hull for an autumn trip to upstate New York and Canada. After another month with Geddes, Frederick's father purchased the Sachem's Head farm for him.

Even after he was established at Sachem's Head and then later at the Staten Island farm, there were numerous returns to Hartford for dalliances of a few weeks or more. Of Frederick's apprenticeship with David Brooks, Charles Beveridge writes: "There he 'studied farming' in the same spirit that he had earlier 'studied engineering' with [Reverend]

Barton."[10] His few months at Yale came to an abrupt end when he suffered spells of something that seemed at the time like apoplexy.[11] And, of his brief career with Geddes, Frederick told Charley Brace, "I have looked on and talked more than I've worked."[12] Even as late as 1849, when Frederick was finally settled at Akerly, the Staten Island farm, his father still had great cause for concern. "I think that your farm will require your *close* & *undivided personal* attention at all times & I hope no extraneous or unimportant matters . . . will take up your mind & time when it should be actively employed on yr farm—."[13]

Even if he had been more an observer than a worker, Frederick nevertheless had the ability to learn by what he saw around him, and so began to grasp the science of farming at Brooks's and certainly at Geddes's (though he apparently would never grasp the *business* of farming). Yet, judging from his letters of the time, what he seemed to gain most out of these two apprenticeships was in fact two powerful reading experiences that were to influence his thinking for years to come. At the Brooks farm he read Johann Zimmermann's *Solitude*, and at Geddes's he read Thomas Carlyle's *Sartor Resartus*.[14] The first called up his own years as an adolescent woodsman—at a time when his "mates were fitting for college"—and reinforced his urge to nourish himself in retreat from the mainstream of society, in essence through a merger with nature in the guise of "natural scenery." The second was a transcendental call to greatness by doing "the duty which lies nearest." The first tended to celebrate "being," the second "doing"—though both romanticized life and affected this aspect of Olmsted's being.[15]

Under the influence of *Solitude*, Olmsted could celebrate the rural attractions near the Brooks farm—going off with his "gun & dog . . . exploring" and finding "some of the most picturesque & sublime scenes I ever saw"; he could even take pleasure in his "voluntary exile to the rock bound head at Sachem." Under the influence of *Sartor Resartus*, he could tell his friend Brace: "There's great *work* wants doing in this our generation, Charley, let us off our jackets and go about it."[16] The latter choice, unfortunately for Olmsted, could only be accomplished within the mainstream of society—within the arena of competitive striving and all the painful personal and professional conflicts from which he inevitably retreated.

When Frederick joined John Hull for a time at Yale in 1846, he was twenty-four and his brother twenty-one. Their letters and the various photographs taken then and a few years later reveal the differences between the two. John Hull had a relaxed, light-hearted air about him and was extremely handsome, with deep-set, shadowed eyes; his eyes, like his mouth, had the beauty of a woman's. His nose was straight and fine. Frederick's eyes were set wide apart and seemed to bulge slightly. He had inherited the noticeable bump at the bridge of the nose and the wide nostrils of his father. Only the mouth was like John Hull's with its fine and sensitive lips. If not handsome in the way John Hull was, Frederick appears nevertheless to have been a good-looking young man, whose whole being, in pictures and in words, was far more intense than his brother's. Photographed with John Hull and their Yale friends—Brace, Kingsbury, and Charles Trask—Frederick is the only one who turned his face away from the camera in both of the two poses that survive, staring at Trask in one, at Brace in the other. It is in the pose in which he is looking at Brace that Frederick seems most open, almost wistful, almost feminine. Fifteen years later, Katharine Wormeley, at Frederick's side when he commanded a small fleet of hospital ships during the Peninsula Campaign, became a student of the myriad expressions of his face, a face that, she said, had "the expressive delicacy of a woman's," that could be "beautiful," but that also harbored something she found "difficult to fathom," something a little too severe.[17]

The New Haven years were also more notable for the emotional attachments and storms that Frederick experienced than for any vocational or academic achievements. The most important of these experiences, in the long run, was the cementing of a friendship with John Hull's Yale classmate, Charles Loring Brace. At Yale, Charley Brace was a rather homely, raw-boned youth with long straight hair and a turn in his left eye. The son of the head of the Hartford Female Seminary, Brace was athletic, studious, and serious-minded. He later contrasted his own his own frugal life with that of his more affluent friends, the Olmsted brothers.[18]

After Yale, Brace studied for the ministry, but as a result of a walking tour of Europe, undertaken with the Olmsted brothers, he began writing travel letters for newspapers in America, then published two books based upon his experiences in Europe. Brace would continue to publish: most notably *The Dangerous Classes of New York, and Twenty Years' Work Among Them* (1872), a record of his work among the urban poor. Brace was an

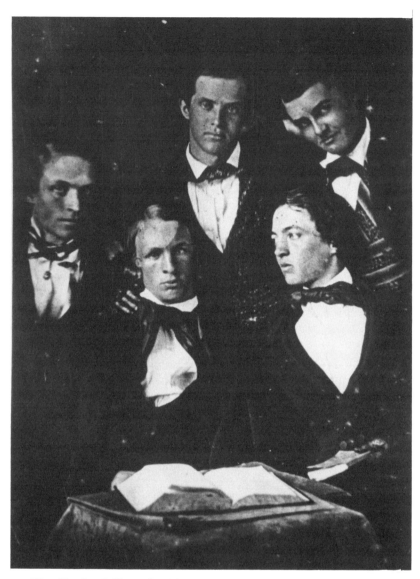

10. The friends of Olmsted's "New Haven days," 1846: (clockwise from upper right) John Hull Olmsted, Frederick Law Olmsted, Charles Loring Brace, Charles Trask, and Frederick L. Kingsbury. Brace and Kingsbury would remain close to Frederick well into his later years. (National Park Service, Frederick Law Olmsted National Historical Site.)

early follower of the Hartford minister Horace Bushnell, whose sermons and writings he urged upon Olmsted, and Brace's career was an enacting of the "social gospel"—the notion that it was a Christian's duty to enact the gospel in the doing of good works. In 1853, Brace participated in the founding of the Children's Aid Society, acting as its Executive Secretary for more than three decades until his death in 1890. His own literary pursuits, his philanthropic work and his diverse family connections gave Brace entrée into the patrician and literary circles of both New England and New York City—a position he used often to help Frederick gain access to and the support of these same circles.[19] In his early years in New York City, Brace, now bearded, took on a more settled, gentle, thoughtful look. Olmsted sometimes employed a harsh, argumentative tone in his correspondence with Brace; but in 1884, Olmsted would write Brace: "You decidedly have had the best & most worthily successful life of all whom I have known."[20]

As noted earlier, it was in the New Haven years also that Frederick became involved with Elizabeth Wooster Baldwin, the daughter of the Governor of Connecticut and highly regarded for her intellectual and religious qualities. She had enormous influence upon Olmsted, who yearned for her with a great and hopeless love. "She's too good for any coarse vulgar *man* merely, is not she?" he wrote Brace.[21] In his 1890 letter to his quondam sweetheart (then Elizabeth Baldwin Whitney), Olmsted told her that she had helped to awaken in him the intellectual and "poetical" part of his nature, suggesting that it was through her influence that he had been led, during those New Haven years, to "Emerson, Lowell and Ruskin, and other real prophets, who have been familiar friends since."[22]

Olmsted continued to fall in love with great regularity over the next few years, in much the same highly idealized way. As John Hull later wrote to Kingsbury: "Fred is finally rather hard up. He won't be content with less than infinity—while he himself is only finite & a farmer."[23] It seemed that Frederick's hopes and needs would at last be fulfilled when, in 1851, Frederick became engaged to Emily Perkins, the niece of Harriet Beecher Stowe. However, very shortly afterwards a letter from Emily's mother announced "a revulsion of feeling in E.," requesting that the engagement be broken off. It was an enormous blow to Frederick's self-esteem and seemed to end in him any real hope of knowing the romantic love of a woman.[24] Indeed, on the eve of his ill-fated affair with Emily

Perkins, he had made (to Brace) an eerily accurate prediction of what lay ahead for him: "I am likely to remain all along a bachelor or to marry believing that the 'highest element of love' is not of earth, and so secure from disappointment if I shall not find it."[25]

In these years, friendship and courtship were interwoven with intense religious speculation. The wave of conversions that swept the New Haven circle in 1846 raised such powerful emotions in these young people that even the most level-headed among them—including John Hull and Fred Kingsbury—succumbed and made public professions of faith. Frederick cheered them on, but he, like his father, never himself converted. He yearned, however, for some great transcendental experience of the heart, which nevertheless eluded him. "My heart has been with you so much for two or three days," he wrote to John Hull as the latter stumbled to conversion, "that I have given myself up to [it?] entirely almost—I have had violent throbbings in my head and other symptoms—warnings which I must not disregard—so today I have been riding most of the forenoon."[26] His familiar "symptoms" had been triggered by the danger inherent in reaching deep into his inner self in order to achieve the longed-for transcendental experience.[27]

For the next few years, Frederick continued to torment himself with the conflicting demands of head and heart, at times driving himself to moments of despair. Olmsted's biographers have done heroic and useful work in trying to make sense out of his long disputational letters of the 1846–1849 period, a period John Hull summed up (not all that jokingly) thus: "Fred Olmsted still continues thinking big thoughts & growing daily more transcendental & perplexed."[28] To his family and friends, Frederick was an "enthusiast," which was true enough. But he also possessed a far more complex and subtle intelligence than any of his peers in the New Haven circle, and he felt in himself the conflict between Romantic idealism and Utilitarian rationalism far more painfully than they. And, in the end, it was the latter that prevailed in matters of religion. Late in 1848, responding to Kingsbury's concern for the state of his "heart and mind," Olmsted asserted: "My own reason must pilot, and if she runs down the Bible, my own heart & my own friends, I cannot take the helm from her."[29] It says something of Frederick's inner self-image that he assigned the feminine gender to his "own reason"—a faculty that, in his time, was considered a masculine attribute.

In 1850, two years after he moved into the Staten Island farm his father purchased for him, a crucial experience took place, through which he would soon leave behind all forms of religious speculation in favor of much enlarged and more secular concerns.[30] However, the inner conflicts that were behind his agonies over head and heart would continue to find expression, first, in his new idiom of social and political speculation and ultimately, in the landscape design projects and urban planning philosophy that were the intellectual and creative achievements of his later years.

The crucial experience of 1850 was the walking trip through the British Isles and the Continent that he undertook with John Hull and Charley Brace. It was the English leg of the walking tour that had a profound effect upon Frederick's search for a career in a number of ways. First, there was his decision, after returning to America, to produce a book based upon his travel journals and the letters he wrote home to family and friends. *Walks and Talks of an American Farmer in England* first appeared in 1852. Its conversational style and acute reportage would provide Olmsted with the credentials for a journalistic career in the mid-1850s; this first, small taste of literary success and his own wish to increase his "power . . . over others" would fire his literary ambitions and turn him fully and finally away from farming.[31] But of greater ultimate importance, surely, was the impact upon his creative imagination of the English pastoral countryside and of the great public parks, such as Birkenhead Park at Liverpool and Eaton Park near Chester. "The country— and such a country!—green, dripping, glistening, gorgeous!" Olmsted wrote in *Walks and Talks*. "We stood dumb-stricken by its loveliness."[32]

In addition, their experiences on the Continent, especially in Germany, seemed to have reinforced in Frederick the appeal of European-style social democracy. (When news of the revolutions of 1848 had first reached Staten Island, Frederick had cheered them on. "I wish I were a German now," he had exclaimed to Brace, adding: "I really revel in a *Righteous War*.")[33] His awakening to the utopian aspects of socialism led Olmsted, in 1852, to visit the Fourierist community in Red Bank, New Jersey. "I have strong respect for them as hard-working, earnest, unselfish livers in the faith of a higher life for man on earth as well as 'above,' " he wrote Brace.[34] The point is, of course, that the Fourierists had renounced all forms of rivalry, economic and social. Olmsted thought that such a way of life would be favorable for many, if not most, Americans—not only the average laboring man, but also "merchants, shop-keepers, lawyers and ministers." But he was honest enough to admit "I am not a Fourierist for myself." Though Fourierism would not "suit" people like him and John Hull, Olmsted said, he had nevertheless come away from Red Bank as more of an "Associationist—a Socialist," than before his visit.

By the time *Walks and Talks* was published in 1852, the sectional storms of the 1850s were in full force. The intensely emotional debate that resulted in the Missouri Compromise of 1850, followed by the passage of the Fugitive Slave Law in September of that year, gave renewed impetus to the abolitionist cause. By the fall of 1850, there were mass meetings throughout the North, and political actions designed to spur resistance to the Fugitive Slave Law. In the following year, there were attempts by abolitionists to rescue fugitive slaves who had been jailed in Northern cities. And in June 1851, installments of Harriet Beecher Stowe's *Life among the Lowly* began appearing in the antislavery paper, the *National Era*, drawing a widespread, emotional response, despite the journal's tiny readership. In March 1852, the serialized novel was published in two volumes as *Uncle Tom's Cabin* and sold 300,000 copies throughout the United States by the end of the year.[35]

That fall, Henry J. Raymond, editor of the year-old *New York Daily Times*, wished to send a correspondent to the South who could objectively report on social and economic conditions in the slave states. Charley Brace proposed the recently published Olmsted as correspondent, the deal was struck, and objectivity was what Olmsted expected to deliver. With an eye on the response to *Uncle Tom's Cabin* and the outpouring of imitations that followed, Olmsted wrote Fred Kingsbury in October 1852 of his intention to produce "a valuable book of observations on the Southern Agriculture & general economy as affected by Slavery," a book that would offer a "matter of fact" contrast to "the deluge of spoony fancy pictures now at its height."[36]

Over the next two years, Frederick made two trips through the slave states, spending a total of some fourteen months on the road. He eventually published seventy-five dispatches, in the form of letters signed "Yeoman", in the *Times* between 1853 and 1854 and in the *New York Daily Tribune* in mid-1857.[37] These, in turn, formed the basis for three books: *A Journey in the Seaboard Slave States* (1856); *A Journey Through Texas* (1857); and *A Journey in the Back Country* (1860). John Hull accompanied his brother on the first leg of the second trip (November 1853 through May 1854) and wrote the *Texas* book based upon Frederick's notes and letters.

"I am no red-hot Abolitionist like Charles [Brace], but am a moderate Free Soiler," Olmsted told Kingsbury, in the 1852 letter cited above. "Going to vote for [Whig presidential candidate Winfield] Scott & would take in a fugitive slave & shoot a man that was likely to get him." The thirty-year-old Olmsted was, in fact, a Hartford Whig who had been washed in the rhetoric of social democracy. He had resisted all of Brace's attempts to convert him to abolitionism, which included bringing abolitionist leaders like William Lloyd Garrison and Theodore Parker out to the Staten Island farm. Indeed, as the *Papers* editors point out, Olmsted had revealed his gradualist philosophy about slavery in *Walks and Talks*, insisting that "it was necessary to educate and civilize the still-barbaric slaves before freeing them" and assigning to the North the role of encouraging the Southern slaveholders to discharge their responsibilities to educate and emancipate their slaves.[38]

It should be made clear that Olmsted never in any way justified the enslavement of the black race, nor did he ever suggest that the slave population was content with its lot. "One thing I am certain of—," he wrote in a letter published June 30, 1853, "if the slaves are satisfied with their present condition and prospects, they are more degraded and debased than I have described them to be." Logical Southerners either had to admit that slavery was "unjust, unnatural and cruel" or believe that "the negro is naturally incapacitated for personal freedom."[39] Olmsted himself clearly believed that no one was thus "naturally incapacitated." But he also could not conceive of the efficacy of the abolitionist solution —*immediate* freedom for the blacks—without first providing them with the education and training with which to properly exercise that freedom. He thought that abolition, "the direct sundering of the tie of master and dependent," might be "impracticable, fanatical, mischievous and unjust." Rather, he sought "Amelioration, the improvement and the elevation of the negro."[40]

Olmsted saw the slave in the same light that his Puritan forebears had seen the small child. "The negroes came to us from barbarism as from a cradle," he wrote in an earlier letter. He saw them as subject to "strong and simple appetites and impulses," to "violent and uncontrollable passions, and altogether undisciplined, uneducated and unchristianized."

Those who had taken on the burden of such a "child" retained a responsibility for the upbringing of that "child"—and it was from this sense of the slaveowner being duty-bound that Olmsted evolved his paternalistic concept of "amelioration" of the slave condition.[41]

When Frederick got the chance, with the help of Charley Brace, to make his journalistic journey through the southeastern states, he was on his way to a final escape from the Staten Island farm. Frederick's literary ambitions burned even brighter in the years following his return from that first Southern trip, in 1853—the more so when Brace introduced him into the literary salons of New York. This was at a time when the Kansas-Nebraska Act of 1854 and the struggle over "Bleeding Kansas" enflamed Northern opinion against the South, especially the opinion of the literary intellectuals to whom Olmsted was drawn, at times more for reasons of his own ambitions than out of admiration of their talents. In mid-1853, Olmsted was paid a "pleasant visit" by the poet Ann Charlotte Lynch, whose salon Olmsted would frequent during this period. "I like her much and shall try to be acquainted with her," he wrote his father afterwards. "She is acquainted with all the distinguished people and her taste is highly cultivated, though her verses are as dull as anybody else's."[42]

Decades later, Mary Olmsted would tell Rick that, between 1854 and 1858, his father had belonged to a circle of young men who "frequented the 'salon' of Anne Lynch." "All were ambitious of social success," she added, "except your father."[43] In fact, as just indicated, Olmsted had at the time rather openly declared to his father his ambition to make important connections at Anne Lynch's salon. The Frederick Law Olmsted who frequented Anne Lynch's salon in the mid-1850s was no longer content to be a "scientific farmer" and an occasional journalist. He meant, through his literary connections, to become a man of influence in his society—and the arena of this influence was to be the Free-Soil movement, the first of the secular causes to which he could devote the intellect and passion that had once been absorbed in religious disputation.

Equally important, Frederick's journalistic activities in the 1850s gave him his first taste of public recognition. As a young farmer on Staten Island when the decade began, Frederick was then still little armed by the world's esteem, still terribly vulnerable in his fragile ego, and still too ready to show his inner self-contempt, as revealed in this description of his New Year's Day, 1850:

Charley [Brace] wanted to call on some stuck up people in Union Sq. whose acquaintance I did not care to begin upon—so I went to a tavern & read the papers—completely disgusted with meeting men the counterpart of myself— Drab overcoats with a corner of a linen [handkerchief] accidentally sticking out of the left breast—black sping'd pantaloons & shiny boots—smooth chin & standing collar—& I bethought how a lady must receive us—"there's another of *them*."[44]

In the intervening years, Olmsted would be a social and professional success on Staten Island (though a financial failure); would travel to England and the Continent and make a book of his journey; and would, with his travels to the South, enter into New York City's world of letters. In 1855 (five years after that New Year's Day of despair), he could strike a far different pose for his father:

I went by invitation Friday to Mrs. Schuyler's to a small party, spent the night and the next day there . . . dining Saturday at Colonel Hamilton's. They are the most capital people—the most finished people that I ever saw. They treated me with a great deal of respect and confidence and I enjoyed the visit very much.[45]

In this letter, Olmsted could note with good humor that Brace was now "hand & glove with all the best people and he and his wife both succeed finely"—for he himself had at last achieved *some* of the stature he had sought and could now feel comfortable among "all the best people" to whom Brace had introduced him.

Although Olmsted's literary ambitions may have provided the emotional context for his Free-Soil enthusiasm in the 1850s, the intellectual catalyst was his second trip through the slave states—the trip he took with John Hull. Perhaps the single most important experience was their visit in Nashville with Samuel Perkins Allison, a Yale classmate of John Hull, whose relatives were major slaveholders in the area. The discussion that took place seemed to stun Olmsted, who made the visit and his reflections afterwards the subject of a long and remarkable letter to Brace.[46] Allison led Olmsted through all the South's grievances against the North; he insisted that the South "*must* have more slave territory," suggesting that California would become a slave state, and that the Amazon would be "a promising field for Slave labor."

Allison particularly attacked the North for its lack of good breeding, getting Olmsted to agree:

There is a great deal of truth in his view. I tried to show him that there were compensations in the *general* elevation of all classes in the North, but he did not seem to care for it. He is, in fact, a thorough Aristocrat. And altogether, the conversation making me acknowledge the rowdyism, ruffianism, want of high honorable sentiment & chivalry of the common farming & laboring people of the North, as I was obliged to, made me very melancholy.

A curious aspect of this encounter is that Olmsted and his brother were, to judge from their letters, formidable debaters. Indeed, several years earlier, Brace had commented on Olmsted's keenness in argument, suggesting that such debates were the principal way in which Olmsted had exercised his intellect.[47] Yet Olmsted now had to admit to Brace that Allison had "silenced us and showed us that our own position was by no means consistent and satisfactory."

Olmsted's response (in his letter to Brace about the Allison visit) was to be cheered by the thought of Peter Cooper—who had recently established Cooper Union for the free education of working people—and of "the Reds" of Europe who had made revolution against their own aristocracy. He favored "the encouragement of a democratic condition of society as well as of government," and he wished to provide for the poor "an education to refinement and taste and the mental & moral capital of gentlemen." What was needed were "institutions that shall more directly *assist* the poor and degraded to elevate themselves." Education must comprise more than "the miserable common schools," Olmsted charged, surely in part from the hurt of his own early schooling experiences. "The poor & wicked need more than to be let alone," he added.[48]

To such an end, Olmsted now urged Brace to go ahead with his Children's Aid Society and to "get up parks, gardens, music, dancing schools, reunions which will be so attractive as to force into contact the good & bad, the gentlemanly and the rowdy."[49] The state, he added, "ought to assist these sorts of things *as* it does Schools and Agricultural Societies." He also thought that some sort of national magazine would be required, one that would have "variety & scope enough for this great country & this cursedly little people"—in other words, a magazine like the *Nation*, of which he was to be one of the intellectual godfathers a decade later.

The position in which Olmsted now found himself as a northern intellectual was one he would share with other gentry intellectuals in America and their counterparts in England—genteel reformers all of them, caught up in the struggle against capitalistic and aristocratic privilege on the Right and popular democracy on the Left. Writing of a "Victorian connection" in the antebellum era, David Hall comments on the fact that so many of the leading American intellectuals were of Puritan heritage, "while among the English an equivalent background in nonconformity turns up again and again." But this genteel leadership had turned from the religious to the cultural sphere: "these secular intellectuals were 'modern missionaries,' carrying on into a new age an ethic derived from nonconformity and evangelicism," Hall writes.[50] Strongly influenced by John Stuart Mill, these intellectuals sought to accomplish two reforms through their published writings: to reveal the essential truths of life, truths not to be found in sectarian Christian orthodox preaching; and to "present 'the best' in art, politics or literature, and thereby overcome the blight of mediocrity."

Olmsted's celebration of European social democracy was an identification with the educated middle classes of Europe, which he took to be in revolt against despotism in 1848 and beyond. Thus, when Olmsted later became responsible for the large work force at Central Park, he would scarcely be egalitarian in his attitudes toward his workmen.[51] On one occasion, a thousand men at an adjoining work site struck for higher wages; two work gangs from Central Park joined in this strike. The striking Central Park workmen were promptly discharged, following which, Olmsted wrote Brace, "there has been the most perfect order, peace & good feeling preserved, notwithstanding the fact that the labourers are mainly from the poorest or what is generally considered the most dangerous classes of the great city's population."[52] That Olmsted was an effective administrator of labor and a fair and decent employer are not to be doubted. But it is equally clear that he regarded the free laborer (free, but not free to strike) in much the same authoritarian, paternalistic manner that he had the "childlike" slave laborer.

As noted earlier, Olmsted was nearly as much a Whig as his father, a fact he himself often acknowledged.[53] What Hall says of the Victorian reformers could be said of Olmsted: both he and they "were a most conservative sort of revolutionary."[54] In fact, Olmsted would say as much of himself during his early days at the Sanitary Commission, when the Union was reeling from the first disaster at Bull Run. Olmsted found the horrendous defeat a crushing personal humiliation and lent his voice to those who thought a revolution was necessary in order to install an intelligent, strong-willed government in Washington. But Olmsted admitted, perhaps ruefully, to Henry Bellows: "I have always been conservative, impetuoso in modo perhaps, conservative in res."[55]

When Olmsted later converted his dispatches from the South into books, he seemed to take a harder line toward the South—an attitude that was dictated less by the South's treatment of the blacks and more by the South's *political* ambitions. That is, his later attitudes reflected a stronger attachment to Free-Soil politics, though he remained opposed to abolition. Thomas Bender argues that Olmsted self-consciously assumed in all his writings, whatever the subject, the role of "the representative man"—representative of his class, that is. Thus, Olmsted's political attitudes as revealed in his successive dispatches and books about the slave states can help "chart the evolution of free soil attitudes" within Olmsted's social and intellectual milieu during the decade preceding the Civil War.[56]

Olmsted's experiences in Texas would cement his commitment to the Free-Soil movement. Thus far in his trips through the South, he had found no group with which to identify: not the plantation owners, not the merchants, not the poor white farmers, and certainly not the enslaved blacks. In West Texas, he would finally make such an identification— with the German Free-Soil settlers he encountered in Neu Braunfels and Sisterdale (near San Antonio). As he wrote to a friend: "We have, indeed, been so much pleased that we are considerably inclined to cast our lot with them."[57] But, of course, he did not and could not.

Partly because of Olmsted's identification with these German emigrants, partly because of his own rising literary ambitions and the political sensibilities he shared with his new friends in the "literary republic," his dispatches from Texas and the book John Hull made from them were to be strongly imbued with the spirit of Free-Soil political propaganda. *Texas* is a morality play that contrasts the highly idealized, educated, and cultivated Free-Soil German settlers of West Texas with a grim portrait of unrelieved coarseness and ignorance among the slaveholders, rich and poor, of East Texas. Caught up in this morality play—almost, at times, as comic relief—are the slaves, who emerge as the most ignorant and debased of all the players on the stage.

Frederick's glorification of the German settlements at Neu Braunfels and Sisterdale (apparent even in his original dispatches) had deeper, more heartfelt roots than Free-Soil politics alone. From the time of his visit to the North American Phalanx to his attempt (during his Mariposa exile) at a masterwork on American civilization, Frederick would idealize a way of life in which men eschewed materialistic competitiveness in favor of a mutual regard for the common welfare. Frederick believed that such a way of life had differentiated the early Puritan settlements of New England from other emigrant communities. Discussing those Puritan colonies in his "Civilization" notes, Frederick observed: "Nowhere has Christian Socialism been more extensively acted upon."[58] Similarly, the Olmsted brothers much admired the communitarian impulse they found among the German settlers in West Texas. Like the New England gentry who had formed Frederick's ideal of a civilized community, these settlers were clean, cultivated, industrious, and supposedly free of the competitive spirit. "There are no capitalists among the Germans," Frederick had stated in one of his dispatches to the *Times*.[59]

To the extent that Olmsted's Free-Soil sympathies were anchored in a certain cultural and religious perspective, that perspective was largely one enunciated by the Hartford theologian Horace Bushnell.[60] In his letter to Brace, following the Allison encounter, it was the notion that it was one's duty to place the welfare of society above one's own welfare that had led Olmsted to urge Brace (and himself) beyond Free-Soil enthusiasm to the doing of good works that would improve every facet of northern society and make it an example to the South. This was the sort of social gospel that Bushnell himself had evolved from his own concept of the organic unity of the family—a concept that had led him to the notion of the organic unity of society and to the existence of a familial mutual responsibility for the good of all.

Olmsted's ambition to join the literary republic; his unnerving debate with Samuel Perkins Allison; his Bushnellian outlook; his disgust with a "barbarous" way of life in East Texas for which he had little sympathy; his empathy for the respectable, civilized, communitarian Germans living in Neu Braunfels and Sisterdale—all of these were factors that combined to make him, for a time, a Free-Soil activist. Olmsted meant *Texas* both as a furthering of his literary reputation and as political evangelism. Indeed, he had cited these very concerns to his father in connection with the completion of his first book on the South, *The Seaboard States*:

> Reputation or notoriety it can not fail to give me—not perhaps friendship but respect I think for while I strike right & left and strike hard I do so respectfully and with the grace of sincerity. . . .

I have said some unpleasant things from a sense of duty—I thought they ought to be said & nobody else appeared to be ready to say them. If they are true they will now make their way—if not it will be discovered.[61]

He had become, in Hall's term, a "modern missionary," a man whose thirst for "reputation or notoriety" and whose "sense of duty" were happily mated in his new vocation as a Free-Soil journalist. To do good work in the world, and to become famous while doing it, was a career far more rewarding, it seems, than those Frederick had first had to choose between—a merchant's life or a farmer's life.

CHAPTER 8

Life in
the Literary Republic

In 1848, just after Frederick had first taken possession of the Staten Island farm, he met Mary Cleveland Perkins, the petite nineteen-year-old granddaughter of one of his new neighbors. She was, he wrote at the time, "just the thing for a rainy day—Not to fall in love with, but to talk to." Some seventy years later, Mary would recall that Frederick had been "perhaps too fond of argument to be altogether pleasing to a willful woman!"[1] In the event, it was John Hull Olmsted—then studying medicine in Manhattan—who courted Mary and became engaged to her in 1850. Shortly after they married in 1851, John Hull discovered that he had tuberculosis; by then a doctor, he would never practice medicine. By the time Frederick and John Hull embarked upon their trip to Texas, John Hull and Mary, together with their son Charley (John Charles), had become co-occupants of the Staten Island farm and responsible for it during Frederick's many absences in pursuit of a literary career.

Toward the end of 1855, Olmsted would seek funds from his father to help with the publication of his first book on the slave states—essentially, Frederick stated, for "a certain private advertizing" of himself. He added that there "is a sort of literary republic, which it is not merely pleasant & gratifying to my ambition to be recognized in, but also profitable." The publication of his book, Frederick wrote, would help him "take & keep a

11. Mary Cleveland Perkins, c. 1850, at the age of twenty—when Frederick knew her in Staten Island. She was the granddaughter of a neighbor. Though Frederick met her first, John Hull courted her and married her in 1851. (Society for the Preservation of New England Antiquities.)

position as a recognized litterateur, as a man of influence in literary affairs."[2]

In this letter to his father, Frederick touched upon the two ambitions that would dominate his life for more than a decade: the ambition to be recognized, to have his opinions respected, to be "a man of influence"; and the ambition to make money, to succeed at practical affairs. Obviously, a great many people are moved by such wishes, but few are driven to the torments these ambitions brought upon Frederick, particularly as he often pursued them in ways that seemed mutually exclusive. For Frederick, both of these ambitions were linked to an insistent need to shore up his damaged self-esteem, to authenticate his worth as an individual—especially the intellectual superiority and creative energies he sensed in himself, but which could only be validated through the respect of others.

Early in 1855, Frederick entered into partnership negotiations with the publishing firm of Dix, Edwards & Company—a venture, underwritten by his father, that Frederick meant to assure him of a place in the "literary republic." By March, John Hull was writing to their father that his brother had been looking for rooms in Manhattan so as to give more time to his duties as managing editor of the Dix and Edwards publication, *Putnam's Monthly*. Frederick's move would leave John Hull and Mary alone at the Staten Island farm as the new owners. "I regret to be left in the lurch," John Hull said, "but I suppose things will go on as they did in his absence last summer."[3] By this time, John Hull was suffering badly from his tuberculosis, and he had little expectation of making the farm succeed financially any more than Frederick had.

In April 1855, Frederick settled into his rooms in the Moffatt Building on Broadway, a few blocks from the Dix and Edwards offices. He was thirty-three, smallish, leaner, and more intense than ever.[4] His hairline was receding, and he may already have added the bushy, handlebar moustache he sported in his Central Park days, possibly a souvenir of his Texas trip. By the end of May, his rooms had been freshly painted and the Park Place office of Dix and Edwards completely renovated. Olmsted found the latter a "very pleasant & a capital place to work in *for the city*."[5] He was now fully launched upon his literary career.

In today's vernacular, publishing was a "growth industry" during the 1850s—an ancient craft that was redefining itself for the modern mass

12. Frederick Law Olmsted in his middle years—probably taken during his tenure as Architect in Chief of Central Park (1857–1861). The handlebar moustache may have been a souvenir of his "saddle trip" through Texas with John Hull. (The New-York Historical Society.)

market.[6] And Olmsted's sense of the opportunities in this new "literary republic" was surely correct. Russell Nye notes that conditions were more favorable to the American writer at this period than ever before. Not only was the reading public growing rapidly, both through population growth and through education, formal and informal, but the new methods of printing and distribution were making possible the rise of the great publishing houses. The new Harper Establishment, which opened in New York in 1853, had been laid out to accomodate the bureaucratic and hierarchical requirements of this new kind of mass market publishing.[7] In the year that Olmsted joined Dix and Edwards (1855), the Association of the New York Publishers honored 153 of "their most popular authors" at a banquet at the Crystal Palace. The American Renaissance was then at full flower: Emerson, Thoreau, Hawthorne, Melville, and Whitman had all published their most important works.[8] It was a "literary republic" indeed, and one that attracted not only Olmsted, but a good many of his gentry peers.

Further, Olmsted came to prominence in New York at a time when, according to Thomas Bender, a transition was taking place in the social and cultural leadership of the city—a transition from the city's patrician-dominated "civic culture" of the early antebellum decades to a "literary culture" of the midcentury decades. This transition was marked by the rise of what Bender calls the "metropolitan gentry," a new generation of New Yorkers, among whom Bender includes Olmsted, E. L. Godkin, Henry W. Bellows, and George W. Curtis. The "metropolitan gentry" found its opportunity for leadership in the broad social changes that had undermined the cultural and political authority once held by the patricians and their intellectual coterie. The "metropolitan gentry" would assert that leadership through—and felt they *deserved* leadership because of—their cultural, rather than their political, authority, an authority they claimed to exert purely "in the interest of civilization."[9] They were, in fact, the most ambitious and careerist examples of those gentry intellectuals whom David Hall called "modern missionaries." Indeed, the magazine that was the cornerstone of the Dix and Edwards enterprise, *Putnam's Monthly*, had been founded a few years earlier to provide a forum for men like these, to speak (as Bender observes) "with a New York voice as the nation's intellectual capital."[10]

It is understandable, then, that Olmsted moved to New York with great optimism and good spirits, almost a manic mood, when the world seemed right and the possibilities unlimited. He had two rooms, a parlor "9 yards by 5" and a bedroom "about half that." He sought carpeting from his father and said he would buy "good strong furniture" at auctions and wholesale houses, hoping to create "a neat and tasteful aspect to the room, suitable to the editorship of the Monthly." Olmsted's regimen was to breakfast in his room on tea and toast made on a gas burner, lunch on crackers and soup at the Astor House, and dine at "the French ordinary" with Charles A. Dana, another member of the "metropolitan gentry" who was both a contributing editor to *Putnam's* and an assistant editor of the New York *Tribune*.[11]

But there remained the question of whether the tumultuous, competitive world of Manhattan might not in the end be more debilitating than exhilarating to Olmsted. "I am not sure [Fred] could stand the life—," John Hull had written his father, "but would like him to try—it *might* be much better for him." And John Hull told Bertha, a month after the move, "it is uncertain how well he can endure it & how his *book* will get on."[12] Indeed, almost at the outset, Frederick told his father of "a rather severe return of the trouble I used to have in my side," forcing him to restrict his writing. The following summer he had to retreat to the farm for a respite, stating: "I have been diseased & congested in [the] brain the last week, better these two days & beginning to write again."[13]

Olmsted's move to Manhattan was, in fact, a major change of lifestyle for him and an abrupt departure from the small town or rural life he had mainly known until them. Olmsted had not really separated from Hartford until he moved to Staten Island in 1849, and after that he had spent the major part of his time either on the farm at rural Southside or traveling through the southern states, visiting Manhattan only for business and social purposes. When Olmsted moved to Manhattan in 1855, it was no longer the compact and manageable little town it had been during his apprenticeship at Benkard and Hutton in 1840–1842. It had more than doubled in population and was totally developed beyond Union Square, several blocks above Washington Square, and had spread northward almost to the nascent Central Park. The area around Union Square and along Broadway was now densely packed with buildings—Washington Square, Union Square, and City Hall Park being the major oases in the incredibly busy canyons of central Manhattan. In the 1850s, Broadway itself was the chief artery of a booming, vital city.[14]

13. Broadway and Duane Street in Manhattan, looking south toward Trinity Church (on Wall Street), 1850s. Frederick's rooms, in 1855–1856, were about two blocks north of this point. The publishing firm in which he was a partner first had offices a few blocks below this intersection, then moved to this block on Broadway in 1856. (The New-York Historical Society.)

A half-dozen blocks east of Olmsted's rooming house was the most notorious section in New York, the Five Points. To New York's elite, the Five Points was a byword for drunkenness, depravity, squalor, and sordidness—really a symbol for the immigrant sections of New York, especially the Irish. Symbol or not, the Five Points (so near to Olmsted's world) was horrible enough. One reporter called it "the great center ulcer of wretchedness—the very rotting skeleton of civilization." The *1866*

Guide stated that the environs were "those of wretchedness and crime; they have been fitly described as 'an exhibition of poverty without a parallel—a scene of degradation too appalling to be believed, and too shocking to be disclosed.' "[15]

The abject poverty raging only a few blocks from his neighborhood was, of course, only one aspect of city life as Olmsted met it each day that he lived and worked on Broadway. This part of Manhattan was also extraordinarily noisy. Lockwood reports that conversation was often impossible because of the roar of traffic on the paving-stone street: the "rumbling noise of the omnibuses' wheels . . . the shouts and curses of their drivers, the sharp sound of hundreds of iron horseshoes striking the stone pavement, and the rattling of boxes and building materials in the wagons." Some fifteen thousand vehicles were estimated to have passed by the corner of Broadway and Fulton Street, in the vicinity of Dix and Edwards, on a weekday in the 1850s.[16]

It is likely that Broadway was a difficult place to live for a man of Olmsted's rural sensibilities—as can be seen by the fact that he cited it as a horrible example when arguing for the sunken transverse roads in Central Park.[17] The park as then planned, Olmsted noted, was equal to the distance between Chambers Street and Canal Street. Just imagine but "one crossing of Broadway," he wrote, and the problem level transverse roads in the park would present would be evident:

Inevitably they will be crowded thoroughfares, having nothing in common with the park proper, but everything at variance with those agreeable sentiments which we should wish the park to inspire. . . .They must be constantly open to all the legitimate traffic of the city, to coal carts and butchers' carts, dust carts and dung carts; . . . ladies and invalids will need special police escort for crossing them, as they do in lower Broadway.

And fifteen years later, in his most important address on the necessity for public parks, Olmsted would reveal vividly the effects of living and working where he had during the 1850s:

consider that whenever we walk through the denser part of a town, to merely avoid collision with those we meet and pass upon the sidewalks, we have constantly to watch, to foresee, and to guard against their movements. This involves a consideration of their intentions, a calculation of their strength and weakness. . . . Our minds are thus brought into close dealings with other minds without any friendly flowing toward them, but rather a drawing from them. Much of the intercourse between men when engaged in the pursuits of commerce has the same tendency—a tendency to regard others in a hard if not always hardening way.[18]

"People from the country," he added, "are even conscious of the effect on their nerves and minds of the street contact." Without some form of relief, Olmsted said, "we should all be conscious of suffering from it." Here is a lasting legacy that was to have a great impact upon Olmsted's philosophy of urban design—a legacy of the clamorous environment he had encountered in his brief years in Manhattan during the mid-1850s. It was a legacy of the hard life of the competitive city, but the lesson may have been one learned as much *inside* the confines of Dix and Edwards as on the streets of Broadway below.

Frederick's chief duty at Dix and Edwards (as John Hull described it) was to act as the "editing publisher" of *Putnam's*, answering letters, receiving literary men, and conducting "the literary side of the business." There was an editor above him (George W. Curtis), who was to remain incognito for the time being and who would "decide on the manuscripts & furnish articles." John Hull felt that "Fred's influence though subordinate is large" and that this was "a capital position for him—one that suits him admirably," provided Frederick's health "holds out in such labor." Frederick himself described his chief business duty as writing to contributors to *Putnam's*, returning manuscripts, and expending much time "waiting to see people and seeing them about all sort of matters."[19]

But Frederick's business situation seems to have been doomed from the start. Within a few weeks of Frederick's becoming a partner in Dix and Edwards, John Hull reported: "Fred is running badly into debt to begin with tho' I hope it will turn out well in the end. Their expenses are enormous & will swallow up all their capital I should think. Fred is worried about it—that is at having incurred so much risk at once." And a few months later, the firm was unable to pay Frederick's salary; he had to borrow from friends in order to meet his own expenses.[20] Frederick finally was compelled to seek from his father the funds required for Dix and Edwards to publish *Slave States*, the preparation of which generally occupied Frederick's mind as much as or more than his business duties. After writing at length upon and rationalizing all the financial details, Frederick burst out:

I am ashamed of myself, excessively ashamed of myself, to be so suffering with these cursed business responsibilities. I am hardly able to think of going on with my quiet writing, when I am responsible for this general business, but feel compelled to give myself wholly to it until it is permanently safe & sound. I wonder how I could have been moved from my repeated resolution not to be a business-man; knowing so well my unaptness for it.[21]

It was only a few weeks after this that Olmsted sought (successfully) to borrow more money from his father in order to finance his efforts to become "a recognized litterateur . . . a man of influence in literary matters." Clearly, the pendulum was swinging between Olmsted's two ambitions at this time, and he now saw himself making his place in the world as a writer and man of letters, not as "a practical man." The yearning to be occupied only with his "quiet writing" seemed to be another form of retreat from the world of commercial striving.

In the event, for two years Frederick lived the life of a literary man and a Free-Soil activist (raising funds both for the German settlers he had met in Texas and for the embattled Free-Soilers in Kansas). In 1856, he spent six months in London, representing his firm in seeking English literary works for American publication. But his publishing firm continued to be ineptly managed, and Frederick spent far too much time in bitter quarrels with his partners as the firm slowly declined into bankruptcy. Frederick's letters, rather than truly focusing upon the financial situation, were preoccupied with two issues that seemed to strike to the heart of his inner needs: resentment at being placed in a subordinate position; and anxiety about maintaining a position of respect and esteem in London. In one letter, Olmsted complained bitterly of being treated as a "very young, undisciplined clerk." The lack of confidence shown in him, Olmsted said, "could have paralyzed all the elements of success in my character & habits."[22] At another point, Olmsted excoriated Joshua Dix's handling of business matters, savaging his hapless young partner:

You are a nervous boy, with an ill-balanced mind, not yet a mature habit of sound reflection. Having a confusion of motives you act vehemently from that which is uppermost, and vainly suppose you are pursuing some purposes & are governed by some ideas of your own you allow yourself to be imposed upon & turned hither & thither by any one who has the capability of personal reflection & the ability to make you believe that his words are your thoughts.[23]

As Elizabeth Stevenson suggests, Olmsted, when confronted with situations that struck deeply to his inner self, often made use of the psychological defense of projection, attributing to others traits and behavior that he feared were true of himself.[24] Was Joshua Dix the only one who could be described as "a nervous boy, with an ill-balanced mind, not yet a mature habit of sound reflection"? Did not Olmsted himself often seem to have a "confusion of motives" and to "act vehemently" from the one that pressed him hardest?

Time and again, Olmsted was engaged in what he seemed to consider mortal combat with the very people with whom he had to cooperate. In this instance, it was Joshua Dix and Arthur Edwards. Very soon after, at Central Park, it would be Egbert Viele and Andrew Green and the Commissioners *en masse*, not to mention his closest colleague, Calvert Vaux. During the Civil War, he would develop wrenching conflicts with Henry Bellows and the Sanitary Commission's Executive Committee, as well his western associate, John Strong Newberry. Time and again, the real issue would be Olmsted's own damaged self-esteem, making him bristle at being put in a subordinate position to anyone—particularly if the other person's regard for him seemed to him insufficient and particularly if that person was a contemporary of his or John Hull's or even younger.

Olmsted's combative outbursts often would be sprinkled with lurid images of self-destruction. This trait is evident in his furious letters to Arthur Edwards and Joshua Dix. In an early letter to Edwards, disputing the latter's sharp business practices, Olmsted had written that he would prefer "to starve or to commit suicide in some less painful manner" than to condone such practices.[25] In a later letter to Dix, Olmsted wrote: "I would rather be shot dead to night than fail to meet the obligations I have undertaken on our mutual account here in England."[26] Such hyperbole can be seen as merely melodramatic posturing. But it suggests also that, in Olmsted's inner world, death itself was preferable to loss of respect from those who mattered so much to his self-esteem.

Olmsted represented Dix and Edwards in London until October 1856. Even after he returned, however, there is no evidence that he ever initiated a searching inquiry into the firm's troubled financial condition, though both his brother and his father had urged him, warned him, to do so. "It's a duty to father that you should know that not only is all above board but thoroughly well done," John Hull had written him.[27] But Frederick apparently continued to neglect his "duty" long after his return to New York. He stayed on in the partnership, continuing to leave his father's money at risk, even though his letters that February (one month after the publication of *Texas*) revealed his certainty that the business would fail. As it happened, Dix and Edwards were forced out of the firm the following April, with George W. Curtis taking over the reins, bringing in a new third partner to himself and Olmsted. Finally, in August, Curtis wrote: "We failed today! It was unavoidable."[28]

It seems clear that it was literary influence that had attracted most of Frederick's energies from the outset of his publishing venture. During the alarming and contentious summer of 1856, John Hull had told Frederick that one reason Dix and Edwards had originally wished him to stay in England was because there was nothing for him to do in New York. "In fact, there never had been," John Hull wrote. "You had always been principally occupied with your own writings. And now there appeared to be no room for you." And in December 1856, Olmsted had written to Edwards that, except when he had been in England, he had never had any "distinct special duties" that required one-tenth of his time. Even now, Olmsted added, he spent half his time reading proofs and "otherwise forwarding my own books."[29] Throughout the first half of 1857, whatever efforts Dix, Edwards, and Curtis may have been making to save the business, Olmsted seemed to be sleepwalking through his business affairs, almost a spectator, while his mind and heart remained firmly fixed only upon journalism and Free Soil.

By the time his publishing venture finally failed in August 1857, Frederick had been left very much alone in New York. John Hull had traveled with his wife and children first to Cuba and then to Switzerland and France, seeking a better climate for his deteriorating health. John Olmsted, touring Europe with his wife and their two daughters, would, in early November, hurry to his son's bedside in Nice, arriving there just as the young man was dying.

Moreover, the spring and summer of 1857 was a period of pervasive social conflict in the nation at large and, more importantly, within the city where Frederick lived and worked. In Utah, Brigham Young and his supporters were defying the Federal government, and federal troops had marched off for a confrontation—the so-called Mormon War.[30] There is no sign that Olmsted had become as alarmed as so many of his fellow New Yorkers, such as George Templeton Strong; but Olmsted seems to have given some thought to going West to cover the story as a journalist.[31]

However, impending chaos would strike even more closely to Olmsted that summer in the form of a "Police War" that touched off rioting in the streets of Manhattan during the summer. This particular "war" was caused by reform legislation, through which the New York State Legislature attempted to curb police corruption. It created a metropolitan police force, under a board of five commissioners, to replace the local forces in several counties, including Manhattan. Mayor Fernando Wood called the new law unconstitutional. He and the municipal police refused to turn over their facilities or control of the streets to the metropolitan police. "Civil War," the *Times* headlined, as the Commissioners placed Mayor Wood under arrest and "Rioting & Bloodshed" took place in the streets. Though Wood eventually capitulated and the municipal force was disbanded, the disruption to public authority sparked collisions between New York's many street gangs.[32]

Finally, in August a speculative bubble burst with the failure of the Ohio Life Insurance and Trust Company. By September, the panic of 1857 was in full swing. "Panic is dreadful in Wall Street," Strong recorded in his diary on September 28. "The banks will probably stand, but failures are multiplying."[33]

Beyond these social upheavals, there were also events that may have rubbed raw Olmsted's pride. Though Olmsted saw business failure all around him, the book business in fact had major successes during that panic year. The *Atlantic Monthly* was inaugurated in 1857, along the lines Olmsted had hoped to establish at *Putnam's*, with a roster of authors he had sought to publish.[34] Also founded that year was *Harper's Weekly*, whose editor was none other than Olmsted's former colleague and partner, George William Curtis. But the hardest to bear may have been the publication in midyear of Hinton Rowan Helper's book, *The Impending Crisis of the South: How to Meet It*. The notoriety of this book far eclipsed anything Olmsted had achieved with his own books, and Helper's theme —that slavery, as an institution, had degraded and impoverished many Southern whites—was similar to one of Olmsted's major theses.

His dream of "practical success" shattered by the Dix and Edwards failure, Olmsted nevertheless hung on to his hopes for literary influence. He seems to have insulated himself from the uproar in New York's streets by immersing himself totally in his Free-Soil labors and in the writing of his third and final book on the South. While street gangs were rioting on the July 4th weekend (and New York City was placed under martial law), Olmsted was writing a long letter to an associate in the Free-Soil movement and another to the Cotton Supply Associations of Manchester and Liverpool, both letters dealing with schemes for colonizing the western territories with antislavery settlers. Neither of these contain any personal references to life in New York, although the first of them was marked "92 Grand Street," Olmsted's lodgings of 1857, several blocks from the worst of the riots. Nor was Olmsted writing to his family abroad at this time.[35]

By late July, Olmsted had fled New York's hot summer, residing for a while at an inn at the seaside resort of Morris Cove, Connecticut, near New Haven, where he could concentrate upon his "quiet writing," hoping to complete *Back Country*. While there, according to Olmsted, he chanced to lunch one Sunday at a table next to one of the members of the new Board of Commissioners for Central Park.[36] This new Board had been created during the Republican State Legislature's reformist attack upon New York City's Mayor, Fernando Wood—the same political conflict that had given rise to New York's "police war." These new Commissioners hoped to elect a superintendent who would be "the Executive Officer of the Chief Engineer with respect to the labor force and would have charge of the police and see that proper regulations were enforced in regard to public use of the Park." The Commissioners thought it desirable that this man be a Republican, and, after some conversation, this Commissioner suggested Olmsted himself might be a candidate. Olmsted immediately undertook a campaign to get himself appointed to the post.

The position described by this Commissioner must have had several appeals for Olmsted: first, it offered a steady income; second, it seemed also to offer prestige and stature; third, there was clearly an appeal to his psyche, another opportunity to assert his identity through "practical success," but success in a benevolent public work, ostensibly far removed from the competitive world of business. It must have been immediately evident to Olmsted that the new park would provide a haven of retreat from the tumultuous city, an escape from the "shafts of malice" endemic to the mercantile world. Ironically, in the months ahead the new park would involve Olmsted in personal conflicts that would dwarf those of Dix and Edwards both in their intensity and in their destructive impact upon his physical and mental state. And the most painful of these conflicts would be with those members of the patrician-gentry elite whom he had expected to support and sustain him.

As noted in the introduction, Stow Persons has defined the American gentry rather broadly as "a self-constituted aristocracy of the best," an elite of talent and taste ("the natural aristocracy"), in contrast with the socioeconomic elite of birth and money ("the actual aristocracy"). It was an elite, Persons notes, that could include professional men of modest means (doctors, lawyers, creative artists, journalists, educated clergymen, college professors) as well as the more cultivated sort of merchants, bankers, and businessmen. Persons also cites Emerson's observation that this natural aristocracy of self-made men was not to be found at the heart of the actual aristocracy but only at its edges.[37]

I would suggest that the "metropolitan gentry" of which Bender speaks, the talented and energetic newcomers to these circles, was a group of men that existed at the "edges" of New York's patrician and gentry aristocracies (whether "actual" or "natural"). The metropolitan gentry may have achieved cultural leadership, as Bender suggests, but this was not the same as achieving social, economic, and political power—and this kind of power escaped most of them, much as they may have wished to see themselves as a sort of "natural aristocracy." I suggest further that members of this metropolitan gentry, men like Olmsted, Brace, Curtis, Bellows, and Dana, achieved success in accordance to the degree to which they helped to meet the needs of the patrician-gentry elite, the degree to which they could enact an agenda actually established by that elite.

Olmsted's constituency, as a public man, had originated within this patrician-gentry elite of New York. In his pamphlet of 1882, *Spoils of the Park*, Olmsted emphasized that his initial supporters for the position of Superintendent of Central Park (in 1857) had included men like Washington Irving, William Cullen Bryant, Peter Cooper, David Dudley Field, and others—men whom Bender assigns to the earlier patrician-dominated "civic culture" of the city. Later on in his pamphlet, Olmsted observed that the early Commissioners of Central Park had included "several men unknown in politics, but of high standing in liberal, benevolent, and unpartisan patriotic movements, [plus] others, who, if known in politics, were unknown as office-seekers, or . . . politicians." It was from this group of commissioners—members of New York's patrician-gentry elite—that Olmsted would receive his early support on the Central Park Board.[38]

In the summer of 1857, it had been Olmsted's task (in order to obtain the Superintendent's position) to marshall his resources within the patri-

14. A bird's eye view of the site of Central Park (1854), looking from the Hudson River toward the East River. The building at left center is the Mount St. Vincent Convent, at about 103rd–104th streets, on the former Boston Post Road, while the old Croton reservoir is in the center of the picture. (Eno Collection, Mirian and Ira D. Wallach Division of Art, Prints and Photographs, The New York Public Library, Astor, Lenox and Tilden Foundations.)

cian and gentry circles of New York, the kinds of people for whom, through Brace's help and his own talents, he was coming to be the "representative man," their delegate. Parke Godwin, a journalist and author whom Bender cites as one of the mediating figures between the older patrician culture and the new metropolitan gentry, urged Olmsted's nomination upon a pivotal commissioner, the Reform Democrat Andrew H. Green. "Let me assure you," Godwin wrote Green, "that I know of no man in the country better qualified then he for such a place."[39]

On the evening of September 11, as the new, Republican-dominated Board of Commissioners was preparing to elect a superintendent for

Central Park, Olmsted passed the time writing to John Hull to tell him of the events of the past few weeks: "I have moved to town & done nothing else . . . but canvass for the Superintendent's office."[40] At an earlier subcommittee meeting, the nomination had narrowly gone to him, Olmsted wrote, but the salary had been reduced from $3,000 to $1,500. This was done apparently to placate the supporters of Chief Engineer Egbert Viele by making Olmsted's salary clearly subordinate to Viele's—thus reducing Olmsted's position to that "of a mere overseer of laborers."[41] (Viele himself had been hired by the original Board, controlled by Mayor Wood's Democrats.) Olmsted said he had thought of turning down the job at the lower salary, but had changed his mind after reflecting, "what else can I do for a living?" He had hoped, also, that the salary would later be increased if he proved "the importance and responsibility of the office." And, he observed finally, the times were getting "worse and worse," with merchants and bankers becoming "horribly blue," fearing a bank riot. In a burst of realism, he somberly noted: "I shall think myself fortunate if I can earn $1500."

In an addendum to the letter, Frederick announced that he had been elected to the position with but one negative vote cast against him.[42] "The strongest objection to me, [is] that I am a literary man, not active," he told John Hull; "yet if I had not been a 'literary man' so far, I should not have stood a chance."

Olmsted had indeed been fortunate. It had been on August 6 that George W. Curtis had written Olmsted the letter that had informed him that their publishing firm failed. Also, since his first two books on the South had been financial failures, Olmsted had had little to hope for, monetarily, from his third. His material outlook that summer had been dismal. "Fred's case is a very hard one," John Olmsted wrote a month later. "Fortunately he has no family."[43]

In the teeth of a panic and with what were, at best, marginal qualifications for overseeing a massive public works project, Olmsted had landed an excellent position, one that made him responsible not only for the construction of the park, but also for its use by the public. "If a fairy had shaped [this position] for me, it could not have fitted me better," Olmsted wrote Vaux six years later. "It was normal, ordinary and naturally outgrowing from my previous life and history."[44]

In fact, both Olmsted and his supporters had built the case for his nomination on his educational background (nonexistent), practical farm-ing experience (as putative owner of two farms, both of which were failures), and his travel writings and observations (excellent, but hardly indicative of his executive abilities). Thus, Olmsted's receiving the posi-tion was hardly "normal" or "ordinary." That he got the job nevertheless is likely due to a combination of circumstances. First, Olmsted's creden-tials seemed a lot better on paper than they had been in reality, especially when backed up with the kind of references Olmsted was able to com-mand. (Even today a strong resume and the right contacts are the best path to a major career move.) Second, as noted above, many of the new Commissioners were of the same patrician-gentry circles as were Olm-sted's referents and friends, people to whom the intense, energetic Olmsted had apparently been able to project himself as an appropriate agent for implementing the social programs to which they all subscribed. Indeed, one of Olmsted's principal supporters on the Board, later to be his rival, was the man recruited by Parke Godwin, Andrew Haswell Green, a man of similar background as Olmsted and equally able to serve as an agent of the needs and wishes of the patrician-gentry elite. Third, it was certainly helpful that Olmsted's friends among the "metropolitan gentry" included such important journalists as George W. Curtis, Parke Godwin, and Charles A. Dana, men who, as Beveridge points out, not only supported him for the position but later championed his views on park matters.[45] And, finally, probably few of the candidates, if any, had any greater qualifications to oversee a totally new kind of public work, especially among those candidates who were acceptable to the Republican majority on the Board. In any event, the fact remains that the position *did* fit Olmsted's psychological needs and intellectual capacities as if tailored to them. The Commissioners could hardly have made a better choice.

It was in November 1857, only a few weeks after beginning work on the park, that Frederick received his last letter from John Hull, who wrote: "It appears we are not to see one another any more." And he told Frederick: "I have never known a better friendship than ours has been & there can't be a greater happiness than to think of that—How dear we have been & how long have held out such tenderness."[46] Constantly sedated with opium, John Hull found it hard "to comprehend the sudden-ness," but he saw the end coming on quickly, as he was now barely able to get out of bed, with little breath left. "I want you to keep something

[of] mine," John Hull wrote, "my watch or cane or something." And he ended with his last words to Frederick: "Don't let Mary suffer while you are alive—God bless you."

Two weeks later, the grieving father, John Olmsted, wrote Frederick that John Hull had felt it "hard to be called to part with life at so early an age as 32," but felt also that he had had a very good life, especially in his marriage and in the "mutual friendship & brotherly love that had existed always" between him and Frederick. "In his death I have lost not only a Son but a very good friend," John Olmsted wrote. "You, almost your only friend—."[47] It was a brutal truth, told with Puritan candor. But the other part of the truth, unsaid and perhaps unknown to the father, was that Frederick had also lost the person who had been the first and most formidable rival of his life.

John Olmsted went on to add that John Hull had left Frederick his watch and anything Frederick could use from his wardrobe, including brand new clothes from Paris that had never been worn. "It will be a pleasure to you I presume to use [or] wear anything that was his." The father then enumerated all the fine items of the younger son's wardrobe that should now be taken on by the older son. It seems very clear from both the father's and John Hull's last letters that it was now Frederick's obligation to take on whatever remained from John Hull's too-short life —including perhaps the responsibility for his wife and children.

Indeed, both Laura Roper and Charles Beveridge have suggested that this was so, that Olmsted's marriage to his brother's widow (eighteen months after John Hull's death) was an act of duty rather than love.[48] The nature of the relationship between Frederick and Mary can be seen in their letters after Frederick went off alone to Washington in the summer of 1861 to begin work on the Sanitary Commission. "I wanted you to go because I thought you would be happier there, than here with me, on the Park," Mary wrote; "if you do not exert yourself to be happy you see I am swindled, besides being as it appears, impoverished."[49]

There were undoubtedly several reasons for Olmsted's leaving Mary and the children behind in New York when he moved to Washington, not the least of which was that Mary was several months pregnant at the time. But Marion was born in October, and a year later Olmsted still had not brought his family to Washington. Instead, he warned Mary that even when he visited New York, he would not be spending much time

15. Mary Cleveland Olmsted, c. 1860. Mary had been left a widow with three children when John Hull died in 1857. In June 1859, she and Frederick were married by the mayor of New York in a ceremony at Central Park. (Society for the Preservation of New England Antiquities.)

with them. Writing of himself in the third person, Olmsted stated: "Fred will come to New-York in a few days, *to work on the park*. That is his object & his only justification for being away from Washington."[50] His use of the third person may well symbolize the extent to which he used his work as a barrier to and replacement for intimate relations.

There were surely reasons enough for two lonely people who had known each other so long to make a companionate marriage. Olmsted's marriage to his brother's widow satisfied his own long-held wish for a wife and the pleasures of family life (whenever he would permit himself to enjoy them). "He had romanticized this condition," Stevenson writes, "and had been supported in his dreams by Zimmerman's *On Solitude*, which is in part a rhapsody in praise of home virtues."[51] And I have already pointed out that their marriage took place only ten days after the death of Frederick's beloved Aunt Maria, the woman who had, more than any other, served as a surrogate mother for him.

But one interesting, perhaps unconscious, motivation for Frederick is suggested by a coincidence of names. The brother whom Frederick was replacing in this marriage bore the same name as their father; the young widow Frederick married bore a name similar to that of his stepmother. Seen in this light, Frederick's marriage to the woman who had been his brother's wife is remarkably suggestive of the fantasy Freud placed at the heart of the Oedipus complex—the little boy's wish to replace the father as the mother's mate. It has already been suggested, in part 1, that the long illness and the carriage accident that followed upon Olmsted's marriage to his brother's widow may have been a self-induced punishment for usurping his brother's place. The shattered leg Frederick sustained as a result of that accident, a symbolic castration, is precisely the form of punishment that, according to Freud, the child fears will result from his fantasy wishes.

Before that accident, before the illness that preceded it, on the day in June of 1859 that Frederick was married to Mary at Bogardus House in Central Park by the Mayor of New York, he had stood at the pinnacle of his mid-life career. He was Architect in Chief of the park and, until that spring, the sole authority over that great public project, a man of growing reputation and increasing respect within the patrician and gentry circles of the city. It had been less than two years since Dix and Edwards had failed. Despite the chaos that had existed in the world around him during that summer of 1857, despite his humiliating failures in the still-thriving "literary republic," despite his own desperate financial condition, and despite the sure knowledge of his brother's impending death, Frederick had not given way to despair. As Fred Kingsbury had prophesied a decade earlier: "Many of his favorite schemes will go to naught—but he'll throw it aside and try another."[52] He had tried again, and he had succeeded. Yet even as Olmsted brought his new family to live in Central Park in mid-1859, his triumph was turning into another bitter defeat.

CHAPTER 9

"Slow Murder"

Olmsted's acquisition of the almost ideal position as Superintendent of Central Park was marked with portents of the rivalries that would deplete and exhaust him throughout these otherwise extraordinarily productive four years, demoralizing him to the point that he felt compelled to submit his resignation in 1861. When he had first applied for the position, the Chief Engineer, Egbert Viele, had treated him as just another patronage-seeker, ignoring him for hours and then dismissing Olmsted's petition with the observation that he would rather have "a practical man" in the job. And in his election-night letter to John Hull, Frederick had commented: "It seems to be generally expected that Viele & I shall quarrel, that he will be jealous of me, & that there will be all sorts of intrigues." Some months later, after being approached by Calvert Vaux with an offer to jointly enter the Central Park design competition, Frederick wrote his father: "I am greatly interested in working with Vaux. If successful, I should not only get my share of $2000 offered for the best [design for Central Park], *but no doubt the whole control of the matter would be given to me & my salary increased to $2500.*"[1] This last statement suggests that he had been gunning for Viele from the outset, with the goal of becoming the sole master of the park.

As noted earlier, it was scarcely a month after Frederick had begun work on the park that John Hull died far away in Nice. It appears that Olmsted mourned his brother by becoming increasingly absorbed in work. In this period, he would find aspects of the brother he had lost in

16. Calvert Vaux (c. 1860), Olmsted's self-effacing partner in the creation of the Greensward Plan, which won the competition for a new design of Central Park and helped to propel Olmsted to the position of Architect in Chief. It troubled Vaux greatly that he never received the public recognition he deserved for his share in the work. (Society for the Preservation of New England Antiquities.)

another younger man, slightly older than John Hull. Calvert Vaux would become his self-effacing comrade-in-work. The two would begin in partnership and work in close intimacy, but, as Vaux himself would later complain, Vaux would find himself subordinate to the man he considered less experienced than himself.

Vaux was a small man, apparently shorter than Olmsted, studious-looking, with his pince-nez eyeglasses, high forehead and scraggly beard. He seems to have been a modest, retiring sort of man—and yet he was almost as emotionally excitable as Olmsted and even more fierce in defense of principle. Vaux had been born in London and trained in England as an architect, emigrating to America to be an architectural assistant to the founder of American "landscape gardening," Andrew Jackson Downing, in Newburgh, New York. He had worked with Downing in designing the grounds of the White House and the Smithsonian Institution. A few years after Downing's death in an 1852 steamboat accident, Vaux moved to New York City, where he helped to lobby and propagandize for the creation of a new and better landscape design for Central Park to replace Egbert Viele's pedestrian, engineering-oriented plan of development. To this end, Vaux urged the Park Commissioners to hold a design competition. When the Commissioners accepted the notion of a competition, Vaux persuaded Olmsted to join him in submitting an entry.[2]

The Greensward plan created by Olmsted and Vaux was one of thirty-five entries submitted in the competition. A few of the entrants described themselves as landscape gardeners, and one competitor would play a major role in the development of the park under Olmsted's supervision: Ignaz Pilat.[3] According to Ian Stewart, the plans were generally of high quality, demonstrating "full awareness of both the classic and current works on landscape design." The competition thus revealed an emergent professional interest in landscape design.[4]

Aside from his desperate finances of those years, Olmsted's ambition was also pulling him in different directions. Ownership of the Staten Island farm had passed to Mary at John Hull's death, but the responsibility of managing it remained with Frederick, as it had since John Hull went abroad. He was in the position, he told his father, of one who was starting in an important new business without any capital and saddled with debt. "I have had to constantly throw back old debts by making new ones."[5] He could perhaps catch a glimmer of the prominence he would

achieve by being both designer and master of Central Park, even while
the residue of earlier responsibilities and ambitions still tugged at him:

the plan of the park which *I have decided to present*, will cost some hundred dollars.
It is certainly *worthwhile for me* to go into this competition; the reward of success
being so large. . . . While attending to the park & the plan—I have also if possible
to complete my book [*Back Country*] for publication, the labor in it being too much
to let slide. Unquestionably I am undertaking too much either one of the
three enterprises being enough for all my talents and strength—but I don't see
from which I can secede.

The words I have emphasized in this letter indicate that Olmsted, unconsciously, had already begun to think of the park design project and its
rewards as uniquely *his*, rather than belonging equally to Vaux.

Within a few months, Olmsted's objectives on the park were achieved.
On April 28, 1858, the Commissioners selected Greensward by Olmsted
and Vaux as the winning design. (Charles Beveridge suggests that the
decision was actually made along political lines: all six Republicans, plus
the Reform Democrat, Andrew H. Green, voted for Greensward, while
the other three Democrats voted for a plan submitted by the park's
Superintendent of Planting, also a Democrat.)[6] On May 12, a resolution
of the Board called upon Olmsted, as Superintendent, to "proceed forth-
with to form working plans for the construction of the Park" and to
employ his partner, Vaux, in the project. On May 17, the Commission
voted that "the duties heretofore imposed on the Chief Engineer and
Superintendent be and the same are hereby devolved on the Architect-in-
Chief," who was to be "the chief executive officer of this Board, by or
through whom all work on the Park shall be executed."[7]

Viele's position was abolished, and he was dismissed from the park,
along with the Superintendent of Planting, whose design had won second
prize. The Republican majority, with Green's help, now had its own
plan for the park and its own man to implement that plan. Viele's later
career, it should be noted, would be quite distinguished, including service
as a brigadier general during the Civil War, a term in Congress, and (most
galling to Olmsted and Vaux) presidency of New York City's Park Commission in 1884. Like another Olmsted antagonist, Andrew H. Green,
Viele was friendly with George Templeton Strong, who thought well of
him.[8]

It had been less than a year since Olmsted had begun canvassing for the Superintendent's position, a position he had secured despite the opposition of the Chief Engineer, Egbert Viele. Now Olmsted had triumphed over Viele and made himself complete master of Central Park and all its laboring men, a position he would hold unchallenged between May 1858 and October 1859 (at which time Andrew H. Green became Comptroller of the Park). "It was," Charles Beveridge has written, "the most intense and the most productive period of park-building in his entire life."[9]

In an 1873 letter to a parks Commissioner, Olmsted described what had been accomplished in the four years following his appointment as Architect in Chief at Central Park:

construction of roads and walks, arches and bridges, the formation of lakes, greens and lawns, the changes of surface and the preparation and distribution of soil on the rocky parts to be planted, [were] principally executed. The main bodies of foliage were brought to a high state of provisional finish; the nucleus of the keepers [Park Police] force was formed and instructed and certain customs of public use were established, the rude and fundamental work needed to the realization of the design was thus in great measure done and some little more.[10]

In later years, Olmsted would occasionally look back on the forces, within and without, that had driven him at Central Park in his middle years to become such "a hard-worker and *doer*." In one of his 1893 letters to Mariana Van Rensselaer, Olmsted enumerated his reasons for throwing himself into the Central Park work with "more than ardor" after his "somewhat vagabondish somewhat poetical" earlier way of living. These included the hopelessness of his brother's condition, his broken-heartedness at John Hull's later death, and the "mortification" and repressed anger caused by the failure of his publishing venture. But he added that his obsessive attitude toward the work at Central Park was also caused in part by "a rapidly growing hatred of New York politicians with whom all my work on the Park was a *war*."[11]

With 130 years of experience behind us, we cannot be surprised that the chief executive officer of a vast public work would feel himself continuously at war with a ruling body of eleven politically powerful men (generally successful businessmen), consisting of "part Republicans, part Wood Democrats, part 'reform' Democrats, part nondescript," as Olmsted later described them.[12] Yet, between the spring of 1858 and the fall of 1859, Olmsted had enjoyed relative autonomy as the new Architect in

Chief of Central Park. Indeed, in September 1859, in the midst of a quarrel with one of these Commissioners (John F. Butterworth), Olmsted revealed the extent to which executive power had been delegated to him: "I have thus far been held to no account of how this power is used, except as evidenced in its results on the park."[13] It was, Olmsted indicated, precisely how he wished things to be.

In fact, Olmsted's accomplishments on the park as Architect in Chief were enormous. But the pride he felt in those accomplishments in later years was very nearly overwhelmed by the anguish and bitterness with which he recalled his continual conflicts with the Commissioners. These conflicts fell into three general areas: various schemes and proposals for altering the Greensward plan; the attempts of various Commissioners to make use of the park for political patronage; and the debilitating struggles with Andrew H. Green for control of the park work.

Some of the design proposals made by the Commissioners were in complete hostility to the Olmsted-Vaux plan—the plan that had been endorsed by the Republican and Reform Democrat coalition. One such was made by Commissioner Robert J. Dillon (with the support of fellow Democrat August Belmont), calling for the creation of a boulevard, something like the Champs Elysée, running from the Fifty-ninth Street entrance of the park on a straight line to the Croton Reservoir at its center, a boulevard that would cross Olmsted and Vaux's proposed new lake by means of a wire suspension bridge. Decades later, Olmsted still remembered with horror how Dillon's avenue would have made "natural landscape . . . subordinate to the stateliness of an effect essentially architectural." And he recalled how he had combatted this idea. He had invited two of the most powerful gentry newspapermen in New York, Henry J. Raymond of the *Times* and Charles A. Dana of the *Tribune*, to breakfast in the park, "in a table tent set on a grand rock in the Ramble, right on the line of the proposed avenue." Olmsted had directed them to "look southward" and consider the destructive effect of Dillon's avenue on the "natural beauty" of the park. "It was a case of natural eloquence versus grandiloquence," Olmsted quipped.[14]

However, it was not park design per se, but rather political patronage that was most often the battleground between Olmsted and the Commissioners (other than Green) during his three-year tenure as Architect in Chief. When Henry G. Stebbins, a banker and Reform Democrat, became a commissioner at the beginning of 1860, Olmsted informed him that from "the first day of my duty to this, I have never been free from the most urgent advice, importunity, warnings, even threats, intended to influence or overcome my judgment as to my duty, either from Commissioners, or from persons coming to me in their name." As much as he tried to act toward the Commissioners with "respect, gratitude and friendship," Olmsted said, he felt his position had nevertheless been undermined, and the confidence of the Board in his judgment weakened, because he had felt "compelled to act contrary to their advice in the matter of appointment." When we consider that it was in June, six months later, that Olmsted would suffer his near-fatal carriage accident, it is rather startling to find him telling Stebbins that should these demands continue to be made, "I am convinced that I could not live through next summer." [15]

In one of Olmsted's final reports to the Board of Commissioners before taking leave to assume his new post with the Sanitary Commission in 1861, he was still seeking to free himself of the demands of political patronage. Just like "the Custom House or the City Hall," Olmsted wrote the Board, "the park has never been free, but has been constantly cursed and disgraced with the vice of politics." [16] For Olmsted, the problem was an example in microcosm of the corruption of municipal government in America. "It is often said that the failure of republican government in application to cities must be conceded," Olmsted wrote in "Passages" in 1873, adding: "But those who do concede it have abandoned the struggle to secure good government." And when his connection to the New York parks came to an end in 1878, Olmsted devoted most of his embittered pamphlet, *Spoils of the Park*, to attacking the evils of the patronage system.

Olmsted's struggle against the corruption of public service was both a courageous and a necessary one—a struggle that he and his peers in gentry circles would evolve into the civil service movement. But his conflict with his one-time supporter, Commissioner Green, was something else again—a long, drawn-out power struggle between two men who had seemed to have every reason to be allies. But of all those with whom Olmsted was at war in his life, Andrew Haswell Green was surely the most severe rival, considering both the intensity of the animosity they developed toward each other and the three-decade duration of their dealings.

17. In M. M. Graff's words, "the men who made Central Park." She identifies them as (from left to right): Andrew Haswell Green, the Central Park Treasurer and Comptroller (and Olmsted's nemesis); George Waring, Jr., responsible for the drainage and sanitary engineering projects; Calvert Vaux; Ignaz A. Pilat, himself a landscape architect, responsible for all the planting at the park; the sculptor Jacob Wrey Mould, responsible for the ornamental stone work at the park (most notably, at the Terrace); and Frederick Law Olmsted, leaning heavily on the railing to relieve the weight on his still-mending thigh, in the wake of his near-fatal carriage accident. Graff, *Central Park*, 66–67. (Prevost Collection, Rare Books and Manuscripts Division, The New York Public Library, Astor, Lenox and Tilden Foundations.)

Andrew Green was, physically, a much bigger man than Olmsted, tall
and broad in the shoulders and chest. He was a handsome, impressive
man with a "Roman head," bushy eyebrows, and a full, neatly trimmed
beard. Green was two years older than Frederick, but from a quite similar
background. He had been born and raised in rural Massachusetts and,
like Olmsted, had acquired his education by diligent reading rather than
through advanced schooling. Like Frederick also, he had been introduced
to the world of commerce as an apprentice clerk to a New York City
merchant. Unlike Olmsted, Green had taken to the dry goods business
and to the keeping of ledgers. Later he studied law and, at twenty-two,
joined the law firm of Samuel J. Tilden, a man who would be both his
mentor and hero. By the 1850s, Green was a fixture in New York City's
patrician and gentry circles. He became president of the Board of Education in 1856 and a member of the Park Commission. In the latter position,
he was both an early planner for Central Park and (as noted earlier) the
only Democrat to support Olmsted's appointment as Superintendent,
continuing to support Olmsted as he assumed the role of Architect in
Chief. Green served as Comptroller of the Park Board, and thus its chief
executive, from 1859 to 1870. He became Comptroller of New York City
in 1871, after the ouster of the Tweed Ring, and was responsible for
restoring the city's finances to fiscal soundness. In the latter part of the
century, Green led the fight, often alone, for merging New York City
with its surrounding municipalities. He would, in 1898, receive a gold
medal as "The Father of Greater New York."[17]

In their own time, Green seems to have been at least as respected as
Olmsted by their gentry society. In an oft-quoted observation, George
Templeton Strong was moved by Green's heroics against the Tweed
Ring to write:

I believe A. H. Green an honest man. People generally think well of him. I
have known him since 1844, more or less. The only person I ever heard speak ill
of him was F. L. Olmsted, who had relations with him in Central Park administration, and Olmsted has a rather *mauvaise langue*.[18]

Ian Stewart, very much an Olmsted admirer, writes of Green: "More
than any other individual, it would be this man who would be largely
responsible for the successful development of the park."[19]

Olmsted and Green, both dedicated to Central Park, began as colleagues, became rivals, and ended as bitter enemies. It could hardly have been otherwise. Both men had sought control over the development and operation of Central Park, and Olmsted had lost to Green in that struggle. It did not help that Green, in the words of his own biographer, was imperious, vain, and parsimonious both in his own and in public finances. As Laura Wood Roper writes, the relationship between the two became, by 1860, that of "one autocrat regularly overborne by another."[20] There is another aspect to their rivalry, too, one that may have given further psychological impetus to their quarrels. Up until June 1859, both men were bachelors who had given over almost their entire lives to the park. It is therefore possible that Olmsted's sudden marriage was also an upsetting factor in their relationship, perhaps a cause of envy on Green's part and occasional jealousy on Olmsted's (Green dined with the Olmsteds "almost every other Sunday" and frequently called at the Olmsted home at Mount St. Vincent's in Frederick's absence).[21]

Green's view was that the early Central Park Commissioners had been distracted by political frictions and thus had been "quite willing to leave the work [of the Park] to anyone who would attend to it"—namely, Olmsted. To correct this situation, he states, the position of Comptroller of Central Park was created especially for him, combining all the executive power of the Board with those of the Treasurer.[22] Olmsted's view was that Green, upon assuming that office, had undertaken "not only to assume more important responsibilities and more valuable duties, but to include all other duties and responsibilities within his own, and to make those of the *inferior office* [Olmsted's position as Architect in Chief and Superintendent] not only completely and *servilely subordinate* but to make them appear of a temporary value and then important only temporarily."[23] The words emphasized reveal Olmsted's anguish at finding himself in a subordinate role to a man who was his peer, a reversal of the kind of supremacy *he* always sought to achieve in such relationships.

Green's ultimate weapon was his smothering control over all expenditures made by the Superintendent. Olmsted complained that "not a dollar, not a cent, is got from under [Green's] paw that is not wet with his blood & sweat." But Olmsted also acknowledged that Green was "honest and sensible in the main" and that "he does, and always has done, a hundred times more work than all the rest [of the Commissioners] together."[24]

Nevertheless, Olmsted essentially invited upon himself his misfortunes with Andrew Green. First, there was Olmsted's inability to control costs on the project, perhaps even to realize how essential it was on a public project not only to do so, but to provide for a rigorously detailed accounting of where the money went. This lack of fiscal responsibility had drawn innumerable lectures from his father during Frederick's two attempts at managing farms in Sachem's Head and Staten Island. John Olmsted, who knew his son well, had been very pleased at the news of Frederick's appointment as Superintendent of Central Park, but also concerned. "This seems to place you in a position which I have no doubt of your ability to fill, hardly knowing however what your duty is," he wrote to his son, adding: "You will of course be cautious not to give offense in your new position & particularly careful in your accounts if there are any to keep."[25] Subsequent events proved that John Olmsted had had every reason to be concerned. The cost overruns, which reached more than a quarter of a million dollars by the end of 1859, certainly undermined Olmsted's position and helped to bring on the election of Commissioner Green as Comptroller.[26]

The second problem was Olmsted's tendency to throw all his energies and passion into his work and then to break down both from exhaustion and the mental strain of personal conflicts. His first breakdown at the park, it will be remembered, came after his marriage to his brother's widow. A brief vacation at Saratoga Springs failed to improve things, and it was only a few days after his return to the job that Olmsted had informed his father: "I feel just thoroughly worn out, used up, fatigued beyond recovery, an older man than you."[27] The solution, either proposed or endorsed by Green, was that Olmsted should make a trip abroad at the city's expense, ostensibly to further study the parks of England and the Continent, but primarily to recover his health.

Unfortunately for Olmsted, while he was gone, Green was formally elected Treasurer and Comptroller and took over active superintendence of the park work—a fact that was duly recorded in complaining letters to Olmsted abroad from his wife and subordinates. One of these reveals not only the nature of Green's management of affairs, but also the secret both of Olmsted's managerial success and of the loyalty he won from his subordinates.[28] "Your successor at the helm [Green] does not know much of human nature," the drainage engineer, Waring, wrote Olmsted. He described Green as acting "cross & crabbed" with everyone, cracking his whip "over good & bad indiscriminately." Consequently, Waring added, it seemed as if every one of the park's employees, from "chief to water-boy . . . does less work than he did under your system of placing some confidence in men's sense of honor & duty."

The escalating costs of the construction also opened the door for the Democrats to attack the management of the park. In an earlier report to the Board, Olmsted had blamed these cost overruns upon the pressure to get the park in shape for public use as fast as possible, which had been accomplished "in fifteen months from the beginning of work, instead of four years, as contemplated in the estimates of the designers [Olmsted and Vaux]."[29] But continued rising costs provided fuel for political attacks on the park management by the Tammany Democrats. The *New York Leader*, a Democratic weekly, would assail the Republican and Reform Democrat Commissioners as "imbecile and corrupt" and claim that "millions of the public money" had been squandered on the work at Central Park.[30] Early in 1860, Olmsted informed his father than a "very energetic and unscrupulous lobby" was at work in the State Legislature at Albany. In fact, Olmsted had recently been informed by an insider that his allies were then fighting two Democratic bills: one to abolish the Park Commission altogether and another that would replace it with a Board including New York City's Mayor, Comptroller, and Street Commissioner. These bills failed, but in mid-April the State Legislature authorized an investigation "into the condition, affairs, and progress" of Central Park.[31]

It was in the midst of the Senate investigation (August 1860) that Olmsted had his near-fatal carriage accident. As the investigation intensified that fall (and Olmsted struggled with Green for authority over the park work), Olmsted was still very much crippled by the accident. He wore a splint and was "tightly bandaged from toe to hip," his knee so stiff that he could not sit in a chair or turn over in bed. When the weather was good, he made an occasional foray around the park, "toted about on the litter chair."[32] The worried Republicans on the Board had every reason to listen to Green's demands for ever-greater cost control and to deliver increasing authority into his hands, authority through which, it seemed to Olmsted, Green attempted to gain full control over the management of the park.

Throughout the growing conflict, Roper writes, "Olmsted strove to behave toward Green with scrupulous subordination."[33] The frustration and anguish Olmsted endured at the park were largely vented through complaints, mostly directed to his new wife, Mary. Just a few months after her marriage to Frederick, Mary confessed that Green "frets me with his manner of thinking himself so much more efficient than you or any body else," but she nevertheless advised her husband not to work himself up "in the absurd manner" to which he was given.[34] But he *did* continue to aggravate himself privately over his submittal to Green, and the suppression of his rage only added to Olmsted's physical ailments.

An example of Olmsted's "scrupulous subordination" to Green may be seen in their disagreement over the destruction of some willow trees to make way for a drainage ditch. "It is quite expensive to get trees on the Park," Green wrote Olmsted, "and I hope nothing in [the] shape of a tree will be cut." After initially dismissing Green's complaint with a simple, dignified note, Olmsted later felt constrained to write a much longer, convoluted, and rather obeisant letter. Olmsted stated that he had always tried to inform Green of his intentions on all park matters and to be guided by Green's opinion, not out of "official courtesy or duty, but only on a sincere respect for your final judgment and a willingness to sacrifice my own convictions in matters of small consequence to maintain a hearty cooperation of will in our work." But Olmsted added that he had nevertheless assumed that where there was a difference of opinion between the two of them in a matter such as this one, his (Olmsted's) judgment should control the decision. "If I am wrong," Olmsted said, "I only desire to be informed of it to more scrupulously avoid the like error in the future," and he indicated that if Green did so inform him, he would be take care not to be "betrayed into neglecting or overstepping" his responsibility.[35]

The succinctness and directness of Green's comment (and of Olmsted's original reply) need only be compared to the flowery circumlocution of Olmsted's second response to suggest the degree to which his problems with Green lay in his own unwillingness or inability to hold to a firm, no-nonsense stance. If Green *had* been bent upon achieving total responsibility for all superintendence of the park work, it seems to me that such a response from Olmsted could only have encouraged him in his ambition, presuming that any resistance from Olmsted would be ineffectual. A more determined executive would either have ignored Green's further comment altogether or simply informed Green firmly that such a decision was the executive's to make until such time as the Board cared to relieve him of his duties. Indeed, M. M. Graff cites the firmness with which Andrew Jackson Downing had handled a similar problem when called upon to design the Capitol grounds and Mall in Washington, D.C. Would Green have behaved differently toward Olmsted and Vaux, she wonders, "if one of them had stood up to him with equal resolution?"[36] In January of 1861, Olmsted did finally take such a course of action, rebelling against the subordinate position in which he had been placed at Central Park. In an effort to regain his lost autonomy, he submitted his resignation to the Board of Commissioners.

The growing rupture between the one-time colleagues Olmsted and Green mirrored the growing rupture in the Union itself, which had been taking place since Lincoln's election in November. By the time of Olmsted's resignation gambit, the secession of six states had taken place. Only the month before, Olmsted had told Brace: "We intend to have two republics, peaceably if we can, fighting, if we must, don't we? *But my mind is made up for a fight.* The sooner we get used to the idea, the better, I think."[37]

Several months later, Olmsted would identify with the Union in an extremely personal way after the disaster at Bull Run. "I am overwhelmed, I have suffered intense humiliation," Olmsted wrote Mary after the defeat.[38] A similar mechanism may have been at work here. Olmsted's obsessive immersion in the work of Central Park may have been a way in which he defended himself against the raging conflicts within himself and with Green—conflicts that were magnified by the similar struggles then taking place within his society.[39] Olmsted's sudden marriage to his brother's widow could be seen as another sort of defense —his personal expression of the social "cult of domesticity," his attempt to create for himself a haven from the conflicts that surrounded him.[40] When such defenses failed, he could well have made up his mind for a fight, for the park as well as for the Union.

In the course of a very long presentation to the Board explaining his reasons for resigning, Olmsted revealed the essence of his inner conflicts and ambivalences, as well as his relationship to the Board and to Green. This presentation also makes it clear, once again, that Olmsted was unable to communicate his anger, his deep hurt and resentment, in blunt, unequivocal terms. Thus he struck out the following passage, which had apparently set forth his dissatisfactions too forthrightly: "The system of the park is in fact one which, in some respects I do not at all approve, which I have no heart in, which I do not myself harmonize with, and in which I feel myself unable to succeed." Further, Olmsted repeatedly struck out direct references to "the Comptroller [Green]" when reciting actual incidents of bureaucratic obstruction.[41] He persistently denied that he had any quarrel with Green as a person, much less as a rival.

However, the presentation did make it clear that Olmsted was suffering not only from Green's domination and harassment, but also from what he took to be the Board's loss of respect and confidence in him. And the presentation made it clear that such respect and confidence was as important to him as the park itself. It is possible that Olmsted had always had a need to prove himself to John Olmsted and to the other representative fathers in his life—to wrest from any and all of them the gratification (acceptance and respect) that he had yearned for from his childhood as an outsider. What Olmsted had sought, and had found in his middle years, was the work that was worthy of this need to prove himself, and worthy also of his other, inner, creative needs.

Olmsted had found such a work first at Central Park and then later at the Sanitary Commission. Having found this work, Olmsted could, in his middle years, turn from the idling "dilletante" into the obsessive hard worker and "doer." And Olmsted would insist on reminding these father figures of the burdens he had been forced to take upon himself in order to so prove himself. Thus, in the course of this resignation letter, he informed the Commissioners that he had worked himself to "the edge of brain-fever" and, frequently, to the kind of exhausted state that had led to his terrible carriage accident six months before. In 1863, as he closed out his two years at the Sanitary Commission, he would tell Henry Bellows that he had labored with all his "brains & blood" to fulfill the Executive Committee's requirements of him.[42] And to the father figure who counted most, to John Olmsted, Olmsted would write (in this same period): "As long as I keep my health, I suppose that you don't care how hard I work."[43] This helps us to understand the full meaning of Olmsted's sad lament upon his father's death: "the value of any success in the future is gone for me."[44]

This need for acceptance and recognition from authority figures was combined in Olmsted's inner world with the demands of sibling rivalry —the need for those representative fathers to recognize his position as first among his siblings, his peers. In his resignation presentation to the Central Park Board, Olmsted placed the Board in the role of the authoritarian father, from whom he had always sought recognition and vindication, casting himself as the good and dutiful son, reminding them of his "personal habit of discipline and loyalty." At the same time, he made it very clear that his sibling rival (Green) had usurped the prerogatives that had been due to Olmsted as the first-born, the first among his peers. "For two years," he reminded them, "I was denominated, I was, your sole executive officer," in which position "I selected, I engaged, and I fixed the pay of every officer, man & boy employed by my department on the park." From that exalted position, Olmsted had had a great fall. And the bitterness of Olmsted's fall can be seen in material he had removed from his manuscript: "I had . . . allowed my self to drift into a position of humiliation . . . I had a severe duty before me, for which I was insufficiently equipped." And, of his decision to resign he wrote: "I will not live thus humiliated in my conscience a single day."[45]

Olmsted's need for respect, for the visible signs of respect, was revealed in an incident involving the Central Park Keepers (park police). In the fall of 1860, as Olmsted was entering the critical phase of his conflicts with Green, he was invited to attend an excursion of the Keepers. In the draft of a note in which he disapproved of the excursion, Olmsted also struggled to explain the reasons for the deference he felt he was due from the Keepers. Olmsted argued that he was not to be deferred to because of his own "station in life" or his superior advantages of birth and education, as the correspondent had suggested. "There is no man among you who has it not in his power to obtain a better education than mine," Olmsted stated. After a passage marked by numerous cross-outs and revisions, Olmsted suggested that his higher station reflected only a "higher responsibility & [graver] larger duty," that must be "respected by you [under all circumstances]." "I require exact and formal marks of that respect," Olmsted stated, "but I require it no more for my own station than I require it for yours from those who are officially [your inferiors] below you in station." Olmsted's struggle in this passage seems to be that of a man who had considered himself (and who in many ways was) a democrat, but who nevertheless yearned for deference, and was trying to find a way to reconcile the two. It was the struggle of a man whose fragile self-esteem would always require "marks of that respect," from those in authority as well as from his own subordinates.[46]

Throughout the last few pages of Olmsted's resignation presentation to the Central Park Board—a rather dissembling discourse devoted to his relationship with Green—Olmsted continued to insist that he had no real quarrel with Green. Olmsted reported that "dozens of people" in the weeks preceding his presentation had asked him about his relations with Green. "I find it difficult to make these people believe that I am *not* at sword's points with Mr. Green," he complained. Olmsted most certainly *was* "at sword's point" with Green, and his use here of a symbol of phallic aggression is surely instructive as to the unconscious fears regarding their rivalry—the conflicts inherent in masculine competitiveness, conflicts related to the question of who will dominate and who will submit.

Three years later, writing to Vaux from his exile at the Mariposa Mining Estate, Olmsted turned to the subject of Green with a passion he had thus far subdued, a passion that mocks the mild words he had used about Green in the resignation presentation of January 1861:

I turned over my letter-book lately and it made me boil with indignation to see how cruelly and meanly Green had managed me—how entirely regardless he was of honor, generosity and truth, and what a systematic small tyranny, measured exactly by the limit of my endurance he exercised over me. It was slow murder. It made my head swim to read my studied and pathetic entreaties.[47]

As always, the superheated language employed by Olmsted signals the intensity of the inner conflicts it represents. It was in fact his own paralysis of will before Green's petty tyranny that made Olmsted's head swim and made him feel the victim of "slow murder." He was not, after all, still the helpless child who had no choice but to suffer the cruelty and meanness, the tyranny, he had found at Boggs's and Joab Brace's boarding schools. He was, theoretically, free to act—and that he had not acted speaks more to own his own weakness in this relationship than to Green's political skills. It was perhaps an unwillingness to face that fact that had led Olmsted for so long to mask the intensity of his anger from others and from himself.

Olmsted's inner feelings regarding his situation at Central Park were also made clear some eighteen months later, during that period at the Sanitary Commission when he persuaded himself that he had at last found an accepting and understanding father figure (Henry Bellows, as representative of the Sanitary Commission's Executive Board), one who had last given him the autonomy and respect he had sought. In a letter to Bellows, Olmsted compared the close scrutiny in petty matters that he had endured at the hands of Green and the Central Park Board with the trust and autonomy that Bellows and the Sanitary Commissioners had thus far shown him.[48] And Olmsted laid bare his relationship to the latter in these graphic terms: "at 40, I have the continuous *delight* of a good boy, in the consciousness that you are worldly wise in dealing with me in just the *unbusiness-like* way you do."

The first phase of Olmsted's long association with Central Park had actually been a glorious achievement. Fresh from his failure at Dix and Edwards and still smarting from his humiliations at the hands of Arthur Edwards and the newer humiliations delivered by Egbert Viele, Olmsted had succeeded as Superintendent of the park in making real the designs he and Vaux had created, had established the Park fundamentally as we know it today. But it was not his successes at the park that he carried forward with him over the next four years. What he carried with him was his bitterness toward the Central Park Board, which had failed to give him the unstinting support and respect he had yearned for. And as he continued to seek fulfillment through obsessive striving in a hotly competitive and conflicted society, his sense of having been defeated and humiliated by Andrew Green—a humiliation far greater than offered by Arthur Edwards or Egbert Viele—grew deeper.

CHAPTER 10

Architect in Chief of Central Park

In considering all that was accomplished during Olmsted's tenure as Architect in Chief of Central Park and the motivations that lay behind both the work and the personal conflicts he engaged in, it is important to distinguish between the two aspects of Olmsted's involvement with the park: design and superintendence. It was the *latter*, the position of Superintendent of the park, that had mattered most to him in the years before the Civil War. I would associate Olmsted's preoccupation with the superintendence of the park project, in great part, with the striving for practical success, for dominance and respect, that was foremost in his mind in the 1857–1865 period. His role as a designer of Central Park, the "art" role, as Calvert Vaux would describe it, was a form of inner retreat, in the way that all creative work is—a lonely sort of work, in which the artist must look into himself, have access to his own unconscious life, to find the materials for creative expression. It was Olmsted's unique genius that both aspects of his psyche contributed to the achievement that was Central Park.

Olmsted felt that the position of Superintendent of Central Park was ideally suited to his own talents and needs. He had campaigned for it and, having obtained it, had stretched it to suit his own nature and ambition. In 1860, Olmsted had told Brace that a Swiss engineer, appointed by the State Legislature to investigate the park project, had found its "organization and superintendence" to be "most excellent," the best by far of any public project in the United States. "I think it important to me that the public should know this & that I should have the credit of it," Olmsted had written. "I am anxious to remain Superintendent of the Park, that is."[1] Ambition for fame and desire for power were thus linked to this position.

On the other hand, as he told Vaux in 1863, the design function had come to him without his planning for it; it represented a "higher ambition" to which he had been brought by the "comradeship" of Vaux.[2] But the design function was much less suited to his needs and talents—"less instinctive, less engrossing and permanent in character." Had he and Vaux lost the design competition, he would still have been content as the Superintendent of the park. In fact, Olmsted said in that 1863 letter, he would never have entered the competition in the first place if he had thought that it might jeopardize the Superintendent position, a position he had acquired without Vaux's help. In making *him* the Architect in Chief of Central Park (rather than Vaux), Olmsted told Vaux, the Commissioners had simply recognized the preeminence of the superintendence function over the design function.

Olmsted tried, in this letter, to make it as clear as possible to Vaux that his need to hold singular and supreme authority over the construction and the public use of Central Park came from the depths of his being:

I am capable of stronger passions than many men and I never had a more desperate passion than that. Such things are not to be explained—It was part of a motive power in me which had its birth, and which I can [see?] had acted upon me long before it took the form in which you are concerned in it. A great deal of disappointed love and unsatisfied romance and downtrodden pride fastened itself to that passion, but there was in it at bottom a special distinctive individual passion of my nature also. All which to you is not only absurd as one man's passion always is to another, but it is childish and contemptible.

This 1863 letter to Vaux makes it clear that Olmsted's passion to be Superintendent of the park was much greater than had been his passion for the young women in his life; that this passion had its source in some more fundamental, perhaps elemental passion; that the motive force for that elemental passion was an intrinsic part of his being, "a special distinctive individual passion of my nature." Olmsted's word choices underline the fact that this "desperate passion" was one that, in its essence, had been created in the earliest years of his life. Its "birth," he says, took place long before it had achieved its present state. I believe that this elemental passion stemmed from his early childhood, from his longing after his lost mother—that the passion that drove him forward in Central Park and could be satisfied in no other way was the passion to be rejoined with his lost mother through the creation of the park.

The superintendence aspect of the Architect in Chief position was significant not only because of Frederick's psychological relationship to Central Park, but also because of his relationship to Calvert Vaux. After the tragic death of John Hull Olmsted, Calvert Vaux may have become the repository of most of what John Hull had meant to Frederick—the younger, better educated and perhaps more artistically talented comrade in arms. The first-born Frederick—predecessor of John Hull in their Hartford family and predecessor of Calvert Vaux in the Central Park project—was forced to assert his own prior rights with Vaux, just as he had with John Hull.

Frederick's chief "property" in Central Park, he told Vaux, was what he had possessed as Superintendent: "the influence and opportunity for the gratification of my own purposes which the position was the evidence of my having gained and of which it was the security." We must remember that it was at bottom the "gratification" of his motive passion that Olmsted was talking about. And it was both in the overt sense of the property of superintendence itself (authority and supremacy) and in the hidden sense of the motive passion invested in it that Olmsted told Vaux bluntly: "In this property you had no rights and you acquired none by arrangement with me." Similarly, in the writing of *Texas*, John Hull had unconsciously acquiesced to a similar claim by Frederick, though the claim had then been an unspoken one. Surely it had been tacitly agreed between them, concerning *Texas*, that the preeminence was to be Frederick's—not only in the credit for the book, but also in the gratification of the motive passion that had fed his need for fame.

While Olmsted clearly gave more weight to the superintendence function (bolstered perhaps by the fact that it was *this* function to which his "rights" were connected) than to the design function, he did have some ambivalence in this regard. When the Board notified Olmsted that he had been appointed Architect in Chief, Olmsted responded by informing them of "the personal feeling and *purposes*" with which he accepted the position. To make those purposes clear, Olmsted cited the words of his identity statement as he had set it forth in *Walks and Talks*.

What artist so noble as he who, with far reaching conception of beauty and designing power, sketches the outlines, arranges the colors, and directs the shadows of a picture upon which nature shall be employed for generations before the work he has prepared for her hand shall realize his intentions.[3]

The new position, then, was one that had fulfilled Olmsted's deepest inner feelings and true self's purposes—that is, it gratified that motive passion with which he had come to Central Park. Moreover, he recognized that he had been summoned to be the "noble artist" who would "sketch, arrange and direct" the great artwork he had set out for nature to execute. The position of Architect in Chief, Olmsted knew full well, was one in which he could satisfy all the elements of his ruling passion—both the need to create and the need for power and respect, both being and doing.

Nevertheless the superintendency was primary for Olmsted in these years. At the outset of the 1863 letter, he told Vaux: "I had a will—an ambition, a plan of life, in connection with the park, by which my conduct had been greatly moved before I knew you. Under its influence I had obtained the position of Superintendent of the Park—this before I knew [you], before I entertained the idea of having anything to do with the design or with you." Moreover, Olmsted said that it was the superintendency that had given him public fame, not the winning of the design competition. Even if he and Vaux had lost the design competition, Olmsted stated, he would still have had the position he was most interested in, Superintendent of the park, and "should have held it in all probability, to this day." In that position, he added near the end of the letter, he would have been "nearly as well known to the public."

Implied by Olmsted's comment was the truth that the public would have loved Central Park no matter whose design had been executed. Clearly, the particular design he and Vaux had created was more important to *them* than to the public, was meant to satisfy their own inner aesthetic rather than a public demand. Thus, as was usually the case with Olmsted, the work itself was more important than the public for whom that work was intended. People at large were worthy of consideration only to the degree to which they could be made to appreciate his creation.

At the outset of his work on the park, Olmsted pointed out to Vaux, he had been concerned only with executing a design he had then supposed would be Viele's. "My office extended in its term beyond that of the execution of the design," Olmsted wrote. "By express terms I was made responsible for the *use* to be made of the completed park—independent of the *designer*." This was to Olmsted the most essential responsibility, because it was crucial to him that the work he was creating be permanent, and this permanence could be obtained only by educating the public in the "customs of usage" of such a park, thus "gaining the public regard and respect for it." Olmsted stated that it was in the exercise of his "natural gift" for this latter task that he had been "worth most to the park." The success he and Vaux had achieved in the design and creation of the park, Olmsted said, "was made much more complete and permanent and unquestionable and advantageous" through *his* success in thus educating the public. In this sense, then, Olmsted the Superintendent had served the interests of Olmsted the designer and had been responsible for the validation of his true self's purposes—a validation that could be accomplished only through "public regard and respect" for the park.

The park Olmsted had sought to create in New York and was so anxious to educate the public to appreciate and to use properly was also the kind of park that had been, and continued to be, his own refuge. Olmsted told Vaux that he (Olmsted) would have been satisfied to be nothing else than Superintendent of the park, if only for the opportunity this position offered for spending a good deal of his life *in* the park, "watching over it and [cherishing?] it in every way—living in it [and] being a part of it." The feeling thus gratified was one of long standing, Olmsted stated. "While others gravitated to pictures, architecture, Alps, libraries, high life and low life, when travelling I had gravitated towards parks," he said, adding:

and this with no purpose whatever except a gratification which came from sources which the Superintendence of [Central] Park would have made easy and cheap to me, to say the least, every day of my life. What I wanted in London and in Paris and in Brussels and everywhere I went in Europe, what I wanted in New York in 1857, I want now *and this from no regard for Art or Fame or Money.* (Emphasis Olmsted's.)

As it happens, Olmsted had cared very much about art and fame, if not money. Yet it is equally true that there was a driving motive that set

18. The buildings at Mount St. Vincent's Convent in Central Park. After his marriage to Mary, Frederick got permission to move his new family into apartments in these buildings. It was an ideal situation for Olmsted—both living in and working on Central Park. (The New-York Historical Society.)

Olmsted to visiting parks when alone in any crowded city—and that driving motive was certainly a more critical one than art or fame or money. It will be remembered that until September 1857, Olmsted had been living and working in the dense, crowded, and noisy center of Manhattan, the major exception being the period of his trip abroad, with its long, lonely, and conflict-filled stay in London. Upon becoming Superintendent of Central Park, Olmsted had taken on new offices far from midtown Manhattan—in an old farmhouse at the edge of the park on Fifth Avenue, opposite Seventy-ninth Street, "which is a graded, paved & lighted street, from the 3rd avenue cars to the door." After marrying John Hull's widow, Olmsted had applied for and had received the right to make his home and office at the Mount St. Vincent Convent on the

Central Park grounds.[4] Indeed what Olmsted had "wanted in New York in 1857" was the refuge, the haven Central Park had so uniquely offered him, a haven made more complete by the acquisition of a wife and family —*John Hull's* wife and family. I am reminded of Christopher Lasch's phrase for the nineteenth-century conception of home and family: "haven in a heartless world." But *this* home had been established in the bosom of the idealized environment mother, Dame Nature.

Calvert Vaux tried hard to measure fully the depths of Olmsted's feelings and the full meaning behind the words of that 1863 letter. In reply, Vaux wrote Olmsted:

> I have received your letter [and] it makes me sick and sad but I know that I have but one feeling towards you which is and always had been sweet and pure. My error seems to have arisen thus. When we went into the competition I knew you were superintendent, but did not attach the meaning to the word that you did.[5]

Vaux added that for all the unique strengths Olmsted had brought to the Park, he (Vaux) had contributed strengths of his own: "to me it seemed that I brought as much as you to the park[,] that I brought education, special fitness to take up new problems, a love of the race, a love of the park and all it meant intellectually and that I worked faithfully and fraternally with you throughout." Now it was more clear than ever, Vaux said, that "we had a joint title you did not believe in."

Renewing the argument sixteen months later, Vaux put the matter more bluntly. Olmsted's attitude, Vaux charged, was: "all theirs is ours[,] all ours is mine—and all mine is my own. . . . I must have the reputation —and I must have it all—and I must have it immediately and I must have it always."[6] In this, Vaux had cut through to the heart of Olmsted's narcissism—his complete absorption in his own needs and purposes, which so often crowded out any perception of the needs and purposes of friends and family. And it was an assessment that Olmsted did not quarrel with or deny. But what, then, had Vaux seen in Olmsted that had led Vaux to value his partner so highly?

I suggest that Vaux very shrewdly had seen in Olmsted an equal measure of Utilitarian and Romantic—the false selfhood of the "doer," the practical man, the Superintendent, and the true selfhood of the "be-er," the creator, the "head artist" (as Vaux called him). Vaux tried in his letters, that spring of 1865, to summon Olmsted once again to a "higher ambition," to call him into the services of art—the only thing that had permanence, the thing by which Olmsted's worth must ultimately be measured.

There was Central Park to be saved from the Commissioners and the new Brooklyn park, which, Vaux wrote early in May, "is all our own."[7] It was their right, in fact, "to control matters from Washington Heights to the other side of Brooklyn." But Vaux first had to summon his quondam partner back from what Vaux rightly saw as an exile. Olmsted had not given him much moral support thus far in this effort, Vaux wrote, adding: "alone I am a very incomplete Landscape Architect and you are off at the other end of the world depriving the public of your proper service." It was the Romantic artist that Vaux was summoning back to prepare for "the day of battle" against the philistine Utilitarians. It had been foolish for Olmsted to use "management against management" in the struggle for the control of the Park's destiny, Vaux said.

Art against Commission is easily understood. Now we can say take your Reports and account books. We will take our Park. I have always upheld your art position hoping that you would some day realise that it was your best foundation to build whatever you want on. You were in too great a hurry I think.

Vaux used, as an example, Olmsted's bitter rivalry with Andrew Haswell Green. Although Vaux disliked Green nearly as much as did Olmsted, Vaux suggested that much of the latter's problems with Green had been self-created. Green's claims for a leading position should have been given consideration, Vaux said: "he had earned it." "I always felt you know that you were a little insatiable in your ambition," Vaux added, "and that your theory left no room for Green or anybody else—and that we ought to have provided for him."

In another letter that May, Vaux got to the heart of his argument.[8] The issue was to discover what was uppermost in Olmsted's nature: the Romantic artist who worked for the public good or the Utilitarian power-seeker who worked only for his own good. Had he really believed that the latter was the real Olmsted, Vaux said, "I would . . . unhesitatingly have set to work to plough you under with the firm conviction that you were no friend to art[,] no friend to the good cause and only a somewhat ambitious self-seeker." Vaux believed that he had had the "perceptive quality" required to see through Olmsted's "course of action to its foundation head" and to find the artist who was hidden behind the man of affairs.

In all this I may be mistaken. You may be no artist. You may be Nap[oleon] III in disguise[,] you may be a selfish fellow—who would like to get power & reputation on other mens brains—You may be a money-grubber[.] You may have no patience &tc &tc—but . . . I am under the impression that the humble artist spirit is within you.

It was between these poles, these opposing perceptions of Olmsted, that Vaux kept oscillating on into the summer of 1865 in his effort to cajole Olmsted out of what all his colleagues seemed to regard as an exile. The argument was the same: give up worldly ambition and devote yourself to art and to the republic. It was not impossible that artists could be "energetic men of affairs also," Vaux wrote in June, so long as art was primary, and this applied "especially to the Park the big art work of the Republic."[9]

In late June or early July, Vaux apparently received letters from Olmsted that set forth a new plan for the park work, but one still based upon the notion that design issues must be subordinated to general management ("a semi-barbaric idea that you share with others," Vaux said). In response to these letters, Vaux returned a final time to his view of the two Olmsteds: "Olmsted the artist & republican with whom I could heartily act and sympathize—and . . . Olmsted the bureaucrat and imperialist with whom I could never for a moment sympathize," bitterly adding:

the realization of 'your plan' is unlikely if by that I understand the conversion of this many sided, fluent thoroughly American high art work into a machine—over which as Frederick the Great, Prince of the Park Police you should preside, and with royal liberality dispense certificates of docility to the artists engaged in the work—all of this side of the affairs is nauseating & odious.[10]

Vaux's comment here about Olmsted offering "certificates of docility to the artists" struck hard at Olmsted's need for deference from his peers, a need, I think, that was akin to claiming the rights of the first-born from one's siblings. Olmsted's new plan, Vaux said, actually represented a return to the past, when Olmsted had taken the Park "out of the region of high art" and "stifled it down to Green's level," only to find that Green had taken it away from them—which Green was after all bound to do "in self defense." Olmsted's new plan still gave Green nothing and was "unrepresentative and undemocratic." Who did Olmsted represent "outside of the Park Police?" Vaux asked: "nobody."

Vaux seemed to long for the sweet and exhilarating intimacy of the days in which they had produced their Greensward design—an equal partnership. But in the months that had followed Olmsted's appointment as Architect in Chief, Olmsted had sought power and dominance. He had sacrificed intimacy, whose principal reward is a sharing of mind, of experience, and of dreams. In a letter of early July, Vaux expressed his view of this aspect of Olmsted in bitter terms. Olmsted had objected to Vaux's plan for their future work on the New York parks, Vaux wrote, "because it involves the idea of a common fraternal effort[,] it is too republican an idea for you, you must have a thick line drawn all around your six [pence?] worth of individuality." And, equally bitterly, Vaux recalled the picture of Olmsted busy as the Architect in Chief of Central Park—"your porcupine arrangement of Foremans reports 70 to each pocket and one in your mouth so that you never had a word to say to a friend." In this same letter, Vaux indicated that Olmsted's "insatiable egoism" would have driven him with "tremendous power" toward an authoritarian role in all park activities, except that his ambitions had been derailed by Andrew Green's "dirty tricks."[11]

Surely, as Vaux says, it was a thirst for power that had turned Olmsted into "Frederick the Great, Prince of the Park Police." And surely, Olmsted's notion of "a common fraternal effort" was one that established *him* as the first among equals. "I am no Fourierist for myself," Olmsted had admitted in 1852. But there was simply no other way for Olmsted to accomplish his deepest purposes except through his obsessive competitive striving. During his first year in Washington, D.C., for the Sanitary Commission, Olmsted would tell Henry W. Bellows: "I am one of those men who work best with a strong head of steam on." He would also take note of the possibility that his "towering ambition" might lead him to "neglect the humbler duties."[12]

But in assessing Olmsted's purposes at Central Park, we should remember Winnicott's observation that we often forgive an individual's aberrations because that person "has so rich a personality that society may gain through the exceptional contribution he or she can make."[13] So it was with Olmsted, whose thirst for power served society's needs. Much as it gratified his thirst for power, the Superintendent's office Olmsted had so coveted had also allowed him to create both a new kind of park and an "ideal audience" for the enjoyment of that creative work. Daniel Dervin has written that the "audience, reader, or patron" for a creative work acts the part of "the idealized adoptive parents" of the artist, who, by accepting the artist's reconstructed vision of himself as expressed in his work, allow him to overcome his narcissistic wounds, his inner sense of being flawed.[14] Ultimately, Central Park would, for Olmsted, stand or fall on the degree to which it satisfied his most fundamental, and largely unconscious, objective: the expression of his own true self, his supreme act of declaring his identity, an act of creativity that was, also, a suitable act of reparation to his lost mother.

Both in the Greensward plan and in the initial reports to the Park Commissioners, Olmsted and Vaux had given due recognition to one of the leading purposes for an urban park—a purpose that had motivated Downing and the patrician intellectuals and civic leaders who had led the fight for Central Park. This was, as David Schuyler points out, that the park would be "an instrument of moral improvement through a theory of social reform [Downing] called 'popular refinement.' "[15] But Olmsted had a more urgent, inner-driven purpose, meeting a far more important psychosocial need: to put within reach of harried city-dwellers a naturalistic preserve totally screened off from the crowded, teeming city adjacent to it. On the massive rectangle of barren, swampy, rock-strewn acreage he had been given, he hoped to create a man-made replication of nature. Not nature as it was to be found helter-skelter in the rural Connecticut of his youth; rather, artfully selected passages of natural scenery, each designed and crafted to offer yet another pleasure to the mind, another form of restoration to the beleaguered psyche. Chief among these and the most restorative in Olmsted's schema was the pastoral scene, the rolling meadow offset by trees and water.

In later years, Vaux stated that Olmsted had from the start seen Central Park as "a finished thing . . . as an oasis, an arcadia in the desert of brick & mortar vibrant with happy life from morning to night." Vaux held that Olmsted's strong point in the design of the park was his recognition of "the human element in it."[16] Though Olmsted himself did not fully evolve or put before his gentry peers a philosophy of urban park design until after the Civil War, it is clear that, as Vaux suggests, he had had his own inner purposes from the start—and that this inner vision stemmed from the motive passion he described in his long letter to Vaux. It is in light of this motive passion that the exhausted Olmsted's words to his father, written in the fall of 1859, must be read: "I feel just thoroughly worn-out, used up, fatigued beyond recovery, an older man than you, and am determined to let the park take care of itself for a while at whatever cost. . . . I have fixed *what I most care for on the park beyond reconsideration* & shall not be so zealous probably in the future." Six months later, after the New York Legislature initiated its investigation into the park's management, Frederick told his father that he did not have much to fear from this inquiry, adding: "at all events they can't destroy the present which is ours—."[17]

Whom did Olmsted represent, Vaux had asked, beyond the park police? "Nobody," he had declared, but that was hardly the correct answer. Olmsted represented the public for which he had become the delegate, but a public that had to be led by him and educated by him (via his rules and regulations for park usage, enforced by the park police), so as to be reborn as the "ideal audience" for his great creative work, his pastoral urban park. If he was their delegate, they would become *his* disciples. And through their discipleship, his work might eventually be appreciated, his true self might ultimately be vindicated.

It was, in fact, *this* aspect of his work on the park that Olmsted had made the heart of his argument in his resignation letter of January 1861 to the Board of Commissioners. Olmsted began that resignation presentation by reaffirming the fundamental truth of his relationship to this great work: "I could nowhere in the world put to better use such talent as I possess, or live with more satisfaction to my taste and inclinations, than on the Central Park."[18] But what is most interesting is that Olmsted was here led to employ the very argument that Vaux would urge upon him four years later: art versus money. Olmsted here put forth the notion that *his* artistic sense and purposes were superior, when assessing the needs of the park, to the Board's dollars-and-cents point of view. In arrogating the ultimate responsibility for the design and the fulfillment of the design to himself, Olmsted assessed the Board's duties as that of "cashiers and accountants" who should leave all the details of the work to the "prudence" and "judgment" of the designer of the park (Olmsted). Twenty years later, a similar argument would become Olmsted's final public word on Central Park in his embittered pamphlet, *Spoils of the Park*.

Olmsted had earlier in the letter to the Board asserted that no proposal of his for the work on the park had ever been made in order to increase his own authority. Moreover, he added, "I have never intimated *my real need*, my personal judgment as to my needs—*to the needs of the work*, in this respect—to the Board . . . that I have not seen evidence that my statements were regarded with incredulity." The words I have emphasized reveal that Olmsted had associated the needs of the park with his own inner needs. The two were necessarily interrelated, for the needs of the park, as he conceived the park, could only be fulfilled when it succeeded *both* as his great reparative work for his lost mother and as the expression of his creative self. It was in this sense that Olmsted spoke a profound truth when he told the President of the Board in this letter, "I don't care a copper for myself, Sir, or for what becomes of me, but I do care for the park, which will last after I'm dead & gone, years & years, I hope." It was to that end, he added, that his superintendence was dedicated—"to have the work well done upon it . . . honestly and surely and carefully and *certainly* well done."

Nowhere, in all of Olmsted's writings, does he lay out the psychological foundations of his attachment to Central Park—its fundamental connection both to his true self and false self and to the existential mediation between them—as clearly as in this passage:

> I shall venture to assume to myself the title of artist and to add that no sculptor, painter or architect can have anything like the difficulties in sketching and conveying a knowledge of his design to those who employ him. . . . *The design must be almost exclusively in my imagination.* No one but myself can feel, and without feeling no one can understand, *at the present time*, the true value or purport of much that is done on the park, or much that needs to be done. Consequently, except *under my guidance* these pictures can never be perfectly realized and if I am interrupted and another hand takes up the tools, *the interior purpose which has actuated me* will be very liable to be thwarted, and *confusion and a vague discord* result. Does the work which has thus far been done accomplish *my design?* No more than stretching the canvas & chalking a few outlines, realizes the painter's.[19]

It was Olmsted's point that what had been accomplished thus far had been merely rude construction work, that the finishing artistic work was still to come. This had been the sense of his comment to Brace a month earlier that it was still too soon "to estimate the merit of the park as a work of Art." Yet he was now asking the Park Commissioners to trust in

19. The northern section of the park in the early 1860s, still under construction, looking southwest from near 102nd Street and Fifth Avenue, toward the new Croton Reservoir in the distance. The Boston Post Road cuts across the middle of the scene. (Prevost Collection, Rare Books and Manuscripts Division, The New York Public Library, Astor, Lenox and Tilden Foundations.)

his vision as an artist even more than in his judgment as an executive. And it was in this same vein that Olmsted complained to a supporter a month later that Andrew Green's tight-fisted budgetary control tied his (Olmsted's) hands "just where it is of the highest importance that I should operate with an artist's freedom and spirit."[20]

The resignation itself and his stance as an artist were certainly tactical ploys aimed at regaining complete control over the park. Olmsted probably chose to put the argument in artistic terms here because it was the only area left in which he could still claim superiority to the judgments of Green and the Board. If his argument were to be accepted by the Board at face value, then it would follow that Olmsted should be given complete control over the work, and a free hand to spend as he saw fit—a *"liberal* superintendence," Olmsted called it. Nevertheless, the argument Olmsted made here was also a genuine expression of an inner selfhood that he was still uncertainly struggling to realize—and it is as a reflection of his *inner* purposes that his words are so revealing.

After more than three years work on Central Park, Olmsted had come to regard it as completely his own, originating "almost exclusively in [his] imagination," meeting the "interior purpose which had actuated" him. It was now *his* design, *his* work, meeting *his* interior purposes, and there was no part in it for the purposes of a Green, a Viele, or even a Calvert Vaux (just as Vaux himself would charge in 1865). If this seems to present Olmsted in a selfish, exploitive light, then I must add that it was precisely because Central Park had come to represent both his necessary reparative work and the expression of his true self (his creative self) that he had accomplished so much under great bureaucratic handicaps and extreme personal stress. In this light, this defense of the work as *his* work was absolutely crucial to the inner survival of his sense of true self. For only in this way could he justify not only his obsessive competitive striving for power, position, domination, but also the price he had had to pay in physical and mental torments.

Indeed, Olmsted had always believed that only the future could judge how well he had succeeded at his task (and in his inner purposes)—something he had made clear to the Board in the letter in which he had accepted position of Architect in Chief. "In the first and highest responsibility of the office," Olmsted had written in April 1858, "I shall steadfastly regard the distant future, when alone it can be fully seen how far I am worthy of [this position]." And eighteen months later, when discussing the park with the publisher of the *Atlantic Monthly*, Olmsted had stated: "in the next century, it must be held a work of Art, or a failure."[21] In other words, it had been bequeathed to future generations to validate his True Self (the artist self) and, thus, his true worth—something that would have been beyond the capacity of Green and the other commissioners to assess.

But Olmsted's words to the publisher may also have pointed to his deepest fear, a fear greater even than loss of the superintendency of the park work—a fear that the work might ultimately be judged a failure after all. I believe that it was in fact such a fear that lay behind a curious passage in his resignation presentation. In this passage, Olmsted stated that the Board had given him certain assignments to accomplish in his role as Superintendent and Architect in Chief, but that there was no hope that he could succeed at these tasks under the limitations imposed by the Board. And his failure to complete those tasks, he said, could only lead one to believe that he was a "swindler" or an "imposter." To such an imagined charge, Olmsted could only cry out: "I am *not* an imposter, Sir. I am *not* responsible in those particulars." If he had sailed under the "false colors" of Superintendent and Architect in Chief, it was the Board that had made them false by taking away his autonomy.[22]

It is also possible that Olmsted had other reasons for fearing that he had been sailing under "false colors" in his role as master of Central Park. Olmsted was acutely sensitive to being thought an "enthusiast" and "impractical"—attributes that had feminine associations in a highly competitive society that made a virtue of "manliness." On one level, therefore, the role of Chief Architect and Superintendent—of the highly organized, tough-minded taskmaster and doer—was perhaps that of a False Self meant to mask that far more sensitive, passive, and vulnerable (and thus more "feminine") child and youth who had so loved to daydream under a tree. And yet, there is nothing essentially wrong with that, if the "screen identity" (false self) is a protector and facilitator, but the hidden identity (true self) actually determines one's crucial decisions and life goals.[23]

Olmsted's impassioned rhetoric suggests the degree of inner (and perhaps unconscious) conflict he felt in regard to the role he had assumed. Did the title of Superintendent and Chief Architect (which he had aspired to, gloried in, and yearned so to hold onto) truly represent Olmsted's identity—not only in the sense of holding real authority on the park, but also in the sense that it accurately reflected his inner selfhood and all that he had aspired to? Was he truly a responsible, practical manager? Or was he an artist, an idealist, a dreamer? And if he was truly the latter, then was not his pose as "doer," a practical man, the man in charge, an imposture, even a swindle?[24]

Moreover, even as an artist, it would have been his duty to achieve perfection in his creative work. For the inability to do so would also raise the fear of being exposed as an impostor, even a swindler: the world at large might see the shortcomings in the work and say, "This is not the work of an artist; we have been cheated." In this light, Olmsted was perfectly sincere when he wrote in his resignation letter that he had never once had been in the lower part of the park without experiencing "shame, disappointment, discouragement," because he felt himself "disgraced" by the failures to fulfill his design intentions that had been occasioned by financial and administrative obstacles. It was surely true that the value of the park to him—as a reparative work and as an expression of his true self—could only be fully realized through perfection. That "thousands & thousands of people" (who were to be his ideal audience) should find less than perfection in this work would surely cause him "disgrace." It was, therefore, just as he had told the publisher of the *Atlantic Monthly:* if future generations were to judge Central Park anything less than "a work of Art," then it would be a failure.

Psychoanalytic theory posits that there are no negatives in the unconscious, and that the more desperate such a cry, the more likely it is to mean the opposite of what has been said. Thus Olmsted's indignant cry —"I am *not* an imposter"—may well have expressed his deepest fear, that in his proud assumption of the roles of Superintendent and Architect in Chief of Central Park, he was indeed an imposter.

In the end, Olmsted's resignation presentation failed in its purpose of reestablishing his supremacy on the park work. He was persuaded to withdraw it while he and the Board continued to negotiate his position during the ensuing weeks. "My deferred crisis is now imminent," he wrote his father in March, and he added that he would rather take his "chances for a living elsewhere, than to stay & be humiliated." [25] And a few days later he asked the Board to appoint a special committee to examine his plans for the park construction, in the hope that he would achieve "the freedom to act efficiently and according to his own necessities without waste of time in matters of form." [26]

At the beginning of June, the Commissioners relieved Olmsted of almost all responsibility for superintending the construction of the park. He was granted only responsibility for "the finishing operations" and given his choice of the staff, from among the park employees, to assist him. He was also granted the power to make expenditures up to $500 without specific authorization from Green. [27] Though it was framed as a concession to Olmsted's demand for autonomy, the Board's action simply confirmed his subordinate position.

Even while he was facing a defeat at the park, however, Olmsted still had other interests to pursue, interests that had the potential to redress the wounds of a loss to Green. In February, Olmsted had contracted with an antislavery journalist, Daniel R. Goodloe, to revise and condense the three books about Olmsted's Southern journeys into a single volume (*The Cotton Kingdom*), to be published by the New York firm of Mason Brothers. The two men corresponded throughout the spring both as to the revisions and about the new material Goodloe would be adding, and Olmsted surely expected (with the secession of the slave states) that the book would advance his reputation both in the "literary republic" and within northern political circles. "I read your letters when they first appeared in the Times," Goodloe, a native of North Carolina, told him, "and I was struck with their accuracy, in giving the very body and spirit of the South."[28]

Even more significantly, in April Olmsted was invited by Henry Bellows to become a member of board of directors of the Central Association for the Relief of the Sick and Wounded of the Army, which would become the Sanitary Commission. In mid-June, Olmsted was elected the General Secretary of the Sanitary Commission and, soon after, left for Washington. He retained the position of Superintendent of the park at half salary ($2,500) and was to receive $2,000 in his new position.[29]

Mary put a very good face on it all in writing to John Olmsted: "The appointment is a great honor to Fred, and the change in employment will do him good." But she apparently had made it clear to her husband that she regarded all this as a surrender to Green. It was an interpretation that Frederick could not accept, writing her: "I think you forget that the main purpose against Green was accomplished, and he doubtless felt himself beaten more than I did." If leaving the park was a form of "surrender," he added, "it is for what we both deem a good & sufficient remuneration —to be allowed to do my part directly in the war."[30] Mary's position, however, was supported by Olmsted's staunch ally, the drainage engineer, Waring, who wrote: "I am sorry that you did not demand the entire control [of the park construction work]; I think you could have received it." Waring advised Olmsted against taking the Sanitary Commission position, despite all the good he could do there, because he was " 'King bolt' to the Central Park."[31]

Indeed, Frederick would later react with an uncharacteristic show of anger toward his father when the latter apparently suggested (in 1863) that Frederick should have made a public fight against Green and the

Commission, rather than give up his position at the park. Frederick declared that there was nothing he would not have done to save that position—not out of pecuniary interest, as his father now urged, but out of "my ambition and pride and more than that—affection for my work and—moral obligation to do all that was possible for me to do to control so valuable an agency of civilization." Frederick insisted that he had devoted all those abilities that had gained him the position "with far greater effort and persistence to retain it." And he concluded: "It pains me that you should have the misfortune of supposing me to be so much less respectable a man than I am."[32] Frederick's response thus summed up so much of what practical success as Superintendent of Central Park had meant to him: competitive striving, self-esteem, the desire to do good work in the world, the wish to be in control, the need to earn his father's respect.

Olmsted's association with the metropolitan gentry—especially with journalists such as Raymond of the *Times*, Dana of the *Tribune*, and Bigelow of the *Post*—certainly gave him the means of appealing directly to the public (as when he had combatted the Dillon proposal to create a grand boulevard in the park). The situation was just as Vaux would state in 1863: "The public has been led to believe from the commencement of the Central Park work to the present time that you are pre-eminently the author of the executed design." The result of this, as Vaux noted in a letter of 1865, was that Olmsted had become "the representative man" of Central Park.[33] Indeed, that is the result Olmsted seems to have been striving for when he told Brace, several weeks before his resignation ploy, that he wanted "the public to know" that the Senate investigation had praised his management of the park work, that he wanted "to have the credit of it" and remain Superintendent of Central Park. A year earlier an English friend had endorsed Olmsted's strategy: "I am delighted to hear that you are so firmly seated on the back of the Public. If you continue to ride that horse right it must win the race against all others, 'Intrigue' 'Trading Politicians' or whatnot."[34]

However, it was surely not the public at large that Olmsted and his associates were referring to. It is true that Central Park had by 1861 become enormously popular—some 75,000 to 100,000 people a day were making use of it, Olmsted estimated.[35] But it is likely that the vast majority of these people had little knowledge of or concern for Olmsted's stewardship, or whether he, Green, or Mayor Wood himself superintended the work. (In the "representative man" letter, Vaux would tell Olmsted that "the majority of those who think of the matter at all suppose you still to be at work there"—that is, four years after Olmsted had left for the Sanitary Commission.) The Democratic press was, as we have seen, aligned against him. But the conservative press could be hostile too, as when the *Herald* observed that the park was "a dead failure," that neither in its "natural nor artificial beauties" did it meet "the requirements of good taste." Papers like the *Herald*, Olmsted felt, promoted the "fallacy of cowardly conservatism"—that is, the notion that respectable people would be driven from the park by the hooliganism of the lower classes flooding into it.[36]

The public Olmsted appealed to and whose support he had enlisted through Raymond, Dana, and Bigelow consisted of the enlightened, civic-minded members of the patrician and gentry classes for whom he surely was the "representative man." George Templeton Strong spoke for such New Yorkers when he pronounced Central Park a success both as a managerial achievement and as a work of art—"*Rus in Urbe*," he called it.[37]

Thus, when the publisher of the *Atlantic Monthly* asked Olmsted who might be qualified to write a suitable appreciation of Central Park, one of those mentioned by Olmsted was "Dr Bellows, who is 'one of yours' " and who had been "watching our work with much interest." Bellows was indeed selected to do the article and was conducted on a tour of the park by Olmsted. In his April 1861 article, Bellows hailed Olmsted as the "original designer, patient executor, potent disciplinarian, and model police-officer" of the park. Bellows also lauded the conception and execution of Central Park—"the beau ideal of a people's pleasure ground," he wrote. For Bellows, Central Park was a triumph of democracy, "developing, both in its creation and growth, in its use and application, new and almost incredible tastes, aptitudes, capacities and powers in the people themselves."[38]

It is therefore not surprising that Bellows enlisted Olmsted for the Sanitary Commission work at this same time, telling Olmsted: "Your acknowledged administrative talent is very much needed" and that "your services . . . cannot easily be dispensed with."[39] But then what was the reaction of Andrew Green and the other Commissioners when they read what Olmsted himself called "the tremendous puff on Fred in the World a week or two ago and the tremendouser one in the Atlantic of April"?[40] It was certainly such articles that would lead Vaux to describe Olmsted's attitude as: "I must have the reputation—and I must have it all."

The interrelationship of the patrician class and gentry elite in public life would be most notable in the organization of the Sanitary Commission. As noted in the introduction, George Frederickson has suggested that "the motives of the elite that ruled the [Sanitary Commission] were more complicated" than the legend of simple benevolence that it created for itself. The Commission, he states, "was a predominantly upper-class organization, representing those patrician elements which had been vainly seeking a function in American society." He argues that the Sanitary Commission was ruled in "supremely authoritarian manner" by a "small but increasingly confident coterie who favored a much more conservative idea of government and society." Such "conservative activists," Frederickson argues, hoped to create cultural institutions in America that would be instruments for "social control" over the population at large.[41]

Certainly, the eastern leadership of the Sanitary Commission (men like George Templeton Strong, Wolcott Gibbs, Cornelius Agnew, and others) not only represented the American gentry as defined by Stow Persons; most of them also represented, as Frederickson suggests, a gentry segment with a decided patrician tinge—men from established families who had, through their own talents, created positions for themselves in the professions of medicine, law, and higher education.

While Frederickson has focused upon the element of social control that lay behind the "educative" function (to use Olmsted's word) of the Sanitary Commission, Thomas Bender points out that almost *all* of the activities of the gentry elite were so inclined—and were encompassed within the broadest possible claims for "the moral authority of cultivation" and undertaken under the assumption that for "individuals who embraced culture (and its cognates, cultivation, education, civilization), the prize was . . . special authority and, perhaps, responsibility."[42] It was to this group that the men of Bender's "metropolitan gentry"—"talented newcomers" like Olmsted and Bellows—aspired through their service to gentry causes. At the Sanitary Commission, both Olmsted, as General Secretary, and Bellows, as President of the Executive Committee, would serve (indeed, help define) the Union cause of the gentry elite.

Olmsted's ability to serve the needs of his wealthier patrons was indicated in his response to the assignment he and Vaux received in July of 1860 from a special commission of the New York State Senate to lay out the upper wards of Manhattan (above 155th Street), generally referred to as the Washington Heights area. One of the attractions of the assignment for Olmsted—beyond the $2,500 fee and the "chance for further employment"—was, as he told his father, the fact that the area consisted of "1800 acres of very rugged & beautiful ground—unpracticable to be brought into the square street & avenue system of the rest of the island."[43] Olmsted detested the gridiron system with which Manhattan had been laid out by the Commissioners Plan of 1811 and which was, by midcentury, immutable in the greatest portion of the island. In his mind, this system served to condense the greatest amount of population and buildings into the smallest possible space, making for a dreary and monotonous cityscape devoid of air and room and sunlight. David Schuyler, a contemporary critic of New York's grid system, argues that Olmsted's Washington Heights plan sought to provide "a residential enclave of villas and cottages" that would "attract those middle-class families who might otherwise move to suburbs in Brooklyn or New Jersey." But Jon Teaford also points out that the 1811 grid plan, while monotonous, was nevertheless egalitarian, "giving preference to no area and creating no preconceived bastions for an urban aristocracy." For Teaford, Olmsted's "suburban schemes laid the foundations for the class-segregated city of the twentieth century."[44]

The only evidence of Olmsted's thinking about Washington Heights, an unfinished letter to one of the Commissioners (and a resident of the area), tends to support Teaford's view that Olmsted sought to create aristocratic enclaves.[45] It is clear from this letter that the purpose of the project itself was to establish and preserve in the Washington Heights area an "elegant rural character" for the villas of wealthy New Yorkers, where they might live in "tranquility and seclusion." Other sections of Manhattan had once been the site of such villas, but these had since been abandoned by their owners. Olmsted blamed the deterioration of such once-rural areas on the extension of Manhattan's gridiron system of street layout, which provided major thoroughfares directly from the center of the city and access roads directly from these thoroughfares to the upper-class villas. Local businesses (merchants, taverns, breweries, and the like) were established along the main thoroughfares, while the side streets blossomed with "cheap tenements & boarding houses" that domiciled the "mechanics & laborers" who worked in the business establishments. Thus each area had turned "gradually from a quiet & secluded neighborhood . . . to be a noisy, dusty, smoking, shouting, rattling and stinking one."

To preserve the tranquil and secluded nature of these neighborhoods of the "rich and cultivated" families, Olmsted suggested (in his Washington Heights letter) that a different system of street design must be employed—one designed, for example, so that local merchants could not use "the heights' roads for any other purpose than to supply the wants of the residents." It would not be objectionable, he thought, to use such roads "for pleasure driving," which would both "confirm that the neighborhood was designed for leisure, not commercial, usage" and provide the residents with "the frequent recognition of friends of their own class." Although the unfinished letter provides few details for the actual design of the villa neighborhoods, Olmsted did, early in this letter, cite the example of fashionable neighborhoods in Liverpool and London, built upon crescents and cul-de-sacs, with gates at the entrances from the main thoroughfares to the access roads that wound through the neighborhood, and with a little park or commons in its center.[46]

Given Olmsted's powerful journalistic connections, and the fact that he had proven himself as one who could so well understand and serve the civic needs of the more aristocratic New Yorkers, the question remains: why did Olmsted not make a public fight against Green and the other Commissioners? In answer, we must remember that Andrew Green was himself well connected to the patrician and gentry circles of New York and that many of the other Commissioners belonged to those circles. It is therefore far from certain that Olmsted would have prevailed in a public quarrel. And to have made the fight public and lost would have been an even greater blow to his fragile self-esteem. Moreover, there was the essential truth that he stated to Commissioner Russell the year after leaving for the Sanitary Commission: to make a public quarrel with Green "would be playing into the hands of the enemies of the park."[47] It seems to me there is no question that, as Olmsted had so often insisted, the survival of Central Park in basic accordance with the Greensward plan (his true self's purpose) was ultimately more important to him than power or position. Pushed to a choice, the good of the park came first.

The Sanitary Commission and Mariposa

Olmsted divided the four years of the Civil War very nearly evenly between two years at the heart of the conflict, in Washington running the Sanitary Commission, and two years of exile in Bear Valley, California, presiding over the doomed Mariposa mining estate. Both enterprises represented a continuation of his ambitions for practical success, further investment in the various screen identities of competitive striving that masked the dreamer behind them. As at Central Park, Olmsted actually achieved remarkable managerial and administrative success in both ventures. And, as at Central Park, Olmsted resigned from both with a profound sense of having failed in his purposes.

The story of Olmsted at the Sanitary Commission is perhaps the richest and most compelling of his long, productive life.[1] The story of his work at Mariposa is, in comparison, quite arid. And yet the Sanitary Commission very nearly depleted his physical and emotional resources, while the Mariposa exile, in the end, facilitated his self-definition, stimulated his artistic and intellectual development, and returned him to the New York parks with his self-confidence renewed and a more integrated sense of purpose than he had ever known before.

The Sanitary Commission was one of the most extraordinary bureaucratic and organizational achievements of the Civil War, an achievement that was, until that time, unique in philanthropic endeavors. Volunteer

20. Olmsted in his forties, probably at the time he was General Secretary of the United States Sanitary Commission. Having already established his obsessive work habits at Central Park, Olmsted now drove himself even harder. One can see the strain and fatigue in his face. (National Park Service, Frederick Law Olmsted National Historical Site.)

societies, composed mainly of women and operating under the aegis of the Commission, contributed perhaps $15 million worth of medical supplies, clothing, blankets, and other materials. The massive organization created by Olmsted efficiently processed and distributed these contributions for the use of Union soldiers and the treatment of the wounded and sick throughout all the theaters of battle. Though public attention was focused primarily upon the Commission's success in dispensing medical and other supplies to the Union forces, Olmsted saw the opportunity also to accomplish perhaps even greater tasks: fostering scientific and medical innovation; inculcating proper sanitary habits in the Northern volunteers, habits that would later be taken back to civilian life; and perhaps most important of all (for Olmsted), educating the Northern public to think in national terms, rather than those of parochial local and sectional interests.

After several months of hammering together the superstructure of the Sanitary Commission and about the time that *The Cotton Kingdom* was published, Olmsted spearheaded an effort by the Sanitary leaders to lobby for legislation to reform the Medical Bureau and to have the elderly and inept Surgeon General, Clement A. Finley, replaced by the youthful and capable William A. Hammond—an effort that succeeded by the spring of 1862.[2] At the beginning of 1862, however, there seemed little chance of success for the reform effort, and Sanitary Commission funds were beginning to be depleted.

At this low point, Olmsted began to pursue other career opportunities —none of which, interestingly, involved a return to Central Park. Olmsted pursued several of these positions simultaneously—an offer from the Mayor of New York City to nominate Frederick as Street Commissioner; a possible position as Commissioner of the proposed Bureau of Agriculture and Statistics; and an intense lobbying effort on behalf of his Port Royal plan for the supervision of the blacks who been liberated through the recent capture of the sea islands off the coast of South Carolina—a plan that included his own appointment as military governor.

The nature of Frederick's search for a public position, and of the inner needs it served, is readily apparent in a letter to his father, which he wrote as it became clear that he would not receive the appointment at Port Royal: "I suppose that if I was determined to have it, and could neglect other matters to devote myself to it, I could get myself appointed Brigadier General, and assigned to duty as Military Governor of the islands, and then have absolute dictatorial control of it."[3] It should be noted that one of his bitterest rivals, Egbert Viele, had by this time achieved military eminence in the war and had been appointed to the rank of Brigadier General. To equal Viele's wartime stature and to have "absolute dictatorial control" over a conquered territory had surely represented a suitable goal for Olmsted's competitive striving. More broadly, Olmsted's letter paints a graphic picture of his busy scramble to find a place for himself, to create a public identity acceptable to himself and worthy of his father's respect.

But it is important to note also that it was not just the desire for power, supreme authority, alone that made Olmsted turn from his duties at the Sanitary Commission to devote so many weeks to the drafting of bills and arguments and the lobbying of persons in and out of government (including Abraham Lincoln and Secretary of War Stanton) in regard to his Port Royal plan. There may well have been another motive, one of perhaps even greater importance: the vindication of his position on slavery. "I shall go to Port Royal, if I can," he wrote his father, "and work out *practically* my solution of the slavery problem as long advocated in my book."[4] In the context of Olmsted's striving for place and respect, the Port Royal plan thus represents a connection to his lingering ambition for membership in the literary republic—one that would turn his idealistic plans into *practical* success.

Moreover, Olmsted's Port Royal plan of 1862, as he described it in a letter to President Lincoln, was also an expression of Olmsted's still emerging Millite social philosophy, especially Mill's notion that government should have an active but limited role in fostering the common welfare—a role confined to "the kind of activity which does not impede, but aids and stimulates individual exertion and development."[5] Olmsted argued to Lincoln that his Port Royal plan would, in part, "*train* or *educate*" the former slaves "in a few simple, essential and fundamental social duties of free men in civilized life," including how to obtain the necessities of life "independent of charity." His plan would also teach them to have a regard for "family obligations" and to learn to substitute submission to the laws of a free labor society for submission to the will of their former owners.[6]

In the event, nothing came of Olmsted's lobbying, nor of his other job-seeking efforts in the early months of 1862. The alternative to pursuing all these various jobs, Frederick told his father, was to try to "build up a landscape gardening business." But he feared that, "even at forty," he was not yet ready to devote himself to *any* career just yet. " 'Wherever you see a head, hit it' is my style of work, & I have not yet sowed my wild oats altogether."[7] As it happened, McClellan's Peninsula Campaign in April 1862 provided Olmsted with a new role to play, as he took personal command of the Sanitary Commission's little fleet of hospital transport ships.

The eleven weeks Olmsted spent on the peninsula—much of it at White House landing on the Pamunkey River—formed his most intensive involvement in the fighting, albeit behind the lines. What confronted him in those weeks was "intolerable chaos" and second-rate, if not callous, treatment of the sick and wounded by the surgeons and administrators of the Medical Bureau.[8] The fact is that the Medical Bureau could not handle the needs of the wounded alone, so Olmsted's cadre of professionals shared much of the work. The most notable of these efforts took place when Olmsted's fleet of hospital ships plied the Pamunkey River, carrying boatloads of sick, wounded, and dying Union soldiers from Fair Oaks and other battles back to base hospitals, treating them *en route* with a mixed crew of professional and volunteer workers. Within his small, dedicated cadre of associates at the peninsula, Olmsted achieved something more than "absolute, dictatorial power." He made himself their "Chief" and won a deference from them all that was almost worshipful—and was earned by his own organizing power and the inspirational force of his driving sense of duty. Katharine Wormeley was mesmerized by her "Chief"—small and lame, yet triumphing over the decided lameness "by doing as if it did not exist." She thought that he was a man of "the most resolute self-will . . . born an autocrat."[9]

The Peninsula Campaign was one of the triumphs of Olmsted's life and an enduring, warming memory. But it cost him dearly in two ways. He once again had worked himself into a state of physical and nervous collapse. Exhausted and suffering from a severe skin disorder, he was ordered by Dr. Agnew of the Executive Committee to convalesce at Saratoga Springs. Even worse, his eleven weeks at the peninsula had left a power vacuum in the running of the Sanitary Commission at large, a vacuum into which the Executive Committee stepped. Opening a permanent office in New York City, this standing committee began to take on

21. The Executive Committee of the U.S. Sanitary Commission: (from left to right) Dr. William Henry Van Buren, George Templeton Strong, the Rev. Henry Whitney Bellows, Dr. Cornelius Rae Agnew, and O. Wolcott Gibbs. Bellows was the president of the Commission and Strong (the Wall Street lawyer and famed diarist) was its treasurer. (MOLLUS-MASS Collection, U.S. Army Military History Institute.)

the responsibilities of leadership that had formerly been left to Olmsted as General Secretary, and the stage was set for the debilitating confrontations that were to be Olmsted's undoing—all the more so because of the bond Olmsted thought he had forged with the Committee members.[10]

For Olmsted, the first year at the Sanitary Commission had been an opportunity to broaden his contacts and his reputation within the intellectual circles and gentry society of New York and New England.[11] Serving with him on the Executive Committee of the Commission were such men as George Templeton Strong and Wolcott Gibbs. Strong, Wall Street lawyer and philanthropist, is remembered today for the extraordinary diaries he kept between 1835 and 1875. Wonderfully cultured, acutely intelligent, and confidently opinionated and bigoted, Strong left behind a detailed portrait of a way of life in a dynamic metropolis, a portrait that rivals the London journals of Pepys and Boswell. As noted previously, Strong had been an early admirer of Central Park and stood in awe of Olmsted's incredible energy in the Commission's work. Olmsted, Strong noted in 1863, "works with a steady, feverish intensity till four in the morning, sleeps on a sofa in his clothes, and breakfasts on *strong coffee and pickles!!!*"[12]

Gibbs was a noted scientist and educator. It was with him, most of all, that Olmsted worked to create the Loyalist Club, which became the Union League of New York. In his written proposal to Gibbs, Olmsted sought to discriminate between prominent patricians like those of the Executive Committee and wealthy New York bankers such as Henry G. Stebbins and August Belmont (who, significantly, had been Central Park Commissioners). These bankers, Olmsted wrote, represented "the other sort," a vulgar moneyed class that would, "if they could, have a privileged class in our society, a legal aristocracy." Olmsted claimed that both *he* and his Sanitary Commission associates, on the other hand, represented the "hereditary, natural aristocracy," "the true American aristocracy, the legitimate descendants and arms-bearers of the old Dukes of our land, of our law-givers."[13]

Their close-knit elite would form the core of the group, Olmsted suggested, and this core would search beyond its own circle to obtain new members for the club. Their search for members, he noted, could canvass among several different groups, including "men of good stock or of notably high character, of legal reputation," especially those with "old colonial names"; men of "established repute in letters and science"; and "clever men, especially those of letters, wits and artists who have made their mark."

This definition of those who could be *canvassed* for the club could have embraced Frederick himself: as a man "of good stock," as a man of "notably high character," and as a man of "established repute in letters or science"—that is, as one of the talented newcomers of the "metropolitan gentry." And yet he had chosen to define himself as belonging among the more "hereditary" elite ("the legitimate descendants and arms-bearers of the old Dukes of our land, of our law-givers")—though he was the grandson of a poor farmer and the son of a small-town dry goods merchant.

Olmsted's belief in a natural aristocracy that embraced both himself and his peers at the Sanitary Commission helped to make him feel, for the first time since his literary republic and Free-Soil days, that he might after all be a "member" of some segment of society, that there might be a group of which he could say (as Raymond Williams writes): their purposes were his purposes.[14] But his bruising disagreements with the Sanitary Commissioners would soon disillusion him. From Olmsted's point of view, the Committee members would prove themselves to be little more enlightened than had the Central Park Commissioners—who had also been "the best men." During his Mariposa exile (two years after producing his Union League proposal), Olmsted would express a far more skeptical view of the "natural aristocracy." His friend the journalist E. L. Godkin (another member of Bender's "metropolitan gentry") had apparently proposed a plan of government that would have given a special representation to this gentry elite. To this Olmsted responded:

I have no faith that government by the Central Park Commissioners, the Sanitary Commission, Trinity Church, the Union League or the Century Clubs would on the whole accomplish as much of the proper purposes of government at as little cost and with as little demoralization of the people [as government by the politicians of the period].[15]

What Olmsted had come to see perhaps was that he was still the outsider, "the hired man," who was just as much at the mercy of his patrician and gentry patrons as of the democratic masses that elite so feared.

At the outset of the Sanitary Commission effort, Olmsted had been given a degree of autonomy such as he had not held since the glorious sixteen months between his appointment as Architect in Chief of Central Park and the appointment of Andrew Green as Comptroller. Like the early Central Park Commissioners, the Sanitary Commissioners had initially looked to Olmsted for leadership; as William Quentin Maxwell states, "their gospel was Olmsted."[16] As late as November 1862, George Templeton Strong still had unbounded admiration for Olmsted, observing that the latter would make an ideal Secretary of War: "Olmsted's sense, energy, and organizing faculty, earnestness, and honesty would give new life to the Administration were he in it."[17]

But there were some warning signs, too. In that same month, Strong noted that were Olmsted "not among the truest, purest, and best of men, we [the members of the Executive Committee and Olmsted] would be in irreconcilable conflict." And only two months later Strong wrote that Olmsted was "in an unhappy, sick, sore mental state," "trying to pick a quarrel with the Executive Committee."[18] By March, Strong came to believe that Olmsted was "unconsciously working to make himself the Commission." And a week later, Strong noted his fear that "Olmsted is mismanaging our Sanitary Commission affairs," adding these ambivalent observations, so tragic in their import for the character Olmsted presented to his associates:

He is an extraordinary fellow, decidedly the most remarkable specimen of human nature with whom I have ever been brought into close relations. Talent and energy most rare; absolute purity and disinterestedness. Prominent defects, a monomania for system and organization on paper (elaborate, laboriously thought out, and generally impracticable), and appetite for power. He is a lay-Hildebrand. . . . incredible as it seems to myself, I think without horror of the possibility of our being obliged to appoint somebody else.[19]

On the same day as Strong's first March entry, above, Henry Bellows was drawing a similar picture of Olmsted's strengths and weaknesses. Olmsted, he wrote, had "glorious and invaluable qualities . . . his integrity, disinterestedness and talent for organization, his patriotism and genius." But he also saw in Olmsted "his impracticable temper, his irritable brain, his unappreciation of human nature in its undivided form." Olmsted, Bellows wrote, possessed "an indomitable pride of opinion," and if he were a priest, "he would be worse than Hildebrand or Laud."[20] The close coincidence of opinions and dates of Bellows' comments and those of Strong suggests that they had only recently discussed Olmsted and had reinforced each other's feelings and language about their General Secretary. When these descriptions of Olmsted are coupled with Vaux's fretting that Olmsted might be a "Nap III" or style himself as "Frederick the Great," a powerful picture emerges of the autocratic style Olmsted presented to those who otherwise most admired him—a style that was clearly a function of his all-devouring narcissistic needs.

In the meantime, Olmsted was becoming emotionally distraught. By May, he was brought to the point of "intense mortification," making the extraordinary statement that "the Sanitary Commission is a monstrous humbug," which "does more to hinder than it does to promote supplies to the sick and wounded." Two months later, infuriated by the appearance of an unauthorized newspaper published by the western branch of the Sanitary Commission, Olmsted told Bellows, "my face flushes, and a real tempest of mortification and shame passes through the fibre of my brain. How can I bear it?"[21] A photograph taken of Olmsted during his tenure at the Commission seems to show the physical and mental toll that the position took upon him: he is still lean, sporting a bushy moustache, but more balding now, with long straight hair hanging down at the back; his face is haggard-looking, and his eyes are edged with large dark circles.

Once Olmsted came to feel, as he did in 1863, that he was actually serving the needs of the Executive Committee, rather than his own deep psychic needs, he was (as he had been at Central Park) put in the position of being, in existentialist terms, nothing more than a servant. "Receiving the money of the Commission, and the continued respect and kind intention of its members," Olmsted told Bellows that summer, "I do require of myself constantly to perform as far as my imagination, sympathy and skill enable me to appreciate it, *the will of the Commission.*"[22] And choosing to be a servant, to devote all his "imagination, sympathy and skill" to fulfilling "the will of the Commission," was, inevitably, choosing to betray his true self. "I am really oppressed beyond endurance by my grief that *the grand purposes which I have had at heart* in the Commission," he wrote Bellows a few days later, "should appear to me to be sacrificed to little personal whims and good purposes of a narrow and ambiguous kind."[23] All the promises that had been made to him (essentially to be given a free hand in the running of the organization) had been broken, "and all with the pretence of religion & love & friendship." He could see no way out, Olmsted added: "Accordingly, I chafe and fume like a caged lion." His sense of despair, of having betrayed the "caged lion" that was his true self, was indeed profound. As he put it bitterly and succinctly in yet another impassioned letter: "My purposes have failed. I have led nothing, to nothing."[24]

As his position at the Sanitary Commission deteriorated, Olmsted suffered a bitter sense of rejection, which helped to drive him into his California exile. As at Central Park, most of the constraints that were now placed upon Olmsted and curbed his autonomy were financial in nature—an attempt to prevent the Commission's expenditures from escalating out of control and to maintain a rigorous accountability for the Commission's supporters. To Olmsted, these constraints were unnecessary and harmful, inhibiting the flexibility and broad outlook that was needed in order to meet the complex and ever-changing needs on the battlefields and in the camps. Moreover, Olmsted felt that the organization he had built had become simply a means for soliciting money and goods from the public and then deploying these where needed. It had not become the grand educational, civilizing, and reforming vehicle he had hoped it would be.[25]

Thus, Olmsted complained to Bellows of "the fetters which bind me here & which cramp & paralyze half my powers." Olmsted added the next day that that his most "comprehensive" measures at the Commission had been "nipped, twisted, turned about or fairly emasculated" by the patrician-gentry elite on the Executive Committee.[26] To lose such a struggle, to be forced to submit to the will of others seems to have represented for Olmsted a loss of his masculine selfhood, a "feminization." Perhaps also it represented a loss of control over his own destiny and a betrayal of his true self, a sacrifice of his authenticity. A *member* can lead an authentic life; a *servant* cannot. The escape to Mariposa, to become an *exile*, was certainly one means by which Olmsted could seek to regain control of his own "helm," to reassert his autonomy and his masculinity, to renew his search for authenticity.[27]

To Olmsted's repeated cries of failure, Bellows finally made a most sensible reply. "It has failed to realize *your* ideal for it," Bellows wrote. "It has not failed to realize that of the Board, or that of the Nation, or that of its Contributors." Bellows added that he did not know what ideal Olmsted had in his own mind, but Bellows did know that the Commission had accomplished "ten times more" than he had hoped when the work had begun: "The war has been vaster, the army ten times larger, the whole field immensely broader than I contemplated." If one focused upon what had been accomplished rather than upon where there had been failures, Bellows wrote, one would consider the work "worthy of great rejoicing."[28] But such a balanced view was impossible for Olmsted to achieve. He was one of those creative people described by Anthony Storr, whose work "contains the whole of [his] self-esteem and sense of self."[29] As Elizabeth Stevenson acutely observes: the essential problem that Olmsted faced at the Sanitary Commission was the same that he had with Andrew Green and the Central Park Commissioners: "it had to be his; it had to be as perfect as he could make it."[30]

Understandably, then, one of the things that lured Olmsted to his Mariposa exile in the summer of 1863 was the promise of "complete, entire, uncontrolled management" of that enterprise.[31] This surprise offer from the Mariposa Board of Directors fired up his grandiosity once again, and the resilience that Fred Kingsbury had noted so long ago came to the fore yet another time. Thus, he wrote to Bellows: "I *know* that I have unusual abilities, unusual, far reaching sagacity. . . . I can't help feeling confident. If the Sanitary Commission had trusted me as it originally proposed to do, it would have accomplished infinitely more than it has done." Olmsted added that if the Mariposa Board of Directors would "really put the management in my hands as they propose, for two or three years, I know (humanly speaking) that I can astonish them."[32]

Trying to turn Olmsted back from "the pecuniary temptation" of Mariposa, Bellows told Olmsted that he was "gradually but surely gaining a place of confidence and respect as a man of statesmanlike mind and character." Bellows said that he did not know "a half-dozen men in the whole North" whose influence would be more critical to the nation over the next five years. He urged Olmsted not to desert "this grand patriotic arena," even though public service would never make him rich, adding, "I am inclined to think you never *ought* to be."[33]

But it was not his net worth that Olmsted was most truly concerned with; it was his sense of self-worth, a sense of self-worth that required the esteem of others for its enrichment. Far from becoming a man of influence, Olmsted retorted to Bellows, he "never, anywhere in the world, [had] been so completely snubbed & set down and made of no account" as he had in Washington."[34] Secretary of War Stanton at least had paid him the respect of hating him, Olmsted wryly told Bellows, but that was the most respect he had received in Washington. His books and views, his proposals for the public arena, Olmsted said, were far better known abroad than within government circles in his own country: "A foreign minister is the only man in Washington who has ever taken the trouble to call upon me on account of the five years' hard study I gave to the practical difficulties of Slavery." Moreover, Olmsted had clearly been stung when Bellows seemed to accuse him of deserting the cause of the Union because of the lure of gold. Olmsted retorted that, were it not for his debts, he would happily stay in the East for a fraction of what he might earn at Mariposa, especially to manage a proposed Loyalist newspaper he had discussed with Bellows and other gentry associates.[35]

Indeed, Olmsted ardently pursued the scheme to establish a Loyalist newspaper throughout his final weeks at the Commission, before the sudden offer came from Mariposa. In June, he and Godkin (who would be editor of this publication when it came into being as the *Nation*) had produced a masterful "Prospectus for a Weekly Journal." The journal, the prospectus said, would be modeled somewhat on the style of the London *Spectator*. Beyond its political purposes, this journal would offer articles on topics "of social, economical, literary or scientific importance," as well as book reviews and news about the cultural, social and political scene abroad.[36] It was a journal, in other words, that would locate Olmsted at the very center of the literary republic—an ambition he had yet to relinquish.

A letter to his father that April had also emphasized that it was not his finances alone that Frederick was concerned about, even though it almost always was the financial aspect he stressed to his father. "On one tack or another, I don't fear that I can find business to which I am suited, in which I can work with a will and earn the livelihood of my family," Frederick wrote. "But none of these doors seem to open to anything better than that." The phrase "better than that" seems at first to refer to his eternal hope of achieving financial independence ("I am accumulating nothing, and see the chance of accumulating nothing," he wrote). But Frederick revealed what was *really* in his mind and hopes a few sentences later: "I have been for some time accumulating notes and materials for a book which I think, if I ever can put six months of library-work upon it, will [be worth] more to the world."[37]

It was the lure of the literary republic that had drawn Olmsted away from the Staten Island farm a decade earlier. And this was the lure that seemed to be very much in his mind now. The notes and materials for a book to which Frederick had referred in his April 18 letter to his father included a series of sketches he had produced during a recent trip through the Midwest and south-central states on behalf of the Sanitary Commission. These sketches are reminiscent of his travel books of the 1850s— reports of places and people seen, ways of life and local culture, and often great chunks of reconstructed conversations. Olmsted may well have conceived of this book at first as a travel book about the midwestern states. But his letter to his father makes it clear that he had begun to move beyond that goal to a more ambitious one; it would in fact grow into a proposed masterwork on the growth of civilization from barbarism.[38]

In late June, Olmsted told his wife that plans for the weekly journal looked promising and there was a good chance they would be living in New York the next winter. "The thing starts so favorably," he wrote, "I shall go into it strong, meaning to succeed." His next letter brought together all his psychic concerns as he told Mary that he would stipulate "absolute control" over the journal, while augmenting his income by writing for various literary and political journals and by "book-making."[39]

It is my belief that when the Mariposa opportunity came along, Olmsted accepted it because the plans for the literary journal seemed to be foundering and because Mariposa seemed to offer, more concretely, another way to satisfy his constellation of needs. It offered at the outset a good income, with immediate provision for his family, and at least a chance of real wealth, as well as "complete, entire, uncontrolled management" (the more so since its Board of Directors would be clear across the continent). But it also offered, far from the hurly-burly of competitive striving in Washington and New York, time to do his "quiet writing," to produce articles for the intellectual journals of the literary republic and to produce his masterwork on civilization. At least one friend, however, would express doubt that Olmsted could be happy in Mariposa. "You don't like exile & isolation as much as I do," Katharine Wormeley wrote, after his departure.[40]

As it happened, Olmsted's exile in California began very badly, Landing at a San Francisco wharf, he managed to get himself kicked in his crippled leg by a horse, which added to his lameness.[41] I wish to be cautious in ascribing an unconscious wish to what could well have been a chance accident. Nevertheless, people *do* unconsciously put themselves in the way of accidents. There is at least the possibility that Frederick, with his farmhand's knowledge of animals, had courted such an incident. He could have been motivated by an unconscious agreement with Bellows's charge that he (Frederick) had deserted the Union cause and had run away to California in search of gold. During the Peninsula Campaign, Olmsted had become upset at the thought that "many shirks" were pretending to be ill in order to be sent home on sick leave. He had been particularly incensed at the officers who had thus behaved "shamefully," trying to "sneak or bully their way onto the hospital boats." And later, at Mariposa, he would write his father: "Are the people [of the North] patient & resolute & prepared for any further necessary sacrifice? That is the dreadful question always before me."[42] As Frederick arrived in California, the "dreadful question" before his inner self may well have been whether he himself was as much a shirker, in leaving his position at the Sanitary Commission, as any officer who had deserted his men and had lied his way aboard the ship that would carry him away from the peninsula battlefront. If so, he may have found on the San Francisco wharf a way to punish himself—with a castrationlike accident, a reenactment of that Central Park disaster of 1860, when he had caused his horse to bolt.

But the pain of his reinjured leg was minor compared to the emotional pain of the bitter disappointment of his arrival in Bear Valley. He wrote his wife that it was a "broken country," marked by general desolation and "a great multitude of children's graves." The landscape was scrubby and uninspiring: "I find it very hard to put up with." Mariposa itself was much smaller than he had imagined, "just a miner's village—no women & everything as it must be where men don't live but merely camp." The population consisted of "roving adventurers, Chinamen and beggars," and whatever buildings there were had only a "temporary character." Though he was grateful for the "health-giving air," he found the "whole aspect of the country detestable," and he admitted to Mary that if he had known what the place was like, he would not have asked her to come. "You must be prepared for a very hard life," he told her; "I can hardly take it. . . . But it is too late to retreat."[43] And to his father, Frederick made the most crushing admission of all: "The estate is in very bad condition, and is paying so poorly—yielding so little in gold—that the suspicion could not be avoided that deception had been practiced upon the company purchasing it."[44] And upon Frederick, too.

One would think, however, that having so much opportunity to write would have taken the sting out of his profound disappointment in the life he had found in Bear Valley. But, although Olmsted tried mightily— producing an enormous quantity of notes and scraps and fragments and a few set pieces—his "quiet writing" no longer proved to be the means of psychological retreat it had once been for him. "Since I left New York the trouble I used to have in my head has been frequently recurrent, so as to be a serious check upon my writing," he wrote to his wife a month after arriving at Mariposa. "Writing seems to aggravate it or to bring on the attacks more than anything else."[45] A San Francisco doctor diagnosed his health problems as being due to an "enlarged heart," telling Frederick he must avoid fatigue, "especially through writing & brain-work."[46]

Mary did bring the family out, and in July 1864 Olmsted had his finest experience of the Mariposa sojourn and perhaps the most extended and rewarding family adventure in the five years of his marriage, when he took his wife and children on a camping trip first to the environs of and then into Yosemite Valley.[47] While there, Frederick wrote a letter to his father, describing what he was beholding as he camped on the banks of Merced, which was at this point "a trout stream with rushes & ferns, willows & poplars—The walls of the chasm . . . a quarter of a mile distant, each side nearly a mile in height." "It is sublimely beautiful," Frederick wrote, "much more beautiful than I had supposed . . . as sweet & peaceful as the meadows of the Avon." On this night there was "a full moon & a soft hazy smoky atmosphere with rolling towering & white fleecy clouds."[48]

The effect of this journey upon his physical and mental well-being and the effect upon both of his subsequent return to Mariposa reveal better than any doctor's diagnosis the real source of his ailments. "I gained health constantly while in the mountains," Frederick wrote his father, "felt better and could ride further without fatigue than before for a long time, but I find the old symptoms returning as soon as I came back to the desk."[49] This statement to his father is strikingly similar to an entry George Templeton Strong made in his diary some two years later (October 15, 1866), upon returning to New York City from a weekend trip to

Trenton Falls, near Albany. It was "a spectacle to be thankful for" he noted, describing the falls as lyrically as Olmsted had Yosemite. The entry concluded with Strong's return to his office on that Monday, a fine fall day: "Felt perfectly well when I went downtown, but that wretched sensation at the pit of my stomach returned soon after I entered Wall Street."[50] The similarity of their experiences and reactions is surely not coincidental. Rather, it says much about Olmsted's capacity to serve as "delegate" for the needs of his gentry peers. The experiences of Olmsted and Strong demonstrate how powerfully nature acted upon these essentially romantic men, offering psychic retreat, a place of refuge, a chance to experience that transcendent, blissful merging with the idealized environment mother that soothes and heals.

However, as Laura Wood Roper notes, it was not Olmsted, but the Mariposa Company itself that was fatally ill. Several times during 1864, Olmsted seemed to have whipped the mines into a paying position, at times vastly increasing production and breaking a strike along the way. But the progress was illusory; the enterprise was a failure, the stockholders had lost money, and Olmsted had been unable to encourage the development of a civilized community at Bear Valley.[51] The truth is that both Olmsted's health and his hopes were at the mercy of the fluctuating and ultimately declining ore production of the mines.

Facing the failure of the mines, he once again found himself casting about for both a career and an identity, intertwined together as they were. As indicated above, the trouble in his head and eyes had prevented him from pulling together his hoped-for masterwork on "Civilization." With the failure of Mariposa hovering on the horizon and his masterwork only a series of random fragments and disconnected essays, Olmsted had begun to despair. "As for your hopes of me, my dear fellow, they had better be dried up," he responded to a worshipful letter from his former deputy and closest associate at the Sanitary Commission, Frederick Knapp. Olmsted added, in a postscript, "Pray keep on thinking of me for what I was (as unfortunate women say)."[52]

As Mariposa declined, Olmsted cast about for other means of reasserting his identity, for achieving a place for himself. In mid-1864, Olmsted had begun work on a landscape project for a cemetery, and the month after his return from his camping trip, he had been named to the Yosemite Commission by the California Governor.[53] But early in 1865, Olmsted seemed to turn again to his hopes for a place within the literary republic. First he cooked up a scheme for marketing low-priced books throughout the nation, a scheme that would give people of little means access to the great books. At the same time, he had a notion of starting a newspaper in California together with Godkin. "I should like very much to go with Vaux into the Brooklyn Park [as Vaux had urged], but fear that I can not," Olmsted told his wife. "I look more definitely to undertaking a newspaper in San Francisco than to anything else." However, in the end Godkin declined.[54]

Ironically, it was as the Union victory back East became ever more assured, and then was accomplished, that Frederick finally reached the edge of an emotional abyss. Two desolate letters to Frederick Knapp provide great insight into Olmsted's inner torments at this time.[55] Both of these letters were written on Sundays, a week apart, each time after returning from church: the first after taking part in a celebration of the Union victory; the second after participating in a memorial service for Abraham Lincoln.

The first letter was motivated by what seemed to Olmsted an inexplicable fact: that he should be so cast down while the Union cause had risen so high. All week he had been receiving the news of "the great humiliation of the enemy" and of "all that makes the triumph, *our* triumph, so complete." In the midst of this triumph, of exuberant public celebration, Olmsted found himself feeling "an unfathomable yearning" for his "poor dead brother," apparently possessed with guilt that he, Frederick, "should have lived to see this day" while his brother had not:

I stood alone and my heart cried back stronger than ever to my poor, sad, unhopeful brother, who alone of all the world, ever really knew me and trusted me for exactly what I was and felt, & tho' I felt more than ever how thoroughly strangers to my real self everybody here is, and how for any purpose that my heart has had in my past life, completely dead and disabled I am.

He had come to realize, Frederick also said, that in all of San Francisco, "there is not a man who knows me . . . who begins to know me; who has the least idea what I am."

What Frederick confronted in this letter was the emptiness his competitive striving had brought him to. His practical ambitions had driven him in California to an inauthentic way of living, based upon the false selfhood of the practical man. Only his lost brother, it now seemed to Frederick, had known and accepted his true self ("exactly what I was and felt"). Thus Frederick now also had to confront the fact that he felt no true intimacy, no shared "sympathy" with anyone in this world, that his closest relationships had come about only through work, through his intense, obsessive, depleting competitive striving. In his April 9 letter, Frederick wrote: "I can't make acquaintance with people with whom I have no close relations of business of duty." But, again, his business life was one based upon the false self, the repression of his true self's purposes ("any purpose that my heart has had"). Thus, he concluded in his letter of April 16: "I hate my business & all I do in it is for my truth's and duty's sake."

It was surely the "unfathomable yearning" for his "poor dead brother" that had impelled Frederick to write to Knapp in the first place. Indeed, Frederick told Knapp, in the April 9 letter, that he had to turn to Knapp in order to regain a sense of "sympathy and fraternity," of "the satisfaction of comradship this side of death." But it seems to me that this goes beyond Frederick's need to reach out, to find a sympathetic, undemanding human response somewhere, and thus to break out of his despair. I believe that in his need for Knapp to replace his brother, Frederick had sought to deny his brother's death. Remember that it was the Union victory and the church service that had aroused Frederick's despair, his emotional numbing (feeling like "a dead man"), and his mourning for his brother—a mourning that was couched in terms of guilt, of the implied question of why *he*, Frederick, had survived while his brother had died. And surely the church service had included some memorial prayer on behalf of the vast number of Union soldiers who had died to bring about the great triumph.

I suggest that Frederick had connected his brother's death with the Union dead and that, in the midst of triumph, he was suffering from what Robert Jay Lifton calls *survivor guilt:*

Where a recognized loss triggers the process, as in reactive depression, the depressed person acts very much like a survivor, and psychic numbing becomes very prominent. Such people often express the feeling that a part of them had died, and that they "killed" the other person in some symbolic way by failing to sustain the other's life with needed support, help and nurturance. The idea of either having killed the other person or having purchased one's own life at the cost of another's is fundamental.[56]

If the Mariposa failure had begun Olmsted's psychic retreat, the Union victory accelerated it by arousing Frederick's deep-seated sense of guilt. Remember that Frederick's chase after a place in the literary republic in the mid-1850s had left John Hull "in the lurch" at the Staten Island farm, where the latter's health had declined. When John Hull was dying in Nice in the fall of 1857, Frederick had been preoccupied with first gaining and then mastering the position of Superintendent of Central Park. And in mid-1863, after Gettysburg, Frederick had left his post at the Sanitary Commission to pursue his dream of practical success on the gold-mining estate of Mariposa, in a sense "abandoning" the Union soldiers whose survival had been his concern for two years. "In my mind," Olmsted wrote Knapp in the April 9 letter, "the Army has become a person and I love it as a person & I think what a happy man you are to be ministering to it as you are."

Frederick had been caught in a deepening sense of depression as his Mariposa's failure become ever more grim and complete. Instead of acting as an antidote to that depression, the Union victory and the celebrations it sparked only added to his sense of being isolated and withdrawn from human connectedness and sympathy. In the midst of triumphal victory celebrations, he had written on April 9, he had felt "more lonely, more like a dead man, and more wanting to be immortal, than for long before."[57]

A week later, Frederick had to confront the death of Abraham Lincoln. It has become commonplace to refer to strong political leaders as father figures. But, as Charles Strozier has shown, by the end of the Civil War Lincoln had assumed a unique role in this regard. A society reeling from four years of enormously destructive warfare, with its 600,000 dead, had a powerful need for an idealized leader. Strozier suggests that Lincoln had "purposely shaped his heroic image to fit a nation longing for unity and greatness."[58] Lincoln had in fact taken on the attributes of the ideal father figure: wise, strong, and forgiving.

Olmsted now had not only to cope with this great loss, but in a sense he also had to relive (in Lincoln's death) the loss of his mother, when he had been confronted with a most unsatisfactory substitute (Mary Ann Olmsted). Indeed, in the April 16 letter Frederick told Knapp: "Mr Lincoln is dead, and we have got a man for President I don't like . . . an essentially uncivilized man, a man of prejudice & bad temper, a very dangerous man." Moreover, Frederick's description of Andrew Johnson recalls the years when, as a boy, he had had to accept the bad-tempered and dangerous Joab Brace as a "deputy father" in place of John Olmsted. The situation seemed to carry Frederick back to a primordial neediness, the neediness of an abandoned child. After discussing (in the April 16 letter) the public mourning for Lincoln, Frederick wrote: "A man may suffer and appreciate his deprivations, and be hungry and express a sense of hungering, knowing what he wants and cannot have, and in all not have a complaining mind, may he not?" He added, further, that this hunger was a function of his own socially immature nature:

Because I am of all men the most slow, and awkward and difficult & inefficient and incapable in social action—at 43, a perfectly shy, unbroken, moody and balky colt—my social instincts are not less strong than any other man's. I think I am all the hungrier because I feed so poorly.

In previous circumstances, Frederick noted, he had dealt with his "social insecurity and the fearful deprivation & misfortune" it caused him by absorbing himself in his work, "chiefly in writing." But now he was unable to write "without great distress," except in "extreme moderation." And when he *did* write, Frederick added, "I only make myself a bundle of contradictions—it don't at all answer the purpose." Frederick's comment here supports the notion that his "quiet writing" once had been for him a safe form of psychological retreat. But now even that safe retreat had failed him, and his retreat to within himself had become inchoate. What he found inside himself was not the artist self but the hungry child —the wounded narcissistic child who lived on within his psyche, "a perfectly shy, unbroken, moody and balky colt," who had been abandoned first by his mother in her death and then by his father in his unawareness of the child's real needs.

Yet in the midst of this psychological retreat, the depressive abyss, Olmsted still showed the resiliency Fred Kingsbury had observed: Olmsted's ability to pick himself up after failure, dust himself off, and undertake still another scheme. Having already said (in his April 9 letter) that his "real self" was hidden from the world and that he felt "completely disabled and dead," Olmsted also told Knapp: "yet it seemed as if you and some others were singing Glory! Hallelujah! too, & that there might be a capacity of life in my dead bones even yet." And in the April 16 letter, Olmsted wrote: "For all that, I can't help feeling that the best part of me is pining here in a sort of solitary confinement."[59]

Thus, Olmsted's hope of resurrection from his psychic retreat seems to have been based upon the assertion of an authentic selfhood, a need to identify and live for his true self's purposes. And this, in fact, was precisely the position that Calvert Vaux took in his many months of intensive letter-writing during the spring and summer of 1865, when he was trying to persuade his quondam partner to return to New York and a career in landscape architecture.

In early April, as Olmsted was sliding toward the emotional abyss, immersing himself in death imagery, Vaux wrote: "I have, perhaps from the accident of temperament—more faith in the future than you & I can see no reason why you should not live for fifty years yet and crystallize all your vagaries & whims and freaks—to say nothing of your aspirations and conditions into a permanent form." "I wish you could have seen your destiny in our art," Vaux wrote in early May, adding, "God meant you should I really believe." It was two days later that Vaux called Olmsted the "Head Artist" of Central Park, staking their claim "unquestionably" to control landscape design in New York "from Washington Heights to the other side of Brooklyn."[60]

On July 21, Vaux notified Olmsted that the embryonic firm of Olmsted and Vaux had been appointed landscape architects to Central Park. The work on the park could now be completed successfully, Vaux told Olmsted; "but it depends on you—and the spirit with which you now approach it." All that Olmsted had hoped to achieve at the park, Vaux said, was "now easily possible." But, Vaux added (in the pungent comment noted in chapter 10), all would be lost if Olmsted persisted in trying to convert "this many sided, fluent thoroughly American high art work into a machine—over which as Frederick the Great, Prince of the Park Police you should preside."[61]

As we have seen, as early as February, Olmsted had told Mary that he "should like very much to go with Vaux into the Brooklyn Park," but feared that he could not. In March, Olmsted had told Vaux: "My heart really bounds (if you don't mind poetry) to your suggestion that we might work together on [the Brooklyn Park]."[62] He greatly admired Vaux's plans for the park: "excellent of course," he said, "You don't play with it, but go at once to the essential starting points." Still Olmsted seemed to hesitate. In answer to Vaux's plea that he come back and take his place as "Head Artist," Olmsted wrote on August 1:

I can do anything with proper assistants, or money enough—anything that any man can do. I can accomplish means to ends better than most, and I love beautiful landscapes and rural recreations and people in rural recreations—better than anyone else I know. But I don't feel strong on the art side. *I don't feel myself an artist*, I feel rather as if it were sacrilegious in me to post myself in the portals of art—yes, I know you are indignant and vexed with me, but I speak the truth, and it has got to be reconciled with all the rest. (Emphasis added.)[63]

Olmsted's astonishing claim "I don't feel myself an artist" was a rejection of the role to which Vaux had called him—the true-self role of the "be-er," the artist and idealist. It was in fact a rejection of the very role he had claimed for himself in his 1861 resignation letter at Central Park, when he had written: "I shall venture to assume the title of artist." In the teeth of the Mariposa disaster, at a time when there were stockholders who may have indeed thought him a swindler, Olmsted nevertheless chose to assert his superior talent as a practical man ("I can combine means to ends better than most"), rather than to answer Vaux's call. This recalls Olmsted's sputtering insistence (in that same 1861 resignation letter) that he was *not* a swindler or an impostor. Perhaps, as at Central Park in 1861, his greatest fear was that if he accepted the role that Vaux had offered him (the very role he had claimed for himself in 1861) and failed at it, then Vaux and all the world might decide that he was indeed an imposter—an imposter at the very core of his being, in his creative self.

Further, Olmsted apparently continued to hope—even while pondering Vaux's call—that he might yet find a place in the literary republic. He had apparently made this clear to Norton. The latter had written to Godkin, a few weeks before Olmsted's August 1 letter to Vaux, that Olmsted could be "induced to come home if a proper place could be found for him here." Godkin may have made Olmsted's decision to join Vaux in landscape architecture somewhat easier by writing to Olmsted that he could supplement his income in that profession by submitting articles to Godkin's *Nation* and Norton's *North American Review*, for which Olmsted would be paid "handsomely." "You have plenty of friends who believe in your capacity," Godkin wrote, and he urged Olmsted "to come on in September without fear or hesitation."[64]

Calvert Vaux, who understood Olmsted so well, had earlier lashed out at what he considered all the false identities Olmsted had pursued. "There are plenty of people to write for 'The Nation'—add one more to the number if you will," Vaux wrote. "There are plenty of Gold mines to superintend but who is going to be the better for the Gold?"[65] In opposition to these careers, Vaux had offered Olmsted a more elevated pursuit, park-making—"an unaccredited but important pursuit" that would be "a direct contribution to the best interests of humanity." From Vaux's point of view, he was trying to call Olmsted away from his false self's concerns to the realization of his true self's purposes. "I used to tell you," Vaux had written Olmsted the year before, "that you would be wanted for the public service in the old romantic way [that is, without thought of money or power], but you would [not] listen."[66]

On August 31, Olmsted informed his father that he proposed to accept Vaux's offer once he was finally relieved of his Mariposa duties.[67] In the end, Olmsted's place in the world had been found by Calvert Vaux, on the Brooklyn Park, and it prepared the way for Olmsted's intellectual and creative gifts to be channeled into his identity as America's premier landscape architect. After Olmsted's return to New York, his services to the *Nation* dwindled and his proposed masterwork on civilization faded into the background. Olmsted's urge for "quiet writing" would be put into the service of his role as the philosopher of urban landscape design for America's great and growing cities.

PART IV

The Landscape Architect

I suppose as long as I live I shall be forced to make long journeys.

FREDERICK LAW OLMSTEAD, 1893

CHAPTER 12

"Civilization"

In keeping with his growing sense of despair about himself and his prospects, Olmsted's ruminations on society, particularly in America, grew more pessimistic by the latter part of 1864, ostensibly because of his observations of social behavior both in Bear Valley and in San Francisco. But it is clear that Olmsted's reflections had as much to do with the state of his inner world as with the world around him. A few of the themes that would be so pronounced in Olmsted's "Civilization" notes of this period were expressed in a long letter to a colleague.[1]

In this letter, Olmsted painted a grim view of the California countryside outside of San Francisco, stating that it was peopled "almost entirely [by] thriftless, fortune-hunting, improvident, gambling vagabonds." Even among those who were by comparison respectable, one found very few "who have a deep abiding faith in living by intelligent industry directed to the essential benefit of their fellow citizens." He claimed that goldmining was the driving force, and all other occupations were founded upon this central industry. Since most mines failed to produce a sustaining profit, he added, life built around them was doomed; villages sustained by respectable white men were already decaying or deserted. The successful (small) businesses were mostly owned by Chinese, "who are content to work for modest wages."

Olmsted had little use for the kind of society that might be created under the prevailing circumstances in places like Bear Valley: "It is *nowhere;* there is no society. Any appearance of social convenience that

259

may be found is a mere temporary and temporizing expedient by which men cheat themselves to believe that they are not savages."[2]

Olmsted's view of San Francisco society was only a little more flattering. Such mercantile centers, Olmsted said, were dependent upon "a vigorous class of men, vigorous in whatever they put their hands to, vigorous and enterprising, daring, audacious, often more than that, *criminally reckless*."[3] Olmsted also allowed that "these qualities are sometimes applied to good, benevolent, religious purposes." Nevertheless, words like "vigorous," "daring," "audacious," and "criminally reckless" reveal his inner vision of an unrestrained commercial city, a buccaneer society —achieving, masculine, utilitarian, competitive, and ruthless.

Olmsted's observations on social conditions in California—bound up as they were in his perceptions of men and human nature—spilled over into several letters of the Mariposa years. But it was in his "Civilization" notes that he pursued this concern most relentlessly and purposefully, reaching deep into his own nature and history to do so.[4] Referring to this projected masterwork, Laura Wood Roper discusses Olmsted's intensive preparation, his massive reading and evidence-gathering (newspaper clippings, journal articles, personal research, and so forth), and describes the projected book as a systematic and scientific inquiry into "the nature and progress of civilized man."[5] But the massive unfinished work was also an attempt at self-realization and self-integration, as well as a final bid for a meaningful place in the literary republic.

Olmsted's central argument in the "Civilization" notes revolved around the concepts of *frontier* and *civilization*, which he regarded as opposing states of existence that might be found anywhere in America, East Coast to West.[6] In the frontier condition, he argued, every man looks after himself and expects to look after himself—a frame of mind that can be appealing in the form of self-reliance, but can also be seen as a dangerous form of selfish individualism, resulting in anarchy. In the civilized condition (which, at his most optimistic, Olmsted associated with true republican government), the ruling spirit is benevolent and cooperative. " 'What can we do for each other?' " Olmsted wrote, "is the question asked by every (civilized) man of every other." Olmsted recognized that these conditions, though apposite, were not mutually exclusive. Aspects of civilization might be found in a frontier settlement, and aspects of the frontier spirit in a civilized community; the frontier settlement could advance, the civilized community decline. Furthermore, he held that the ethnic immigrant enclaves of America's large cities (such as the Five Points in New York City) were each as much a barbarous "frontier settlement" as any in Texas or Bear Valley.

Olmsted asked himself why such paradoxical phenomena should occur. His answer was that there were two "strains" in the nature of every American—one toward barbarism and one toward civilization. Influenced by Horace Bushnell's sermon on "Barbarism," Olmsted believed that men from civilized communities tended to revert to barbarous habits under pioneer or frontier conditions. Olmsted already had seen at first hand some memorable examples of this during the "saddle trip" he had made to Texas with his brother, John Hull. They note, in *Texas*, that the condition of the young men they had encountered in East Texas "appeared to incline decidedly to barbarism," citing a group of drovers and their neighbors, all of whom were "polite and respectful" toward the Olmsteds, though among themselves "their coarseness was incredible."[7]

With the unleashing of the barbarous strain, the strong dominate the weak, and the only restraint upon "appropriating the property of others, and for not injuring others where any pleasure is to be secured by doing so, is the danger that the injury may be avenged or punished." In contrast, the "highest sentiment" of the civilizing strain is the desire to cultivate self-denial, constraint, and "benevolent impulses." The presence of such a sentiment in individuals, Olmsted believed, is what makes possible the movement toward civilization even in a frontier condition. Pioneers "may be extremely coarse, rude and simple in their wants," with a hatred of "refinement and conventional ornament and courtesy," but they are nevertheless marked with the civilizing spirit if they have "the quality of self control, of temperance, of industry, [and if they are] provident . . . or forehanded in their habits." "The grand distinction between the savage and the civilized state," Olmsted summed up elsewhere, "is that the repulsive forces of man's nature are stronger in the first than the last."

Self-denial, self-constraint, and self-control: these are the real hallmarks of the civilizing spirit for Olmsted. Thus, Olmsted's theorizing about frontier and civilization is cast in terms similar to the classic Puritan confrontation with the state of one's own soul—the tug of war between the savage and the saintly in every man. If a man does not have sufficient self-restraint or self-control, the puritan believed, all of the base desires that boil and bubble within the recesses of the human mind might break loose in licentious excess and savage outrage.

Nevertheless, in his most optimistic moments, Olmsted was confident that the chasm between frontier and civilization *could* be bridged. One should not compare the common man in America with the most favored few among the privileged classes of Europe, Olmsted observed early in his "Civilization" notes, but rather take note of how far the common man here had progressed above the peasant classes from which he had come. Even more optimistic was Olmsted's comment: "Nowhere has Christian Socialism been more extensively acted upon or better vindicated by success than in the new settlements of America."

The most interesting section of his Mariposa essay is where Olmsted struggled to put into words the motivating characteristic within men that could permit them to bridge the ideological (and emotional) chasm between self-indulgent individualism and an other-directed spirit of cooperation. In this section of the essay, Olmsted gave a name to this motivating characteristic: communitiveness. He defined it as "a combination of qualities which fit [a man] to serve and to be served by others in the most intimate, complete and extreme extend[ed] degree imaginable."[8] Olmsted's use of the word *intimate* in the last phrase is, I think, crucial and signals the degree to which communitiveness represented the combination of qualities in himself that he hoped would eventually come full flower, eventually permit *him* to benefit from and to be capable of human relationships that were "intimate, complete and extended."

Olmsted imagined a scale of measurement upon which one could rank various men, from the most barbarous to the most civilized. The greater the degree of communitiveness within a person, the higher he would be upon that scale. As an example, Olmsted cited four of his neighbors at Mariposa. Two of these he placed near the bottom, with very little difference between them: a "dull, silent, stupid savage" and a white Kentuckian of English stock, an idling "gamester." Far above these two, but no more than half way up his scale, Olmsted placed, close together, a Chinese servant and a German shoemaker—"steady, plodding, short-sighted, frugal workers." He had ranked these latter two no higher, Olmsted explained, because his scale was based upon something other than "industry, well-balanced demand and supply . . . sobriety and inoffensiveness." His scale was, in fact, based upon the degree to which the men he measured possessed the motivating characteristic of communitiveness. He had found, Olmsted wrote,

not merely less of a community but less possibility of community, of communitiveness, here among my neighbors of all kinds than in any other equal body of men, I ever saw. And the white men, the Englishmen the Germans, and other civilized men do not possess [it] often in as high degree as the Mexicans Chinese and negroes—nor do the good men always possess as much of it as the rogues, the wild fellows.

Communitiveness clearly is a significant concept, in its own right as well as in Olmsted's thinking. It comes as much from his penetration into his own motivating forces as from his observations of other men. Indeed, his fascination with "the rogues, the wild fellows" around him may well reflect his own concern about himself. The matter had immediacy for Olmsted precisely because he knew himself to have been a wanderer and a vagabond and perhaps because he feared his own savage tendencies. It was out of that same kind of fearful self-knowledge that Olmsted could write to an associate about men who "cheat themselves to believe that they are not savages."[9] And this was also the acute self-knowledge of the rueful comment Olmsted would make a decade later to Charles Eliot Norton: "Ah! well, I'm afraid we none of us have advanced so very far from the simplicity of savage life. We are all alike crazy when our blood is up, and it seems to get up without our knowing it."[10] Olmsted's extensive ruminations on the savagery of men on the frontier represent Olmsted at his most pessimistic and Hobbesian.

At another point, Olmsted described the situation of native Americans who had settled in the eastern cities, apparently law-abiding "good citizens." Yet, he argued, their Indian "propensities and habits" had actually become stronger in them because of the "prolonged suppression to which they [had] been subject."[11] Occasionally, Olmsted went on, such an Indian gives in to these suppressed propensities and indulges them "in a furtive solitary way." In some cases, an assimilated Indian will eventually and suddenly wander off to a place, likely the frontier, where he might escape "from the restraint of organized society" and indulge his "independent, vagabond [gambling] proclivities."

That Olmsted was not talking about Indians alone was made clear in a passage immediately following, in which he commented that white men brought up "in mature communities" might be found with the same proclivities. Under favorable circumstances, they might be "controlled" or "restrained" and thus cause "little harm"; under other circumstances, these proclivities could turn such men into "gamesters" or "gamblers," whose ostensible profession was that of "speculators." The inevitable comparison must be made to Olmsted's own recent history. It was Olmsted himself who had made his way to the frontier, where he had regained the independence that had been so constrained by his peers at the Sanitary Commission and where he was now engaged in speculation (gambling) in gold and oil. And do we not recognize a youthful version of Olmsted, the vagabondish "dilettante," in Olmsted's observation: "if they are industrious, it is in some irregular unmethodic way, involving so much risk, guess work and shifts." Indeed, in the letter to his associate, cited above, Olmsted wrote that had circumstances been different, he himself might have found his amusement in gambling. Thus, the youthful vagabond he had been was still a part of his inner self—"the rogue, the wild fellow."

I would suggest, in fact, that Frederick's boyhood exile from home had provided the metaphors both for his Mariposa exile and for his explorations of barbarism and civilization (within himself and within the world around him). Recall Frederick as an adolescent, wandering in the Connecticut backwoods, alone with his gun, totally unrestrained by adult supervision or responsibilities, and the prism through which Olmsted later viewed the "frontiers" of Texas and California becomes apparent. The emotional meanings of exile along the frontier had been internalized from his boyhood years in rural Connecticut. And the man who in his middle years had become such a "doer," who had come to praise self-restraint as the essence of civilization and civilization as the highest good, still carried within himself the memory and longings of an idling, unconstrained boyhood on the Connecticut "frontier."

This image of himself as a vagabond, an adolescent wanderer, was one that Olmsted could nevertheless accommodate, looking upon that aspect of himself with tolerant amusement, even wistfulness. His deeper concern was for the suppressed "proclivities" of the savage that slumbered beneath one who outwardly seemed so law-abiding, so civilized in his habits—savage proclivities that could erupt at any time. This aspect of his self, the savage aspect, had an origin far earlier than the idling, dreaming wanderer of adolescence. Its origin is revealed in an Olmsted comment that comes late in the Mariposa essay files. The central element of a savage or barbarous nature, Olmsted wrote, is "a simple unwise shortsighted selfishness—the selfishness of a child." Perhaps Olmsted saw the source of his own savage, barbarous urges in the wounded narcissistic child he once had been.

This was the fearsome core of his inner self, the self that had to be contained within Victorian self-restraint and punishing, obsessive, hard work. Though the nature of Olmsted's psychological wounds were, of course, particular to him, his need to constrain his passions within the oppressive bonds of compulsively hard work was a trait he shared with his contemporaries. As it happens, I find the moral earnestness, self-discipline, and industriousness of many Victorians to be rather attractive qualities—virtues that contributed greatly to society. But, as with any virtue, it is carrying it to an extreme that gives cause for alarm. On a visit to the United States in 1882, Herbert Spencer noted the terrible effects of the "the gospel of work" among the American gentry. "In every circle I have met men who have themselves suffered from nervous collapse, due to stress of business, or named friends who had crippled themselves by overwork," Spencer commented.[12]

It was this same fear of his own inner self that underlay Olmsted's concern that even the most civilized of the men from older communities who migrate to the frontier "are falling back very rapidly." The frontier, Olmsted knew, only brought out what was already there—the gambling man, the vagabond, the savage beneath the skin. In fact, those two "strains" found in every American—barbarism and civilization—were opposing movements along the continuum of communitiveness, the former being its almost total absence, the latter its presence in the highest degree. The most frightening aspect of the frontier condition, for Olmsted, was that it threatened whatever gains an individual might have made in fostering his own communitiveness, in mastering his own savagery. There were more meanings than one behind the confession Olmsted made to his wife as he contemplated undertaking the superintendence of the Mariposa mining estate: "I hate the wilderness & wild tempestuous, gambling men, such as I shall have to master.'[13]

The inner wildness harbored in every human mind was to be found in cities as well as on the frontier, and in the cities in perhaps even more insidious and dangerous ways, since cities were meant to be the full flowering of man's urge to communitiveness. Thus, the contending models of human existence Olmsted had struggled at Mariposa to define in his hoped-for masterwork—between frontier and civilization, between an individualism that could explode into rivalrous savagery and a communitiveness that fostered mutual concern and cooperation—would remain the central concern of his emergent philosophy of urban landscape design, as it took shape in the postwar years.

It was no wonder that Olmsted never completed either his masterwork or his essay on Mariposa: he was seeking to reconcile conflicts, within himself and within society, that could not be reconciled—he was seeking solutions to the human condition that have yet to be found one hundred and thirty years after he was writing. Yet, in communitiveness, Olmsted had worked his way toward an answer for one of the central problems of his time and ours—how to set a limit to human destructiveness, how to "contain hate in a framework of love."[14] If his emergent philosophy, as he would expound it during the five year period between 1865 and 1870, offered no final answer, it offered at least a beneficial program. One might not be able to prevent the effects of unrestrained individualism, Olmsted seemed to realize at last, but one could perhaps ameliorate those effects.

Olmsted's projected masterwork was a rejection of the utopian social democracy with which he had once toyed, the kind of socialism found in the North American Phalanx of the Fourierists or the Neu Braunfels of the German Free-Soilers—both of which he had already rejected for himself. Returning to New York in the fall of 1865, Olmsted had also rejected, for himself and for society, the nonconformist existential roles of exile and rebel. He had chosen conformity—either a hoped-for membership or else a settled-for servanthood—in his competitive Utilitarian society. In place of either a permanent exile from his society or of a radical restructuring of that society, Olmsted now would offer a different solution. He would try to make the conditions of membership (or of servanthood) bearable.

If there was a grand design beyond that immediate goal, it was perhaps to create conditions in his urban parks and suburban settings for the impulse of communitiveness to be nurtured within the men who would frequent them, in the hope that communitiveness would be carried outward into the larger community and exert a civilizing influence there. In this way, Olmsted would at the same time nourish the impulse of communitiveness within himself, foster his own civility and strengthen his conforming social self against his feared anarchic shadow self.

It seems to me that an ideological-existentialist conflict had taken place all through the nineteenth century and had intensified as Victorianism settled into Olmsted's generation—a conflict between idealism and materialism, between Romanticism and Utilitarianism, between what had been defined as the feminine in life (being) and what had been defined as the masculine (doing). Urban, pastoral parks were at the psychic heart of that struggle, and Olmsted was its agent. Olmsted had not come forward as a soldier of Romanticism, not even, originally, as an artist. It had been Calvert Vaux who in 1865 had called him to that duty, but Olmsted had accepted it and had come at last to define himself that way. Yet Olmsted was something more than an artist, something more than the "representative man" of Central Park. He was, even more, the representative man of the nineteenth-century struggle to live an authentic life.

It has been a fundamental thesis of mine that in his urban design career, Olmsted served as a delegate (the "representative man") for meeting certain psychic needs and achieving certain social aspirations of those gentry and patrician men who upheld Romantic idealism as a more than literary force in American life. Leo Marx speaks of the "pastoral ethos" that had been such an important strain in Romantic thought. "The renunciation of worldly striving in favor of a simpler, more contemplative life always had been the core of the pastoral ethos," he writes. In America, where, in Emerson's words, "the whole land is a garden," that ethos seemed more credible than ever before.[15] Olmsted's task (his *chosen* task) was to respond creatively to the shared needs, both conscious and unconscious, that gave rise to the pastoral impulse and to offer what seemed to his peers to be valid ways of meeting those needs.

Neither as a delegate nor as an artist nor as an idealist was it required that Olmsted pioneer or innovate in either his actions or his thinking. Indeed, men like Andrew Jackson Downing and William Cullen Bryant had carried the pastoral impulse into the heart of the city and had championed the cause of Central Park long before Olmsted had awakened to the need; Calvert Vaux had created the essence of Prospect Park in Brooklyn while Olmsted despaired in Mariposa; and Vaux had seen, before Olmsted, that their calling of urban design was "the big art work of the Republic." But Olmsted was to give greater immediacy to the

22. Bird's eye view of the lower part of Central Park. The formal mall can be seen (at center) with the Ramble beyond, between the mall and the old reservoir. (The New-York Historical Society.)

needs that lay behind the pastoral impulse and was to offer a more complex and truer vision of modern urban life than Downing, Bryant, Vaux, or any of the Emersonian Romantics.

In 1869, Clarence Cook noted that the growth that had transformed New York from a small town into a great metropolis had been "almost without precedent for suddenness."[16] The demand for building lots had been such, he stated, that "it was with difficulty [that] even the public squares, reserved for air and recreation, could be preserved inviolate." Such had been the necessity of the time, he added, that "every new building meant so much less light." Cook then cited the progress of the park movement in New York and described Viele's original plan for Central Park as "just a matter-of-fact tasteless affair as is always produced by engineers . . . when they attempt anything of ornamental design." Cook hailed the advent of Olmsted and Vaux, "both well known and highly esteemed by a large and cultivated circle in this community," and he lauded the design that had won the Central Park competition, particularly the notion of the underground transverse roads.

It is clear from Cook's account that Olmsted and Vaux both could be seen as delegates of their gentry and patrician circles in the creation of Central Park. "It could hardly have been possible to find in our community two men better fitted by education, by experience, and by a combination of valuable qualities," Cook wrote, "to carry out so difficult and so important an undertaking as that of the Central Park." He thought that it might have been fate that had made "like to mate with like" and had made "the fruit of such a union its own best praise."

In 1893, when Mariana Van Rensselaer was working on her *Century* profile of Olmsted, he wrote her: "I hope you will not fail to do justice to Vaux and to consider that he and I were one."[17] Cook's observations make it clear that Olmsted and Vaux had been as "one" in the minds of their peers. And it also clear that Vaux had been as visionary as Olmsted, as Vaux was, for example, in his notion of what the two of them might bring about "from Washington Heights to the other side of Brooklyn." During three decades, their combined passion and skills came very close to achieving the green belt they had dreamed of: in Brooklyn they established Ocean Parkway, Eastern Parkway, Prospect Park, and Fort Greene Park; in Manhattan, Central Park, Morningside Park, and Riverside Park.[18] And if Olmsted had come to prominence over Vaux as *the* delegate of their peers, this owed at least something to the fact that Olmsted was *Vaux's* delegate—the "Head Artist" on the park work and its "representative man."

It was clearly Olmsted's administrative and organizational abilities, his passion for the work in all its details, that drew the gentry elite to him and made them seek him out as their delegate in the great works to be done. Thus, recall Bellows recruiting Olmsted as General Secretary for the Sanitary Commission on the strength of his superintendence of Central Park.[19] When he was leaving the Commission, Louisa Lee Schuyler told Olmsted how "restful" it had been to have him running the Commission for the past two years: "To know everything was right, 'because Mr. Olmsted was there.' " Later, when someone was needed to head the new Freedmen's Bureau in 1864, George W. Curtis urged Olmsted to take the position: "you are the only man to whom we all so instinctively turn." And, as we have seen, Norton had urged Godkin, in July 1865, to help him "find a place" for Olmsted, to convince the latter to return from California.[20] Clarence Cook, in his appreciation of Central Park (1869), described Olmsted as "an American of Americans." Cook lauded Olmsted's Central Park reign as Superintendent, noting how much was owed to Olmsted's "quiet earnest zeal, to his integrity, and to the abundance of his resources." "Few Americans in our time have shown so great administrative abilities," Cook added. Finally, during their inept machinations in 1872, a splinter group of Liberal Republicans put forth a "conscience ticket," of William Slocum Groesbeck for President and Olmsted for Vice President.[21]

Neil Harris observes that after the Civil War, the nature of cultural institutions in the United States underwent a significant transformation. Antebellum cultural activities had been participatory—were meant not only to entertain, but to bring together "representatives from all social grades in the pursuit of intellectual, aesthetic, and moral improvement." After the war, these institutions were made to serve other purposes: to become "refuges for the best that world culture had produced" and a means for the elite to "certify" their own standards of taste and cultivation. As a part of this process, cultural institutions (museums, symphonies, and the like) were given over to the hands of professional, and authoritarian, managers who would enforce the elite's cultural standards rigorously and efficiently.[22]

Those managers, of course, were not the peers of the elite, but rather their employees—were not *members*, but *servants*. This is the role that Olmsted came to fill in his post–Civil War career as a landscape architect. It was a role he shared with others of "the metropolitan gentry": E. L. Godkin, the voice of gentry concerns in the *Nation;* George William Curtis, equally their voice in his public orations and in the pages of *Harper's* and other publications; Charles Loring Brace, the representative of the gentry conscience at the Children's Aid Society. It was a role he even shared with the more patrician of the gentry intellectuals—men like Charles Eliot Norton and Wolcott Gibbs, who, in their later careers at Harvard, became prototypes of the professorial intellectuals of what Thomas Bender refers to, in its New York guise, as "Academic Culture."[23]

Upon his return to New York in 1866, Olmsted would have little to do socially with the patricians of George Templeton Strong's circle. Even his wartime friendship with Wolcott Gibbs was to grow tenuous. It was a friendship, the *Papers* editors note, that had not stopped Gibbs from assailing Olmsted's stewardship of the Sanitary Commission. "Do you remember how I used to abuse you & caricature you in the Commission?" Gibbs had written in 1867. What seemed to be left between them, as the Gilded Age settled in, was merely their wartime bond. "I see but little of you my dear old Olmsted as we grow older and our paths in life are so different," Gibbs wrote in 1879, "but I always keep you in cherished remembrance and your old mug often smiles at me from my album."[24]

But Olmsted's executive ability, his success as a doer, had never alone attracted his gentry peers; he had attracted them because they believed Olmsted shared their basic assumptions, would accomplish what they wanted to have accomplished. "I feel that you and I are one in political opinion and feeling," Gibbs had written Olmsted in 1863 (at the time of their Union League proposal).[25] Even more, the gentry connection with Olmsted was a response to something they could only sense in him—*his* true self's purposes, an inspiration and vision that gave an aura of significance to their shared work. It is true that, despite all his sneering at the "Frederick the Great" image of Olmsted the doer, Vaux also wanted his partner's executive ability for the Brooklyn park work; but this was, even more, a recognition of Olmsted's executive ability linked to something grander than "bossing jobs." It was linked to a vision of the park as an artistic enterprise and one of great social meaning. "This is what you are gifted to foresee & design as well as and probably better than architecture or Planting or both together," Vaux told Olmsted, "but it is all art work of the pure sort, and places you on the platform with the rest of the guild."[26]

Robert Lewis has drawn attention to the intellectual rapport among the "genteel triumvirate" of Olmsted, Godkin, and Norton, even claiming that the latter two had a shaping influence upon Olmsted's thought as reflected in his "Civilization" notes. He also observes that Olmsted "shared the assumptions of many other Northeastern genteel thinkers that social progress required the complete integration of all the diverse groups and classes in the United States to form a cosmopolitan whole"—what Godkin called "the promotion of assimilation."[27] It was men like Godkin, Norton, and Olmsted whom David Hall had referred to as "modern missionaries." Genteel reformers, Hall writes, spread a social gospel with two purposes: to reveal the essential truths of life and to "present 'the best,' whether in art, politics or literature, and thereby overcome the blight of mediocrity."[28] Additionally, as Geoffrey Blodgett points out, Olmsted was one of the founders of the American Social Science Association, whose charter, Blodgett reports, "stressed the 'responsibilities of the gifted and educated classes to the weak, the witless, and the ignorant.' "[29]

It is true, as Lewis and Blodgett observe, that Olmsted shared most of the basic assumptions of his gentry peers and patrician patrons. But *their* agenda was not ipso facto his. He certainly employed the language of his peers in enlisting their support for his urban design projects, but that is not where his passion and his purposes were. When Olmsted spoke of his own purposes, he spoke to those patrician and gentry men whose needs and tastes were most closely aligned with his own (George Templeton Strong, Charles Eliot Norton and, even, Calvert Vaux), as well as to those middle-class men who also shared those needs and whose tastes could be elevated, could be *educated*, to the gentry level.

Blodgett writes that the "superb achievements" of Olmsted's urban design career insulated him from the "stigma of failure" attached to his colleagues in conservative reform. "Yet his parks may be understood to reflect as accurately as civil service reform or tariff reform or Mugwump journalism a common group desire to counter the headlong popular impulses of the Gilded Age," Blodgett states.[30] I would submit that the parks Olmsted designed, with Vaux in New York and with his stepson and others in Boston, have endured as triumphs of urban design because they were energized by the validity of Olmsted's vision, deriving from his own deeply felt inner needs—a validity in *human* terms, not class or gender terms.

During a bitter period in 1878, when the ailing Olmsted had gone abroad and Vaux was feuding with Godkin and Olmsted's family over credit for Central Park, Vaux told Godkin that Olmsted's "strongest point in the park" had been "the human element in it." Vaux said that Olmsted had seen it from the start in its finished form and that the image Olmsted had had was of "an oasis, an arcadia in the desert of brick & mortar vibrant with happy life from morning to night." Now, with the park's integrity under attack from the politicians once again, Vaux said, Olmsted should speak out, *"not as a Servant, but as a Master."*[31] Within a few years, almost destroyed by his final controversies on the New York parks and in the midst of his transition to Brookline, Olmsted did what he had never done before in his quarrels at the park or at the Sanitary Commission: he did at last "go public" with his pamphlet, *Spoils of the Park.* Its reception more than disappointed him, and he thought that the New York parks would be ruined and his vision destroyed.[32]

"You are preaching truth far above the comprehension of our generation," Norton wrote to Olmsted during this painful period.[33] This was something that Norton was coming more and more to believe about his own life. In the last two decades of the century, Norton would gradually retreat from public affairs and exile himself into the idealistic world of art and art history, dividing his time between academia (Harvard) and rural retreat (his country estate). Several months after that letter to Olmsted, Norton wrote another colleague of the decline in what Olmsted had called communitiveness:

Men in cities and towns feel much less relation with their neighbors than of old; there is much less civic patriotism; less sense of a spiritual and moral community. This is due in part to other causes, but mainly to the selfishness of individualism in a well-to-do democracy.

And, fourteen years later, Norton had given up all hope. He predicted, rather stoically, the worst of what Olmsted had considered the opposing "strains" in American life; "I fear that America is . . . likely to become more and more a power for disturbance and barbarism." "The Old America," he added in an 1898 speech, "the America of our hopes and our dreams has come to an end." All he could do now was to mourn for "the very pleasantest little oasis of space and time" that had been New England early in the century.[34] It was surely men like Norton that Stow Persons had in mind when writing: "The successor to the nineteenth-century gentleman is the alienated intellectual."[35]

As noted earlier, Olmsted's Sanitary Commission experience had soured him upon the notion of government by the "best men." Indeed, he and Godkin would quarrel over the Mugwump idea that Liberal Republicans should align themselves with Reform Democrats such as Samuel J. Tilden and his New York ally, Andrew H. Green.[36] But Godkin would continue to represent the narrowest claims of the "best men"—men who, he felt, deserved to lead the republic because of their cultivation. Such cultivation, Godkin noted, "comes of the protracted exercise of the faculties for given ends, under *restraints* of some kind, whether imposed by one's self or other people," and it could properly be described as "the art of doing easily what you don't like to do at all." As such, cultivation represented more than simply what a man knew; it represented his character. Godkin noted that the process of cultivation owed a great deal to "the old Calvinist theology, against which . . . the most bumptious youth hit his head at an early period of his career, and was reduced to thoughtfulness and self-examination, and forced to walk in ways that were not always to his liking."[37]

With such notions, it easy to see why Olmsted and Godkin were bound to part ways intellectually. Godkin had come more and more to embrace

what was, for Olmsted, only one side of his own painful inner paradox—
the claims of civilizing self-discipline versus the yearning for a more
unrestrained, "poetical" and authentic way of life. I suspect that, for
Godkin, as for Olmsted, the principle of self-restraint was the ultimate
defense against the barbarism within oneself and one's society. Moreover,
as Bender notes, men like Godkin and Olmsted "were concerned to
establish their opinion in public; they were not interested in a public or
political sphere that served as an arena for competing ideas and interests."
They believed (as proper Millites, I might add) that superior men—such
as one would find within the membership of the American Social Science
Association—could discover social truths "scientifically" and could dispense these truths to the masses, who ought to accede to the moral
authority of their intellectual superiors. When the realities of life proved
otherwise, Godkin withdrew into his (and his peers') defenses. "By the
late 1880s," Bender writes, "some of the narrowness and prejudice of his
journalism had become apparent; Godkin had brought Liberalism to a
shrill negation, always choosing pessimism over tolerance."[38] Thus Godkin had given himself over to his inner defenses almost totally. But
Olmsted would not, could not, withdraw from the public struggle for his
principles, his true self's purposes, even though he feared and hated that
struggle.

    If by 1882 Olmsted had traveled, intellectually and psychologically, no
farther than Norton and Godkin had tried to lead him, then he too might
have retreated into exile, to his new estate in Brookline, bemoaning the
passing of "the very pleasantest little oasis" of an idealized golden age.
But Olmsted had come through his catharsis of exile and inner retreat in
Mariposa much stronger than that and with a much deeper sense of his
own true self's purposes. He had enough strength to become reengaged
in the struggle for communitiveness in post–Civil War America, the
struggle to recreate the "pleasantest little oasis" that had been the New
England of *his* boyhood within the modern competitive, commercial city.
In this, Olmsted was helped by his future-mindedness, his belief in
scientific and technological progress and that tomorrow could be made
better than today.

    Far from harboring sentimental feelings about the rigorous discipline
of a Puritanism gone by as Godkin had, Olmsted celebrated the passing
of Calvinism as a sign of human progress. In 1887, recuperating from the
railroad accident that had reinjured his damaged leg, Olmsted was moved

by a letter from Brace to recall with great distaste their "Sartor Resartus days" in New Haven—the heated religiosity of their youth and the kind of religious speculation "that used to be such a terrifically cruel burden upon me." He believed it was "a mark of the amazing progress of New England" that he never thought about such things anymore. And he added: "What a different, happier and better life I should have had, had it always been so." Thus he could conclude that, "in spite of the growth of a wretched leisure class" and the consequent "spread of anarchism," the world had still advanced far more since his youth "than in any half century before." "In the old language," Olmsted told Brace, "I feel that we have been exceedingly blessed."[39]

But, in that letter to Brace, Olmsted also took note of the demands of travel and work with which he continued to burden himself. "I should like to feel free to undertake less," Olmsted wrote. The reason he could not "feel free" was inadvertently revealed in the midst of repenting his youthful obsession with "superstitious meandering." He had no time now for such nonsense, Olmsted commented, because he was "occupied enough with 'the duty that lies nearest to you.' " Thus, while the Transcendental preoccupations of his youth had long since faded, unmourned, Olmsted remained in thrall to the essential message he had taken from them—the claims of "duty" as it had been espoused in *Sartor Resartus*. While Godkin insisted upon the privileges earned through a Calvinistic upbringing, Olmsted insisted upon the responsibilities it had imposed.

Olmsted could be as clear-eyed as Godkin or Norton about the problems of the materialistic capitalism in their time—and as depressed as they by its impact upon the quality of life in America. But Olmsted's essential optimism, combined with his almost oppressive sense of responsibility, kept him in the struggle, fired up his resiliency time and again, and sustained his belief that *his* work *could* make a difference. In an important essay on the use of trees in the cities (1882), Olmsted would voice a sentiment similar to Norton's. The growth of cities, he would write, had created conditions that tended to "impoverish" the minds and tastes of Americans, to deprive them of what, "under our older village habits, [was] productive of a great deal of happiness . . . a most important source of national wealth." But he would characteristically add that through the planting of trees on village streets and in town parks "one can resist this tendency."[40]

Olmsted clearly recognized that his true self's purposes had not become less important to the burgeoning society around him—as it seemed to Norton and Godkin that *their* inner purposes had become irrelevant—but rather had grown even *more* important, and more important to an even broader constituency. Olmsted became, in fact, the epitome of a modern missionary, preaching a doctrine of salvation, of psychic salvation from the punishing pace and environment of the new metropolises. It was a gospel that, as the century wore on, would no longer be reserved for the patrician and gentry classes alone. And it was a gospel whose essentials Olmsted worked out in the first few years after his return from California.

CHAPTER 13

A Philosophy of
Urban Landscape Design

When Olmsted brought his California exile to a close in the fall of 1865 and returned to the New York parks, he was not simply returning to the work he had left in 1861. That work had been intensely personal; it had not required Olmsted, thus far, to evolve a defining philosophy for a life's work. However, after his failed attempts at practical success in New York, Washington, Mariposa, and San Francisco, Olmsted was ready to create out of his inner struggles a philosophy of urban landscape design to meet the needs of other men who were also struggling in that masculine world of commerce.

The social philosophy that had evolved in the course of Olmsted's "Civilization" notes served to bring his public pronouncements on urban design more into line with his own inner needs and purposes. Those needs and purposes had not changed during the period of his labors at the Sanitary Commission and his exile at Mariposa; if anything, they had become even more imperative. But Olmsted's immersion in his "Civilization" notes had enabled him to conjoin his own needs to those of his society in both intellectual and psychological terms. As a result, the nature of Olmsted's public discourse on the purpose of parks and upon urban design would become more comprehensive, more deeply felt, and more profound.

Both before and after the Civil War, Olmsted frequently cited the benefits of the park's natural scenery as a civilizing agent. After his upsetting visit in 1853 with the Southern aristocrat, Samuel Perkins Allison, Olmsted had suggested to Brace that the lower classes could be improved by association with more civilized classes: "get up parks, gardens, music, dancing schools, reunions which will be so attractive as to force into contact the good & bad, the gentlemanly and the rowdy."[1] Five years afterwards there would be an echo of this notion in Olmsted's description of Central Park, published in the Commission's second annual report, in January 1859: "The Park is intended to furnish healthful recreation for the poor and the rich, the young and the old, the vicious and the virtuous, so far as each can partake therein without infringing upon the rights of others, and no further."[2] In 1860, Olmsted commented to Henry Bellows that one could already see how Central Park "thus far justifies the highest hopes which have been entertained for its moral influence."[3] After the war, in his 1870 address to the American Social Science Association, Olmsted noted that the park "exercises a distinctly harmonizing and refining influence upon the most unfortunate and lawless classes of the city."[4] Statements like these were meant to validate his parks for the reformist gentry he was addressing—but they have precious little of the passionate immediacy of his lengthy passage, from that same 1870 speech, on the debilitative effects of both city life and commerce— the nerve-shattering and "hardening" effects of each.

   Whether talking about the benefits of association between classes of the population or of the moral influence of the park's natural scenery, Olmsted was merely reflecting the commonplace sentiments of the time. Joining William Cullen Bryant's crusade for a major New York park in 1848, Andrew Jackson Downing had stated that public parks "soften and humanize the rude, educate and enlighten the ignorant, and give continual enjoyment to the educated," breaking down the "artificial barriers" between classes. In 1851, in "The New York Park," an essay published in the *Horticulturist*, Downing expanded upon the notion of the benefits of association between classes: "they enjoy together the same music, breathe the same atmosphere of art, enjoy the same scenery, and grow into social freedom by the very influences of easy intercourse, space, and beauty that surround them."[5] These goals were the essence of "our republican profession," Downing had proclaimed in another *Horticulturist* essay several years earlier, specifically charging his fellow landscape designers to use their art to establish "a larger and more fraternal spirit in our social life."[6]

Since Downing was highly regarded in the Olmsted family (where his *Horticulturist* was read regularly) and was extremely influential upon Olmsted, it can be assumed that Olmsted was familiar with these ideas, which were commonly shared among the patrician and gentry members of his circle. These were sentiments in which Olmsted surely believed and which fit within his philosophy of the benefits of association. But such sentiments did not strike to the center of his being or of his experience.

On the other hand, it is easy to picture Olmsted himself during his literary republic years in the 1850s, walking the streets of Broadway to his lodgings or his work, caught up in the urban throng and having "constantly to watch, to foresee, and to guard against their movements." It is clear who was in Olmsted's mind when he spoke (in his 1870 ASSA speech) of "people from the country," who were so conscious of the effect of city life "on their nerves and minds." It was the gentry man, forced to compete in the hard and mad-paced city, for whom Olmsted had his truest and deepest compassion. It is worth recalling that Olmsted had told Calvert Vaux that he had once expected to spend most of his life both *working and living* in Central Park.[7] Upon his return from California, after several months in a boarding house on East Fourteenth Street in Manhattan, Olmsted moved his family to a house in rural Staten Island, from which he commuted by ferry to his work on the Brooklyn Park. It was only after the breakup with Vaux in 1872 that Olmsted moved his family into the combination home and office at 209 West Forty-sixth Street in Manhattan, which he would occupy until moving permanently to Brookline in 1882. The decade between, the final years of his intimate connection with the New York parks, would be one of continual conflict, aggravation, and illness.[8]

Ironically, as Ross Miller has observed, it was the restorative purposes of Olmsted's public parks that ultimately proved to be the more realistic. The notion that urban parks would serve a democratic end, breaking down the barriers between classes and "civilizing" the poor, proved to be utopian. The landscape architect "could easily make the city more livable," Miller writes, "but he could not redeem it, or change its basic commercial character." Parks had been expected to be the living symbols

23. The Terrace Bridge and Bethesda Fountain, c. 1894. This is perhaps the area of the park that most perfectly blends the architectural vision of Calvert Vaux with the idea of natural beauty that Olmsted carried with him from his Connecticut boyhood. (Museum of the City of New York.)

of gentry culture, democratizing and civilizing. But that was asking too much of them. Nevertheless, parks could and did become "a prominent source of relief from the persistent demands of urban life."[9] In fact, the parks as restorative refuges were the essence of Olmsted's contribution to urban life, a contribution that derived from his own psychological struggles.

Indeed, it was psychological recuperation that was the subject of the very first report issued on the Brooklyn park (1866) after Olmsted's return to New York. This "*unbending* of faculties," the report stated, was central to the task the designers had undertaken, and it could only be secured "by the occupation of the imagination with objects and reflections of a quite different character from those which are associated with their bent condition."[10] Recuperation is the stated goal here—not elevation of faculties nor refinement of tastes. The restorative purposes of the park represented a *democratic* goal only to the extent that people of various classes might have needed such "unbending." Olmsted, however, had in mind mainly *men*—gentry men, as well as perhaps men of the new middle and professional classes. "Men must come together, and must be seen coming together, in carriages, on horseback and on foot, and the concourse of animated life which will thus be formed, must in itself be made, if possible, an attractive and diverting spectacle," the report states. I suspect that the diversion to be found in "men coming together" is a diversion from the ruthless competition with which men confronted one another elsewhere in the commercial city. It is meant to be a triumph of the "strain" to communitiveness over the "strain" to barbarism.

If permitting people "to come together for the single purpose of enjoyment" was one goal of urban park design, the second was providing scenery that offered "the most agreeable contrast to that of the rest of the town."[11] Pastoral scenery, the report continued, would consist of "combinations of trees, standing singly or in groups, and casting their shadows over broad stretches of turf, or repeating their beauty by reflection upon the calm surface of pools." Here again, the purpose of that scenery was surely not to edify or elevate the mind, but rather to produce an effect that would be "to the highest degree tranquilizing" to the visitor. Thus, the restorative purposes of the park were accomplished both through a noncompetitive, nonthreatening "coming together" and through the restful contemplation of natural scenery.

Olmsted was not wrong in assuming the debilitating effects of urban life, no matter how subjective his assumption was. But it is important to understand that Olmsted's views *were* subjective—representing the singular interest of a man habituated to the rural life and to the passive enjoyment of natural scenery; of a man weary and wary of the city; a man intellectually assured enough (or perhaps obsessed enough) to believe that *his* viewpoint was the only correct one. Olmsted had considered it one of his primary duties, he had told Vaux, to instruct the public on the *correct* use of the park. Thus, as Geoffrey Blodgett has suggested, Olmsted found that his own view of passive, contemplative, genteel recreation as the most appropriate for his parks was at odds "with the demands of the active young working-class male." Olmsted, Blodgett adds, responded only "grudgingly to their desire for 'manly and blood-tingling recreations,' 'boisterous fun and rough sports.' "[12] Clearly, Olmsted believed his views were entitled to prevail over the democratic working out of the various notions, held by various publics, of what a park should be.

True to the gentry class to which he belonged, Olmsted could not conceive that in a democratic republic the people have a right to be wrong. For Olmsted, this was no mere intellectual civics debate, but rather, as he had stated to Mariana Van Rensselaer, it was warfare. It was not a political issue, but a moral one. And thus it became a powerfully felt mortal struggle. It became the war of civilization against barbarism. It is rather tragic that Central Park—which Olmsted saw as a place of retreat from the furious competitive struggles of the great city—should itself have become one of the fiercest battlegrounds of his strife-filled life, leading to his physical and mental breakdowns in 1859–1860 and 1878–1879.

Even Walt Whitman, the great celebrator of "Manhatta," had left New York in 1862, never again to make his home or career there. It was in this period, according to David Cavitch, that Whitman came to feel that his "Oedipal striving for equality with his father [was] pointless: not purposeless, just futile." Whitman had "no recourse," Cavitch adds, "except to align himself in partial defeat but secure intimacy with the feminine side of his nature." One aspect of that feminine alignment was the role he assumed in wartime—the "wound-dresser" who spent those years in Washington, taking up "an arduous routine as a volunteer hospital aide, comforting young soldiers in their pain, loneliness, and, often, their final agony."[13] As much as Whitman continued to celebrate "Manhatta," that great city of Oedipal striving was no longer the place in which he could fulfill his psychic needs.

Certainly Olmsted's personal experience of New York was valid and necessary, and it inevitably fed a creative impulse that left that city with one of its grandest legacies, Central Park. Yet behind that creative impulse, was a darker one. Beyond the fear of the thrusting physicality of that enormous city itself—of its din and dirt, sidewalks and paving stones and sky-screening buildings, crowds and carts and omnibuses—was a psychic fear, a fear of what the city represented, was a mecca for, celebrated and rewarded: a fear of the driven, competitive spirit in mankind and in himself. And it was a similar impulse that gave rise to the more Hobbesian moods of Olmsted's "Civilization" notes, yet enriched the social philosophy he had evolved therein.

The philosophy Olmsted began constructing at Mariposa for his masterwork on civilization would be transformed into a rationale for urban landscape design, a rationale that was expounded piecemeal during the first few years of his return from California through a series of reports dealing with the design of parks and suburbs in San Francisco, Berkeley, Brooklyn, and Chicago.[14]

The driving principle of Olmsted's emergent public philosophy was that great cities were the focal point of Western civilization; that they were bound to increase greatly in size, in terms of both population and geographic reach, swallowing up neighboring suburbs or creating new ones; and that scientific and technological advances had occurred, and would continue to occur rapidly, that could make these great cities more livable, but only if these advances were harnessed to sound urban planning.[15]

The underlying motivation for both his public work and its justifying philosophy, however, was first and foremost to provide his fellow *men*— especially the patricians and the genteel intellectuals whose delegate he was—with a retreat from the torments that he and they had suffered in their city life. Though he never named the concept again, I believe that Olmsted's parks were meant to appeal to that strain of communitiveness he thought present in *all* men; were meant to offer men a way to find intimacy, completeness, and psychological retreat, at least for a time; and were meant to provide men with a restorative respite from the competitive world of commerce.

The intensely personal origins of the broad vision Olmsted now began to present to his public is revealed in a passage from a report on Prospect Park published in 1868.[16] Toward the end of this report, Olmsted argued the case for creating a boulevardlike parkway, running from Fort Hamilton (overlooking the Narrows of New York harbor) through the Brooklyn park to the East River.[17] Olmsted argued that creation of such a parkway would encourage the development of well-to-do communities in the area, that the parkway would be flanked by "detached villas each in the midst of a small private garden." Olmsted described the ideal candidate for the purchase of such a villa as a "country boy" of "superior calibre"—one who would have come to the city seeking those "enlarged opportunities" that would make him wealthy. "Trees and grass are, however, wrought into the very texture and fibre of his constitution," Olmsted wrote, observing that such men would look for the means of adding "the old country flavor" to their city lives in order to make those lives "palatable as well as profitable." Olmsted suggested that a ruralized suburb, such as he envisioned along his Brooklyn parkway, would be the ideal place for such men to make their homes.[18]

The "city-bred country boy" described by Olmsted draws heavily upon his own experience. It was Frederick, that country boy of superior caliber, who had been irresistibly drawn to New York, to the publishing company of Dix and Edwards, where he had hoped to find both a place in the literary republic and relative wealth. Further, Fairsted, the home that Frederick would purchase in Brookline more than a decade later, became the kind of home he had in mind here: a "villa" in a ruralized suburb of a major commercial city (Boston). And of whom could it be more fittingly said than of Olmsted that "trees and grass [were] wrought into the very texture and fibre of his constitution"?

The personal history behind the public philosophy can also be seen in Olmsted's proposal for a San Francisco park.[19] San Francisco, Olmsted wrote, was destined to be a major city, with "many millions of people" and a more certain future than even the older cities of New York and Boston. Clearly, that dynamic city, buccaneer society and all, had held a great attraction for Olmsted during his Mariposa exile; he had even thought of settling there, perhaps publishing a newspaper. It was, therefore, largely his own experience he drew upon when arguing the need for a major rural park in San Francisco. Olmsted claimed that the more important part of that city's population (that is, gentry men) "is wearing itself out with constant labor, study, and business anxieties, at a rate which is unknown elsewhere." Such a claim recalls Olmsted's reported bouts of "brain fever" during his California labors, especially in light of his comment: "Cases of death, or of unwilling withdrawal from active business, compelled by premature failure of vigor of the brain, are more common in San Francisco than anywhere else."

Olmsted's proposed solution was the one to which he himself had turned at Central Park and at Yosemite: a psychic retreat to the bosom of nature. He called for the creation of "a spacious and attractive public-ground" businessmen would visit daily for "healthful recreation."

Refreshing pictures of sylvan scenes, and of a multitude of animated, pleasure-seeking men, women, and children, thus crowd in upon the general daily experience of men strained with the eagerness of competition, or anxiously intent upon the means of meeting their engagements and preserving their integrity.

Those who continued to work obsessively, he added, would find that they could not depend upon "others so misusing their strength." Without recourse to such a park, he argued, work-obsessed men would eventually be forced into a premature retirement from the business world.

But, once again, it was Olmsted himself who was the admitted obsessive "hard worker" and who had been told that he must, for his health's sake, retire from an active business life. It was Olmsted himself who had been "strained with the eagerness of competition," who had been "anxiously intent upon the means of . . . preserving [his] integrity." What was personal to Olmsted, however, was also relevant to the gentry elite, the class of men whom he represented and whose delegate he had been. We remember that in 1858 George Templeton Strong recorded in his diary: "Improved the day by leaving Wall Street early and set off . . . to explore the Central Park." *Rus in Urbe*, Strong called it, after touring the Ramble and climbing the observation tower that was then atop the summit of Vista Rock.[20]

Consideration of the inner sources of Olmsted's emergent philosophy of urban design should not obscure the valid application of his own psychological needs to the psychological needs of the community at large. Nor should it obscure the sometimes breathtaking foresight of Olmsted's visionary planning. Roper points out, for example, that Olmsted had called for a grand promenade in his San Francisco pleasure ground (to be located near the center of the city), which would also serve as a firebreak. Olmsted's plan was rejected for reasons of economy. Forty years later, however, the dense city blocks that lined the area Olmsted had designated as his promenade-firebreak were dynamited "as a last desperate resort to stop the ruinous blaze that followed the earthquake of 1906."[21]

The second of the reports that had their birth in Olmsted's California exile, his Berkeley campus proposal of 1866 (never implemented), took his emerging philosophy into the another area of urban design that preoccupied him in these years: suburban neighborhoods.[22] The principal requirements of Olmsted's plan were supposedly to be directed toward the needs of students, but he quickly introduced the persons he was most truly concerned about: those men who would "gain wealth" in growing San Francisco, men for whom "a large number of residences [would] be needed . . . suited to a family life in accordance with a high scale of civilized requirements." Olmsted thought the vicinity of a college campus an ideal place to secure those requirements of civilized suburban life. Thus, the first of his principal requirements for his college was that the plan "should present sufficient inducements to the formation of a neighborhood of refined and elegant homes"—that is, the same sort of inducement for the construction of gentry "villas" that would be offered by his 1868 proposal for a majestic Brooklyn parkway.[23]

Beyond the community itself, Olmsted also addressed the requirements of the ideal home, noting that the proper design of a residence would take into account something more than just "human comfort"— would in fact give as much or more attention to the degree to which the *health* of the "inmates" was favorably affected by the design. All homes provide shelter; good homes also provide adequate sunlight and fresh air. Olmsted thought it ironic that the more luxurious the home, the more often it was deficient in these latter respects.

In a curious and difficult passage of this proposal, Olmsted argued the need for "attractive open-air apartments" (single rooms or suites of rooms within the houses he had been discussing).[24] His notion was that people ought to be able to spend "hours at a time" in such apartments, with all necessary "convenience and ease," so that ordinary occupations need not be interrupted, nor conversations disrupted, in order to engage in activities required to preserve "health and cheerfulness." When such apartments are lacking, even in the most luxurious of homes, the occupants are likely to be troubled by "languor, dullness of perceptions, nervous debility or distinct nervous diseases." Indeed, if the interior design of the home is really poor, one might have to travel abroad to preserve one's health; or one might be tempted into indulging in "unhealthy excitements" or even to develop "depraved imaginations and appetites, and . . . habits of dissipation."

Here again, it would seem that Olmsted's artist self had drawn its creative imperative from the oppressive experiences of his competitive striving self. One must think of the flat that Frederick had rented on Broadway after moving from the roomy, spacious, and bright farm house on Staten Island—a flat that was in the midst of all the noisy and lurid temptations of Manhattan life. And we remember the unhealthy life that Olmsted had lived in Washington, when his work day embraced the middle of the night and his office too often served as his bedroom. But also Olmsted directly appealed to his gentry peers in the assertion that

24. Fairsted—Olmsted's home and office in Brookline, Massachusetts, to which Olmsted relocated in 1882, a few years after he was dismissed from all connection with the New York parks. Like the Mount St. Vincent Convent, Fairsted fulfilled Olmsted's ideal for a residence—airy and open to daylight, surrounded by trees and shrubbery. Alongside of one wing (not visible here) is a magnificent elm tree. (National Park Service, Frederick Law Olmsted National Historical Site.)

persons poorly domiciled might eventually be forced to travel abroad for their health—a practice that both he and they were well acquainted with.[25]

Olmsted's accommodations on Broadway and in Washington stand in stark contrast to the domesticity and airiness and openness of the "apartments" at the Mount St. Vincent Convent in Central Park, where Frederick had both home and office and could apportion his day between the two at his own will. As with the villas described in the Brooklyn parkway report, Mount St. Vincent likely set the pattern for the home that Olmsted finally sought and found at Fairsted in Brookline—a home that, as any visitor today might judge, fits all the prescriptions of the passage cited above. Olmsted's home at the Mount St. Vincent convent in Central Park combined within itself *both* of the aspects of urban landscape design that Olmsted would be so concerned with after his return to New York in

1865. That is, Mount St. Vincent had offered a "domestic beauty" that was at once both a suburban setting and an urban park.

Both Mount St. Vincent and Fairsted, in their grounds as well as in their surrounding neighborhoods, fulfilled Olmsted's prescription for the ideal suburban setting—that it must supply "fresh air in abundance, pleasant natural scenery, trees, flowers, birds, and, in short, all the essential advantages of a rural residence." It was not enough that one's private grounds be spacious and well landscaped, Olmsted said; one should also have "good *out-goings* from the private grounds," both socially and environmentally.

As we have seen, Olmsted's preliminary thoughts on suburban neighborhoods were first presented in his 1861 letter concerning the development of Washington Heights—[26] then were further elaborated in the Brooklyn parkway and Berkeley reports discussed above. His most thoroughly considered discussion of the subject was contained within an 1868 proposal for a "suburban village" near Chicago, to be called Riverside.[27]

Olmsted began this report with a familiar theme: the unprecedented growth of the great commercial cities in the modern era. This, he added, had been accompanied by a "concurrent, and probably identical . . . unprecedented movement of invention, energy, and skill, toward the production of certain classes of conveniences and luxuries, which, even yet, can generally be fully enjoyed by great numbers of people only in large towns." But Olmsted now discerned the recent growth of "a countertide of migration, especially affecting the more intelligent and more fortunate classes," toward the "separation of business and dwelling streets, and toward rural spaciousness of the latter." The demand for country homes and estates had been spurred by the growing conviction that the advances that had occurred in large towns had been made "at too great a sacrifice of certain advantages," which could, at present, only be found in "semi-rural" surroundings.

In his proposal for Riverside, Olmsted stressed the same purposes that had been earlier suggested for the Brooklyn park. Indeed, the Riverside proposal stemmed from the same design philosophy that had called forth the pastoral scenery of the park. Riverside would achieve "secluded peacefulness and tranquility" through the "tasteful and convenient disposition of shade trees" throughout the entire suburb, providing the community with "the charm of sylvan beauty." When combined with streets that curved to follow the natural topography, the overall effect would be "positively picturesque," contrasting vividly with the "constant repeated right angles, straight lines, and flat surfaces" that characterized the great commercial cities.

But inasmuch as Chicago has severe winters, such charm and tranquility would be available only half the year. Thus Riverside offers another example of the continuing dominance of Olmsted's imagination and psyche by his psychosocial fetish: the trees of summer. Similarly, one description of a pastoral scene for the Brooklyn park (in the Olmsted and Vaux report) speaks of "combinations of trees . . . casting their shadows over broad stretches of turf" and their "beauty" reflected in the nearby "pools." Here again, it is the tranquility of a summer day that is being summoned up. Where were "town-strained" men to find their psychic retreat during a Brooklyn winter? Apparently, it was only the image of the feminized summer shade tree that had the power to restore.

The Riverside proposal suggested that "to ensure success" the ideal suburb must have two other qualifications (beyond the requisite pastoral influence of trees). The first qualification was "domicilation of men by families," by which Olmsted evidently meant privacy and seclusion to promote family intimacy and retreat from the encroaching world. But the strain toward communitiveness could not be promoted, even within oneself, by retreating into one's own home. Thus, Olmsted's second qualification was for "the harmonious association and co-operation of men in a community, and the intimate relationship and constant intercourse, and inter-dependence between families." To promote the latter purpose, Olmsted returned to the image of the idealized New England village of his boyhood—an image that was, in fact, exemplified by his mother's hometown of Cheshire. He called for public grounds with "the character of informal village-greens, commons and play-grounds, rather than of enclosed and defended parks and gardens." In providing for such amenities, Olmsted wrote, the inhabitants would prove that "they are Christians, loving one another, and not Pagans, fearing one another," because they had taken the care to have the means of "coming together, of being together, and especially of recreating together on common ground."[28] That is, their ability to "come together" in social harmony rather than in hostile competition would be proof that the "strain" toward Christian communitiveness was winning out over the "strain" toward pagan barbarism and savagery.

The phenomenon Olmsted had discerned—the "counter-tide of migration" in which upscale families began to seek "semi-rural" homes—was surely accelerating in the years following the Civil War.[29] And it was a phenomenon to which Olmsted would be particularly sensitive, for it was, again, reflective of his own inner need, the same inner need he had expressed nearly three decades earlier, when, as a boy of eighteen serving an unhappy apprenticeship with a Manhattan merchant, he had written his stepmother: "Oh, how I long to be where I was a year ago, midst two lofty mountains, pursuing the course of the purling brook . . . under the sweeping willows, & the waving elms."[30] The source of Olmsted's resonant identification with the flight to the suburbs, as well as city dweller's need for pastoral parks, was in his own desire to flee from the *masculine* world of commerce to the symbolic breasts, the flowing milk, and the sheltering skirts of the lost mother—as represented by the *feminine* world of nature, by rural life as opposed to urban, by *being* as opposed to *doing*. As pronounced as this need was in Olmsted, because of his singulai psychodynamics, it represented also a romantic vision shared by a very large number of mid-nineteenth century Americans.[31]

Olmsted's social theorizing throughout the latter part of the 1860s was fed by his own conflicting needs both to make his career in the city ("doing") and to find his tranquility in the country ("being"). This inner conflict between (in nineteenth-century terms) Olmsted's "masculine" active, achieving self and his "feminine" passive, contemplative self has been noted by Thomas Bender:

[Olmsted's] life history reveals a longing for a freer, more authentic, and less competitive way of life than American society, particularly in the larger cities, offered. Yet one also finds him seeking opportunities for the exercise of his powers and the exertion of influence on the course of events that could only be found in the world of the city.[32]

The existential paradox in Olmsted's psyche was fed by his ambition, his inner feeling of being "cruelly prodded up" to take more upon himself "than he was equal to."[33] In Eriksonian terms, this drive for success and recognition represented the universal desire of sons to supplant their fathers. But in Olmsted this drive, as I have observed, also represented a need to defend his birthright as the first-born (the first among equals) against the competition of John Hull, who had the "advantage" of being named for their father.

Both drives—to supplant the father and to defend his place against his brother—involved destructive, aggressive unconscious wishes (savage and barbarous wishes) that demanded repression (self-restraint). For Olmsted, this demand could only be met by nurturing the feminine element of "being" within himself, the strain toward communitiveness. How was he to be both "doer" and "be-er," to both yield to his aggressive ambitions and at the same time to repress the destructive wishes they represented? The answer, taking final form after 1865, was to turn his false self's ambitions to his true self's purposes: to undertake the grand design of his reparative creative work; to become the agent for the amelioration of the effects of competition.

Olmsted's philosophy of urban landscape was put forth in its most complete form thus far—one of the most complete expressions of it he would ever make—in the important paper he had been asked to deliver at a meeting of the American Social Science Association at the Lowell Institute in Boston on February 25, 1870.[34]

Olmsted began with his usual recitation of the trend to urbanization, aided and abetted by technological advances, which, together with cultural riches, had made town life seem more desirable than rural life and had made the great cities the focal point of civilization. The leitmotif for the remainder of the address was set when Olmsted turned to the hazards of city life, which corrupts the body and spirit in various ways. One's lungs, Olmsted noted, are corrupted by foul air, which "tends strongly to vitiate all our sources of vigor." But, he added, there is an even more serious cause of "irritation and waste" of physical powers and of damage to "the mind and the moral strength." This characteristic ordering of Olmsted's priorities would be even more evident in his 1882 essay, "Trees in Streets and in Parks," where he would state that both the "air purifying value" and the "decorative motive" of planting trees wre *subordinate* to its paramount object: to offer a restorative, often unconscious, "solace and comfort" to town-strained minds.[35]

It was at this point in his 1870 address that Olmsted made the observation about city life that I have already discussed:

whenever we walk through the denser part of town, to merely avoid collision with those we meet and pass upon the sidewalks, we have constantly to watch, to foresee, and to guard against their movements. This involves a consideration of their intentions, a calculation of their strength and weakness. . . . Much of the intercourse between men when engaged in the pursuits of commerce has the same tendency—a tendency to regard others in a hard if not always hardening way. . . . This is one of the many ways in which . . . men who have been brought up . . . in the streets, who have been most directly and completely affected by town influences, so generally show, along with a remarkable quickness of apprehension, a peculiarly hard sort of selfishness.[36]

This "peculiarly hard sort of selfishness" is of course Olmsted's familiar *bête noire*, barbarism. The tragedy in this is that "every day of their lives" such men have met "face-to-face . . . thousands of their fellow-men, and yet have had no experience of anything in common with them." In fact, Olmsted observed, these townsmen have devoted all their calculation to drawing away from one another, rather than experiencing a "friendly flowing" toward those with whom they have come into contact in the course of their affairs. The strain toward barbarism in the harsh urban world overcomes the strain toward communitiveness; fear obviates fellowship. The result is debilitation, mental exhaustion, for all but the hardest of men. Furthermore, Olmsted warned, "every evil to which men are specially liable when living in towns, is likely to be aggravated in the future, unless means are devised and adapted in advance to prevent it."

One solution, Olmsted stated, would be to plant trees by the sides of at least some streets, even in the commercial quarter. Trees would both purify the air and offer temporary seclusion and "escape from conditions requiring vigilance, wariness, and activity toward other men." However, when he contemplated the actual fate of trees in urban areas, Olmsted suddenly exploded into a passion of indignation, thus suggesting the significance of trees—Olmsted's psychosocial fetish symbol—for his self-representation:

Thousands and tens of thousands are planted every year in a manner and under conditions as nearly certain as possible to either *kill them outright*, or so to lessen their vitality as to prevent their *natural and beautiful development*, and to cause *premature decrepitude*. Often, too, as their lower limbs are found inconvenient . . . they are *deformed by butcherly amputations*. If by rare good fortune they are suffered to become beautiful, they still stand to be *condemned to death* at any time, as obstructions in the highway.[37]

To understand the depth of self-revelation here, one need only contemplate the calm language with which Olmsted normally described, for example, the plight of working-class men and women in his various reports. Nowhere else in this paper does his language reveal such passionate resentment. The imagery, I believe, was drawn from his own life and torments. Consider that a child who had been sent away from home to rude, often cruel, boarding schools might well be said to have been "planted" in such a way as to prevent his "natural and beautiful development." It is possible, also, that as a child Olmsted had feared that the purpose of his abandonment was to "kill him outright." Anger that cannot be directed toward its provoking target (as in the case of a puritanically raised child and his remote, powerful, imposing father) must eventually be directed inward. Aggressive wishes evoke self-condemnation and self-punishment, as had occurred in Olmsted's carriage accident, when one of his "inconvenient" lower limbs was "deformed" and very nearly lost to "butcherly amputation."[38] Finally, Olmsted suffered under the continual fear that as much as he had overcome his obstacles and succeeded in life ("become beautiful"), he might yet be found to be an "obstruction" and "condemned to death." Was that not precisely the outcome—an outcome Olmsted would claim to have welcomed—of his 1893 anecdote of the honey locust and the axeman? In that anecdote, the beautiful tree he had planted as a boy had been felled in its splendid maturity, not because of any defect in the tree, but because it had outlived its usefulness. And in this same 1870 ASSA paper, Olmsted included a scornful note about the proposed felling of a stately tree that had stood in the center of "the oldest town in New England" since its founding. The tree was to be cut down even though it was "perfectly healthy and almost as beautiful as it [was] venerable." This tree, he said, was an American elm.

There is yet another analogy to be found in Olmsted's plea that room must be made for trees in the crowded commercial cities—trees grown to the full beauty of their natural development. This was a plea also that men's true selves might be given room to flourish.[39] It represented, also, the fear that the false self of accommodation (of convenience and necessity) would take over, an ugly and deformed caricature of the person that might have been—and that the true self, obstruction that it was to the busy highway of commerce, would suffer a premature death.

As with the San Francisco and the Brooklyn parks, Olmsted proposed two forms of relief, two forms of "receptive recreation." Olmsted had already distinguished between "exertive" and "receptive" recreation, citing both chess-playing and ball-playing as examples of the former and appreciation of the fine arts as an example of the latter. He made brief reference to the need for cities to accommodate exertive recreation through smaller, satellite parks, rather than in the large pastoral park—so that the peaceful, pastoral acres required for the receptive recreation of the many would not be sacrificed to the exertive recreation of the few (as in sacrificing meadowlands for ball fields).

The first form of *receptive* recreation, which Olmsted discussed only briefly, he called "gregarious." This was his familiar concept of people "coming together"—in this case, in large numbers in one place, simply for the pleasure of being there together. In the New York parks, he said, one might see a "hundred thousand people" thus assembled, "poor and rich, young and old, Jew and gentile," gathering "with an evident glee in the prospect of coming together, all classes largely represented, with a common purpose . . . *competitive with none*, disposing to jealousy and spiritual or intellectual pride toward none, each adding by his mere presence to the pleasure of all others."[40] Simply to assemble thus in pleasurable friendliness, "in pure air and under the light of heaven," was in itself a healthful influence "directly counteractive to that of the ordinary hard, hustling working hours of town life." This democratic form of recreation could be met mainly through promenades, Olmsted suggested.

Gregariousness, however, could at best be only a *minor* stimulus to communitiveness, for there was no cooperative endeavor here, no give and take, no real intercourse. It was largely ceremonial, a way for men to reverse their usual pattern of engaging each other in "hard if not always hardening" ways in the struggle to dominate, control, or subdue one another. Through the ceremony of the promenade, men could smile at each other in mutual enjoyment, wanting nothing from the other, without fear of the other. Gregariousness would be, in today's vernacular, a form of behavior modification.

The rest of Olmsted's address dealt mainly with what he considered to be of the deepest and most restorative psychic value: the "neighborly" form of receptive recreation. It was this form that would most encourage development of the strain toward communitiveness in men and thus would most effectively counteract the barbarism of city life. Rather than a ritual coming together in large groups, neighborliness involved coming together in small, intimate groups; it encouraged domesticity; and it fulfilled the highest purpose of Olmsted's pastoral parks. The impulse to neighborliness was, in fact, another incarnation of his notion of the strain toward communitiveness.

Olmsted claimed that too many young men satisfied this impulse by gathering with their peers "on the curb-stones or in the dram shops," under conditions little conducive to developing "a spark of admiration, of delicacy, manliness, or tenderness." Other men, however, satisfied this same impulse by gathering around "the tea-table with neighbors and wives and children, and all things clean and wholesome, softening and refining." The latter example suggests Olmsted's projection of the idealized home of one's childhood, a home everyone wishes to have had—the fantasy that had become, in fact, the cornerstone of the Victorian cult of domesticity. Moreover, the adjectives Olmsted employs here, notwithstanding the almost compulsive Victorian use of *manliness*, are almost all those associated with femininity.[41] It was this latter, feminine, means of satisfying the neighborly impulse that Olmsted hoped to foster and accomplish with his pastoral urban parks.

Thus, Olmsted's philosophy of park design—a projection of his own need for psychic retreat—accepted the necessities to which men of nineteenth-century urban America were driven, accepted the hard realities of competitive masculine life. But if Olmsted accepted, however reluctantly, the fact that there should be masculine and feminine spheres in his society, he also saw (was made to see, by inner compulsion) the need for these spheres to merge, at least for a time. Olmsted's ideal was, once more, the "familiar domestic gathering, where the prattle of children mingles with the easy conversation of the more sedate, the bodily requirements satisfied with good cheer, fresh air, agreeable light, moderate temperature, snug shelter." For Olmsted, only this highly idealized, impossibly perfect, feminine sphere of "family life" could "stimulate and keep alive the more tender sympathies, and give play to faculties such as may be dormant in business or on the promenade." Pastoral parks, with their "clean greensward . . . and a sufficient number of trees," were to be public realization of the feminine, domestic quality of a loving, sheltering home. They would provide "the greatest possible contrast" with those aspects of city life "which compel us to walk circumspectly, watchfully, jealously."

The great, pastoral urban parks, then, would be family life writ large. Where women provided for a pleasant domestic setting within the home, nature herself would furnish the park with "the beauty of the fields, the meadow, the prairie, of the green pastures, and the still waters." For him, both the home and the parks he championed served the same end: "tranquility and rest to the mind."

In this speech, in the urban design philosophy Olmsted fashioned out of his inner needs and psychic conflicts, nature had become the idealized mother, providing the great sheltering environment reminiscent of the home of tranquility, security, warmth, and love that for him may never have existed in reality, but that in his unconscious fantasies had been provided by his lost mother.[42] Olmsted's plans for ideal suburban life—homes with "open-air apartments," situated on spacious landscaped grounds, along winding tree-shaded streets—were to be the ultimate embodiment of this fantasy. But it was to urban parks that he devoted most of his later career and for which he would become the "representative man." It is noteworthy that the nurturance to be provided by pastoral parks, their beneficial restfulness, were to be only temporary refuges from the demands of urban life, perhaps as Olmsted's own periods of domestic happiness—as a child and as a man—were only temporary intervals in his life of wanderings and turmoil.

CHAPTER 14

Defending the Vision

The men who had tried to respond to the great variety of needs of the
growing constituency for the New York parks were by no means simply
hack politicians and demagogues, and few, if any, were working for
corrupt purposes. Indeed, it was probably even more frustrating to Olmsted
that opposition to *his* views of the park's purposes and needs was so often
endorsed by men he would otherwise admire. As Olmsted told Vaux in
1883, "every year in [Central Park's] history some project of ruinous
tendency has had the warm support of many good men." But as far as
Olmsted was concerned, the true purposes of Central Park had not
changed in twenty-six years: to provide near at hand to its potential users
"natural, verdant and sylvan scenery for the refreshment of town-strained
men, women and children, especially in those conditions of life that
preclude resort to scenery of absolutely [unrestrained and] unsophisti-
cated nature."[1] And, as he had been telling Vaux since 1863 at least, "the
nature of the park depends upon gradual education of public opinion in
appreciation of its natural scenery." But the struggle to propagate and
defend this vision of the New York parks became increasingly difficult in
the latter part of the century: the public was many times larger than in
antebellum New York and far more diverse; public tastes were changing,
defined by men younger than Olmsted.

In 1886, even as the nearby constituency of the uptown New York
parks had become increasingly mixed, the current New York park management solicited Olmsted's help in enlarging and greatly extending the

roads to be used for carriage-riding in and between the three parks. Olmsted declined to be involved in such a project, attacking the idea as yet another misguided intrusion upon the basic purposes of the park.[2]

In opposing the project, Olmsted used his reply to the President of the Park Department as an opportunity to recall the fundamental design principles of the original Central Park plan. One basic principle, he said, was that "there should be great numbers of trees with a spread of branches and standing in relations to one another that could not be expected to be attained in less time than forty years." He added that all other design considerations, especially roads for vehicular traffic, had been subordinated to that fundamental principle. But as time had passed and the management of the park continually changed hands, the original purposes had begun to be overlooked; a series of little things had been done to the park that, collectively, had proved "disastrous to the original ends of the work." Most of these were features that had been thought desirable for some special segment of the public: the "riders, the drivers, the walkers, the skaters, the curlers, those who are fond of croquet, or archery or lawn tennis, or cricket or baseball; those who have a special interest in exotic plants, in flowers, in perennials, in specimen trees; those who think the park is too shady, those who think it is too sunny and so on."

No revisions of the original plan should ever be made, Olmsted insisted, that would subvert the longstanding, primary purpose of the park, which he now stated once again: "to provide for the mass of the population unable to go as much out of town as would be desirable, a retreat as completely rural in character as the circumstances would admit." Noting the changing circumstances of the city, Olmsted pointed to a paradox: the number of "carriage visitors" could be expected to continually increase, but their proportion would continually *decrease* relative "to those who use it on foot"—an observation I take to be a recognition of the increasingly middle-class usage of the park. Thus, Olmsted came down more emphatically than ever before in favor of the priority of the "neighborly" pastoral park over "gregarious" forms of recreation:

The fact is that the enjoyment of rural scenery, or of any approach to rural quiet and tranquility [that is, the primary object of the park], cannot well be provided for in the midst of a city by arrangements that will also provide in a perfectly satisfactory way for the pleasure that people take in great throngs, in making displays of fine dresses, equipages, horses and horsemanship, and in watching such displays. . . . We cannot have our cake and eat it.

With three-fourths of the forty years required to bring the park into its full "rural charm" now having passed, Olmsted urged the Board not "to throw away the advantage that has thus been gained."

In Boston, where Olmsted's work was just getting under way, similar demographic changes were then taking place. Sam Bass Warner describes the growth of Boston and the development of the three southerly suburbs (Roxbury, West Roxbury, and Dorchester) that gave need to the park system and provided both the rationale and the land for the "emerald necklace" of parks and parkways that resulted. After the panic of 1873, a "gigantic boom" in the 1880s and 1890s brought to these suburbs great numbers of middle-class commuters "whose jobs remained in old sections of Boston."[3]

While working on the Boston park system in 1886, Olmsted took note of a similar rise in middle-class usage of Prospect Park, owing to the advent of street cars. "The larger part of the people to whom the Brooklyn Park has thus proved unexpectedly helpful," Olmsted wrote in a Boston report, "are the very best sort of frugal and thrifty working-men, their wives, and their children."[4] Clearly, Olmsted assumed that the same phenomenon would be seen in the "rural parks" of the Boston system—especially in Franklin Park, located in West Roxbury.

In Franklin Park, Olmsted had the opportunity to design for both the "neighborly" and the "gregarious" forms of recreation—in an almost literal realization of his 1870 address to the ASSA. The key to the design, as discussed by Cynthia Zaitzevsky, was the creation of *two parks* on the site.[5] The first (using two-thirds of the total acreage available) was "the Country Park . . . to be used solely for the enjoyment of natural scenery." The second (smaller) park was the "Ante-Park," which would contain not only a grand mall "for promenading on foot, horseback, and carriage," but also various and quite sizable athletic facilities, a zoo, and a small playground for children.

Many of the facilities designed for the Ante-Park reflected the kinds of changes in park use that Galen Cranz associates with the transition from the "Pleasure Ground" stage of park development to the "Reform Park" stage after the turn of the century. But, as we have seen, most of these demands (which Cranz assigns solely to this later stage) actually existed from at least the post–Civil War decade; it was only the priorities that had changed.[6]

Olmsted's plan for Franklin Park suggests that he had become more accommodating to some of these demands. Or at least, he had understood that he and his associates must set aside space to meet such needs, if his pastoral parks were not to be cannibalized, as he feared was happening in New York. In Boston, however, Olmsted had the chance to work with an unusual coalition of Brahmin patricians, gentry Mugwumps, and civic-minded Irish-American politicians. The latter had taken power in the city in 1885—much to Olmsted's dread—but had sought a "functional rapport" with the "Yankee elite" in the Mugwump wing of the Democratic Party.[7] The plan for an Ante-Park in Franklin Park seems to suggest an accommodation to the various constituencies thus represented ; but it was the Country Park," the pastoral park, that would fulfill Olmsted's True Self purposes.

Given the psychic processes through which, according to Olmsted, people would most benefit from sceneric surroundings, it is very clear that only the Country Park could serve his purposes. In his 1882 essay, "Trees in Streets and in Parks," Olmsted tried, somewhat awkwardly, to differentiate between the conscious and the unconscious forms of recreation offered by parks and scenery. Conscious recreation, he stated, was a reaction to the kind of scenery that calls people "to a halt, and [causes them] to utter a mental exclamation of surprise or admiration." He held that this reaction was both inferior to and interruptive of unconscious recreation. The "highest value" of a park, he wrote, was in the "simple and natural" aspects of scenery that touch us so quietly that we are hardly conscious of them; yet they have been "solace and comfort" not only to the most "intelligent and cultivated" of men, but also to "cottagers in peasant villages."[8]

A decade later, in keeping with this notion, Olmsted told Mariana Van Rensselaer that, while he had "early had a rather remarkable easy enjoyment of natural scenery," he had, paradoxically, never been what was commonly called "a lover of Nature."[9] Perhaps, he added, that was because "laziness" had kept him from "any such study of nature." But in reality, this laziness had been simply his "wandering, contemplative, daydreaming" nature, a habit much like the one men satisfy in "listening to music and gazing upon scenery." Thus he linked his vagabondish boyhood habits to unconscious recreation, the superior form of recreation.

In an earlier letter to Van Rensselaer, Olmsted had written that "a disposition was born in me, or early became fixed, to vagrancy, to day-

dreaming, to find my pleasure in an intellectually inactive or not consciously directed contemplation of natural scenery." Olmsted added that
an attempt to make him a merchant had failed, because "it was not in my
nature that it should succeed," and that his time at sea had only confirmed
and made more deep-seated his disposition to "reverie and day-dreaming
—day-dreaming being the soul of designing." Olmsted harkened back to
his days in London for Dix and Edwards ("in that miserable book business"), when he had turned to London's parks for his own psychic retreat
("a citizen seeking rest, refreshment, [unconscious] recreation"). He had
then, Olmsted said, no idea of "ever being a park-maker." It had all
happened so unintentionally, through various "unconscious influences"
and through his own habit "of day-dreaming about rural scenery, a habit
favorable to poetic moods and the development of a *designing* habit." [10]

Raymond Williams uses the term *vagrant* to identify a rather passive
mode of nonconformity: the "maximum demand" of the vagrant is that
"he should be left alone." [11] It would surely have been a term of opprobrium among the Puritan ministers and burghers among whom Olmsted
grew up—and it was as a term of opprobrium that he had used it in
"Civilization." But I would suggest that there was a singular need within
Olmsted's adult artist self to justify *his* hidden vagrant self, a lingering
adolescent self. And there was an inner need also to continually recreate
the surroundings, the *environment* of that youthful vagrant self—to continually seek to bring the woodlands of a rural Connecticut boyhood into
the heart of the commercial city.

The world of nature, however, was a feminine world; there still had
been a masculine world to be challenged, a masculine identity to be
asserted. Thus, even in this retrospective musing at the age of seventy-
one, Olmsted reminded Van Rensselaer of the importance of his practical
self, the "doer" and Oedipal striver. His passive daydreaming nature,
Olmsted noted, was "twist[ed] in with a certain degree of native intelligence, activity of mind and what is called organizing, administrative and
executive ability." The latter were all, of course, masculine attributes in
Victorian society. The curious phrase Olmsted used for the mixture of
active masculine and passive feminine attributes—"twisting in" together
—signals the tortured nature of the accommodation he had sought to
make between them, the lingering effect of what Robert Stoller calls
symbiosis anxiety, the male's fear of his own inner feminine identification

with his mother—an anxiety Olmsted shared with most men in his society.[12]

Olmsted's need to accommodate the opposing genderized aspects of himself can be seen in almost all the careers he had undertaken. If the milieu he chose to work in was feminine, his role would be masculine. If farm life existed within the female natural world of "being," his role would be that of "doing"—a farmer, and of a *scientific* farmer at that. If the world of letters was a part of the feminine world of art, his role would be the most masculine of the literary arts—journalist and publisher. If the Sanitary Commission was engaged in the feminine tasks of nurturing and succoring, his role would be the masculine one of chief administrator and organizer. If at Central Park he was to practice landscape design as an art (feminine) within the idealized maternal, domestic environment of nature (also feminine)—an environment that he was creating, bringing forth (again feminine)—then his preferred identity in that work would be the domineering masculine role of chief executive.

Olmsted's letter to Van Rensselaer also suggests that in the final decade of his career, the false self of the "doer" had at last come to serve the true self's purposes of the dreamer. Olmsted had not conquered his inner conflicts, but he *had* created an identity—as America's premier landscape architect—that was the best accommodation he could make, an accommodation that permitted him to choose to be, and be chosen as, the delegate for men who suffered from those same inner conflicts. He could —while paying a terrific price to do it—stand before his peers as a kind of Romantic idealist hero in a ruthlessly Utilitarian materialistic society.

In the last few years of his career, it would be Olmsted's task to defend that identity and to defend his true self's purposes against the smothering pervasiveness of the materialistic standards of his society. Indeed, Olmsted was led continually to argue for his principles of landscape design on the basis that his work represented good art and that the *market value* of higher forms of art (such as his) was not only immediately greater, but would go on increasing "century after century."[13] Olmsted was obviously not alone among Romantic artists in struggling with the materialistic standards of the potential audience for his work.[14] But Olmsted was hardly being grandiose in his estimation of the future market value of *his* works of art. A four-color advertisement that appeared in 1987 (for a luxury "condominium residence") featured a gorgeous aerial photograph of Central Park in its summer guise, offering apartments with "views of the Park that are yours forever." The price tag for this forever view ranged from $2.5 milion to $4 million.[15]

At the outset of this study, I took note of the singular honors Olmsted received in 1893: the simultaneous doctoral degrees conferred by Harvard and Yale; the handsome tributes by Charles Eliot Norton and D. H. Burnham during the latter's testimonial dinner; the biographical and critical study by Mariana Van Rensselaer for Richard Watson Gilder's *Century* magazine. It seemed as if the remnants of the American gentry, in academia, in the professions, in the literary world, had roused themselves in recognition of their most enduring, and arguably most successful, representative in American public life.[16] But in the last decade of the nineteenth century, Olmsted had turned seventy and was wearing out in the struggle, even though his determination, and his obsessions, remained at fever pitch. All of the old concerns remained fresh in his mind; all of the old struggles remained critical to his psyche; and the potential failure to achieve all of his grand objectives haunted him—haunted him most grievously during the long, sleepless nights. In that final decade of the nineteenth century, Olmsted's fears and hopes focused primarily upon the last two great works to which he would personally commit himself: George W. Vanderbilt's Biltmore estate at Asheville, North Carolina, and the great Columbian Exposition (World's Fair) at Chicago.

The Columbian Exposition was to be a celebration of the advent of Chicago as a commercial city of international stature; a demonstration of the vitality and abundance of American capitalism; and an announcement that the young country was ready both to shed its reputation for provincialism and to become a trading and investment partner of the great nations of the world. To accomplish these aims, the Exposition, under the overall supervision of Daniel H. Burnham, deliberately turned its back on the indigenous, vigorous, and innovative architecture that had evolved in Chicago—as reflected in such landmarks as Louis Sullivan's auditorium and John W. Root's office building, "The Rookery"—in favor of what many have seen as a retrograde neoclassicism, a rather vulgar triumph of Beaux Arts excess and eclecticism.[17]

Since the buildings were temporary, Laura Wood Roper notes, the Fair's architects "might have dared to be daring"; instead the buildings were "conventional in construction and soothingly classical in appearance."[18] The scale was colossal, not only in the massiveness of the buildings but also in such embellishments as the statuary and colonnades of the entrance gates and walkways. Burnham and his associates decreed that the buildings would embody a uniformity of theme—all of them plastered with stucco facades and painted white. The Fair grounds came to be called the White City, dazzling in the sunlight of the summer days, glittering at night from myriad electric lights and reflections in the extensive waterways. It is considered the first public expression of the City Beautiful movement.

The Columbian Exposition was constructed upon parts of South Park, principally the section called Jackson Park, a sandy, marshy flatland bordering Lake Michigan. As it happened, South Park was the site upon which, two decades earlier, Olmsted and Vaux had proposed a public park for Chicago.[19] It was Olmsted who recommended that Jackson Park be made "the centre of the Fair," in opposition to those members of the Exposition Board who had favored a site in closer proximity to downtown Chicago. As Olmsted later told Edouard André, the French landscape architect whom he so admired, his reason for choosing the Jackson Park site "was simply that it was bordered by the Lake, the only natural feature of scenery of interest near the city."[20] In adapting his old plan for the Exposition, Olmsted retained two key features in particular: the augmentation of the dunes, which would now become the sites for the central Exposition buildings; and the dredging of the swamps to create the canals and lagoons that would give the Fair grounds a Venetian ambience.

In his overall landscape design for the Exposition, Olmsted was most concerned with providing the Fair-goers both with visual relief from the sensory overload and with physical relief from mental and physical exhaustion. It was indeed a "white city," much whiter than he would have preferred, Olmsted told a colleague: "I fear that against the clear blue sky and the blue lake, great towering masses of white, glistening in the clear hot, summer sunlight of Chicago, with the glare of water that we are to have . . . will be overpowering." Thus they must depend upon "dark green foliage" for "all the relief that we can possibly provide." And he called for large stretches of "apparently natural scenery" whose "quieting influence" would counteract the effect of "the artificial grandeur and the crowds, pomp, splendor and bustle of the rest of the Exposition." So essential was the restful effect of green foliage that he urged that colorful flowers be used only discreetly: "flecks and glimmers of bright color imperfectly breaking through the general greenery." He further recommended that, wherever practical, the landscapers should "hide bare tree trunks and branches" with foliage, vines and creepers.[21] Olmsted seemed to emphasize the feminine aspect of his psychosocial fetish (trees) in order to counteract the all-pervasive masculinity of the great Exposition buildings and of the competitive commercial society they represented.

But Olmsted's most important design contribution was certainly the Wooded Island and the large lagoon that surrounded it—a feature he later described in a report to American Institute of Architects:

> near the middle of the lagoon system there should be an island, about fifteen acres in area, in which there would be clusters of the largest trees growing upon the site; . . . this island should be free from conspicuous buildings and . . . it should have a generally secluded, natural, sylvan aspect.[22]

Olmsted fretted constantly over the development of the island and its lagoon, struggling to keep them free of disturbing intrusions. The most alarming of these proposed intrusions was the Music Hall Burnham had thought would be a festive addition to the island. Olmsted told his young partner, Henry S. Codman, that such an intrusion would be "a great misfortune," for nothing that could be introduced to the island could be worth nearly as much as its being "a place of relief from all the splendor and glory and noise and human multitudinous of the great surrounding Babylon." But Olmsted also cautioned Codman that he did *not* wish to make a fight over the issue—an indication of Olmsted's concern to maintain his alliance with this new commercial and architectural elite. "If the calamity is inevitable," he told Codman, "we will accept it and make the best of it with a good grace."[23] This operating philosophy would guide Olmsted not only at the Exposition, but also at Biltmore, where (as will be shown) the stakes within his psyche were much higher.

In the end, Olmsted had to accept a Japanese temple and garden upon the island. Fortunately, as he told the AIA, these were intrusions of a rather discreet and complementary sort. Nevertheless, he added, even this subtle intrusion still had "much injured the island for the purpose . . . it was intended to serve." Had it been avoided, Olmsted observed, the Exposition would have made a "much more agreeable general impres-

25. A bird's eye view of the World Columbian Exposition, Chicago, 1893. The so-called white city—created under the leadership of D. H. Burnham—is considered the inauguration of the neoclassical City Beautiful movement. Olmsted's work here was his most ambitious attempt to "marry" the principles of naturalistic landscape design to the requirements of stately, formal architecture with its monumental buildings. His principle Romantic contribution to the Exposition was the man-made lagoon and the wooded island (lower left), an echo of his work at Central Park. (The Bettmann Archives.)

sion upon visitors of cultivated sensibility to the influence of scenery." And Olmsted went on to list other ways in which the original landscape design had been compromised and in which his proposed scenic effects— "intended to serve for the relief of the eye from the too nearly constant demands upon attention of the Exposition"—had been subordinated to "the more massive elements." [24]

Olmsted's dissatisfaction with the compromises he had had to accept and with the Exposition as it had been realized led him to draft a highly critical letter to Burnham while the Exposition was still underway and some changes could still be made. The need for such improvements, Olmsted told Burnham, was evident in the "melancholy air" that seemed to pervade the sight-seeing throngs, who went about the Fair grounds with more of a sense of duty than of gaiety. Olmsted said that he had seen in the faces of the crowds, while he himself was visiting the Exposition, expressions that were "too *businesslike, common, dull, anxious and care-worn*."[25]

In other words, the Fair-goers seemed much like the "town-strained" men and women for whom he had designed his urban parks. As with his New York City experience, Olmsted seems to have been projecting, at least in part, his own "anxious and care-worn" feelings onto the faces in the crowd. Nevertheless, Olmsted's personal reactions to the Exposition had surely not misled him. Rather, they had awakened him both to the humanistic failings of the great Exposition and to creative avenues of relief for burdened minds and bodies—much the same as his own experience of the tumultuous streets and harsh competitive life in New York had led him to the development of his urban design philosophy.

Several months later, however, Olmsted's view seemed to become far more positive. Looking back on the work that had been done, Olmsted was moved to write Burnham of "the leading thought" that had been in his mind in regard to the Exposition. This "leading thought" turned out to be the same one that preoccupied him during his exile at Mariposa: the contrast between the "frontier condition of society" and "old and well-organized" communities. He had lived in pioneer communities, Olmsted told Burnham, and he knew from first-hand experience that it is "a primitive state of life." It had been his hope that the Exposition would stand as a work of "Fine Art" and, as such, would "demonstrate that the United States is well advanced in its emergence from the distinctive necessary hardship of pioneer life."[26] A few weeks later, Olmsted was apprised that a leading English authority on landscaping had criticized the design of the Fair grounds — in particular, the Wooded Island and lagoon. Olmsted admitted to his friend Stiles that compromises had indeed been made, but insisted that, from his personal experience, "the verdict of the public, and of the intelligent and cultivated and capable public . . . [had] fully sustained and justified" those compromises in the final design. The large lagoon, which had so disappointed this critic, was, Olmsted said, the one thing at the Exposition "by which people were the most fascinated, and which is remembered most vividly & with more pleasure."[27]

I would suggest that Olmsted had made himself something of a propagandist for the idea of the Exposition's success, culturally and artistically, even though he knew full well that it had fallen far short of his wishes for it, both aesthetically and as an embodiment of his true self's purposes in the promotion of psychic relief and of communitiveness. The reason for this was made clear both in his letter to Stiles and in his AIA speech.

Olmsted told Stiles that the most significant aspect of the Exposition—in fact, "an important historical circumstance"—was the ability of men like Root, Burnham, Codman, Hunt, and other architects to rise above "the jealousies and suspicions" to which men are especially prone "when they divide into classes and professions." Now, with the work concluded, Olmsted was able to look back with greatest satisfaction on all he had done to "repress an attitude of antagonism between Building and Landscape Architecture and for the cultivation of fraternity."[28]

Similarly, he told the AIA that it was "a notable circumstance that there should have been so little friction; so little display of jealousy, envy and combativeness, as has appeared in this enterprise." He thought this had been due to "the industry, skill and tact" of Burnham, "the master of us all," and was only possible "in a country which was in a high degree socially as well as politically, a republic."[29]

Thus, it was not the Exposition itself, nor the impact upon even the most cultivated Fair-goer, that Olmsted truly had in mind when he had spoken of the Exposition as a triumph of civilization. Rather, it was the fraternity of the designers, the mutual respect and collegiality of this community of artists, that had made Olmsted feel so positive—for it was *only* within this small community that he had perceived the triumph of the spirit of communitiveness over the "strain" to barbarism (that is, masculine competitiveness and peer-rivalries).[30] It was for this that Olmsted had been prepared to yield even in his true self's creative purposes and to celebrate the comprised design of his centerpiece, the Wooded Island and lagoon, despite his awareness of how much less successful it had been than he had wished.

As Olmsted concluded his work on the Columbian Exposition, there were still two great public works projects taking place in the United States with strong claims upon him professionally and psychologically: the Boston park system and, almost to the very end, the New York parks. But Boston was becoming more and more the domain of his young partners, while New York had been left to Calvert Vaux a decade earlier. The aging and ailing Olmsted had been reaching the point of exhaustion insofar as public projects were concerned. The endless fights to hold the various parks and parkways to his principles against the encroachments of political hacks and well-meaning civic leaders alike were now simply repetitions of the past three decades. In fact, when Olmsted wrote in opposition to a proposed broadening of the pleasure roads in Franklin Park, he informed the President of the Boston Park Commission that it was much the same struggle he had had at Central Park several years earlier.[31] And Olmsted had to make much the same point now as he had then. The single most important purpose of Franklin Park, Olmsted wrote, was to give Bostonians "means for the enjoyment of the highest degree of rural scenery that it is practicable to give them in a place to be occupied in great numbers." The broader they make the roads, Olmsted warned, "the less will be the enjoyment of rurality to be obtained in the Park." Several months later, he declined to help John Charles in a confrontation with Boston's Mayor and Park Commissioners over their plans for new and more extended bridle paths in Franklin Park. Olmsted complained that such projects were "preposterous & hateful" to him and that he had already opposed them for years at Central Park; "it makes me sick to begin over again."[32]

In New York, where Calvert Vaux was undergoing constant harassment by the proponents of neoclassical design (the City Beautiful movement), Olmsted and his firm were continually being asked to consult on one project or another. But, much as the New York parks maintained their psychic hold upon him, Olmsted no longer seemed to have the energy for the struggle. Hearing a rumor that Vaux had retired, Olmsted told John Charles and Eliot that if this was true, "ought we not at once to think of enlarging our organization and having a strong branch in New York?" He noted that there was a great opportunity there—three thousand new acres of public parks to be laid out—but that it would also involve a great public struggle: "Tammany vs our reputation." And he added wearily: "I can't say that I have any appetite for the fight that would be inevitable."[33]

Later on, Olmsted was invited to consult on plans for further development of Prospect Park and spent three days in New York (during which time he did not contact Vaux, who was still landscape architect for the New York parks). It was a depressing experience. The new plans for Prospect Park were heavily influenced by the monumental-minded, neoclassicists Stanford White and his partners, Charles Follen McKim and William R. Mead. Recognizing the implications of what was taking place, Olmsted wrote Vaux that their principal duty in Brooklyn was "to hinder, delay, and resist operations further upsetting the original [Olmsted and Vaux] design, while we wait and seek opportunity to urge and advance restorations and recoveries."[34] Olmsted could not contemplate a head-on collision with the likes of Stanford White and his associates—who, David Schuyler notes, were then introducing structures and gardens into the park that, while certainly handsome, were terribly destructive of the park as a rural retreat. "The City Beautiful invaded the naturalistic landscape," Schuyler writes, "and so littered it with mock temples and statuary that instead of becoming an alternative to the urban environment the park became an extension of it."[35]

As the proponents of the City Beautiful movement and of Beaux Arts classicism became ever stronger, Olmsted was reaching the end of his physical and mental resilience. Indeed, he had gone much further than anyone could have expected, to the amazement of his contemporaries. "I am truly grieved to learn that you suffer as you describe," H. W. S. Cleveland, another leading American landscape architect, wrote Olmsted in 1892, "and wonder at your courage in continuing to travel & work as you do."[36] It could have only saddened Olmsted greatly and heightened his own fears for himself to be solicited soon after on behalf of a fund to provide support for Cleveland and his wife, as Cleveland was now "very nearly insane."[37] And for three years, Olmsted heard the tales of Vaux's torment on the New York parks—that Vaux was being driven to "the verge of insanity" and that he now had to swallow these indignities or face a retirement in poverty.[38] Then, in 1893, Olmsted's young partner, Henry Sargent Codman, suddenly died only months before the opening of the Exposition upon which he had been a driving force. "I am standing on a wreck and can hardly see when we shall get afloat again," Olmsted wrote Gifford Pinchot, with perhaps more meaning than he was conscious of.[39]

Now seventy-three, suffering physically and mentally and constantly reminded of his own mortality, Olmsted became dominated by a steadily growing obsession with the Biltmore estate in the final months before his own breakdown—an obsession in which he saw Biltmore both as a validation of his true self's principles and as a training school for his son, Rick. Moreover, the purposes with which Olmsted was obsessed at Bilt-

26. The Biltmore estate at Asheville, North Carolina. The chateau on the hill was designed in the neoclassic, Beaux Arts manner by Richard Morris Hunt, which forced Olmsted to adopt a formal landscaping of the grounds immediately surrounding the chateau, though he endeavored to maintain a more naturalistic feeling elsewhere. (National Park Service, Frederick Law Olmsted National Historical Site.)

more further strengthened his need to make common cause with the representatives of neoclassicism, a school of design that was so foreign to his own aesthetics and purposes. At Biltmore, Olmsted had to come to terms with that school of design, if he was, with Vanderbilt's money behind him, to fulfill his hopes. And his hopes were profound indeed. The Biltmore work would be "criticised and reviewed and referred to for its precedents & for its experience, years ahead—centuries ahead," he told John Charles and Eliot.[40]

George W. Vanderbilt was "an ardent conservationist," with considerable interest in experimental farming, forestry, and horticulture. Biltmore was to be built upon an enormous tract in the farmlands and forestlands near Asheville, North Carolina. The main grounds were to be dominated by the largest country house in America, a house Richard Morris Hunt was creating in the mode of a great French chateau. This huge structure set the theme for the estate and required Olmsted to design the surrounding grounds and gardens in a more formal, neoclassical style than he preferred. But Olmsted intended his work on the rest of the estate—the scenic pleasure drives, the forest lands, and, most of all, the arboretum— to provide both a laboratory for and a demonstration of American natural landscaping.[41]

Olmsted was almost totally preoccupied by Biltmore when, early in 1895, he received an invitation to serve on a advisory committee to oversee "the landscape and architectural features" of Calvert Vaux's Harlem River Drive. Others on the committee would include Stanford White, Richard Morris Hunt, and Augustus St. Gaudens, as well as William A. Stiles of *Garden and Forest*, friend to Olmsted and Vaux.[42] Olmsted declined, on Stiles's advice, but he told Stiles that he had thought of accepting because he feared that the committee would be "packed against natural landscape and against Vaux" and because a minority report issued by himself might "have weight in forming public opinion."[43]

Olmsted felt that White and his followers would be much stronger opponents than he had ever faced before in his career as a landscape architect—far more "fanatical." He assured Stiles that there was "a strenuous fight coming between those of our side and those who are disposed to revise every body of public land that has been laid out regardfully of natural beauty with the object of transforming it as far as possible into a field of architectural beauty." It was as if "war had been formally declared" over Prospect Park in the past year, Olmsted wrote, a war against the naturalistic motives that heretofore had guided the creation of the Brooklyn park. White "distinctly hates these older motives," Olmsted charged, adding that White would love to replace the naturalistic effects that Olmsted and Vaux had created with "sentimental passages of 'Nature' " such as one might find in the Petit Trianon or in Versailles. And Olmsted then whipped himself up into a rhetorical passion:

We have an organized enemy before us. . . . They have struck down Vaux and are doing their best to kill him in the name of the Lord and of France. They are strong; they are sincere; they are confident; they are cultivated gentlemen to be dealt with courteously, but they are doctrinaires and fanatics and essentially cockneys, with no more knowledge of nor interest in real rurality than most men of Parisian training and associations.

After some reflection on all this, Olmsted cooled down and confided to Stiles: "You know that these men of the enemy are my friends; that here and at other points, at Chicago, for example, I have worked in hearty, active, friendly cooperation with them."[44] That might seem an "anomaly," Olmsted told Stiles, but "there is a place for everything." That is, the apparent anomaly could only be explained by Olmsted's determination to win such gains as he could for naturalistic landscape within a cultural scene increasingly dominated by neoclassical architecture. At Chicago, he noted, "we tried to reconcile a picturesque motive of natural scenery with the formal stateliness that [they] our architectural associates were determined to have in the buildings, and we succeeded to their satisfaction." The word in brackets was struck out and the following three words were added to the sentence as an afterthought by Olmsted, reflecting his continued ambivalence between an "us versus them" mentality and his wish for fraternal association with these powerful "men of the enemy."

Turning to Biltmore, Olmsted said that he had managed to reconcile the requirements of Hunt in his "Renaissance" buildings with "a generally picturesque natural character in the approaches, and in the main landscape features." Olmsted played down the formal gardens that he had created in the surrounds of that great country house, referring off-handedly to the "more or less formal spurs and outworks of architectural motive," which, Olmsted suggested, had been worked into an otherwise naturalistic setting. And, he added, once you got away from "the transcendent architectural features, there is not in the whole 9000 acres a suggestion of any other than natural landscape motives."

In this letter to Stiles, Olmsted applauded the seamless harmony that had existed between himself and Hunt. At Olmsted's request, Hunt had "aided in marrying the two motives," extending, modifying, and altering architectural outworks in accordance with Olmsted's suggestion. The image of a "marriage" between neoclassical and naturalistic design seems the ultimate idealization of the policy of accommodation Olmsted had pursued in these later years. But naturalistic design was (by nineteenth-century standards) the accommodating feminine principle, while the ponderous and rather overwhelming Beaux Arts assertiveness favored by Hunt for the great chateau accurately reflected the dominating masculine principle. Tellingly, Olmsted confided to Stiles: "I am taking heavier risks in this respect here than I did at Chicago."[45]

Perhaps the greatest risk, as he later told Rick, was that he was working

in idioms that were foreign to his nature and about which he felt both he
and his young partners were totally ignorant—such as with the "exotic
gardening" of the Terrace Gardens near the mansion.[46] When doing such
work, Olmsted told his son, he felt "ashamed and culpable" in his ignorance, as if was "treading on the verge of quackery"—the specter of the
imposter rising again. He had tried to fix the responsibility for such areas
on Hunt and the others, Olmsted wrote; but if anything went wrong,
"Mr. Vanderbilt will blame us." It was the situation Olmsted hated most,
one that he had cried out against so long ago during the Peninsula
Campaign—where "the lines of responsibility [are] undefined, inexact."
But it was where his necessary policy of accommodation had brought
him. "This is a sad state of things," he told Rick, "and I don't want you
to inherit it." The answer was for Rick, his chosen delegate, to do what
he himself had been unable to: become "much more the master of all the
branches of your profession than anyone else has had opportunity of
being before"—and to use that mastery to defend the principles of natural landscaping.

By midspring, Olmsted became increasingly anxious and all his hopes
for Biltmore seemed to be crystallized in the arboretum, where, as he
wrote to Eliot, the problem of "combining purposes of Science and
purposes of Art on so large a scale . . . is a very difficult one."[47] The
weight of his "perplexing duties" at Biltmore were greatly increased
"because of depression of health," he admitted to Eliot. Indeed, it was
only a week earlier that he had confided to John Charles: "my memory as
to recent occurrences is no longer to be trusted," though he assured his
stepson that there was "no reason to think that I have lost capacity in
respect to invention, design or reasoning powers."[48]

A few months later, John Charles had assumed full command and
removed his stepfather from any effective involvement in the business.
Now Rick was Olmsted's only connection to Biltmore, and his hopes for
Rick and his hopes for Biltmore became one and the same. He needed to
know, Olmsted wrote that summer, that the work was going well and
that Rick was reaping the benefits he had been sent to Biltmore to obtain.
Beyond that, Olmsted added, "I more want [your letters] that I may see
things with your eyes."[49] And by the fall, he wrote Rick, "I am thinking
more of you, these bitter days, than anybody and all else." The only
thing that relieved his feeling of desolation, Olmsted wrote, was "the
assurance that you are taking up what I am dropping."[50]

Six months later, Olmsted was in England, being nursed by his wife and his daughter, troubled by a "noise in his head." Mary Olmsted wrote her sons that "the best we can hope for is imbecility," and she urged them to write their father cheerful letters about Biltmore.[51] In September 1898, Olmsted was confined to the McLean Hospital in Massachusetts, whose site he had consulted on decades earlier. A short time after Olmsted's admittance to McLean, the Medical Superintendent addressed to Rick these heart-breaking words:

At the best I suppose we must expect him to be discontented, but we will do what we can to see if there is anything more to be done to relieve the monotony of his life. *Of course his desire to be usefully occupied is quite impracticable.*

In the same letter, the Superintendent commented that Olmsted "certainly writes a remarkably good letter considering his mental failure." He supposed that Olmsted had passed through "an acute stage in his long illness" and was now in an improved state.[52] It would seem that ignorance, if not arrogance, was to fulfill Mary Olmsted's pessimistic prediction that "imbecility" was all they could hope for.

As we have seen, the strain on Olmsted's mind and body of maintaining his sense of identity through these final decades, of holding together this accommodation of conflicting selfhoods, had been enormous, and he had constantly been plagued by a sense of failure in realizing his true self's purposes. As he weakened under the strain, Olmsted chose his own delegate, the one who would be designated to assume those true self's purposes and allow them a "rebirth" at some future date—his son, Rick.

When we consider the long travail Olmsted had endured in defense of his vision on the New York parks, in the Boston suburbs and at Biltmore, we understand more fully the passion of Olmsted's lengthy letters to Rick in 1895, his desperate need not only to bind Rick over as his delegate, but also to make Rick understand the precise nature of the task bequeathed to him.[53] Deep within his psyche, Olmsted surely had known what lay ahead. Olmsted had come close to the psychic abyss in April 1865, but, with the resiliency Kingsbury had noted in him, had rebounded. He had come close to that abyss once again, with his attack of blindness in 1873, several months after his father's death. And once again, he had rebounded, pushing himself onward in his "long journeys" for two more decades of exceedingly fruitful work and of preeminence as a landscape architect. Olmsted, as a landscape architect, had practiced a public art.

And through his art, Olmsted had remained committed to his existential and social struggle far longer than any of his gentry peers. But in 1895, at seventy-three, Olmsted began his slow and final slide, deep into the abyss, deep into the only form of exile he could then permit himself— the mental illness that enfolded him during his last eight years of life. The magical ivory object had come apart one last time, never to be rejoined again; doing yielded to being; the long, long Oedipal struggle gave way to a final psychic retreat.

Afterword

In certain ways, Rick succeeded at the task bequeathed him by his father more quickly and more completely than the latter could ever have hoped. Even before the senior Olmsted's death in 1903, his son had become a major force in the now respected profession of landscape architecture. He had become John Charles's partner in the family firm, had continued his father's work on Biltmore and had taken over Charles Eliot's role on the Boston Park system after the latter's death—all of this before the century was out and he had reached his thirtieth birthday. He then became an instructor of landscape architecture at Harvard in 1901 and was made a professor there in 1903.[1]

In 1901, Rick was one of those invited to address the annual convention of the American Institute of Architects—a convention purposely held in Washington, D.C., to address the proper architectural development of the capital city in commemoration of the one hundredth anniversary of its founding. This was less than a decade after Rick's father had addressed the same group on the planning for the Columbian Exposition. Shortly after the AIA Convention, Rick was named to the newly created Senate Park Commission for the planning of the capital center, along with Daniel H. Burnham and Charles Follen McKim—those same "men of the enemy" with whom his father had worked on the design of the Exposition a decade earlier.[2] Rick coauthored the report of this Commission, a report John Reps describes as the nation's "first city planning document." As Reps observes, Rick was "rapidly succeeding to his father's position as the outstanding landscape architect of America."[3]

The 1902 plan of the Senate Park Commission would be the first attempt to implement the notions of the City Beautiful movement on a citywide basis. Indeed, the plan created by Burnham, McKim, and Rick Olmsted would become, as David Schuyler observes, the symbol "of the neoclassical civic form that supplanted the midnineteenth century vision of a naturalistic urban landscape."[4] One critic has suggested that the Senate Park Commission's plan was "no more than an attempt to transplant the Chicago Fair to Washington."[5] Thus, the first major public project that Rick had undertaken on his own was one that repudiated the most important mission his father had urged upon him: to take up the task of defending his father's vision of naturalistic landscape design.

Rick's position within the planning triumvirate must, of course, be considered. He was junior by more than two decades to Burnham and McKim, men of great accomplishment and reputation, and he certainly had not learned to be a rebel at his father's side.[6] More to the point, however, was Rick's own emerging philosophy of urban landscape design —a philosophy most appropriate for a young man establishing his professional place in the Progressive Era (and in Theodore Roosevelt's capital city). This was made clear in Rick's speech at the AIA Convention, when he called for a plan for the capital center that would hew closely to the original plan that had been created by Pierre Charles L'Enfant in 1791. Such an approach, Rick stated, would project "the grandeur, power, and dignified magnificence which should mark the seat of government of a great and intensely active people." Reps observes that Rick's AIA address "clearly and forcefully announced that the principles of Romantic landscape design, almost synonymous with the Olmsted name, patently were inappropriate in such a setting as Washington."[7]

As Carol Christensen notes, L'Enfant's layout of central Washington was particularly well adapted to the "sweeping vistas, grand malls, axial arrangements and formal neoclassical composition" that were the essence of City Beautiful urban design.[8] But the irony is that in implementing this neoclassical approach, Rick's landscape plan for the capital center obliterated the work done fifty years earlier by the man who had inspired both his father and Calvert Vaux—Andrew Jackson Downing.

The capital center was the heart of L'Enfant's plan for the city—an L-shaped arrangement of the Capitol, the Washington Monument, and the White House. Downing's midcentury plan called for turning the Mall

27. View from the plan prepared by the Senate Park Commission, 1902, showing the planned development of the mall between the Washington Monument and the Capitol. The proposed mall was largely Rick Olmsted's responsibility—his first independent work—and it echoes the Central Park mall created by Olmsted and Vaux, including rows of elm trees on either side. Rick was then thirty-two, already one of America's preeminent landscape architects. (The Bettman Archives.)

between the Capitol and the Monument into "a national Park" consisting of several smaller parks and gardens, interconnected by "some of the most beautifully varied carriage-drives in the world."[9] This road system, one critic notes, "reached gently down to the banks of the Potomac" and was "purposely separated from the surrounding system of streets by a continuous curtain of greenery . . . as if the park were intended as an enclosed entity, an alternative to the city."[10] Thus, Downing's Mall, obliterated by Rick's landscape plan, had served the same purpose of escape from the city that the New York parks of Olmsted and Vaux later served.

In replanning the great Mall between the Monument and the Capitol, Rick and his associates decreed that it was to be a uniform width of sixteen hundred feet for its entire length, bordered by "buildings devoted to scientific purposes and for the great museums."[11] What commands attention most forcibly is the explicit homage Rick paid to his father in the design of this Mall. The axis of the Capitol and Monument, the report states, was to be "clearly defined by an expanse of undulating green a

mile and a half long and three hundred feet broad, walled on either side
by elms, planted in formal procession four abreast." The report adds that
the "two plantations of elms traversed by paths are similar in character to
the Mall in Central Park, New York, which is justly regarded as one of
the most beautiful features of that park." The report, further, justified
the use of the American elm in part with imagery that reinforces its
appropriateness as a bisexual symbol—citing "the architectural character
of its columnar trunk and the delicate traceries formed by its widespread-
ing branches."

In describing *their* Mall in the Greensward plan, Olmsted and Vaux
had noted that there would be little "dignity of effect" to be produced by
such an avenue unless it led to "some grand architectural structure, which
itself, and not the avenue, is the ultimatum of interest." For Olmsted and
Vaux, the natural beauty of the park would provide that "ultimatum of
interest," for which the Promenade would serve as "an open air hall of
reception."[12] It will be remembered, also, that their Mall was built on a
line pointing directly across the Ramble to Vista Rock, a natural architectural structure. The focal point of *Rick's* Mall would be the Washington
Monument, which the Commission report hailed as "at once so great and
simple that it seems to be almost a work of nature."

The fundamental difference between the purposes of the young Progressive planner, Rick Olmsted, and those of his father, as much a
Romantic artist as an urban planner, can be seen most vividly in the
handling of the transverse roads that cut across the Mall at several points.
Reps finds it inexplicable that Rick did not propose the use of sunken
roads at these points:

The [Commission] report suggested that "the play of light and shade where the
streets break through the columns of trees, and the passage of street cars and
teams give needed life to the Mall." Possibly in this pre-automobile era this
statement may have had some justification. Yet it is difficult to understand even
under those circumstances. Almost a half-century earlier the elder Olmsted, faced
with a similar long and narrow park site in the middle of a great city, had
provided four sunken transverse roads in his magnificent design for Central Park
in New York. It is strange indeed that his son did not insist on similar treatment
in a situation where aesthetic as well as functional reasons dictated this solution.[13]

Where the Mall in Central Park was designed to be a vestibule mediating between the city and the natural beauty within the park grounds,

Rick's Mall *was* the park—what his father would consider an "urban public ground" of accommodation to the city as opposed to a "rural public ground" of escape from the city.[14] Nor had Rick's park been intended—as had his father's—to be "an oasis, an arcadia in the desert of brick & mortar."[15] Rick's Mall, *his* park, was intended to be an architectural structure designed as a stage setting for other, even grander, and more inspiring architectural structures.

Though Reps is critical of Rick's usage of the transverse roads, he nevertheless admires the Commission's "sweeping and noble plan" for its "power and majesty," its "disciplined monumentality." But Reps also notes that there were those who felt "perhaps like Jefferson, that this is not the appropriate atmosphere for the capital of a democracy."[16] In 1908, an editorial in the Washington *Evening Star* charged that the Commission plan would destroy "all the noble shade trees in the People's Park from the Capitol to the river to make way for a sixteen-hundred-feet wide track of desolation as bare and as hot as the Desert of Sahara."[17] However beautiful or noble Rick's Mall, it surely was not, and was never intended to be, what Downing's Mall had become—"the People's Park."

It would take more than three decades for the Senate Park Commission's plan to be realized on the ground. A more immediate effect was to project Daniel H. Burnham into the role of the nation's leading urban planner. "Make no little plans," Burnham later said; "they have no power to stir men's souls."[18] In the years following the Commission's work, Burnham had the opportunity to put that philosophy into effect in major urban planning projects in Cleveland, Manila, San Francisco, and Chicago. In 1910, Burnham attended the Town Planning Conference in London, presenting himself not as an architect, but as an urban planner, displaying models of the plans for Washington and Chicago.

By this time, Burnham was already under attack by young Progressives taking up the new discipline of city planning, who questioned the usefulness of "showy civic centers of gigantic cost." The committee of public and private leaders who sponsored a new Civic Center in St. Louis had argued that it would provide great inspirational and educational value for the people of the city—would foster the spirit of democracy by creating the sort "of neighborhood feeling, which in these days of specialization has grown weak." But the reformist critics of such projects, in effect, questioned the attention given to the creation of magnificent civic plazas, grand boulevards, and mammoth public buildings when there were pressing human needs to be met in the increasingly over-crowded cities of America. Was not the enthusiasm shown by urban political bosses and local commercial and financial leaders for such aggrandizing projects motivated, at least in part, by the need to deflect the growing demands for genuine civic reform and urban planning? Was not "inspiration" meant to blind the citizenry to municipal neglect of more humdrum and basic urban problems? [19]

The London Conference itself was more strongly focused upon European rather than American models, with the Garden City movement of England and the avant-garde street systems of Germany evoking the greatest interest among the participants. Burnham's review of urban planning projects in the United States, illustrated by those with which he had been connected, paid special attention the role of the private sector in providing the impetus and the patronage for massive civic improvement undertakings, for making technological and aesthetic progress an urban reality on a vaster scope than most Europeans had ever envisaged. But the words he spoke were those of the patrician and gentry leaders of the post–Civil War society in which he had matured—the Millite language of Charles Eliot Norton and E. L. Godkin. "Four hundred of your best men animated by one purpose," he stated, "are like a Greek phalanx, which was irresistible against barbarians." His words invited a response from one critic of the Left not too dissimilar from those of the young Progressives back home. " 'Four hundred of the best men' are not exactly 'the democracy,' " this critic pointed out, arguing the superiority of small English garden cities to the "gigantic architectural schemes" celebrated by Burnham. [20]

Burnham's City Beautiful ideology would be condemned by succeeding generations of urban planners in America. Lewis Mumford would later charge that Burnham had been a "promoter of land values . . . like the merest salesman or advertising agent," serving the needs of the merchant princes who were the sources of capital for his grandiose schemes. [21] As Mario Manieri-Elia points out, Burnham was really a transitional figure, standing between the park movement as practiced by men like Olmsted and H. W. S. Cleveland and the onset of the professional city planners of the Progressive Era for whom the City Beautiful movement represented an "ideology of power" that they rejected. Manieri-Elia pro-

poses the powerful metaphor of the sinking of the *Titanic*—"a floating
City Beautiful"—as marking the end of the ideology and the patronage
that had supported Burnham. Burnham died in 1912, only a few months
after that tragedy, bemoaning the fact that the "old World's Fair crowd is
thinning out."[22] In the two decades between those two events, Burnham
alone had achieved the stature and moral authority that Olmsted had once
possessed in the arena of public works—had become the "delegate" of *his*
commercial patrons.

Who would come after Burnham? Who would next seek the place in
public works that Olmsted had sought in the middle of the nineteenth
century? Given the increasingly technical and complex nature of public
problems, Robert Wiebe points out, political leaders after the turn of the
century were far more inclined to turn to the "new-middle-class-expert"
for advice and proposals.[23] But few of these "experts"—city planners
among them—obtained public stature in their own right. Where the great
cities were concerned, as Sam Bass Warner has shown in his study of
Philadelphia, these professionals were by and large the servants of the
political, commercial, and social elites that controlled the planning boards
even in the Progressive Era.[24] Their inability to obtain a higher priority
for public needs than for private interests doomed urban planning for the
great cities, Warner concludes, adding: "The industrial metropolis failed
to create the necessary institutions to control the city's growth and to
allocate the city's public investments effectively."[25]

But the problem of "the private city" versus the public needs had not
arrived with the twentieth century. Olmsted had grappled with it several
decades before the Progressive city planners arrived on the scene. In his
and Vaux's report on Prospect Park in 1868, Olmsted observed:

What is everybody's business is nobody's, and although of late years experts,
with professional training in special branches, are not unfrequently engaged by
municipal bodies to study particular requirements of the people, and invent
means to satisfy them, still, as a general rule, improvements have come in most
cities, when they have come at all, chiefly through the influence of individual
energy, interested in behalf of special mercantile or speculative enterprises, by
which the supineness of the elected and paid representatives of the common
interests of the citizens has been overborne.[26]

Eight years later, in a report on laying out the Twenty-Third and Twenty-
Fourth wards, Olmsted lamented the absence of sound city planning in

Manhattan, adding that when such a plan was formed, "it would be inexcusable that it should not be the plan of a Metropolis," serving the interests "not of ordinary commerce only, but of humanity, religion, art, science and scholarship."[27]

There would be attempts at such planning for New York during the 1920s, but their long-range impact would be minimal. One such a plan was sponsored by the same sort of patrician and gentry reformers who had helped the elder Olmsted to his positions at Central Park and the Sanitary Commission—"The Regional Plan of New York and its Environs," produced under the auspices of the Russell Sage Foundation and set forth in several reports issued between 1927 and 1931.[28] The Sage Foundation was created by a wealthy widow, Margaret Olivia Sage (assisted by her friend Louisa Lee Schuyler, Olmsted's friend and associate at the Sanitary Commission), and was concerned with improving the social environment as a way to eliminate poverty and its effects. Rick Olmsted had earlier served as the landscape architect for the Foundation's "garden city" development in Forest Hills, a New York City suburb described by one critic as "a model suburban development for the well-to-do." And Rick was one of the principal participants in devising the new Regional Plan.[29]

A competing plan was put forth in the same period by the Regional Planning Association of America, a group of architects, planners, sociologists, and economists that included Lewis Mumford. The latter was a more progressive and perhaps more utopian group that sought to impose a new way of looking at the needs of a metropolitan region.[30] But neither plan, in the long run, was successful in imposing a visionary public agenda upon the chaotically developed, self-interested "private city." As one historian has observed, it is doubtful that any political or social movement in the twentieth century was capable of shaking "the attachment of Americans to the institutions of private property and the profit motive . . . an ideological attachment that ran through the great majority of Americans, whether farmers, labor, union men, or members of the aspiring lower-middle economic classes."[31] Without the support of such Americans, where was comprehensive social planning for the great commercial cities to obtain its constituency? The young patrician Gifford Pinchot, who had been Olmsted's protégé at Biltmore, was able to create such a constituency for the cause of conservation, based upon his role as

Theodore Roosevelt's Chief of the Forestry Bureau and as one of the President's closest confidantes. "Nothing permanent," Pinchot said, "can be accomplished in this country unless it is backed by a sound public sentiment."[32]

As it happens, it was not a long-range plan produced by any coalition of progressive experts and patrician-gentry committees that had the most significant impact upon New York City and its environs. Rather, it was the activities of a single man: Robert Moses, the real successor to the public careers of Olmsted and Burnham. Moses was made President of the New York Park Commission in 1930. In the next two decades, he increased the Park Department's recreational facilities fivefold throughout the city. But these were not Olmstedian "pleasure grounds"—nineteenth-century pastoral parks and promenades. They were playgrounds and ballfields and picnic grounds, marked by the architectural use of "practical" industrial building materials, which the *New York Times* described as "Robert Moses' brick-and-tile lavatory style." As Galen Cranz notes, Moses scorned academically based large-scale urban planning. "Moses considered himself a realist," she writes, "who expanded and built not according to a 'radical plan of decentralization,' " as in the RPAA regional plan, but according to practical objectives.[33] Parks were placed helter-skelter throughout the city, without any master plan; they were placed where they were in response to neighborhood needs, political realities and budgetary opportunity.

Yet Moses is not remembered—as is Olmsted—as a park-maker. Rather, he is today recalled as, in Robert Caro's label, "the Power Broker," the man who held an amazing variety of public positions at the same time: New York City's Construction Coordinator and Chairman of the Triborough Bridge and Tunnel Authority, the State Power Commission, the State Parks Council, and the Mayor's Committee on Slum Clearance. "He was not a total czar—there were officials above him—but in practice mayors and governors tended to defer to him," Paul Goldberger writes. Moses, not the elected officials, set the agenda for an enormous variety of public projects, including almost all the major parkways and highways on Long Island, the Triborough and Verrazano-Narrows bridges, the New York Coliseum, and his masterpiece, Jones Beach—the "people's palace beside the sea."[34]

Caro has rightly assailed the arrogance with which Moses could run roughshod over local needs and destroy still-vibrant neighborhoods (as in the construction of his Cross-Bronx Expressway, one of New York's great monstrosities). But, as Goldberger points out, the great majority of his projects (particularly the early ones) "were works conceived in optimism, full of belief in the future of New York and the importance of the public realm." Moses, he adds, "would have had no patience with the spirit of privitization that is [now] afoot in the land." Roger Starr has noted that Moses's success was due in part to "his sublime self-confidence, his apparent imperviousness to criticism." It was the former quality that had propelled Olmsted, but he had suffered greatly because he was deficient in the latter quality.

The spirit of a time can surely be seen in the kinds of people who become its "delegates" in public service and cultural activities. Olmsted had served the needs of his earnest Victorian gentry peers. Burnham had served the self-confident business leaders and politicians of the eras of budding American imperialism and the "New Nationalism." And Moses served the "build-it-now, build-it-bigger, get-it-done" sentiment of the age of the automobile and the skyscraper. He was successively the agent of the Progressivist impulse of management by experts; the New Deal public welfare mentality; and the post–World War II public construction renaissance. To contemplate the careers of Olmsted, Burnham, and Moses is to take a journey across the differing tastes and differing needs of successive generations of Americans. As each new public figure flourished, the name of the "delegate" who came before was forgotten or even (in Burnham's and Moses' cases) fell into disrepute.

In the new century, despite the long continuation of his firm under his son, Rick, Olmsted's name faded into an even greater obscurity than today bedevils Calvert Vaux. Even more, the parks that were to realize his true self's purposes had been led, by successive managements, further and further away from those purposes.

In Boston, as Cynthia Zaitzevsky observes, hardly had Franklin Park been built, "than it became a battleground for competing interests"; all those "undesirable activities that Olmsted had feared began to encroach almost immediately." The park has had to yield, over the years, to the demands of the zoo, more bridle paths, a golf course, a hospital, a stadium and increased automobile traffic. In Brooklyn, Jeffrey Simpson and Mary Ellen Hern note, the changes to Prospect Park have included "overly grand and ornamental buildings," as well as asphalt playgrounds, a skating rink and "lamps and paved walkways [that] interrupted the illusion of countryside." And, from the point of view of the goals of Olmsted and Vaux, Central Park suffered more from the cement and chainlink fence mentality of the public-spirited era of Robert Moses than it had from any of the scandal-prone administrations of the previous fifty years. In the words of one critic, "Moses had no understanding of the value of a natural landscape," and his commissionership was characterized by "a steady stream of poorly designed intrusions on the original landscape"—intrusions that have included the Wollman skating rink that so offends park naturalists to this day. And everywhere, as Zaitzevsky notes, the combination of mismanagement, insufficient funds for maintenance and police, and increasing demands on the spaces themselves combined to make urban parks shabbier and more dangerous.[35]

Stephen Rettig asks why British parks have been so well taken care of, "even during periods of economic stringency," while American parks have been permitted to "run down steadily." The answer lies, Rettig feels, with "the greater emphasis placed upon private property at the expense of public good" in America, as compared with "the still powerful tradition of civic pride and social responsibility among the British."[36] This is true, but so is the corollary fact that deference to patrician leadership continued until the current era in England, a hundred years after the complex pressures of pluralistic politics had curtailed patrician influence in America.

Today, while Burnham's name has faded from public memory and Moses' name is in disrepute, we are reminded everywhere that there is an "Olmsted renaissance" underway. Public and private groups are devoting more funds and time than they have in decades to the rehabilitation of the parks associated with Olmsted, and watchdog groups have developed all across the country to advocate and/or defend various philosophies on how this should be done.[37] In New York City, the Koch administration —whatever the quarrels of specific constituencies—showed concern about the well-being of Central Park, signaled by naming Elizabeth Barlow, an Olmsted biographer and a leader of the privately funded Central Park Conservancy, to the new post of Administrator for the park.[38] Barlow is eloquent on the age-old difficulty of meeting the needs of the park's various constituencies. "I'm delighted that Olmsted is on everyone's lips,"

Barlow says, "but where modern people are attached to things in the park —even architecturally unfortunate things like the Wollman rink—it is political suicide to suddenly change them." One can try to be true to "the principles of Olmsted and Vaux," she adds, but it is just not realistic to try to "completely Victorianize the park."

If the Koch administration was hospitable to the Olmsted and Vaux heritage of Central Park, at the same time it created an ever-greater need for the restorative benefits the designers intended the park to offer. Attacking "creeping gigantism" in New York City architecture and construction, Ada Louise Huxtable notes that there is now "a climate in which zoning controls developed and tested over 70 years no longer have credibility or support," with the result that the city is now "wide open" for exploitation by real estate developers. "Greed has never been so chic," she comments acidly; "The public interest has never been so passé," and the New York City skyline is being "recast" for the worse. She writes that the city is "selling itself to the highest bidder," creating a "Frankenstein monster that now crowds and darkens the city's streets, straining services, civility and art."[39] Similarly, Paul Goldberger has observed: "The exquisite balance that long characterized Manhattan—between skyscrapers and brownstones, between immensity and intimacy, between greed and grace—has become shaky, and in many places it is but a memory."[40]

Huxtable and Goldberger are not anti-urban, and they are not turned off by skyscrapers. Nor was Olmsted, per se, turned off by an urban skyline. In his 1870 ASSA address, he likened skyscrapers to mountains offering a "picturesque" beauty, a beauty associated with "very rugged ground, abrupt eminences." And he suggested to his audience:

Openness is the one thing you cannot get in buildings. Picturesqueness you can get. Let your buildings be as picturesque as your artists can make them. This is the beauty of a town. Consequently, the beauty of the park should be the other. It should be the beauty of the fields, the meadow, the prairie, of the green pastures, and the still waters.[41]

What writers like Huxtable and Goldberger suggest, and I concur with, is that the skyscrapers of New York are becoming more mountainous than ever before, but assuredly no longer picturesque. What the redesign of the New York skyline in the last two decades has been about

28. Central Park and the surrounding skyline of uptown New York. In an 1870 speech, Olmsted said that the tall buildings of a city should be "as picturesque as your artists can make them," while the park should represent the contrasting "beauty of the fields, the meadow, the prairie, of the green pastures, and the still waters." Many consider the contrast shown in this 1947 photograph to have been almost ideal, but fear that the views of and from the park will soon be overwhelmed by the "creeping gigantism" of an overdeveloped city. (The New-York Historical Society.)

is not picturesqueness nor beauty nor elegance nor a desirable quality of life. The rebuilding of the New York skyline is about *power*. Thus, it is fitting that the archetypal Oedipal city is characterized by skyscrapers ever more thrusting and rapacious—devoid of any feminine grace whatsoever. And what is happening in New York is happening elsewhere, Brendan Gill has noted. Citizens of New York, he writes, share with citizens of other cities a sense of "common disaster" and the grip of a "common fear":

The disaster is that of an aggressive, seemingly unstoppable process of overbuilding, with the consequent destruction of the scale on which our cities have hitherto been constructed; the fear is that, in their new, colossal scale, these cities are becoming not only unrecognizable but uninhabitable.[42]

To counteract the impact of oppressive city life on "town-strained" minds, Olmsted offered pastoral parks that would provide those minds with essential "tranquility and rest." If we are in the midst of an "Olmsted renaissance," it is perhaps because he is today *our* delegate, as he had once been the delegate for his own times. His torments are our torments. The city life that was too much with him is even more so with us. No matter how much New York changes, Jan Morris has written, there is something that stays the same: "perpetual and almost hysterical flux, never satisfied, apparently never fulfilled."[43] The thrusting, crowded, demanding, exhausting "private city" was then and is now.

Olmsted knew about the Oedipal thrust for power in men; he knew of the evils of an unrelenting materialistic, individualistic society, a society in which aggression is exalted and codified as an achieving competitiveness. "I speak from experience," he had cried in his "Civilization" notes.[44] Olmsted understood the physical and spiritual destructiveness of such a society, and he knew that we all need physical and spiritual respite from it. Central Park, Olmsted's most driving passion and most crucial work, stands as a double symbol. It is a symbol for the possibility that a municipal government can place civic welfare above the claims of private interests. And it is a symbol for psychic retreat from the pressures and punishment of city life, something we all need from time to time if we are to survive those pressures. Frederick Law Olmsted is now, as much as he ever was, the necessary delegate both of the existential torment we all experience and of the cry for relief we all long to make.

Abbreviations

Listed below are the abbreviations used when citing the basic primary and secondary sources on Olmsted and his times.

Barlow and Alex, *Olmsted's New York*
Elizabeth Barlow and William Alex, *Olmsted's New York*. New York, Praeger, 1972.

Beveridge, "Formative Years"
Charles E. Beveridge, "Frederick Law Olmsted: The Formative Years, 1822–1865." Ph. D. dissertation, University of Wisconsin, 1966.

Fabos, Milne, and Weinmayr, *Founder*
Julian Gy. Fabos, Gordon T. Milne, and V. Michael Weinmayr, *Frederick Law Olmsted, Sr.: Founder of Landscape Architecture in America*. Amherst, Mass.: University of Massachusetts Press, 1968.

Fein, *Cityscape*
Albert Fein, ed., *Landscape into Cityscape: Frederick Law Olmsted's Plans for a Greater New York City*. Ithaca: Cornell University Press, 1967.

FLOP
Frederick Law Olmsted Papers, microfilm ed. (60 reels). Washington, D.C.: Library of Congress.

Graff, *Central Park*
M. M. Graff, *Central Park/Prospect Park: A New Perspective*. New York: Greensward Foundation, 1985.

Kelly, Guillet, and Hern, *Olmsted Landscape*
Bruce Kelly, Gail Travis Guillet, Mary Ellen W. Hern, eds., *Art of the Olmsted Landscape*. New York: New York City Landmarks Preservation Commission and The Arts Publisher, 1981.

McLaughlin, *Papers*
Charles Capen McLaughlin, series ed., *The Papers of Frederick Law Olmsted*, 4 vols. Baltimore: Johns Hopkins University Press, 1977.

Nevins and Thomas, *Strong Diary*
Allan Nevins and Milton Halsey Thomas, eds., *The Diary of George Templeton Strong*, 4 vols. New York: Octagon Books, 1974.

Olmsted & Kimball, *Forty Years*
Frederick Law Olmsted, Jr., and Theodora Kimball, eds., *Frederick Law Olmsted, Landscape Architect, 1822–1903: Forty Years of Landscape Architecture*, 2 vols. New York: Putnam, 1928.

Olmsted & Ward, *Olmsted Family*
Henry K. Olmsted and George K. Ward, comps., *Genealogy of the Olmsted Family in America: Embracing the Descendants of James and Richard Olmsted and Covering a Period of Nearly Three Centuries, 1613–1912*. New York: De La Mare, 1912; reproduced, 1980.

Roper, *FLO*
Laura Wood Roper, *FLO: A Biography of Frederick Law Olmsted*. Baltimore: Johns Hopkins University Press, 1973.

Schuyler, *Urban Landscape*
David Schuyler, *The New Urban Landscape: The Redefinition of City Form in Nineteenth-Century America*. Baltimore: Johns Hopkins University Press, 1986.

Stevenson, *Park-Maker*
Elizabeth Stevenson, *Park-Maker; A Life of Frederick Law Olmsted*. New York: MacMillan, 1977.

Sutton, *Civilizing*
S. B. Sutton, ed., *Civilizing American Cities: A Selection of Frederick Law Olmsted's Writings on City Landscape.* Cambridge: MIT Press, 1971.

White and Kramer, *Olmsted South*
Dana F. White and Victor A. Kramer, eds., *Olmsted South: Old South Critic/New South Planner.* Westport, Conn.: Greenwood Press, 1979.

Wormeley, *Other Side of War*
Katharine Prescott Wormeley, *The Other Side of War: With the Army of the Potomac.* Boston: Ticknor, 1889.

Zaitzevsky, *Boston Parks*
Cynthia Zaitzevsky, *Frederick Law Olmsted and the Boston Park System.* Cambridge: Harvard University Press, 1982.

Following are two important reference works cited throughout.

CDAB
Concise Dictionary of American Biography. New York: Scribner's, 1977.

DAB
Allen Johnson and Dumas Malone, *Dictionary of American Biography.* New York: Scribner's, 1930.

Notes

Introduction

1. Lewis Mumford, *The Brown Decades: A Study of the Arts in America, 1865–1895* (New York: Dover, 1959), 85 and 93.

2. Erik H. Erikson, *Identity: Youth and Crisis* (New York: Norton, 1968), 156–7.

3. Mumford, *Brown Decades*, 93.

4. Unless otherwise noted, biographical material is derived from these sources: John Olmsted's journal and travel diaries and the papers and letters of Olmsted, his family, and his associates, *FLOP* and McLaughlin, *Papers; Connecticut Courant* and *Hartford Daily Courant;* Olmsted & Ward, *Olmsted Family;* Olmsted & Kimball, *Forty Years;* Roper, *FLO;* Stevenson, *Park Maker; DAB* and *CDAB.*

5. Law was the Hartford postmaster and a man with interests in literature and gardening. Frederick's middle name came from this man whom he later identified as an important influence. Law was said to have adopted Charlotte, though her own parents were to outlive her.

6. The children of John Olmsted's marriage to Mary Ann Bull were: Charlotte (1829–1832), Mary (1832–1875), Bertha (1834–1926), Owen (1836–1838), Ada Theodosia (1839–1846), and Albert Henry (1842–1929).

7. When John Hull was ten, he joined thirteen-year-old Frederick for a few months at Joab Brace's puritanical school in Newington. Frederick had boarded there since he was nine.

8. FLO to Charles Loring Brace, July 30, 1846, *FLOP*, reel 3. Similarly, he told his father: "The fact is I have not had but very few hard days work this summer." FLO to JO, August 12, 1846.

9. More than two dozen of these letters, superbly annotated, appear in McLaughlin, *Papers*, vol. 2, from which most of my facts about Olmsted's southern travels have been drawn.

10. JO to FLO, November 28, 1857, *FLOP*, reel 5.

11. CV to Edwin Lawrence Godkin, March 17, 1878, ibid., reel 33.

12. FLO to the Board of Commissioners of Central Park, January 22, 1861, ibid., reel 31.

13. See "Introduction," McLaughlin, *Papers*, 4:1–69; and William Quentin Maxwell, *Lincoln's Fifth Wheel: The Political History of the U.S. Sanitary Commission* (New York: Longmans, Green, 1956).

14. Olmsted and Vaux correspondence, April through July 1865, *FLOP*, reels 9, 32, and 33.

15. Frederick Law Olmsted, *Public Parks and the Enlargement of Towns* (Cambridge: Riverside Press, 1870); rpr. in Sutton, *Civilizing*, 52–99.

16. *Spoils of the Park: With a Few Leaves from the Deep-Laden Notebooks of "A Wholly Impractical Man"* (1882), reprinted in Fein, *Cityscape*, 391–440.

17. The latter has included, over the years, such proposals as: locating Grant's Tomb there, establishing a race-track around the perimeter, erecting various cathedrals and public buildings, taking some of the land for residential construction, etc. See the reprint of the article "If 'Improvement' Plans Had Gobbled Central Park" and adjacent cartoon, ibid., opposite p. 388.

18. Stow Persons, *The Decline of American Gentility* (New York: Columbia University Press, 1973).

19. Journal entry of June 18, 1838, in William H. Gilman, ed., *Selected Writings of Ralph Waldo Emerson* (New York: Signet, 1965), 73.

20. Entries of September 1843 and January–March 1844, ibid., 117 and 119.

21. Robert H. Wiebe, *The Search for Order, 1877–1920* (New York: Hill and Wang, 1967), xiii–xiv, 111–32.

22. Thomas Bender, *New York Intellect: A History of Intellectual Life in New York City, from 1750 to the Beginnings of Our Own Time* (Baltimore: Johns Hopkins University, 1987), 169–205.

23. Persons, *American Gentility*, 134–35 and 150. See also Thomas Bender, *Community and Social Change in America* (New Brunswick: Rutgers University Press, 1978), 17 and 108–20.

24. CEN to Chauncey Wright, September 13, 1870, in Sara Norton and M. A. De Wolfe Howe, eds., *Letters of Charles Eliot Norton*, 2 vols. (Boston: Houghton Mifflin, 1931), 1:399; journal entry, May 15, 1873, ibid., 1:504; CEN to S. G. Ward, April 26, 1896, ibid., 2:244.

25. *DAB*, 13:568–72. Kermit Vanderbilt, *Charles Eliot Norton: Apostle of Culture in a Democracy* (Cambridge, Mass.: Belknap Press, 1959).

26. CEN to CW, September 13, 1870, and CEN to J. B. Harrison, July 23, 1882, in Norton and Howe, *Norton Letters*, 1:399 and 2:135.

27. Entries of May 5, 1839, and May 27, 1844, Nevins and Thomas, *Strong Diary*, 1:104 and 236.

28. JWH to SGW, December 18, 1856, in Maud Howe Elliott, *Uncle Sam Ward and His Circle* (New York: MacMillan, 1938), 446–47; WI to SCW, February 7, 1843, ibid., 367.

29. Henry Adams, *The Education of Henry Adams* (New York: Modern Library, 1932), 22, 26, 247, 280–81, 343–44.

30. *FLOP*, reel 41. Like Adams, Olmsted had a great tendency to associate his own vicissitudes with those of the nation itself. At the end of the passage on the selfishness of businessmen, he first wrote, then crossed out, the cry: "I speak from experience."

31. FLO to CLB, March 15, 1887, ibid., reel 21. In place of *world*, Olmsted had written *word*.

32. David D. Hall, "The Victorian Connection," in Daniel Walker Howe, ed., *Victorian America* (Philadelphia: University of Pennsylvania Press, 1976), 84–85. Carlyle and Ruskin had particular impact upon Olmsted. See for example: FLO to JO, August 12, 1846, and FLO to JHO, December 13, 1846, *FLOP*, reel 3; McLaughlin, *Papers*, 1:271–81; and Roper, *FLO*, 72 and 394.

33. John Stuart Mill made an enormous impression upon Olmsted. *The Cotton Kingdom* (1861)—a revised and augmented collection of his travel books—was, in fact, dedicated by Olmsted to Mill, for the latter's "services in the cause of moral and political freedom in America" and as acknowledgement of the author's "personal obligations to them." Frederick Law Olmsted, *The Cotton Kingdom* (New York: Modern Library, 1969), lix.

34. Hall, "Victorian Connection," 88–89.

35. John Stuart Mill, "On Liberty," in *The Utilitarians* (Garden City: Anchor Books, 1973), 543.

36. Ibid., 552, 585, and 590.

37. Roper, *FLO*, 283–87. The citation is from Olmsted's report, "Yosemite and Mariposa Big Pines," delivered to Yosemite Commission of the State of California, August 9, 1865, ibid., 287.

38. J. G. A. Pocock, *The Machiavellian Moment: Florentine Political Thought and the Atlantic Political Tradition* (Princeton: Princeton University Press, 1975), 545–49.

39. George Forgie points out that in considering the careers of those who came to adulthood before the Civil War, it is extremely important to take note of their own mindset and the political, social, and cultural beliefs that helped to shape their mentalities and their activities. Thus, he finds it much more useful to refer to the first half of the nineteenth century as the "post–heroic age" rather than the "antebellum" years. The latter would obviously have had no meaning at all to those who lived through those decades. Rather, they expressed "their perception of their place in historical time . . . in terms of their relationship to the American beginning—the founding age—rather than any age or events to come." George B. Forgie, *Patricide in the House Divided: A Psychological Interpretation of Lincoln and His Age* (New York: Norton, 1979), 6–7.

40. Persons, *American Gentility*, 219. Martin Duberman, *James Russell Lowell* (Boston: Beacon Press, 1968), 3–4.

41. Daniel J. Wilson, "Neurasthenia and Vocational Crisis in Post–Civil War America," *Psychohistory Review* 12, 4 (1984):35. Wilson makes interesting use of

the sociological theories of Everett C. Hughes (on life cycles and society) and the psychological theories of Kurt Lewin (on the interrelationship between the individual and his psychological environment).

42. Norton and Howe, *Norton Letters;* Duberman, *Lowell;* Bliss Perry, *Life and Letters of Henry Lee Higginson* (Boston: Atlantic Monthly Press, 1921), 111, 115 and 118; Nevins and Thomas, *Strong Diary.* See also *DAB*, vol. 7, part 1, 569–572; 6:458–64; 9:109–11; vol. 4, part 2, 99–100; vol. 2, part 2, 614–16; vol. 5, part 1, 12–13.

43. *FLOP*, reel 43. McLaughlin, *Papers*, 1:98.

44. FLO to Charles Eliot, March 20, 1894, and FLO to Frederick J. Kingsbury, May 18, 1894, *FLOP*, reel 23.

45. Roper, *FLO*, 396; CEN to FLO, May 11, 1883, *FLOP*, reel 20; CEN to John Simon, Norton and Howe, *Norton Letters*, 2:91–92 (1879). "I am half-starved here," Norton told Simon.

46. Cited in Persons, *American Gentility*, 153.

47. Nevins and Thomas, ed., *Strong Diaries*, 4:460–61 (1873).

48. Adams, *Education*, 210. In this section, Adams was recording the struggle of his generation to find a place in American society. Of himself, he wrote: "Adams saw no road; in fact there was none."

49. Raymond Williams, *The Long Revolution* (New York: Harper, 1966), 84–100.

50. Ibid., 87 and 89.

51. D. W. Winnicott, *The Maturational Process and the Facilitating Environment* (New York: International Universities Press, 1965), 140–52. An object relations theorist, Winnicott holds that the achievement of that emotional maturity which permits expression of the true self is a function of the child's nurturance during its earliest years, when it must receive at least "good enough mothering." Ibid., 46–50. Full development of the true self's potential requires that a child's basic *needs* must be fulfilled, needs that Alice Miller lists as "care, protection, security, warmth, skin contact, touching, caressing, and tenderness." Alice Miller, *Thou Shalt Not Be Aware: Society's Betrayal of the Child* (New York: Farrar Straus Giroux, 1984), 316. And Peter Blos reminds us that the father's role is as essential as the mother's to the development of a sense of security and to what Erik Erikson refers to as a basic trust in the essential goodness of life. The little boy's "early experience of being protected by a strong father and caringly loved by him," Blos writes, "becomes internalized as a lifelong sense of safety" Peter Blos, *Son and Father: Before and Beyond the Oedipus Complex* (New York: Free Press, 1985), 10–11. It is the "sense of safety" that enables the individual to give free expression to his true self.

52. Erik H. Erikson, *Childhood and Society* (New York: Norton, 1968), 157. Alice Miller puts the case for interrelation between psyche and soma most strongly when she writes: "The truth about our childhood is stored up in our body, and although we can repress it, we can never alter it. Our intellect can be deceived, our feelings manipulated, and our body tricked with medication. But someday the body will present its bill." Miller, *Betrayal of the Child*, 318.

53. Williams, *Long Revolution*, 87.

54. See Charles E. Rosenberg, *No Other Gods: On Science and American Social Thought* (Baltimore: Johns Hopkins University Press, 1976), 98–108. See also Howard M. Feinstein, "The Use and Abuse of Illness in the James Family Circle: A View of Neurasthenia as a Social Phenomenon," in Robert J. Brugger, ed., *Our Selves/Our Past: Psychological Approaches to American History* (Baltimore: Johns Hopkins University Press, 1981), 228–43; Wilson, "Neurasthenia," 31–38; and Persons, *American Gentility*, 285–92.

55. Fein, *Cityscape*, 150–51; Sutton, *Civilizing*, 40.

56. George M. Frederickson, *The Inner Civil War: Northern Intellectuals and the Crisis of the Union* (New York: Harper 1968), 98–112.

57. Another weakness in Frederickson's argument, I believe, is that he treats this group of men almost totally in the wartime environment, then virtually abandons them in his treatment of the Gilded Age.

58. FLO to William Henry Hurlburt, January 31, 1863, McLaughlin, *Papers*, 4:508–10.

59. During a political squabble with the Army's Medical Bureau, George Templeton Strong wrote that the Executive Committee members were at first disposed to resign, but had decided instead to "define our positions and shield ourselves from blame." Nevins & Thomas, *Strong Diary*, 3:215, entry of March 28, 1862.

60. HWB to FLO, August 18, 1863, *FLOP*, reel 8.

61. Albert Fein, *Frederick Law Olmsted and the American Environmental Tradition* (New York: Braziller, 1972), 6–8 and 18–19.

62. Roper, *FLO*, xiv.

63. John G. Sproat, *The Best Men: Liberal Reformers in the Gilded Age* (New York: Oxford University Press, 1968), 4–10.

64. Gilman M. Ostrander, *American Civilization in the First Machine Age, 1890–1940* (New York: Harper, 1970, 1972), 90–91. Ostrander refers to Olmsted's America as "the Protestant Republic," 43–80.

65. FLO to O. Wolcott Gibbs, November 5, 1862, *McLaughlin Papers*, 4:466–71.

66. Geoffrey Blodgett, "Frederick Law Olmsted: Landscape Architecture as Conservative Reform," *Journal of American History* 62, 4 (March 1976):871–72.

67. Albert Fein, "The Olmsted Renaissance: A Search for National Purpose," in Kelly, Guillet, and Hern, *Olmsted Landscape*, 100 and 107.

68. Geoffrey Blodgett, "Landscape Design as Conservative Reform," in ibid., 111 and 122. This is a revised version of the Blodgett article cited in n. 66, above.

69. Jon C. Teaford, "Landscaping America," *Reviews in American History* 15, 4 (1987):656–61; W. Edward Orser, "The Contested Terrain of Nineteenth-Century Urban Landscape Design," *American Quarterly* 40, 4 (1988):550–55. Both of these are essay reviews of David Schuyler's book, *The New Urban Landscape*.

70. Paul Goldberger, "Square Deal for Columbus Circle?" *New York Times*, October 18, 1987, 2:1 and 41.

71. Howard W. French, "New Yet Old Tableau for Noble Road," *New York Times*, August 5, 1987, B1 and B3.

72. Thomas J. Lueck, "Battling Urban Development With Parks," *New York Times*, March 18, 1987, B1 and B4.

73. Schuyler, "Parks, Parkways, and Park Systems," *Urban Landscape*, ch. 7, 126–46. See also Zaitzevsky, *Boston Parks*.

74. FLO to EBW, December 16, 1890, *FLOP*, reel 21.

75. The concept of role delegation has been employed by Helm Stierlin to describe that mode of family dynamics in which the child is bound by the parents to meet their own unconscious needs. For example, an unruly child in an otherwise highly organized household may be acting out the parents' own repressed wishes to behave "wildly." Stierlin, *Separating Parents and Adolescents* (New York: Quadrangle/New York Times, 1974), 51–66. Anna Freud writes: "Some parents, for pathological reasons of their own, seem to need an ill, disturbed, or infantile child" and block the way to treatment of such children. Freud, *Normality and Pathology in Childhood* (New York: International Universities Press, 1978), 48.

76. Raymond Williams, *Culture and Society* (New York: Harper, 1958, 1966), 110–58.

77. CEN to JRL, November 24, 1873, and CEN to J. B. Harrison, July 23, 1885, in Norton and Howe, *Norton Letters*, 2:21 and 135.

1. The Olmsted Legend

1. *Ecclesiasticus* 44.

2. Olmsted & Kimball, *Forty Years*, 1:37–38; *FLOP*, reel 22.

3. Quoted in Theodora Kimball's introduction to "The Boyhood of Frederick Law Olmsted: Some Auto-Biographical Passages," a manuscript in *FLOP*, reel 46. Kimball was very likely the first editor of the Olmsted papers, working with them circa 1920 and augmenting them with notes based upon interviews she had conducted with both his widow and his son. Her efforts helped to produce Olmsted & Kimball's *Forty Years*.

4. Mariana G. Van Rensselaer, "Frederick Law Olmsted," *Century* (October 1893):860–67. The article is reproduced in *FLOP*, reel 45.

5. FJK to FLO, July 18, 1893, *FLOP*, reel 22.

6. Sutton, *Civilizing*, 18. Thomas Bender, *Toward an Urban Vision: Ideas and Institutions in Nineteenth-Century America* (Lexington: University of Kentucky Press, 1975), 185.

7. The second volume of Olmsted & Kimball, *Forty Years*, is devoted mainly to the senior Olmsted's long involvement with Central Park, reprinting or excerpting many of the more important documents and letters. This work was later supplanted by Fein's *Cityscape* and McLaughlin, *Papers*, vol. 3: *Creating Central Park: 1861–1863*.

8. See, for example, the review article by Dana F. White, in the fall 1987 *Newsletter* of the NAOP, 8–10. Stevenson's work has been neglected despite the

fact that Stevenson herself has been associated with the NAOP. The Stevenson reference cited is in *Park-Maker*, p. 148.

9. The inevitable impression—after reading Fein, *Cityscape*, and Sutton, *Civilizing*—is that one has been reading Olmsted's papers, though all but a few of those presented in these works were coauthored with his various partners, most usually Calvert Vaux. The editors do not omit Vaux, but he is clearly incidental to their purposes and their discussions. Yet it must be noted that Olmsted surely did most of the writing for the Olmsted and Vaux partnership, as Calvert Vaux held that to be one of Olmsted's strongest gifts. It is sometimes difficult to sort out the notions that were expressions of Olmsted's individual philosophy from those that were developed jointly or which belonged primarily to Vaux.

10. Quoted in Diedre Carmody, *New York Times*, May 17, 1982, B3. Carmody refers to Graff as "a writer who is described even by her critics as a fine horticulturist and—up to now, at least—as an eminent park historian."

11. Graff, *Central Park*, 88–89. This passage is also cited in the Carmody article noted above. Graff's book is dedicated to doing justice to these men and the roles *they* played in the creation and maintenance of Central Park in particular —roles, Graff suggests, that were at least as important as Olmsted's. Such a corrective is surely useful even if one feels that Graff is overly hostile toward Olmsted. And her book is also a splendid analysis of the design aesthetics of these two parks, as well as a justifiably angry documenting of their neglect.

12. Jon C. Teaford, "Landscaping America," *Reviews in American History* 15, 4 (1987):656–61. As noted in the introduction, n. 69, this is in part a review of David Schuyler's *New Urban Landscape*. Though Teaford greatly admires Schuyler's book on urban park planning and suburban landscape design in the nineteenth century, he is disturbed by Schuyler's "uncritical" admiration of Olmsted.

13. "The first author of the Lincoln legend and the greatest of the Lincoln dramatists was Lincoln himself," Hofstadter wrote. Richard Hofstadter, "Abraham Lincoln and the Self-Made Myth," in Hofstadter, *The American Political Tradition and the Men Who Made It* (New York: Knopf, 1973), 93.

14. See for example Fein, *Cityscape*, 47–62; Olmsted & Kimball, *Forty Years*, vol. 1; the manuscript fragments reproduced in *FLOP*, reels 43–47; and Olmsted's letters to MGVR of June 1893, reel 22.

15. FLO to MGVR, May 22, 1887, *FLOP*, reel 22.

16. Frederick Law Olmsted, *Spoils of the Park: With a Few Leaves from the Deep-Laden Notebooks of "A Wholly Impractical Man"* (1882), in Fein, *Cityscape*, 424–5. He also set forth the pedigree (in shorter form) of Calvert Vaux (424).

17. Olmsted had been shown a draft version of at least the first half of this article—that is, of the section that discussed his childhood, youth, and early career. See FLO to MGVR, May 22, 1893, *FLOP*, reel 23, and the draft itself on reel 60. Though the final article varies in many details from this draft version, factually incorrect statements that appear in the printed version *also* appear in the draft itself, when Olmsted could still have had them changed.

18. Lewis Mumford, *The Brown Decades: A Study of the Arts in America, 1865–*

1895 (New York: Dover, 1959), 85. Even as late as 1967, the traces of Olmsted's romanticized view of his training can still be seen in the biographical sketches of Albert Fein and of Fabos, Milne, and Weinmayr. See Fein, *Cityscape*, 4–6; and Fabos, Milne, and Weinmayr, *Founder*, 10–15.

19. The letter was prompted by an unusual show of independence on the part of Rick—one more typical of Olmsted himself as a youth than of his son. Rick had sided with the superintendent of the Biltmore nursery in a dispute with Olmsted regarding the use of certain plants. FLO Jr to FLO, December 9, 1894, *FLOP*, reel 52. Olmsted's reply—January 1, 1895—is given in original handwritten draft on reel 52 and in typed manuscript on reel 23. The version of his youth that Olmsted gives in this letter is substantially correct in fact and in essence.

20. Olmsted did not give here the correct age for when he had entered into his publishing venture (April 1855): he was actually thirty-three. This sort of underestimation was a habit with Olmsted. For example, he had been an apprentice at the firm of Benkard and Hutton, the position his father had obtained for him, from eighteen to almost twenty. In a letter written after Olmsted's death, Fred Kingsbury commented that Olmsted had been "rather old for youngest boy in a store." FJK to FLO Jr, November 4, 1903, ibid., reel 23. The Van Rensselaer article, and other sources based upon Olmsted's recollections, give his age at the store as sixteen—an indication of Olmsted's sensitivity on this issue.

21. Lucian W. Pye, "Personal Identity and Political Ideology," in Bruce Mazlish, ed., *Psychoanalysis and History* (New York: Universal Library, 1971), 166.

22. Van Rensselaer, "Olmsted," 867. Olmsted was thirty-five at the time of his appointment to the Central Park position.

23. FLO to JO, February 29 [March 1], 1850, *FLOP*, reel 4; McLaughlin, *Papers*, 1:337–41; emphases Olmsted's.

24. Sutton, *Civilizing*, 4.

25. McLaughlin, *Papers*, 1:337.

26. Mumford, *Brown Decades*, 93.

27. Van Rensselaer, "Olmsted," 867.

28. It should be noted that Frederick J. Kingsbury (1823–1910) had been a classmate of John Hull Olmsted and Charles Loring Brace at Yale in the 1840s, becoming a close friend of both the Olmsted brothers and maintaining a searching correspondence with each for nearly a decade. He resumed his correspondence with Frederick in their later years, and his letters and reminiscences, provided to Olmsted's widow and son, are the source for considerable information on the early life of Frederick and his brother. Kingsbury trained for a legal career, but married a daughter of a partner in the Scovill Manufacturing Company, becoming first a banker and then president of Scovill. He maintained an interest in the humanities, becoming an active member of the American Social Science Association. See McLaughlin, *Papers*, 1:80–83.

29. FJK to MCO, August 30, 1903, *FLOP*, reel 23.

30. Graff, *Central Park*, 31. Graff notes that Parson's comments were "based upon intimate knowledge of the two men." But it should also be noted that

Parsons did not come on the scene until decades after the Greensward Plan had been designed and fundamentally implemented and that he had been Vaux's partner in the 1880s. Graff does not cite the source of this passage, but it was likely from Parson's book, *Memories of Samuel Parsons*, edited by his daughter, which she mentions elsewhere (63).

31. Beveridge, "Introduction," in McLaughlin, *Papers*, 3:11–14.

32. Mumford, *Brown Decades*, 85–88. The only other landscape architect Mumford gave due recognition to was the protégé of Olmsted's later years, Charles Eliot, Jr. Mumford stated that the two of them had "contributed more to the improvement of town and country then any dozen of their contemporaries." Mumford did not believe that "later schemes of civic improvement" had accomplished nearly as much as the work of these two. "Above all, they made their contemporaries conscious of air, sunlight, vegetation, growth," he concluded. "If we still defile the possibilities of the land, it is not for lack of better example." (ibid., 95–96.)

33. Roper, *FLO*, 291 (emphasis added). I have relied upon Roper's reading of this passage, because the microfilm edition of this letter (FLO to MGVR, June 11, 1893; *FLOP*, reel 22), which I will be citing elsewhere, is blotted and smudged at this point. Roper cites this passage, then says that Olmsted "may have been overstating his debt to Vaux."

34. CV to FLO, October 19, 1863, *FLOP*, reel 8.

35. CV to FLO, January 18, 1864, ibid.

36. Vaux's letters to Olmsted of this period are contained in reel 32, Olmsted's to Vaux on reel 9. They will be dealt with at length in part 3, chapter 10. See also Stevenson, *Park-Maker*, 268–73; Roper, *FLO*, 291–3. Stevenson's more thorough treatment of the relationship between Olmsted and Vaux here and elsewhere (see 256–58, for example) is typical of their differing approaches to the personal side of Olmsted. M. M. Graff was particularly annoyed by the notion expressed, in *Forty Years*, by Olmsted's "worshipful son" (Rick) and Theodora Kimball, that Vaux's 1865 campaign consisted of "friendly letters." Graff comments that "only a resolutely rose-tinted editor" could have construed as friendly these "sharply critical and even bullying" letters, whose overall tone was "one of disparagement and reaction." Graff, *Central Park*, 119. But Graff omits, or imputes to coercive flattery, all that was positive and exhortatory in Vaux's letters. For as Rick and Kimball observed, Vaux had indeed tried to persuade Olmsted "of his superior fitness for the work and of his clear duty to return to Central Park." On the other hand, Roper's treatment of the Vaux letters is also rather rosy-hued—virtually ignoring all of Vaux's complaints. Roper, *FLO*, 291–93. Again, the letters will be treated in detail in part 3.

37. It is useful to recall that Vaux originally had come to America to collaborate, in a clearly subordinate role, with Andrew Jackson Downing, the country's first landscape architect.

38. CV to FLO, May 12, June 1 and 3, and July 8, 1865, *FLOP*, reel 32.

39. CV to FLO, May 12 and July 8, 1865, ibid., reel 32. Interestingly, despite

the patriotic outlook suggested here, neither Vaux nor Olmsted—in that which survives of their correspondence from this period—made any reference to the colossal events of recent weeks: namely Lincoln's assassination, the end of the Civil War, the beginning of Reconstruction. Olmsted's other correspondence, however, does deal with these matters—so the obsessively narrow focus is likely to have been Vaux's.

40. Stevenson, *Park-Maker*, 344–45. See also Roper, *FLO*, 361.

41. JCO to CE, August 25, 1887, *FLOP*, reel 21. John said his stepfather had suggested that an arrangement could be made "as the next best thing for the preservation of Central Park & the proper planning of the new one & the uniting of the friends of both Mr. Vaux and himself." This arrangement, clearly, was meant to give Olmsted full authority for the design direction while appeasing Vaux with the actual office of Landscape Architect for the New York parks. In the event, Vaux got the position in 1888, while Olmsted finally retreated from any direct consulting relationship, except for some temporary work on the Riverside and Morningside parks. Stevenson, *Park-Maker*, 372.

42. FLO to MGVR, December 21, 1887, *FLOP*, reel 21.

43. See Graff, *Central Park*, 120. Roper, *FLO*, 294, acknowledges that it was Vaux's design which was implemented in Prospect Park. Stevenson handles the issue this way: Olmsted "had added his part to the design which Vaux had originated, and he knew, from the moment ground was broken, that his part would be larger than Vaux's in bringing the plan into physical shape. He considered no design set as long as work was being done." *Park-Maker*, 277. I think Stevenson's judgment is correct, but this hardly justifies Olmsted's rather cavalier statement to Van Rensselaer insofar as the Brooklyn park was concerned.

44. FLO to MGVR, September 23, 1893, *FLOP*, reel 22.

45. The sections compared below are from the draft version of Van Renselaer's article, "Olmsted," 23 and 27, and the printed version, 863, 865, and 867, *FLOP*, reels 60 and 45, respectively. It should be reiterated that the thirty-two-page draft manuscript encompasses only the first half of the material covered by the article. We have no way of knowing whether that was all Olmsted was shown, or whether the rest of it was given to him, but is now missing.

46. *Greensward* was the name that Olmsted and Vaux gave to their proposed plan for "the improvement of Central Park" in the 1858 design competition. See Fein, *Cityscape*, 63–88, and McLaughlin, *Papers*, 3:119–87. The specifications for the sunken transverse roads will be found in *Cityscape*, 68, and *Papers*, 122.

47. Beveridge, "Introduction," 16.

48. Bruce Kelly, "Art of the Olmsted Landscape," in Kelly, Guillet, and Hern, *Olmsted Landscape*, 34. Elsewhere in this essay, Kelly also states that "divided roadways for crossing one road over another were invented by Olmsted and Vaux and promoted by Olmsted" (70). Kelly also states that "the New York City landscape owes more to Calvert Vaux than to Frederick Law Olmsted," but he adds that it "is Olmsted whom we remember" (69).

49. Fabos, Milne, and Weinmayr, *Founder*, 17–29.

50. Stephen Rettig, "Influences Across the Water: Olmsted and England," in Kelly, Guillet, and Hern, *Olmsted Landscape*, p. 82.

51. Frederick Law Olmsted, *A Journey Through Texas: Or, a Saddle–Trip on the Southwestern Frontier* (1857) (Austen: University of Texas Press, 1978). The following comments of Olmsted, John Hull, and Larry McMurtry are all from the various forewords to this volume.

52. The reviews of the book praised only Frederick and made no mention at all of John Hull, who had nurtured literary ambitions of his own. JHO to FLO, November 10, 1856 (emphasis JHO's), FLO to JHO, February 17, 1857, JHO to FLO, February 15, 1857, transcripts of extracts from reviews in several newspapers, JHO to FLO, July 6, 1857, all in *FLOP*, reel 5.

53. Ibid., reel 60, 14; reel 45, 862.

54. Mary Olmsted to JHO, September 22, 1848, ibid., reel 4. "Downing" of course refers to Andrew Jackson Downing, editor of the *Horticulturist*. Downing was much admired in the Olmsted household and became both friend and mentor to Frederick.

2. *"The Price I Have Paid"*

1. FLO to MGVR, May 22, 1893, *FLOP*, reel 22 (emphasis added).

2. FLO to EBW, December 16, 1890, ibid., reel 21. Elizabeth Baldwin (later Whitney) had had enormous influence upon Olmsted, who had yearned for her with a great and hopeless love. Whitney had been moved to write Olmsted, after they had been parted for several decades, by an article she had read about him. Olmsted responded with this very long and quite fascinating letter, one of several such documents from Olmsted's old age. Olmsted begins this passage by quoting from James Russell Lowell's "The Vision of Sir Launfall":

> Earth gets its price for what earth gives us;
>   The beggar is taxed for a corner to die in,
> The priest hath his fee who comes and shrives us,
>   We bargain for the grave we lie in.

3. McLaughlin, *Papers*, 1:134. *FLOP*, reel 23, the letters of MCO to FLO Jr and JCO during 1896.

4. MCO to FJK, February 25, 1886, ibid., reel 20.

5. FLO to FJK, September 6, 1893, ibid., reel 22.

6. JO to JHO, undated, ibid., reel 4.

7. Stevenson, *Park-Maker*, 179–86, 324, and 340–48; Roper, *FLO*, 146–50 and 358. Roper ignores the 1873 illness and treats the others in far less detail than does Stevenson.

8. Roper's version of Olmsted's illness and accident are given in *FLO*, 146–50. The difficulties with Commissioner Green will be explored more fully in part 3, chapter 9.

9. FLO to JO, September 23, 1859, *FLOP*, reel 6.

10. *New York Tribune*, August 9, 1860.
11. *FLOP*, reel 47, July 16, 1920.
12. McLaughlin, *Papers*, 3:302–3.
13. The *Tribune* article states that Olmsted's quick recovery was noticeable two days after the accident, leading to the hope "that in a few weeks he will be restored to the active discharge of his duties."
14. The description of the accident that follows is taken from Olmsted's letter to his father, November 7, 1854, McLaughlin, *Papers*, 2:331–37; *FLOP*, reel 4. The details of John Hull's situation and Frederick's are from this letter and the correspondence between JHO and JO, July–December 1854, ibid.
15. Olmsted & Kelly, *Forty Years*, 1:16; Stevenson, *Park-Maker*, 317–18.
16. John Olmsted's accident and death were recorded in his journal by his widow, Mary Ann Olmsted, who took up the journal at this point and kept it up sporadically until 1881. *FLOP*, reel 1. The other details were reported in FLO to FJK, January 28, 1873, ibid., reel 13. At the end of the Kingsbury letter, Frederick commented that an examination of his father's papers revealed to him that John Olmsted had felt the likelihood of his death "and has meant to have everything clear."
17. Ibid.
18. JO to FLO, October 29, 1868, *FLOP*, reel 11; FLO to FJK, January 28, 1873, ibid., reel 13.
19. In fact, John Olmsted's father, Benjamin, had died in 1832, by which time John's dry goods store was thriving. The nagging sense of guilt revealed here had been longstanding. In 1847, when Fred was about to move into his first farm, John Olmsted commented to John Hull that few children realize "that their aged parents are solitary & lonely & how much it is in their power to smooth the downhill path." He had tried to do as much, if not more than most people, to make his parents comfortable in their old age, John Olmsted said: "& yet after they were gone, I felt as if I had not done half enough & if they were only back how much more I could have done for them . . . & this feeling remains to this day." JO to JHO, February 7, 1847, *FLOP*, reel 4.
20. FLO to Frederick N. Knapp, January 28, 1873, ibid., reel 13.
21. Kingsbury Memoir, ibid., reel 47.
22. AHO letters to FLO, February 26, March 30, April 15, May 28, July 28, August 4, and September 11, 1873, ibid., reel 13. The August 4 letter told of the probate hearing, which Olmsted had not attended and which was determined in the sons' favor. Albert called the attack of his mother's lawyer upon Frederick "outrageous and scandalous." See also MAO to FLO, August 18, 1873, ibid., in which she complained of Frederick's lack of attention to her.
23. FLO to FNK, August 26, 1873, ibid.
24. AHO to FLO, September 11, 1873, and FLO to SHW, September 17, 1873, ibid. Olmsted enclosed, with the Wales letter, his own suggested bylaw amendments regarding the position of Landscape Architect—which would place "under his orders" the Chief Engineer, Architect, and Landscape Gardener.

25. O. C. Bullard to FLO, November 7, 1873, ibid. Bullard was a Brooklyn park commissioner. Olmsted's eye problems were first mentioned in a letter of Albert's, October 13, 1873, ibid. The treatment Olmsted was undergoing is revealed in letters from his friend, Frederick N. Knapp, October 23 and November 5, ibid. In the first letter, Knapp made a psychologically striking comment when he stated: "I trust that rest (which I imagine will be about as novel a treatment for your eyes—individually—as amputation would be for your legs) will very soon restore their use." The jest contained a true, if unconscious, analogy—for both are stark castration symbols.

Three months later, Olmsted's colleague, the noted landscape architect, H. W. S. Cleveland, wrote that he was grieved to learn of Olmsted's long suffering, adding: "I ought rather to rejoice that you have escaped blindness, than mourn that your eyesight has been impaired." HWSC to FLO, February 2, 1874, ibid., reel 14.

26. Stevenson, *Park-Maker*, 354. FLO to CLB, December 21, 1873, *FLOP*, reel 13. This letter had evidently been inspired by Olmsted's mistaken belief that Brace had written an editorial in the *New York Daily Times* that unfavorably compared John Stuart Mill with Louis Agassiz—casting the former as an "unbeliever," the latter as a "devout Christian." Though Olmsted was clearly alluding to the case of Mill in the "suicide" reference, he had made equally clear his own identification with Mill. It thus seems highly probable that he was talking about himself in his own depressive moods, as well as about Mill. As it happens, Olmsted—when beginning his farmer's life on Staten Island—had written a letter expressing suicidal thoughts to Fred Kingsbury. FLO to FJK, October 14, 1848, ibid., reel 47.

27. Katharine Prescott Wormeley (1830–1908) was with Olmsted during the Peninsula Campaign, a relationship she described in *The Other Side of War*, her book about these experiences. She also wrote the official record of the Sanitary Commission and became a noted translator of French writers, particularly Balzac. *CDAB*, 1212. KPW to "Miss Brace," February 20, 1904, *FLOP*, reel 23. Katharine Prescott Wormeley, *The Other Side of War with the Army of the Potomac. Letters from the Headquarters of the United States Sanitary Commission during the Peninsula Campaign in Virginia in 1862.* (Boston: Ticknor, 1889).

28. KPW to FLO, January 15, 1874, ibid. Wormeley noted the date of *his* letter in her reply, commenting that she got it in time for her birthday. She quotes or paraphrases the text of his letter liberally in hers. In the letter to "Miss Brace" cited above, Wormeley remarks that she had destroyed all of Olmsted's letters to her.

29. See George H. Pollock, "Anniversary Reactions, Trauma, and Mourning," *Psychoanalytic Quarterly* 39 (1970):347–71.

30. These are actually a series of untitled fragments, *FLOP*, reel 47. In a note included with these and other fragments for the book he intended to produce, Theodora Kimball, the early editor of Olmsted's papers, dates them to 1892 or 1893 and thought them to have been written in his Brookline home, "when

confined to the house with ill health or on sleepless nights." She said that Olmsted's widow thought they might have been written at the Biltmore estate, where he "often had to go to bed for a week after the journey down." July 30, 1920, ibid. These fragments often deal with the same material discussed in Olmsted's two earlier efforts at autobiography in 1860 and 1873, but in variant form. Some of these 1893 recollections make up the bulk of the material reproduced in McLaughlin, *Papers*, 1:113–19.

31. *FLOP*, reels 21 and 22.

32. FLO to MGVR, June 17, 1893, ibid., reel 22.

33. This was the first of Olmsted's three major efforts at autobiography and is headed "Biog. Olmsti F. L. Notes for Consideration." *FLOP*, reel 47. The references made in these notes to his work on Central Park as contemporary events date these as written in the 1859–1861 period. His bed-ridden weeks of recovery from his carriage accident seem to offer an occasion of available time and motivation for reflection. The handwriting is consistent with Olmsted's other samples of that period. The notes begin in a half-mocking, stream-of-consciousness manner dealing with the "multiplicity of elements" in his genealogy. They turn serious with the section on his birth, early upbringing, and later career. These notes have considerable psychological significance, which will be dealt with in part 2, chapter 5.

34. Except that his stays at Eastman's in Saybrook occurred during the summers of 1836 and 1837, with the year at home (in Hartford and East Hartford) in between them. Another major error is that the ages given, starting at thirteen, all seem to have happened one year later than Olmsted reports (for example, his year at home, after Brace's, was at ages fourteen to fifteen, and he was at Barton's at ages sixteen and seventeen.

35. Frederick's report card from the Hartford Grammar School, at age eight and a half, described a bright little boy who was too fond of play to achieve excellence in school work. *FLOP*, reel 1.

36. Ibid., reel 47

37. The notion that Frederick's eye problems were what had kept him from going on to college—accepted by all of his biographers—was most strongly supported by material that Rick Olmsted and Theodora Kimball attributed to John Olmsted's journal, but that had in fact been concocted by them (most likely by Rick, working from the family legend). Rick must have known that the subject was important enough to his father, so that he (Rick) felt the family legend needed evidentiary support. Olmsted & Kimball, *Forty Years*, 58–61. For a more complete discussion of this material and the use made of it by various biographers, see my "In Memory of the Summer Days: The Mind and Work of Frederick Law Olmsted," Ph.D. dissertation, New York University, 1988, appendix C: "A Case of 'Sumach Poisoning.' "

38. September 27 and October 7, 1838, *FLOP*, reel 3. The first, from September 10, 1838, is cited in part 2, chapter 4; it is the letter in which John Olmsted informed Frederick of the death of his half brother, Owen.

39. Stevenson believes Olmsted decided to try the merchant's life in New York at least partly in envious reaction to John Hull's being sent to France to study (in 1840). Stevenson, *Park-Maker*, 13.

40. Beveridge, "Formative Years," 39.

41. JO to FLO & JHO, December 30, 1845, *FLOP*, reel 3. John Olmsted was as much concerned for John Hull's health, since his college career had been interrupted by illness. He advised both his sons to develop regular habits, which he enumerates ("wholly eschew coffee and smoke").

42. FLO to FJK, June 12, 1846, McLaughlin, *Papers*, 1:243–44.

43. See Charles E. Rosenberg, *No Other Gods: On Science and American Social Thought* (Baltimore: Johns Hopkins University Press, 1976), 98–108; Howard M. Feinstein, "The Use and Abuse of Illness in the James Family Circle: A View of Neurasthenia as a Social Phenomenon," in Robert J. Brugger, ed., *Our Selves/Our Past; Psychological Approaches to American History* (Baltimore: Johns Hopkins University Press, 1981), 228–43; Daniel J. Wilson, "Neurasthenia and Vocational Crisis in Post–Civil War America," *Psychohistory Review* 12, 4 (1984): 31–38; Stow Persons, *The Decline of American Gentility* (New York: Columbia University Press, 1973), 285–92.

44. Rosenberg, *No Other Gods*, 98–100; Persons, *American Gentility*, 287.

45. Persons, *American Gentility*, 287.

46. Feinstein, "Use and Abuse of Illness," 229.

47. Persons, *American Gentility*, 285–92.

48. Wilson, "Neurasthenia," 35.

49. Feinstein, "Use and Abuse of Illness," 241–42.

50. KPW to FLO, January 5 and November 22, 1877, *FLOP*, reel 16 (emphasis Wormeley's).

51. Roper, *FLO*, 365–66.

52. FLO to CLB, March 15, 1887, *FLOP*, reel 21.

53. FLO to KPW, December 10, 1893, ibid., reel 23. The draft is almost unreadable on microfilm.

3. A Sense of Failure

1. FLO to CLB, November 1, 1884, *FLOP*, reel 20.

2. Roper, *FLO*, 393.

3. In correspondence with the French landscape architect Edouard André, Olmsted had stated several years earlier (1879) that he was "doing but little professionally," pointing with pride only to his public works—the U.S. Capitol grounds, the Back Bay (Boston) park, and, especially, Niagara Falls, where he hoped for "the restoration of natural conditions." FLO to EA, June 6, 1879, *FLOP*, reel 17. At the time of the Brace letter, late 1884, the U.S. Capitol and Niagara Falls projects were basically concluded and Olmsted's public works were generally small scale. Olmsted & Kimball, *Forty Years*, 23, 27, and 28. Thus his

statement that his work had grown smaller may also have represented his own inner perception of private work as being less significant than public work.

4. FJK to CLB, January 10, 1885, *FLOP*, reel 20. Brace had apparently sent Kingsbury Olmsted's letter of November 1, 1884. This passing along of letters within their circle had been common during their youth.

5. See introduction, n. 43.

6. FLO to CE, March 20, 1894, *FLOP*, reel 23.

7. FLO to FJK, May 18, 1894, ibid.

8. Stevenson, *Park-Maker*, 371–73; Roper, *FLO*, 402–3. See also the series of letters between May 20, 1886, and August 26, 1887, *FLOP*, reels 20 and 21. This is the incident referred to in chapter 1 (see n. 41), when Olmsted was being drawn into a prospective consultancy on the New York parks against Vaux's wishes.

9. FLO to CV, July 5, 1887, *FLOP*, reel 21.

10. Cited in Fein, *Cityscape*, 418. (emphases added).

11. FLO to CV, July 9, 1887, *FLOP*, reel 21 (emphasis added).

12. Roper, *FLO*, 146; McLaughlin, *Papers*, 3:230.

13. FLO to JO, September 23, 1859, *FLOP*, reel 6.

14. FLO to CV, August 1, 1865, ibid., reel 9.

15. FLO to John Charles Olmsted and Charles Eliot, October 2, 1893, ibid., reel 21. Muddy River was a highly complex drainage project, vital to the creation of the "Emerald Necklace" the Olmsted firm had designed—a series of parks, parkways, and nature preserves that stretched from the Boston Common, around the city, to Franklin Park in Dorchester. See Zaitzevsky, *Boston Parks*.

16. FLO to William A. Stiles, March 10, 1895, *FLOP*, reel 22. Stiles was a young journalist, influenced by Olmsted, who became the first editor of *Garden and Forest*, a moderately influential weekly that Olmsted helped to found. Roper, *FLO*, 404.

17. Schuyler, *Urban Landscape*, 184–88. Olmsted's work on the Chicago Exposition and his relationship to the architects of the City Beautiful movement will be discussed in part 4, chapter 14.

18. Roper, *FLO*, 464.

19. FLO to WAS, September 18, 1894, *FLOP*, reel 23. Stiles was keeping him informed of the happenings in New York during this period.

20. FLO to FLO Jr., December 23, 1894, ibid.

21. FLO to FLO Jr., July 11 and 23, 1895, ibid., reel 52. The first letter is also to be found, in typescript, in reel 23.

22. October 14, 1895, ibid., reel 52. In an undated letter, probably of the same period, Olmsted told Rick: "I am also thinking . . . with perturbation and apprehension, of what this proceeding of John's, in taking the good will of the business, is going to do for you. I hope that it is coming out all right, but when my will was made it is certain that neither I nor my legal counsel took into account the affect of such a possible *coup*." (Ibid.)

Roper says that Rick told her, in later years (October 1948), there was never any indication that his father's suspicions actually had any substance. Roper, *FLO*, 470.

23. MCO to JCO, August 17, 1876, and July 16, 1879, *FLOP*, reel 15 (emphases added). It is perhaps useful to recall again that John Charles had been five when his father died and less than seven when his mother married his uncle. Further, John Charles had often been separated from his parents for long periods of time during the father's terminal illness. See ibid., reel 5. This is the psychoanalytic prescription for a very angry little boy—one whose anger, however much repressed, would smoulder far into adulthood, seeking opportunities for expression. His mother's "put-down" of his abilities (particularly in respect to those of his stepfather) could hardly have helped matters.

24. Stevenson, *Park-Maker*, 423.

25. JCO to FLO, September 2, 1895, *FLOP*, reel 23.

26. Roper, *FLO*, 338, and Stevenson, *Park-Maker*, 308 and 326, are both somewhat vague about the timing of this name-change. Roper implies that it took place about the time of the family's move to Manhattan, when the boy was a toddler (1872). But the family letters of 1875–1879, *FLOP*, reels 15–17, documented the sequence I have indicated.

27. FLO to FLO Jr., January 1, 1895, *FLOP*, reels 23 and 52. (See also chapter 1, n. 19.)

28. FLO to FLO Jr., December 23, 1894, ibid., reel 23 (emphasis added).

29. FLO to FLO Jr., July 31 and August 13, 1895, ibid.

30. FLO to FLO Jr., undated (late 1895), ibid. (emphases Olmsted's).

31. FLO to FLO Jr., undated (late 1895), ibid. In a letter dated October 15, 1895 (someone has appended a note to the files contesting that date), Olmsted wrote: "Here I am at home again, dear Rick . . . still with the expectation of being taken out to England to die, by Mother and Marion." He asked for "Codaks" of the work at Biltmore, noting: "I suppose that it will be some months before the advance of my malady will make these of no value to me." Ibid.

32. FLO to FLO Jr., November 7, 1895, ibid.

33. Olmsted & Kimball, *Forty Years*, 40. FLO to FLO Jr., December 4, 1895, *FLOP*, reel 23 (emphasis Olmsted's).

34. Fabos, Milne, and Weinmayr, *Founder*, 87. Plans are currently underway to restore the gardens and parks of the Biltmore estate itself, a National Historic Landmark Property of eight thousand acres operated by Vanderbilt's grandson. To replace many of the plants on the property, a new nursery is being established, similar to the one Olmsted had maintained in the 1890s. The curator notes: "Many of the plants that Olmsted tried did not prove suitable for thi climate'" and therefore will not be replaced. Suzanne Brendel-Pandich, Curator Biltmore Estate, in a communication published in *National Association for Olmste Parks News Update*, undated, received September 1985.

35. FLO to CV, March 25, 1864, *FLOP*, reel 3. Two decades later, Olmste was still saying the same thing. The Greensward plan, he told the president c the New York Parks Department in 1886, "was devised with reference not in th

least to what the city then was or to the manifest wants of the day but to what the city might be expected to be and its probable wants after a period of forty years." FLO to H. K. Beekman, June 10, 1886, *FLOP*, reel 20. See also part 4, chapter 14, n. 2.

36. McLaughlin, *Papers*, 3:313. This was his letter of resignation as Architect in Chief of Central Park, January 21, 1861, previously cited in chapter 2. It is quite an important letter, and I will deal with it in depth in part 3 chapter 10.

37. Cited in Harry Guntrip, *Psychoanalytic Theory, Therapy, and the Self* (New York: Harper, 1973), 152.

38. Raymond Williams, *The Long Revolution* (New York: Harper, 1966), 89.

39. Roper, *FLO*, 467–68. Olmsted worked in tandem, at Biltmore, with Richard Morris Hunt (1827–1895), who designed the estate's palatial country house in French Renaissance style. Mumford refers to Hunt as "the most fashionable architect of the Gilded Age . . . building French chateaux on Fifth Avenue." Lewis Mumford, *The Brown Decades: A Study of the Arts in America, 1865–1895* (New York: Dover, 1959), 110. It is ironic that there is, at Central Park, a monument to Richard Morris Hunt (built into the wall on the Fifth Avenue side at Seventy-first Street) but there is none anywhere in New York City for Olmsted or Vaux. One could argue, of course, that the park itself is their monument.

40. FLO to MCO, April 16, 1865, *FLOP*, reel 9. The manuscript shows that Olmsted originally wrote: "to be saved from growing *weaker & more incapable*" (emphasis added).

4. The Wounds of Childhood

1. The 1820 census showed Hartford with 6,901 inhabitants, with another 3,373 persons living in East Hartford across the river. *Connecticut Courant*, July 30, 1822. See also *The Pocket Register of the City of Hartford* (n.p., 1825) and *City Directory for 1828* (Hartford: Ariel Ensign).

2. JO journal, 1825, *FLOP*, reel 1. (John Olmsted's extant journals begin with this year, although references are made, in these annual journals, to records he had kept in earlier years.) The establishment of Washington College, and its curriculum, was announced in the *Connecticut Courant*, September 7, 1824.

3. *FLOP*, reel 47.

4. JO to FLO, August 13, 1836, and JO to JHO, November 2, 1847; ibid., reels 3 and 4.

5. Ibid., reel 1.

6. From "Passages," ibid., reel 43. See also McLaughlin, *Papers*, 1:98–99.

7. Roper, *FLO*, 5.

8. *FLOP*, reel 1. Charlotte's journal probably has been overlooked because it occupies the second part of the little book in which John Olmsted had recorded an 1819 trip of his own, to Niagara Falls. The note identifying this as Charlotte's journal is in John Olmsted's handwriting. He apparently had given the book to her for the occasion of her 1820 trip, which suggests that they may have been

affianced by then. John Olmsted's note identifies all the members of the party except Mary Ann Bull. The references to "Mary Ann" in the journal, however, seem clearly to describe the young woman who was then Charlotte's friend.

9. Col. Charles H. Weygant, ed., *The Hull Family in America* (Hull Family Association, 1913), 495. See also Edwin R. Brown, *Old Historic Homes of Cheshire, Connecticut* (New Haven: C. H. Ryder, 1895), 106–8; genealogical notes by John Olmsted, 1835, JO journal, *FLOP*, reel 1; *Connecticut Courant*, June 12, 1821.

10. Donald Winnicott—in his discussion of "good-enough mothering"—underscores Freud's observation that the infant learns to love from his mother loving him and showing that love through physical affection (for Winnicott, "holding"). Winnicott writes that the mother must be able to identify with what her infant is feeling and, through that identification, practice "a lively adaptation to the infant's needs." D. W. Winnicott, *The Maturational Process and the Facilitating Environment* (New York: International Universities Press, 1965), 48–55.

11. For the little boy, there are two keys to the successful resolution of the rapprochement crisis. First is the continued availability of the mother to reassure the child of her love and affection, while encouraging his efforts toward autonomy. Second is the presence of a forceful father figure who encourages the separation from the mother and who provides a role model for the little boy in his effort to become an independent individual.

The work of Margaret Mahler and her colleagues at the Master's Children's Center in New York has enormously influenced American psychoanalytic thought in the past two decades. Two books set forth the principal concepts of this group: Margaret S. Mahler and Manuel Furer, *On Human Symbiosis and the Vicissitudes of Individuation: Infantile Psychosis* (New York: International Universities Press, 1968), and Margaret S. Mahler, Fred Pine, and Anni Bergman, *The Psychological Birth of the Human Infant: Symbiosis and Individuation* (New York: Basic Books, 1975). For the sake of simplicity, I will refer to the collective work of this group as that of "Mahler" or the "Mahlerians."

12. All children, Mahler notes, must deal with "experiential factors" and "accidental events" that can turn the rapprochement crisis into an "unfavorable fixation point, thus interfering with later oedipal development." Mahler, Pine, and Bergman, *Psychological Birth*, 107–8, 120, and 230. I believe that the continuing trauma and stress that beset Frederick between the ages of three and seven made such a fixation and consequent interference in Oedipal development even more likely in this case.

13. See my "In Memory of the Summer Days: The Mind and Work of Frederick Law Olmsted," Ph. D. dissertation, New York University, 1988, part 2, chapter 1, for the details of John Olmsted's business problems that summer of 1825.

14. The conversion experience was shared by Charlotte; her sister, Stella Law; her friend and John Olmsted's second wife, Mary Ann Bull; fifteen-year-old Harriet Beecher (Stowe), then a boarder in the Bull household, and her sisters, Catharine and Mary; and Naomi Rockwell, who within two years would be

Frederick's teacher. The grim and depressing experience itself was described in detail in Harriet Beecher's later recollections. Charles Edward Stowe, ed., *Life of Harriet Beecher Stowe Compiled from Her Letters and Journals* (Boston: Houghton Mifflin, 1889), 30–37. The church catalog also describes the conversion process. *Catalogue of the Officers and Members of the First Congregational Church in Hartford* (Hartford: Case, Tiffany 1882), 6.

15. Twenty years later, in discussing Charlotte's last hours, Mary Ann Bull Olmsted wrote that she and Charlotte "had together made a profession of religion just about three weeks before that time." MAO to JHO, April 14, 1846, *FLOP*, reel 3. John Olmsted's journal, which gives the date of Charlotte's death, implies that she became ill on February 24. Ibid., reel 1.

16. Ibid., reel 47.

17. MAO to JHO, April 14, 1846, ibid., reel 3.

18. One must also be conscious of the tremendous sense of rage with which a small child would have responded to the death of his mother—a rage comprised of many elements, partly against the mother who abandoned him, partly against the father who allowed her to die. See Winnicott, *Maturational Process*, 86–87; and Mahler and Furer, *Human Symbiosis*, 50–51. Throughout his life, Olmsted was possessed of an omnipresent sense of injustice that turned to outrage far too easily and often inappropriately.

19. Erna Furman, *A Child's Parent Dies* (New Haven: Yale University Press, 1974), 56–57. "Some young children's pain was so poignant that adults could not allow themselves to observe it," she writes. "Sometimes this was due to the surviving parent's being unable to mourn."

20. *FLOP*, reel 1.

21. JO to FLO, September 10, 1838, ibid., reel 3. Frederick, then fourteen, was at a boarding school in Andover, Massachusetts. The letter was likely misdated, as John Olmsted's journal (ibid., reel 1) shows Owen to have died on September 4. September 10 would have been the child's second birthday. See also Olmsted & Ward, *Olmsted Family*, 60.

22. David E. Stannard, *The Puritan Way of Death: A Study of Religion, Culture, and Social Change* (New York: Oxford University Press, 1977), 171–74.

23. Winnicott, *Maturational Process*, 221. Melanie Klein writes: "Infantile death-wishes against parents, brothers and sisters are actually fulfilled when a loved person dies." Melanie Klein, *Love, Guilt, and Reparation & Other Works, 1921–1945* (New York: Delta Books, 1977), 354. See also Furman, *Parent Dies*, 123.

24. John Bowlby, *Attachment and Loss*, vol. 3: *Loss, Sadness, and Depression* (New York: Basic Books, 1980), 22. Bowlby's comments are based upon the extensive observation of such children.

25. Soon after his mother's death, Frederick began school at Mrs. Jeffrey's, which he attended for the rest of that year (1826).

26. JO journal, *FLOP*, reel 1, John and Mary Ann were married on April 25, 1827; Frederick's fifth birthday was on April 22.

27. Stowe, *Harriet Beecher Stowe*, 30. The description of Mary Ann Bull recalls

the note in Charlotte Olmsted's travel journal: "Mary Ann is in bed singing Sarah and myself to sleep." *FLOP*, reel 1.

28. In an autobiographical fragment, Olmsted refers to the "busy, bothering little chap as I must have been," which sounds awfully much like the description one or more of his adult caretakers had imposed upon him. *FLOP*, reel 47.

29. Ironically, Mary Ann's brother, Watson Bull, did a thriving business in Madeira wine, brandy, gin, and all sorts of "choice wines and liquors." See, for example, his ads in the *Connecticut Courant*, October 22, 1822, and January 22, 1827.

30. Mary Ann Olmsted continued to travel widely and alone well into her eighties, to Philadelphia, Boston, and the Midwest. In 1880, she recorded proudly: "I went to the top of the Capitol Dome—500 steps above the elevator—79–½ years old." MAO journal, entry for September 20, 1880, *FLOP*, reel 1.

31. JO journal, ibid.

32. It is possible that Mary Ann Olmsted had initiated the change of schools because of Naomi Rockwell's having made a profession of faith at the Center Church.

33. JO journal, *FLOP*, reel 1; *Connecticut Courant*, March 2, 1829.

34. The details of Olmsted's schooling, and so on can be found in my "In Memory of the Summer Days," part 2, chapter 2, and appendix C.

35. Stevenson, *Park-Maker*, 8. See also Joseph F. Kett, *Rites of Passage: Adolescence in America, 1790 to the Present* (New York: Harper 1977), 16–18. Kett notes that by the 1840s, the influence of reformers like Horace Bushnell (who in those years was the Olmsteds' neighbor) supported the notion that children were best kept at home. Indeed, the Hartford Grammar School ran an ad promoting the idea of combining the virtues offered by a superior local school with those offered by residency at home. *Connecticut Courant*, July 15, 1828.

36. In "Passages," Olmsted referred to the rural ministers with whom he had boarded as a child as his "fathers by deputy."

37. Roper, *FLO*, 9.

38. Olmsted, "Passages."

39. Beveridge, "Formative Years," 7.

40. FLO fragment, undated, *FLOP*, reel 43 (words in brackets struck out). There is no indication of the age at which this occurred, but it seems most likely that Boggs was his schoolmaster at Ellington High School when he was nine. As will be shown later, Frederick had to be removed from this school after a short stay because of the severe cruelty toward him of one of the schoolmasters.

41. Kett, *Rites of Passage*, 49–51 and 111–12.

42. Graff, *Central Park*, p. 22.

43. Emanuel Klien, "Psychoanalytic Aspects of School Problems," *Psychoanalytic Study of the Child* 3–4 (1948):369–89. Klein discusses the school problems encountered by "narcissistic children" (that is, children, often bright or gifted, who have suffered damaging narcissistic wounds in early childhood). To compensate for scholastic failures, to minimize the narcissistic hurt, the narcissistic child

ridicules schoolwork as being worthless and looks for other ways to demonstrate the superiority he feels within himself. Indeed, his need "to succeed without studying" is his way of proving to himself that he *is* superior, that he is "fortune's favorite child," despite all the psychic blows he has received. The narcissism itself is his primary mechanism for denying these narcissistic blows from earlier childhood. With great relevance to Olmsted, Klein notes that such children often grow up to seek "success and glory" through careers as writers.

44. Olmsted, "Civilization Notes," *FLOP*, reel 41. This section of his notes were written during the early years of the Civil War.

45. Ibid., reel 47. The longer citation is also in McLaughlin, *Papers*, 1:116.

46. FLO to MGVR, June 17, 1893, *FLOP*, reel 22. The fragments cited above were written during this same period of his life. The anecdote of walking to Cheshire (in this Van Rensselaer letter) was prompted by reference to his mother, Charlotte Hull Olmsted, and his grandfather, Samuel Hull, whom he "dimly" remembered. "Much more clearly I recall," he wrote, "the great fireplace of a house of my Aunt Brooks my mother's sister, in which house and in the brooks flowing by it, I spent many happy months."

47. Entry of October 28–29, 1842, ibid., reel 1. Frederick had been alone on this walking trip, since John Hull had commenced his studies at Yale only the month before, on September 28, 1842. The distance to Cheshire, and those following for Windsor and Ellington, are taken from *Geer's Hartford City Directory for 1844* (Hartford: Elihu Geer), 136–38 and 167–68.

48. Fanny Olmsted to JHO, February 4, 1846, *FLOP*, reel 3.

49. Ellington High School was then a newly formed school, advertising for students in the *Connecticut Courant* of January 19, 1830. It was endorsed by Reverend Hawes, the Olmsted's minister and by John Olmsted's cousin, Professor Denison Olmsted. The ad for Ellington High School also noted its philosophy of "strong discipline."

Kett notes the growth of high schools in this era, but gives the typical ages of students as being anywhere from eleven to nineteen. Kett, *Rites*, 127. Since Frederick was scarcely nine, and small for his age, he would have been keenly aware of his size among sixty other boys.

50. A "ferrule" was a cane used for whipping students, usually on their bottoms. Erik Erikson observes that it is too easy to speed past a person's brief, often stoic recall of incidents such as this, accepting them as a natural fact of life— unless one puts oneself in the place of the small child and suffers his pain. Such brutality is not natural. "It takes a particular view of man's place on this earth, and of the place of childhood within man's total scheme, to invent devices for terrifying children into submission," Erikson writes. Erik H. Erikson, *Young Man Luther: A Study in Psychoanalysis and History* (New York: Norton, 1962), 68–70.

51. It is also possible to associate significant psychosexual imagery with the preference that Olmsted expresses here: to have his ear pulled until it bled (a vivid castration image) rather than receiving a caning. Such associations are discussed in part 2, chapter 6, of my "In Memory of the Summer Days," See n. 27 therein

for the possible relationship between these images and others recorded by Olmsted—
including his memory of life "at Boggs's."

52. The story of the walk to Cheshire also calls to mind the story of "Hansel
and Gretel"—a story in which two children are abandoned in the woods by their
callous stepmother, with the reluctant agreement of their loving, but weak, father.

53. See the discussion of the "sumach poisoning" incident in part 1, chapter 2.

54. McLaughlin, *Papers*, 1:41.

55. Stevenson, *Park-Maker*, 7

56. From the time that Freud's fundamental psychoanalytical theories began to
take their mature form, at the turn of the century, there have always been two
aspects to classical psychoanalytical developmental concepts. The first—and the
aspect that tended to be emphasized by Freud and his most orthodox followers—
has been the instinctual: the sexual and aggressive drives and the vicissitudes of
instinctual development through the oral, anal, and genital stages, culminating in
that great drama of childhood, the Oedipus complex. The second aspect has been
the child's socially oriented development—a development that is largely a function of the child's growing perceptions of and interactions with its environment,
especially the significant "others" in its expanding universe (parents, siblings,
relatives, household help, and so on).

Contemporary object relations theorists emphasize this second aspect of development, and they tend to see Oedipal conflicts (generally at ages 4–5) as sympto-
matic rather than uniquely causative and as themselves resulting from disturbances in the child's earlier psychic development. Not only can failure to achieve
adequate object relationships in early childhood impair one's human interrelation-
ships and lifelong social functioning; it can also critically damage one's own self-
image. A more complete discussion of object relations theory is to be found in
appendix A of my "In memory of the Summer Days."

57. FJK to JHO, May 8, 1847, *FLOP*, reel 4.

58. FLO to FJK, July 14, 1846, ibid. reel 3.

59. FLO to JHO, April 7, 1846, ibid.

60. FLO to FJK, [April 1, 1846], McLaughlin, *Papers*, 1:235–37 (emphasis
Olmsted's).

61. FLO to FJK, August 22, 1846, *FLOP*, reel 3.

62. Henry W. Bellows to FLO, August 18, 1863, ibid., reel 8. Henry Bellows
was the man who recruited Olmsted to be executive secretary of the Sanitary
Commission and who had the difficult task of supervising him on behalf of the
Commissioners.

63. Psychic maturation, for the Mahlerians, depends upon resolution of the
rapprochement crisis. Such maturation develops with the next and final "open-
ended" phase of the separation-individuation process, which Mahler refers to as
the "consolidation of individuality" and "the attainment of emotional object con-
stancy"—that is, the child's continuing, evolving ability to be separated from its
mother and to endure the ordinary frustrations of life without reversion to primitive emotional behavior. This maturational evolution not only takes us through

the Oedipus complex, but is in a sense lifelong. Mahler, Pine, and Bergman, *Psychological Birth*, 109–20.

As the child grows through the pre-Oedipal years, one hopes it is developing a healthy sense of self, of its own autonomy and of the autonomy of the important people in its life. Such a sense prepares the child, psychically, to deal with the difficulties of the Oedipal years—since the growing sense of autonomy of self and of others carries with it, inevitably, the concept of competition. For, if the important people in the child's life are totally independent of its psychic control, then the child must soon develop the notion of competing for the love, attention, and favor of these people. The child begins to feel that it must compete with each parent for the love and attention of the other—the competition with the father for the mother's love ultimately forming the Oedipus complex. Equally important, it must compete with siblings for the love and attention of both parents. Thus, the final outcome of individuation in the child is realization of and preparation for the competitive nature of life.

5. Memories and Symbols

1. FLO to Edward Mott Moore, January 26, 1889, *FLOP*, reel 21.

2. FLO notes, undated, ibid., reel 47.

3. *FLOP*, ibid. Emma Plank has noted that some creative writers produce childhood memories "quite late in life and under considerable emotional distress." The fact that these are written "in response to an irresistible inner urge" gives "special weight to their contents." Emma N. Plank, "Memories of Early Childhood in Autobiographies," *Psychoanalytic Study of the Child* 8 (1953):385.

4. In the manuscript, the words *stray into* were written over an erasure; after the word *crisis*, several words were erased and a heavy line drawn through the resultant empty space, with the word *of* coming after this space; the words *therein occurring* were added as an afterthought. The thoroughness with which Olmsted obliterated the original words in this segment was extremely rare, perhaps even unique—suggesting that while part of Olmsted's psyche was seeking to get at the core experience here, his defensive mechanism was seeking to repress it. It is my assumption that the more a given passage has been worked over by Olmsted (emended, erased, crossed out, and/or repeated in many variations), the more important the content was to him.

5. Sigmund Freud, "Childhood and Concealing Memories," (1904), *The Basic Writings of Sigmund Freud* (New York: Modern Library, 1938), 65. Sigmund Freud, "Screen Memories," (1899), *Collected Papers*, (New York: Basic Books, 1959), 5:47–69. See also Otto Fenichel, "The Economic Function of Screen Memories," in Hanna Fenichel and David Rappaport, eds., *The Collected Papers of Otto Fenichel* (New York: International Universities Press, 1953), 113–14; and Phyllis Greenacre, *Trauma, Growth, and Personality* (New York: International Universities Press, 1969) 188–203.

Olmsted himself puzzled over the nature of his own screen memories, asking at one point: "What should have led me to remember these incidents several years after their occurrence, when I could not remember others following them of greater importance?" FLO notes, undated, *FLOP*, reel 47.

6. FLO to MGVR, June 13, 1893, *FLOP*, reel 22.

7. Sigmund Freud, "Analysis of a Phobia in a Five-Year-Old Boy," (1909), *Collected Papers*, 3:154.

8. Phyllis Greenacre makes a similar point in her analysis of Lewis Carroll. Phyllis Greenacre, *Swift and Carroll: A Psychoanalytic Study of Two Lives* (New York: International Universities Press, 1977), 245.

9. Phyllis Greenacre, "The Childhood of the Artist: Libidinal Phase Development and Giftedness," *Psychoanalytic Study of the Child* 12 (1957): 57–58. Margaret S. Mahler, Fred Pine, and Anni Bergman, *The Psychological Birth of the Human Infant: Symbiosis and Individuation* (New York: Basic Books, 1975), 71.

10. *FLOP*, reel 47 (emphasis added).

11. JO journal, ibid., reel 1. *Connecticut Courant*, August 28, 1826.

12. Otto Fenichel states that screen memories carry within them, symbolically, the trauma that has been repressed—so that the suppressed traumatic memory may be deduced by analyzing the content of the screen memory. *Collected Papers*, 113–14. In my "In Memory of the Summer Days: The Mind and Work of Frederick Law Olmsted," Ph. D. Dissertation, New York University, 1988, I demonstrate how the linked memories of the "tragic scene" and the three "trivial memories" may be analyzed to reveal deeper, hidden images of pain and anxiety—psychosexual imagery that, in male children, is suggestive of castration anxiety (which to Freudian theorists is central to the development of Oedipal conflicts). See part 2, chapter 3. However, as I note in that chapter, Robert Stoller, the gender theorist, links castration fears to an even greater fear—the feared destruction of one's selfhood. Robert J. Stoller, "Symbiosis Anxiety and the Development of Masculinity," *Archives of General Psychiatry*, 30 (1974):169. In the dissertation's discussion of Olmsted and castration anxiety, it is this aspect I stress.

13. I refer to this central conflict as the conflict between "Oedipal striving" and "psychic retreat." Erik Erikson has cast the psychosexual stages of pre-Oedipal and Oedipal development in psychosocial terms, and it is in these terms that I refer to "Oedipal striving." For Erikson, the major task of the pre-Oedipal years is the development of a sense of autonomy upon which identity can be built: "the very courage to be an independent individual who can choose and guide his own future." In the Oedipal stage, the principal task is to develop "a *sense of initiative* as a basis for a realistic sense of ambition and purpose." In the little boy, for Erikson, this "realistic sense" arises from his growing rivalry and identification with his father—which set the boundaries for his "ambition and purpose" at this stage. The sense of initiative that develops in this stage carries with it both dreams of glorious achievement and conquest and fear and envy of the rivals who can thwart those dreams. Erikson comments that if we "overlook or belittle the phenomenon of childhood, along with the best and the worst of our childhood dreams, we shall have failed to recognize one of the eternal sources of human

anxiety and strife." Erik Erikson, *Identity: Youth and Crisis* (New York: Norton, 1968), 112–22 (emphasis Erikson's). It is the tendency to seek refuge (usually temporary refuge) from this "human anxiety and strife" that I refer to in the phrase "psychic retreat"—a tendency all the greater in one whose psyche is still marked by the scars of the Mahlerian rapprochement crisis.

14. FLO, 1893 autobiographical notes, *FLOP*, reel 47. Some of the associations in the following analysis were developed in the Psychohistory Forum's "Historical Dream Workshop," May 3, 1986, directed by Paul H. Elovitz, and derive from suggestions by made by him, Jerrold Atlas, Flora Hogman, Joel Newman, Peter Petschauer, Robert Saunders, and Deborah Tanzer. Possible meanings connected both with the imagery of this dream and with an associated memory described by Olmsted—of falling asleep with his eyes open while standing watch on a ship—are pursued in greater depth in my "In Memory of the Summer Days," (part 2, chapter 4).

15. Olmsted here wrote several versions of what he had said to the surgeon. As previously noted, whenever Olmsted struggled to get an incident or a record of his feelings precisely right, attempting a number of versions in the process, I have assumed that the subject was of great psychic significance to him.

16. D. W. Winnicott, "Transitional Objects and Transitional Phenomena," *Through Pædiatrics to Psycho-Analysis* (London: Hogarth Press, 1975), 229–42. See also M. Wulff, "Fetishism and Object Choice in Early Childhood," *Psychoanalytic Quarterly* 15 (1946):450–71. Fred Busch, "Dimensions of the First Transitional Object," *Psychoanalytic Study of the Child*, 29 (1974):219, 224.

17. Winnicott, "Transitional Object," pp. 233, 236–37, and 241–42. Phyllis Greenacre, "The Fetish and the Transitional Object," *Psychoanalytic Study of the Child* 24 (1969):162.

18. William G. Niederland, "Psychoanalytic Approaches to Creativity," *Psychoanalytic Quarterly* 45, 2 (1976):188.

19. Phyllis Greenacre observes that the mental processes the child goes through in its symbolic usage of the transitional object make such objects a paradigm for "every truly artistic product which the gifted person arrives at." "The Transitional Object and the Fetish," *International Journal of Psycho-Analysis* 51 (1970):455.

20. Phyllis Greenacre, "Further Considerations Regarding Fetishism," *Psychoanalytic Study of the Child* 10 (1965):187–94; and "Fetish and Transitional Object," 160–62.

21. The psychodynamic usefulness of the tree as a symbol may be seen in its inclusion as one of three devices employed in a projective test for psychiatric analysis, called the House-Tree-Person Test. Through his drawing of a tree, one authority says, the subject conveys to the analyst "his felt impression of himself in relation to his environment." John N. Buck, "The H-T-P Test," *Journal of Clinical Psychology* 4, 2 (1948):155. What is most pertinent to my thesis is the concept that a tree, which is a living thing in its own right, is so suitable for representing a person's self-image.

22. The material to be focused upon here is primarily drawn from Olmsted's 1873 and 1893 memoirs (*FLOP*, reel 43 and 47) and his June 17, 1893, letter to

Mariana Van Rensselaer (ibid., reel 22). The detail of lying beneath the elm's leafy boughs, with its echoes of the third of the three "trivial memories" (and its feminine associations), is given in the two 1893 sources. In his 1873 memoir, Frederick is simply walking with his grandfather. The image of lying down and looking up at the leafy boughs is also suggestive of the infant lying in the crib and contemplating its mother's face.

23. FLO, 1893 autobiographical notes, ibid., reel 47. The words in brackets were struck out by Olmsted.

24. Bruno Bettelheim, *The Uses of Enchantment: The Meaning and Importance of Fairy Tales* (New York: Vintage, 1977), pp. 102–11 and 129.

25. FLO, 1860 notes, *FLOP*, reel 47. See chapter 2, n. 33.

26. Olmsted & Ward, *Olmsted Family*, 12–15.

27. Ibid., vii. *New Practical Standard Dictionary*, Brittanica ed. (New York: Funk & Wagnall's, 1954), 1:616.

28. Nicholas had come to Hartford with his father, James, as a member of Thomas Hooker's founding colony. His house and land were located along the Connecticut River, on what in Frederick's time was about 30–34 Front Street. Mary Ann Olmsted's father, Isaac D. Bull, lived not far from the site (at 47 Front Street). Olmsted & Ward, *Olmsted Family*, 12–13. Gardner's *Hartford City Directory for 1838*, (Hartford: Case, Tiffany), 13.

29. A more in-depth analysis of possible conscious and unconscious associations, including psychosexual imagery, in these and other sections of the 1860 autobiographical notes are discussed in part 2, chapter 5, of my "In Memory of the Summer Days."

30. McLaughlin, *Papers*, 2:114–15. The editors indicate Stowe may have used Olmsted's material—either from his letters or his later book about this first trip south—in her own book, *Dred: A Tale of the Great Dismal Swamp* (1856). Ibid., 93. Olmsted visited her in 1856 at her request, while she working on this book. He had earlier told Charles Loring Brace—who was closely connected to Stowe—"I would rather give $50 than go to the Dismal Swamp." FLO to CLB, December 22, 1852, *FLOP*, reel 5.

31. Remember that Frederick—like Nicholas—had already achieved some distinction in earlier years. He had previously published his *Walks and Talks of an American Farmer in England* (New York: G. P. Putnam, 1852), in which he described a visit to Olmsted Manor in Essex.

32. Also, one cannot overlook the psychosexual imagery here—the sexual adventures, real or fantasied, that the young bachelor had or wished he had.

33. Melanie Klein, *Love, Guilt, and Reparation & Other Works, (1921–1945)* (New York: Delta Books, 1977), 333–34.

34. The outbuilding in fact had been destroyed by fire during the "dry season" —that is, in August.

35. FLO, 1893 autobiographical notes, *FLOP*, reel 47.

36. The definitions cited are from William Morris, ed., *The American Heritage Dictionary of the English Language* (Boston: Houghton Mifflin, 1976), 188 and 1299. See also n. 39 below.

37. Greenacre comments: "The fetish is conspicuously a bisexual symbol and also serves as a bridge which would both deny and affirm the sexual differences." "Fetish and Transitional Object," 150. See also Robert C. Bak, "The Phallic Woman: The Ubiquitous Fantasy in Perversions," *Psychoanalytic Study of the Child* 23 (1968):15–36.

38. It is rather fitting, I think, to refer to *Leaves of Grass* in seeking Olmsted's association with "tussocks of Calamus." R. B. W. Lewis refers to *Leaves of Grass* as Whitman's "strange, sometimes baffling, stream-of-consciousness poem," a single "life-long book," devoted to "the drama of the psyche or 'self' in its mobile and complex relation *to* itself, to the world of nature and human objects, and to the creative act." Lewis, "Always Going Out and Coming in," in Harold Bloom, ed., *Modern Critical Views: Walt Whitman* (New York: Chelsea House, 1985), 100–6. This beautiful statement is akin to what I believe about Olmsted's autobiographical writings, especially these 1860 notes. Whitman was born in 1819, three years before Olmsted, and was also raised in rural surroundings (on Long Island) before his family moved to Brooklyn.

Citations of Whitman's poetry are (unless otherwise noted) from Walt Whitman, *Complete Poetry and Collected Prose* (New York: Library of America, 1982).

39. Justin Kaplan, *Walt Whitman: A Life* (New York: Simon and Schuster, 1980) 233–39. Drawings of the calamus plant, facing p. 97, clearly show the phallic thrust of the calamus flower and also its "blade-like leaves." See also David Cavitch, *My Soul and I: The Inner Life of Walt Whitman* (Boston: Beacon Press, 1985), 125–26, 129–30, and 133–35. Stephen Black sees the poet's imagery of a wished-for, idealized relationship with various young men (expressed in the "Calamus" poems) as "desexualized" and Whitman's own sexuality as self-directed that is, auto-erotic. Stephen A. Black, *Whitman's Journey into Chaos: A Psychoanalytic Study of the Poetic Process* (Princeton: Princeton University Press, 1975), 44–49 and 175–82.

40. Cavitch, *My Soul and I*, 134–35. The lines are from "Long I Thought That Knowledge Alone Would Suffice," a poem whose title in itself is expressive of a disenchantment with rationally based Oedipal striving.

41. Olmsted & Ward, *Olmsted Family*, 16 and 23. They were deacons in Hartford's First Church—the one John Olmsted later belonged to during Frederick's childhood and in which Charlotte Hull Olmsted was converted.

42. The shoe leather and snow water reference is expanded upon in the 1893 recollections, while the reference to his grandmother, Content Pitkin Olmsted, is in the Van Rensselaer letter of June 17, 1893. *FLOP*, reels 47 and 22.

43. Andrew Jackson Downing, *A Treatise on the Theory and Practice of Landscape Gardening Adapted to North America* (1841) (New York: A. O. Moore, 1859). Downing was the pioneering authority in American landscape gardening. As previously noted, he was an important influence upon Frederick, who contributed a number of articles to the *Horticulturist*, while Downing was editor. Downing favorably reviewed Olmsted's book, *Walks and Talks*, a later edition of which Olmsted "humbly and reverently inscribed" to Downing's memory. It will also be remembered that it was through Downing that Olmsted met Calvert Vaux.

44. Downing, *Treatise*, 129.

45. Graff, *Central Park*, 76–77 and 85–86. The prominence and single-mindedness of this design feature are clearly shown in the portfolio of early Central Park lithographs and photographs reproduced in McLaughlin, *Papers*, vol. 3; see 376, 377, 385, 401, 406, and 442. Bruce Kelly notes that some three hundred of the American elms are still in place, "which may be the largest stand left in the world," owing to the ravages of Dutch Elm disease. Bruce Kelly, "Art of the Olmsted Landscape," in Kelly, Guillet, and Hern, *Olmsted Landscape*, 12.

46. McLaughlin, *Papers*, 3:153–54.

47. CV to FLO, May 22, 1865, *FLOP*, reel 32. Vaux was making the point that Olmsted, at forty, not only had both the ambition and impatience of a much younger man, but was also rather a novice at landscape architecture; thus "allowances had to be made by an old hand like me."

48. Roper, *FLO*, 390.

49. Olmsted's home and office in Brookline are now a National Historic Site, maintained by the National Park Service. The physical features of the property are shown in a plan drawing, April 3, 1904, obtained at the site. (I greatly appreciate the tour of the house and offices given me by Shary Page Berg, Park Manager.) A plan of the ground floor interior of the house and office may be seen in a booklet, *Fairsted: The Frederick Law Olmsted Home and Office*, available from the Frederick Law Olmsted Association, New York City.

50. Indeed, the establishment of a tree nursery was perhaps one of his more successful achievements on the Staten Island farm in the early 1850s.

51. McLaughlin, *Papers*, 3:133, 151, and 162–75.

52. Roper, *FLO*, 466.

6. *Images of Mother*

1. As noted in chapter 4, Frederick left for Geneseo April 20, 1828, two days before his sixth birthday.

2. In the surviving draft of this segment in "Passages," Olmsted first wrote, then struck out, the word *baby* before using *child* in the last sentence. Elsewhere, in what is apparently a vestige of a discarded previous version of this segment, he wrote *infant* at the end of the sentence. The words *and looking up at her* were added as an afterthought. *FLOP*, reel 43.

3. Arthur Spencer, "The Art of Frederick Law Olmsted," *Craftsman* (November 1903), in *FLOP*, reel 45. This appreciation of Olmsted, still unsurpassed, was written upon his death.

4. In earliest childhood, the infant not only takes in nourishment with its mouth, but also "takes in" whatever it sees within its field of vision. Erik Erikson, *Identity: Youth and Crisis* (New York: Norton, 1968), 98. In classical psychoanalytic theory, Olmsted's stress on eyes, vision, scenery, and so on, would represent the "taking in" of oral-passivity. His disputatiousness and argumentativeness would represent the later oral sadistic phase of infancy. The former is *being;* the

later is *doing*. In the nineteenth century, the former was linked to Romantic idealism and emotionalism ("feminine"); the latter to empiricist logic and reason ("masculine").

5. Margaret S. Mahler, Fred Pine, and Ann Bergman, *The Psychological Birth of the Human Infant: Symbiosis and Individuation* (New York: Basic Books, 1975), 55. She also notes that at this stage, the mother "still is the center of the child's universe."

6. D. W. Winnicott, *The Maturational Process and the Facilitating Environment* (New York: International Universities Press, 1965), 30–31.

7. See, for example, his *Mount Royal* pamphlet, an excerpt of which is reprinted in Sutton, *Civilizing*, 199.

8. This discussion is based substantially upon Winnicott's similar distinction between the *environment mother* and the *object mother*. Winnicott, *Maturational Process*, 76–77.

9. Sigmund Freud, *Three Essays on the Theory of Sexuality* (New York: Basic Books, 1962), 96.

10. Frederick Law Olmsted, "Trees in Streets and Parks," *Sanitarian* 10, 14 (September 1882), in *FLOP*, reel 45.

11. FLO to CLB, November 12, 1850, ibid., reel 4; McLaughlin, *Papers*, 1:358–62. Brace had remained in Europe.

12. In the final version of this recollection from "Passages," Olmsted struck out *lovely*. The words in brackets (following) were also struck out; the slashes have been added by me to separate different drafts. The importance of this section—his father's response to Frederick's comment about the star—is underscored by the many erasures, emendations, and strike-outs (including a few heavily crossed out). *FLOP*, reel 43.

13. Barbara Welter has quoted this 1852 paean to women's virtue: "Purity is the highest beauty—the *true pole-star* which is to guide humanity right in its long, varied, and perilous voyage." (emphasis added). Welter, "The Cult of True Womanhood: 1820–1860," in Esther Katz and Anita Rapone, eds., *Women's Experience in America: An Historical Anthology* (New Brunswick: Transaction Books, 1980), 198.

14. Winnicott, *Maturational Process*, 82.

15. Melanie Klein, *Love, Guilt, and Reparation & Other Works, 1921–1945* (New York: Delta Books, 1977), 336–38.

16. Winnicott, *Maturational Process*, 65.

17. FLO to MAO, March 20, 1841, *FLOP*, reel 3; McLaughlin, *Papers*, 1:127–29; (emphasis added). Olmsted seemed embarrassed by the outburst of poetic feeling that began with this material, and he tried to make a joke of it—yet the words he chose to use, in poking fun at himself, are also quite revealing: "Ahem! —I say; I did that, I did. That was I, & nobody else. It's mine." I believe this "joking" reveals that his true self had indeed spoken this flight of poetic (and "feminine") fancy. That neither the poetic flight nor the joking afterword was a casual outburst can be seen by referring to the manuscript, which is written very

neatly and carefully, without his usually cross-outs and emendations. This letter was likely a copy he made from a first draft and thus likely had been carefully considered.

18. Ibid., 129.

19. Ibid., 131; *FLOP*, reels 3 and 4; Roper, *FLO*, 59 and 80; Stevenson, *Park-Maker*, 136.

20. FLO to "Parents," November 20, 1843, *FLOP*, reel 3; McLaughlin, *Papers*, 2: 170–73.

21. There is no hint of the plans for marriage in the Olmsted family correspondence of the time. Immersed in the myriad details deriving from his position as Architect in Chief of Central Park, Olmsted wrote very few personal letters in 1858 and 1859. See *FLOP*, reel 5. John Olmsted's journal notes only the actual marriage itself (to "Mary Cleavland, Mrs. JHO"), and earlier noted even more laconically the death of his sister. Ibid., reel 1.

22. Olmsted, *Walks and Talks of an American Farmer in England*, (New York: G. P. Putnam, 1852), 2:155–56 (emphasis added). Evidence of the problematic nature of this material is to be found in the fact that Olmsted excised it from the 1859 edition of *Walks and Talks* (Columbus: Joseph A. Riley). All of the other material that directly precedes and follows the cited passages is identical in the 1852 and 1859 editions, but the material I will be discussing has been omitted from the later edition (see p. 327). The passage *is* included in Olmsted & Kimball, *Forty Years*, 1:108–9, among excerpts from *Walks and Talks*. Charles Beveridge has also noted the importance of this passage, citing it both in "Formative Years," 127, and in his introduction to McLaughlin, *Papers*, 3:22. It should be noted also that the tone of the passage is distinctly Emersonian.

23. One remembers the tendency of Charlotte Law Olmsted to withhold her inner self and feelings from her 1820 travel journal.

24. Writing to Brace, Olmsted said of his first great love, Elizabeth Baldwin, "She's too good for any coarse vulgar man merely, is not she?" FLO to CLB, March 27, 1846, *FLOP*, reel 3. He asked later, "Could an angel love a man?" January 27, 1847, McLaughlin, *Papers*, 1:283–86.

25. FLO to H. W. Beekman, June 10, 1886, *FLOP*, reel 20; FLO to W. L. Fischer, August 6 and 11, 1889, ibid., reel 21. Beekman was at this time president of the Department of Public Parks for New York City; Fischer was in charge of planting for the Boston park system. Olmsted had also pointed out to the architect Charles Follen McKim: "It is much harder to realize a simple, modest lady-like and convenient idea of a place than to carry out elaborate, showy and costly plans." December 24, 1883, ibid., reel 20.

26. This is what Olmsted had written of himself as an adolescent in his 1860 stream-of-consciousness notes. See chapter 2, n. 34.

27. Beveridge, "Introduction," in McLaughlin, *Papers*, 3:18.

28. FLO to MCO, September 25, 1863, *FLOP*, reel 8. This vivid image is another reminder of Frederick's "outhouse" memory—the shafts of sunlight playing in the musky darkness.

29. FLO to Ignaz A. Pilat, September 26, 1863, in Olmsted & Kimball, *Forty Years*, 2:343–49.

30. The use of the word *maturity* here suggests Olmsted's association of a sexual kind of excitement only with adolescent longings. The other words—*rest, tranquility, deliberation*—are of course the main themes of his life's work, his major landscape designs.

31. Graff, *Central Park*, 103.

32. Olmsted, *Walks and Talks* (1852), 2:155–56.

33. Melanie Klein writes that the conflicting emotions with which the small child must deal early in life are "unbearably burdensome to the weak ego; the only escape is flight through repression, and the whole conflicting situation, which is never cleared up, remains alive in the unconscious mind." Klein, *Love, Guilt*, 173. Kept alive in this way, these unconscious conflicts then play a role both in one's response to the events of later life and in determining the nature of the relationships one has with significant figures encountered throughout one's life.

34. FLO to FJK, October 14, 1848, *FLOP*, reel 47. The letter seems to have been prompted by Olmsted's loneliness in his new home on Staten Island and the recent death of a friend. One can see that it was Olmsted's fear of actually realizing this wish, of achieving loss of self, that generated his lifelong insomnia. Even more, it prefigures his final psychic retreat, that mental illness that closed in upon toward the end of his life—a mental illness that was, most of all, a form of not-knowing, of total loss of selfhood.

35. Olmsted, *Walks and Talks* (1859), 112.

36. Spencer, "Art of Olmsted," 112 (emphasis added).

7. *The Making of a Free-Soil Journalist*

1. FLO to EBW, December 16, 1890, *FLOP*, reel 20.

2. FLO to CLB, June 22, 1845, ibid., reel 5; McLaughlin, *Papers*, 1:215.

3. FLO to JO, June 10, 1845, *FLOP*, reel 5. John Hull had just returned to Yale after a bout of illness and was forced by illness to leave school again ten days later. McLaughlin, *Papers*, 1:216, n. 1.

4. FLO to JHO, June 23, 1845, ibid., 217–20; *FLOP*, reel 3.

5. Charles Lockwood, *Manhattan Moves Uptown* (Boston: Houghton Mifflin, 1979), 12–89; Allan Nevins, "George Templeton Strong: The Man and the Diarist," in Nevins and Thomas, eds., *Strong Diary*, 1:x.

6. Whitman, "Crossing Brooklyn Ferry" (originally "Sun-Down Poem").

7. FLO to JHO, August 29, 1840, *FLOP*, reel 3.

8. FLO's journal for March 1843, ibid., reel 1.

9. "I have to complain of no personal ill treatment," Frederick wrote his father, though he noted that he got his share of abuse. "Coming out when not sick, I was happy enough," Frederick added, "half the time enjoyed myself, I

presume, better than anybody aboard." FLO to JO, December 27, 1843, Mc-Laughlin, *Papers*, 1:183–85. After the voyage, Frederick was one of those who testified against the captain and the first mate in a lawsuit over the mistreatment of another cabin boy. Ibid., 133–34. John Hull also went to sea for three months in 1844, as a passenger, sailing with a cousin to the West Indies.

10. Beveridge, "Formative Years," 29.

11. See also part 1, chapter 2. Whatever was troubling Frederick at the time cleared up pretty quickly once he was home. "Fred has been well & is a good deal with the ladies," John Olmsted wrote to John Hull on January 29, 1846. *FLOP*, reel 3.

12. FLO to CLB, July 30, 1846, ibid. Similarly, he told his father: "The fact is I have not had but very few hard days work this summer." FLO to JO, August 12, 1846, ibid.

13. JO to FLO, January 29, 1849, ibid., reel 4 (emphasis John Olmsted's).

14. See, for example, FLO to JO, February 2, 1845, and August 12, 1846, McLaughlin, *Papers*, 1:202–6 and 271–75; *FLOP*, reel 3. See also Beveridge, "Formative Years," 31–33 and 72–73.

15. Roper, *FLO*, 35, merely mentions Zimmermann in passing, giving it no place at all in Olmsted's intellectual development. However, both Stevenson and Beveridge are convincing concerning *Solitude*'s influence upon Olmsted's thinking, and his letters of the time demonstrate its emotional impact. Stevenson, *Park-Maker*, 28, and Beveridge, "Formative Years," 31–33.

16. FLO to CLB, January 27 and July 26, 1847, *FLOP*, reel 4.

17. Wormeley, *Other Side of War*, 59–60.

18. McLaughlin, *Papers*, 1:67–71, 265. Brace's father, John Pierce Brace, be-came the editor of the *Hartford Courant* in 1849. John Olmsted was a director of the Hartford Female Seminary.

19. McLaughlin, *Papers*, 2:49–52; Thomas Bender, *Toward an Urban Vision: Ideas and Institutions in Nineteenth-Century America* (Lexington: University of Kentucky Press, 1975), 136–57.

20. See for example, FLO to CLB, April 8, 1851, and February 8, 1853, *FLOP*, reel 4. FLO to CLB, November 1, 1884, ibid., reel 20.

21. FLO to CLB, March 27, 1846, ibid., reel 3; McLaughlin, *Papers*, 1:232–35 (emphasis Olmsted's). See also part 2, chapter 6, n. 24.

22. FLO to EBW, December 16, 1890, *FLOP*, reel 20.

23. JHO to FJK, February 9 or 10, 1849, ibid., reel 4.

24. JHO to FJK, April 16, 19, 27, and 28 and May 26, 1851, ibid. See also Beveridge, "Introduction," in McLaughlin, *Papers*, 3:10.

25. FLO to CLB, January 11, 1851, McLaughlin, *Papers*, 1:368; *FLOP*, reel 4.

26. FLO to JHO, April 3, 1846, ibid., reel 3.

27. As Stephen Black suggests in connection with Walt Whitman, too deep an immersion in one's inner world entails risking madness; too little access to it entails risking sterility. Stephen Black, *Whitman's Journey into Chaos: A Psychoanalytic Study of the Poetic Process* (Princeton: Princeton University Press, 1975), 43.

The rational Olmsted and the transcendental Olmsted were at war with each other.

28. JHO to Clinton Collins, December 8, 1847, in Roper, *FLO*, 53.

29. FLO to CLB, March 25, 1848, *FLOP*, reel 4; McLaughlin, *Papers*, 1:313–18.

30. Frederick's religious speculations of the 1846–1849 period are dealt with in greater detail in my "In Memory of the Summer Days: The Mind and Work of Frederick Law Olmsted," Ph.D. dissertation, New York University, 1988, appendix D: "Head and Heart."

31. McLaughlin, *Papers*, 1:336–37; FLO to CLB, January 11, 1851, ibid., 365–72.

32. Frederick Law Olmsted, *Walks and Talks of an American Farmer in England* (Columbus: Joseph H. Riley, 1859), 70 and 112.

33. FLO to CLB, March 25, 1848, McLaughlin, *Papers*, 1:316–17.

34. FLO to CLB, [c. July 26, 1852], McLaughlin, *Papers*, 1:375–87; *FLOP*, reel 4 (emphasis Olmsted's). The Red Bank community was called the North American Phalanx and, according to the *Papers* editors, was located fifteen miles south of Olmsted's Staten Island farm. They also note that by the time of Olmsted's visit, "the Fourierist phase of American social reform had almost run its course." The year of Olmsted's visit was the last year of success for the Red Bank community, which ceased to exist by early 1856.

35. Milton Rugoff, *The Beechers: An American Family in the Nineteenth Century* (New York: Harper & Row, 1981), 317–22.

36. FLO to FJK, October 17, 1852, McLaughlin, *Papers*, 2:82–85.

37. More than two dozen of these letters, superbly annotated, appear in McLaughlin, *Papers*, vol. 2, from which most of my facts about Olmsted's southern travels have been drawn.

38. Ibid., 4–5.

39. Ibid., 172–82.

40. Ibid., 179–80.

41. Ibid., 187: dispatch published July 8, 1853.

42. FLO to JO, May 19, 1853, *FLOP*, reel 4. Ann Charlotte Lynch Botta (1815–1891) presided in her New York home over the "first important salon" in the history of American letters and was the friend of such figures as Edgar Allen Poe, Horace Greeley, and Margaret Fuller. *CDAB*, 98. The editors of McLaughlin, *Papers*, note that Olmsted had been introduced to her by Brace, but they add that she had known Olmsted as a child in Hartford. They had both attended Miss Rockwell's School in 1828, when he was six and she was thirteen. McLaughlin, *Papers*, 2:274–275, n. 1.

43. MCO to FLO Jr, undated, *FLOP*, reel 5.

44. FLO to JO, January 4, 1850, ibid., reel 4 (emphasis Olmsted's).

45. FLO to JO, February 7, 1855 (misdated by Olmsted as 1885), ibid., reel 5. James Alexander Hamilton, the third son of Alexander Hamilton, was a lawyer and a politician—a one-time Tammany follower and partisan of Andrew Jackson

and Martin Van Buren. *CDAB*, 395. He assisted Olmsted in his Free-Soil activities and, in 1857, originated one of the petitions on Olmsted's behalf for the Central Park position. Mrs. Schuyler was later to be associated with Olmsted on the Sanitary Commission. (McLaughlin, *Papers*, 2:237, n. 16.)

46. FLO to CLB, December 1, 1853, *FLOP*, reel 4; McLaughlin, *Papers*, 2:231–38. Charles Beveridge has also called attention to the seminal importance of the encounter with Allison for Olmsted's evolving social philosophy. Beveridge, "Formative Years," 208–10.

47. Emma Brace, ed., *The Life of Charles Loring Brace, Chiefly Told in His Own Letters* (New York: Scribner's, 1894), 61–62. This was stated in a letter of 1849.

48. FLO to CLB, December 1, 1853, *FLOP*, reel 4; McLaughlin, *Papers*, 2:231–38.

49. Ibid.

50. David L. Hall, "The Victorian Connection," in Daniel Walker Howe, ed., *Victorian America* (Philadelphia: University of Pennsylvania Press, 1976), 82–89. Hall derives the term *modern missionaries* from Charles Eliot Norton's description of the cultural role played in 1855 by George William Curtis. Curtis was to be the real editor of *Putnam's* magazine during Olmsted's stewardship in 1855–1857, while Norton would later become Olmsted's ally in many social and political struggles of the 1870s and 1880s.

51. See, for example, McLaughlin, *Papers*, 3:296–97, an 1861 notice to workingmen of Central Park, from Olmsted as architect in chief. This notice dealt with the rights (and the responsibilities) of the laborers.

52. FLO to CLB, December 8, 1860, *FLOP*, reel 6 (emphasis Olmsted's). Olmsted would also have to break a strike during his tenure as managing supervisor of the Mariposa Mining Estate.

53. To Kingsbury, Olmsted once described himself as "a vigilant neck or nothing *foxy* Whig." FLO to FJK, September 22, 1847, McLaughlin, *Papers*, 1:302–5. The family letters suggest, in fact, that Frederick and his father generally saw eye-to-eye in politics, indicating that his father was something of a liberal for his generation, while Frederick was something of a conservative for *his*.

54. Hall, "Victorian Connection," 94.

55. FLO to HWB, October 3, 1861, McLaughlin, *Papers*, 4:211–13.

56. Thomas Bender, review article of McLaughlin, *Papers*, vol. 2, in *Agricultural History* 20 (1986):109–11.

57. Letter of March 12, 1854, *FLOP*, reel 4.

58. Ibid., reel 41.

59. Published June 3, 1854. McLaughlin, *Papers*, 2:299–306.

60. Both Brace and Olmsted had come under the influence of Horace Bushnell quite early in life. Brace's father had belonged to Bushnell's North Congregational Church in Hartford, while the Olmsteds had been Bushnell's neighbors and landlords on Ann Street (and Olmsted's father later left Joel Hawes' Center Church to join Bushnell's congregation). Bushnell's enlightened and Romantic theology was a precursor of the Social Gospel and both this and his concept of

"unconscious influence" were important to the social philosophy of Brace and Olmsted. See Russell Blaine Nye, *Society and Culture in America, 1830–1860* (New York: Harper, 1974), 301–2; Daniel Walker Howe, "The Social Science of Horace Bushnell," *Journal of American History* 70, 2 (September 1983):305–22 (esp. 319–20); and Thomas Bender, *Toward an Urban Vision: Ideas and Institutions in Nineteenth-Century America* (Lexington: University of Kentucky Press, 1975), 136–38 and 164. Incidentally, Bushnell himself was representative of the kind of Whig liberalism that motivated Olmsted. As Howe notes, Bushnell's ideas "were intended to strengthen the social order, not to promote individualism" (310).

    61. FLO to JO, November 8, 1855, *FLOP*, reel 5.

8. Life in the Literary Republic

    1. FLO to FJK, May 10 and July 16, 1848, and MCO memoir, *FLOP*, reel 47.

    2. FLO to JO, December 9, 1855, ibid., reel 5; McLaughlin, *Papers*, 2:375–76.

    3. John Hull told his sister, Bertha, that he was not a farmer and would prefer "to do literary or medical work rather than agricultural or real estate-istical," but "it seemed to fall upon" him to undertake the management of the farm. This was the way his father wanted it, he said, and "of course he has all his own way in such things." May 6, 1855, *FLOP*, reel 5. In her biographical sketch of Olmsted, M. M. Graff cites John Hull's words to Bertha, but she construes them as describing Frederick's autocratic behavior: "as his unhappy brother John had noted, 'Of course he gets all his own way in such things.' " Graff, *Central Park*, 28 and 61. However, a review of the letter of May 6 shows that, just prior to this remark, John Hull was discussing the proposal his father had made to him, and it is very clear that this remark refers to the fact that his father, John Olmsted, was the one who always got his way. Nevertheless, Graff in not wrong in suggesting the Frederick usually got "his own way" in the Olmsted family. See also Roper, *FLO*, 108, and Stevenson, *Park-Maker*, 134 and 141, for their views on Frederick's manipulation of John Hull in this matter.

    4. Olmsted moved to New York on April 2, 1855. JHO to Mrs. Perkins, April 1, 1855, *FLOP*, reel 5. His thirty-third birthday was three weeks later, on April 22, 1855. See also Roper, *FLO*, 107n.

    5. FLO to JO, May 28, 1855, *FLOP*, reel 5 (emphasis added).

    6. Ronald J. Zboray, "Antebellum Reading and the Ironies of Technological Innovation" *American Quarterly* 40, 1 (1988):65–82.

    7. Russell Blaine Nye, *Society and Culture in America, 1830–1860* (New York: Harper, 1974), 75–76. Zboray, "Antebellum Reading," 69.

    8. Nye, *Society and Culture*, 71–157; Zboray, "Antebellum Reading," 65–66.

    9. Thomas Bender, *New York Intellect: A History of Intellectual Life in New York City, from 1750 to the Beginnings of Our Own Time* (Baltimore: Johns Hopkins University Press, 1987), 173. By the 1860s, another sort of literary circle had

formed—a more bohemian group that met in Pfaff's Beer Cellar near Bleecker Street rather than the Astor House. It included Walt Whitman, Thomas Bailey Aldrich, Fitz-James O'Brien and Artemus Ward. Justin Kaplan, *Walt Whitman: A Life* (New York: Simon and Schuster, 1980), xx. Thomas Bender cities Olmsted as an example of the new "metropolitan gentry"—ambitious young intellectuals who sought to make an important place for themselves in New York society through their literary gifts. He cites Whitman, in contrast to these young men, as the champion of a more democratic culture. Bender, *New York Intellect*, 173–75.

10. Ibid., 164–65.

11. FLO to JO, April 1 and April 27, 1855, *FLOP*, reel 5. On the back of the April 1 letter (a letter that had described Frederick's planned purchases) there is a note in John Olmsted's handwriting that states: "irrecoverably sold for Taxes & lost."

12. JHO to JO, March 9, 1855, JHO to BO, May 6, 1855, ibid. (emphasis John Hull's). The book referred to is *Slave States*, which Frederick was endeavoring to write at the time.

13. FLO to JO, April 27, 1855, and undated note, ibid.

14. Charles Lockwood, *Manhattan Moves Uptown* (Boston: Houghton Mifflin, 1979), 92–231, offers a rich description of Manhattan as it was during Olmsted's partnership in Dix and Edwards, 1855–1857.

15. Lockwood, *Manhattan Moves*, 108–10; *The 1866 Guide to New York City* (New York: Schocken Books, 1975), 9–10.

16. Lockwood, *Manhattan Moves*, 129.

17. McLaughlin, *Papers*, 3:121, from the Greensward Plan.

18. Sutton, *Civilizing*, 65–66. The passage is from "Public Parks and the Enlargement of Towns," a paper that was originally prepared as an address to the American Social Science Association at the Lowell Institute, February 25, 1870. It was afterwards published by the Association as a pamphlet. This important speech will be discussed in greater depth in chapter 13 of part 4.

19. JHO to BO, May 6, 1855, FLO to JO, April 27, 1855, *FLOP*, reel 5.

20. JHO to JO, April 27, 1855, ibid.

21. FLO to JO, November 23, 1855, ibid.

22. FLO to Joshua A. Dix, August 3, 1856, McLaughlin, *Papers*, 2:385–90. See also Roper, *FLO*, 117; Stevenson, *Park-Maker*, 147–48. A more complete description of this incident and other details of Olmsted's problems at Dix and Edwards is given in my "In Memory of the Summer Days: The Mind and Work of Frederick Law Olmsted," Ph.D. dissertation, New York University, 1988, Part 3, ch. 3.

23. FLO to JAD, September 4, 1856, *FLOP*, reel 5.

24. Stevenson asserts that this letter "reveals more about Frederick Olmsted than of Dix and Edwards." Stevenson, *Park-Maker*, 148–49.

25. FLO to Arthur T. Edwards, August 7, 1855, *FLOP*, reel 5.

26. FLO to JAD, September 4, 1856, ibid. Olmsted was then handling the firm's affairs in England, where his books on slavery would soon make him a man

of some influence. See Roper, *FLO*, 112–16; Ralph Colp, Jr., "Charles Darwin: Slavery and the American Civil War;" *Harvard Library Bulletin* 26, 4 (1978):472–73 and 486.

27. JHO to FLO, July 28, 1856, *FLOP*, reel 5; also JO to FLO, December 28, 1856, ibid.

28. JHO to FLO, November 10, 1855, ibid.; FLO to ATE, December 25, 1856, ibid.; FLO to JO, February 17, 1856, ibid.; note of April 23, 1857, ibid.; GWC to FLO, August 6, 1857, ibid.

29. JHO to FLO, July 10, 1856, ibid.; FLO to ATE, December 25, 1856, ibid. Indeed, at the time of this letter, Olmsted was completing the preface he intended to add to John Hull's manuscript for *Texas*, almost ready for publication. This is a masterful polemic, surely the best thing written by Olmsted on the Free-Soil issue and as good as one is likely to read.

30. Actually, the incident never came to war, but was nevertheless a near-disastrous confrontation between the Mormons' defiance of federal authority, in an effort to preserve religious and civil autonomy, and the federal government's use of troops to extend its control over the new Utah territory. Armed conflict was averted through the efforts of the new territorial governor and a private intermediary, who preferred negotiation to fighting. In the end, federal authority was peacefully asserted as the territorial governor took office in 1858 and the Mormons were assured of religious freedom. One of the factors that had determined President Buchanan to send troops to Utah was public indignation aroused by inflammatory anti-Mormon propaganda. See Allan Nevins, *The Emergence of Lincoln: Douglas, Buchanan, and Party Chaos, 1857–1859* (New York: Scribner's, 1950), 1:314–25. See also, *New York Times*, May 11, May 13, May 18, May 19, May 20, May 25, June 11, and August 3, 1857.

31. During the course of the year, Strong became so aroused with anti-Mormon feelings that he later wrote that it was "fortunate" that the Mormons had defied civil authority, enabling "us to wage war upon [Mormonism] without stirring up a claim of religious persecution." December 12, 1857, in Nevins and Thomas, *Strong Diaries*, 2:376.

32. The *New York Times* referred to these episodes variously as the "Police War," the "Civil War" and the "German Riots". May 26, June 17, June 18, June 19, July 4, July 6, and July 14–16, 1857. Strong viewed all this almost as a public entertainment, looking to the "excitement of the present civil war" to rouse him out of a fit of "incorrigible lethargy and stolidity." He held himself "indifferent" as to the choice between "the two gangs" of police officers. During the riots of July 4th weekend and July 14–15, the irrepressible Strong strolled about "looking for a mob." Nevins & Thomas, *Strong Diary*, 2:341–43 and 347–48.

33. Ibid., 355; Lockwood, *Manhattan Moves*, 233–35. Lockwood reports that the crisis had eased in Manhattan by the spring of 1858.

34. An advertisement for the *Atlantic Monthly* featured Emerson, Bryant, Longfellow, Hawthorne, Whittier, Holmes, and Lowell, as well as such *Putnam's* authors as Melville, Rose Terry, and George W. Curtis. Nevins, *Emergence of*

•

Lincoln, 35. Thomas Bender feels that the successful founding of the *Atlantic Monthly*, even as *Putnam's* was failing, symbolized an ascendancy of Boston over New York, insofar as cultural leadership was concerned, an ascendancy that was to last several decades. This was, Bender writes, "a shift from the concreteness, toughness and diversity of New York's urbanity to the evocation of state of mind, a mind of cultivation and rectitude, but in the realm of the ideal rather than of the reality of the city." Bender, *New York Intellect*, 168.

35. FLO to Samuel Cabot Jr, July 4 and 6, 1857, McLaughlin, *Papers*, 2:436–45. In a letter dated August 11, 1857, John Hull chastised Frederick for not writing. *FLOP*, reel 5.

36. A letter to Samuel Cabot, dated July 26, 1857, is inscribed from this location. McLaughlin, *Papers*, 3:445 and 447. The story of the meeting at the Morris Cove Inn is related by Olmsted in "Passages," *FLOP*, reel 43.

37. Stow Persons, *The Decline of American Gentility* (New York: Columbia University Press, 1973), 2–3, 8, and 42–47.

38. Fein, *Cityscape*, 425 and 435; McLaughlin, *Papers*, 3:81, n. 2. Remember also that James Alexander Hamilton circulated a petition supporting Olmsted for this position (see chapter 7, n. 45, above).

39. Bender, *New York Intellect*, 164–65. McLaughlin, *Papers*, 3:201, n. 1.

40. FLO to JHO, September 11, 1857, *FLOP*, reel 5. Olmsted wrote from the office at 53 Liberty Street in Manhattan of Frederick Kapp, a colleague from the German-American Free Soil movement.

41. The editors of McLaughlin, *Papers*, state that Olmsted was indeed given a salary of $1,500, which was $500 less than Viele's. It thus does not seem reasonable that the Commission had seriously considered a $3,000 salary for the Superintendent position. Olmsted asserted that one party of the Board wanted the Superintendent to be a man who could replace the Chief Engineer "in case of his removal or death." Olmsted also suggested that the lower salary had been proposed by those who favored another candidate, hoping that it would induce Olmsted to withdraw. McLaughlin, *Papers*, 3:81, n. 5.

42. The sole vote cast against Olmsted was that of Tammany Democrat Thomas C. Fields, who voted for one Edwin Smith, a former city surveyor and a "practical man." Olmsted also described several other candidates, the strongest of whom he considered Joel Benedict Nott, an educator and son of the president of Union College in Schenectady, New York. McLaughlin, *Papers*, 3:80–84, n. 24, 26, and 28.

43. JO to OPO, September 12, 1857, *FLOP*, reel 5. Frederick had been elected Superintendent for the Park the evening before this letter was written, but of course his father, in Europe, had not yet even known that Frederick was a serious candidate for the position.

44. FLO to CV, November 26, 1863, ibid., reel 2.

45. Charles E. Beveridge, "Introduction," in McLaughlin, *Papers*, 3:3. Beveridge also observes that Olmsted's "qualifications for the post of superintendent were questionable" and attributes his success in obtaining the post in large part to

the nature of his support and the fact "that he was a Republican who was not politically threatening to the Democratic members of the board."

46. JHO to FLO, November 13, 1857, *FLOP*, reel 5.

47. JO to FLO, November 28, 1857, ibid. A few days earlier, John Olmsted had written to his family as he was sitting next to John Hull's "cold remains." The father said that in the last fifteen minutes of his life, John Hull had "breathed very gently & died without a struggle." He had carried out "to the end his quiet ways." Now John Hull was to be buried in the Protestant cemetery in Nice, in a bricked-up vault with a slab stone over it. JO to MO, November 24, 1857, ibid.

48. Roper, *FLO*, 133. Beveridge, "Introduction," in McLaughlin, *Papers*, 3:61–62.

49. MCO to FLO, August 4, 1861, *FLOP*, reel 6. In this letter, Mary urges that on his next trip home he should "stay a fortnight at least if you love me." And she observed that his last letter was mere "rhodomontade," rather than a proper letter "to a wife."

50. FLO to MCO, October 11, 1862, McLaughlin, *Papers*, 4:458–62 (emphasis Olmsted's).

51. Stevenson, *Park-Maker*, 176–77.

52. FJK to JHO, May 8, 1847, *FLOP*, reel 4.

9. "Slow Murder"

1. Olmsted, "Passages," *FLOP*, reel 43; FLO to JHO, September 11, 1857, and FLO to JO, January 14, 1858, ibid., reel 5; McLaughlin, *Papers*, 3:113–15 (emphasis added).

2. Ibid., pp, 63–68; Graff, *Central Park*, 15–20.

3. Ian R. Stewart, "Central Park, 1851–1871: Urbanization and Environmental Planning in New York City," Ph. D. dissertation, Cornell University, 1973, 160–161.

4. Ibid., 167. Stewart writes that most of the competitors prepared plans derived from "popular picturesque principles visible in the European parks." Only one was a plan for a formal park (164).

5. FLO to JO, February 2, 1858, *FLOP*, reel 5; McLaughlin, *Papers*, 3:115–16.

6. Charles E. Beveridge, "Introduction," in McLaughlin, *Papers*, 3:26–27. Beveridge adds that the commissioners had likely used the competition to "reward 'their own,' " since the first three prize winners were all employees of the park. Waldo Hutchins, the sole American Party commissioner, cast his vote for the fourth-place winner—a designer of cemeteries and suburban projects.

7. Roper, *FLO*, 137. Resolution of the Board of Commissioners, May 12, 1858, *FLOP*, reel 30. McLaughlin, *Papers*, 3:192, n. 1, cites the minutes of the board, May 17, 1858.

8. *DAB*, 10:268–69; McLaughlin, *Papers*, 3:69–71. See also Nevins & Thomas, *Strong Diary*, vols. 3 and 4. Viele was outraged at his dismissal and sued the City

of New York, arguing that he had been discharged illegally and that he was owed compensation for his topographical survey and his own designs of the park—designs he claimed had been copied by Olmsted and Vaux. In 1864, the jury found for Viele, awarding him $8,625, plus costs and interest. Viele would continue, for the rest of his public career, to proclaim himself the real designer of Central Park. Ian Stewart notes that Viele's plan did not provide the "radical treatment" required to make up for the "sparseness of natural riches" in the Central Park site. Stewart, "Central Park," 140. M. M. Graff observes that Viele's "botched plan" reveals that his "unquestioned competence in the field of road-making did not extend to that of art." Graff, *Central Park*, 19–20.

9. Beveridge, "Introduction," in McLaughlin, *Papers*, 3:40. Beveridge points out that in those months, Olmsted "brought construction of the lower park to virtual completion and laid the basis for the form of the upper park." He supervised as many as 3,800 men on work that cost more than $2.5 million.

10. FLO to Philip Bissinger, July 15, 1873, *FLOP*, reel 13.

11. FLO to MGVR, June 7, 1893, ibid., reel 22 (emphasis added).

12. Olmsted, "Passages." *Wood Democrats* refers to those who had been associated with Mayor Fernando Wood. It will be remembered from chapter 8, above, that Olmsted had given a far more flattering description of these commissioners in *Spoils of the Park*.

13. FLO to JFB, September 12, 1859, *FLOP*, reel 6; McLaughlin, *Papers*, 3:228–29.

14. FLO to WAS, March 10, 1895, *FLOP*, reel 23. Olmsted added that he had had to fight the idea all over again a decade later, when Dillon again reintroduced it in 1868. See also Beveridge, "Introduction," in McLaughlin, *Papers*, 3:24–25. Olmsted had been appointed to the new position on May 17, 1858. The Dillon proposals were incorporated in a resolution introduced the following day—only a few weeks after the Greensward Plan itself had been approved. Ibid., 44, n. 67.

15. FLO to HGS, January 13, 1860, ibid., 244–46.

16. FLO to the Board of Commissioners of the Central Park, March 28, 1861, *FLOP*, reel 31; McLaughlin, *Papers*, 3:334–38.

17. Roper, *FLO*, 145–46; Graff, *Central Park*, 66–67; *DAB*, 4, part 1, 535–36; McLaughlin, *Papers*, 3:55–59; Samuel Swett Green, "Andrew Haswell Green—A Sketch of His Ancestry, Life, and Work," *Proceedings, American Antiquarian Society*, new series, 16 (1903–1904):200–20. John Foord, *The Life and Public Services of Andrew Haswell Green* (Garden City: Doubleday, Page, and Company, 1913), 7–33.

18. Nevins & Thomas, *Strong Diary*, 4:385. This entry, of September 15, 1871, was written at a time when Strong was recording the beginning of the end of the Tweed Ring. As will be shown later, Strong—basically an admirer of Olmsted's—had had his own troubles with the latter during the Sanitary Commission years.

19. Stewart, "Central Park," 227.

20. Green, "Sketch," 217; Roper, *FLO*, 154.

21. FLO to John Bigelow, February 9, 1861, McLaughlin, *Papers*, 3:323–27; MCO to FLO, October 10, 1859, *FLOP*, reel 6.

22. Green's account is written in the third person and is reproduced in Green, "Sketch," 207–8. It must be remembered that this account was probably written decades after the events of 1858–1861, and long after Green and Olmsted had become bitter antagonists. Green had held the office of comptroller of the park until ousted by the Tweed Ring in 1870.

23. FLO to Charles H. Russell, November 12, 1861, *FLOP*, reel 7; Mc-Laughlin, *Papers*, 4:226–28 (emphases added). Russell was a Central Park commissioner, identified by Olmsted as "the only arboriculturist on the Commission."

24. FLO to John Bigelow, February 9, 1861.

25. JO to FLO, September 27, 1857, *FLOP*, reel 5. John Hull wrote his father (September 30, 1857) that he was glad that Frederick had "settled for a while in something" and hoped that his duties would not entail "book-keeping and paying." Ibid.

26. Beveridge, "Introduction," in McLaughlin, *Papers*, 3:29. Beveridge points out that the overage was based upon the original estimate for completion of the Greensward Plan and did not account for changes that had been made to the plan later. Nevertheless, Olmsted failed to estimate the impact of these changes or to perform the kind budgetary "trade-off" analysis essential to keep costs within estimates. One must also acknowledge that this has been a common failing on public works down to our own day.

27. FLO to JO, September 23, 1859, *FLOP*, reel 6.

28. George E. Waring, JR, to FLO, October 17, 1859, ibid. See also MCO to FLO, October 10, 18, and 24, 1859, and A. J. Dallas to FLO, October 3, 11, and 25, 1859, ibid. These letters state that the "hiring & firing" done by Green in Olmsted's absence was subject to a subcommittee of three commissioners. In the Stebbins letter referred to above (n. 15), Olmsted was upset about the possibility of a similar committee being appointed over him in January of 1860, but such a committee never came into being. McLaughlin, *Papers*, 3:246 n. 3.

29. FLO to the Board of Commissioners of the Central Park, July 5, 1859, ibid., 221–28.

30. Cited in Ibid., 294 n. 4 (editorial of December 15, 1860). The editorial made the absurd claim that the public money had been spent "in defacing whatever natural beauty the grounds of the Central Park may have originally possessed"—that is, the shanties, swamps, scrub brush, and bare boulders that had originally marked this tract of land.

31. FLO to JO, March 12, 1860, and J. E. Van Nort to FLO, February 7, 1860, *FLOP*, reel 6. McLaughlin, *Papers*, 3:247–8 n. 2.

32. FLO to JO, October 21, 1860, *FLOP*, reel 6; McLaughlin, *Papers*, 3:274–76.

33. Roper, *FLO*, 146.

34. MCO to FLO, October 10, 1859, *FLOP*, reel 6.

35. FLO to AHG, November 15 and 16, 1860, McLaughlin, *Papers*, 3:284–85.

Olmsted's original response was, in full: "I have enquired about the willows referred to in your note of the 12th. None were cut except as I had designated—worthless, of course." Ibid.

36. Graff, *Central Park*, 13–14. Downing had been accused of extravagance and evasion of duty, Graff notes. At a cabinet meeting called by President Fillmore (at Downing's request), Downing presented his plans and delivered an ultimatum: he was to be permitted to implement these plans unhindered or he would "roll up his plans and leave."

37. FLO to CLB, December 8, 1860, *FLOP*, reel 6; McLaughlin, *Papers*, 3:287, emphasis mine.

38. FLO to MCO, July 29, 1861, McLaughlin, *Papers*, 4:130–133.

39. See for example Charles Strozier's discussion, "The Group Self and the Crisis of the 1850s," in his *Lincoln's Quest for Union: Public and Private Meanings* (New York: Basic Books, 1982), 182–203. Strozier notes that the American social and political condition had been marked, from its inception, by fierce competition, suspicion, and conflict among groups and regions and by inflated and heated rhetoric. Early in the antebellum period, however, the cohesive forces in the group self had been stronger than these fundamental "tensions and splits." An effective consensus had been fostered on a variety of cultural, social and political issues—such as the extension of suffrage, westward expansion, internal improvements, the importance of republican "virtues," and so on. By the 1850s, the forces of fragmentation began to overwhelm the forces of cohesion: "In a matter of a few years a largely stable, cohesive society disintegrated into separate and warring parts."

40. Ibid. Olmsted's marriage could also have served as a psychic defensive tactic in another way. At a time when he was being humiliated, defeated by a sibling rival (Green), the marriage provided him with a "victory" over his original sibling rival—"usurping" John Hull's place with his wife and family. But this was a Pyrrhic victory—inducing a guilt that had to be redressed through his near-fatal carriage accident that summer.

41. FLO to the Board of Commissioners of the Central Park, January 22, 1861, *FLOP*, reel 31; McLaughlin, *Papers*, 3:297–323. This document seems to have been in part a letter to the President of the Board (the first few pages of the draft, which are in the hand of a copyist) and in part the presentation he planned to make, or had made, to the board in person (the remainder of the draft, forty-one pages in all, in Olmsted's handwriting and marked "Draft of remarks addressed to the Executive Committee . . . Central Park giving reasons for my resignation. January, 1861"). In dealing with this letter in this chapter and chapter 10 following, I will use the text given in *Papers*, vol. 3, except for references to significant variations in and material deleted from the original manuscript, as it appears in the microfilm version.

42. FLO to HWB, August 16, 1863, McLaughlin, *Papers*, 4:695–703.

43. FLO to JO, April 19, 1862, *FLOP*, reel 7; McLaughlin, *Papers*, 4:309–13.

44. FLO to FJK, January 28, 1873, *FLOP*, reel 13.

45. See the manuscript version of the resignation presentation, ibid., reel 31.

46. FLO to J. P. Walker, November 1, 1860, ibid., reel 6 (words in brackets struck out). See also McLaughlin, *Papers*, 3:276–78. Earlier, Olmsted had consulted with Green on the matter, who disapproved of the Keepers taking part in such an outing. See ibid., 278, n. 1.

47. FLO to CV, March 25, 1864, *FLOP*, reel 3.

48. FLO to HWB, October 3, 1862, McLaughlin, *Papers*, 4:441–48 (emphases Olmsted's).

10. Architect in Chief of Central Park

1. FLO to CLB, December 8, 1860, *FLOP*, reel 6; McLaughlin, *Papers*, 3:286–87.

2. FLO to CV, from the Mariposa Mining Camp in California, November 26, 1863, *FLOP*, reel 2. This was the most important letter that Olmsted ever wrote about his wishes in undertaking the design and superintendence functions at Central Park. Vaux had initiated the correspondence (October 19, 1863), complaining to Olmsted that he (Vaux) had never been given credit for his contributions to Central Park and that Olmsted bore much of the responsibility for this—beginning with his assumption of the Architect-in-Chief title. Olmsted responded with his intensely felt thirty-three-page letter. At the end of it, he told Vaux: "I . . . have taken pains to expose to you, carefully, fully and unsparingly everything in my mind from top to bottom." See also Charles Beveridge's excellent discussion of the respective contributions of Olmsted and Vaux in the first years at Central Park, "Introduction," 11–14, in McLaughlin, *Papers*, vol. 3.

3. FLO to the Board of Commissioners of Central Park, May 31, 1858, McLaughlin, *Papers*, 3:191–92. Olmsted changed the wording somewhat in this version. See part 2, chapter 6.

4. FLO to JO, February 2, 1858, *FLOP*, reel 5; AHG to FLO, August 9, 1859, ibid., reel 30; FLO to JO, September 23, 1859, ibid., reel 6. See also McLaughlin, *Papers*, 3:115–16 and 230–31.

5. CV to FLO, January 18, 1864, *FLOP*, reel 8. See also Stevenson, *Park-Maker*, 257.

6. CV to FLO, May 22, 1865, *FLOP*, reel 32.

7. CV to FLO, May 12, 1865, ibid.

8. CV to FLO, May 22, 1865, ibid.

9. CV to FLO, June 3, 1865, ibid.

10. CV to FLO, July 6 and July 31, 1865, ibid.

11. CV to FLO, July 8, 1865, ibid.

12. FLO to HWB, October 3, 1861, McLaughlin, *Papers*, 4:211.

13. D. W. Winnicott, *The Maturational Process and the Facilitating Environment* (New York: International Universities Press, 1965), 65.

14. Daniel Dervin, "A Dialectical View of Creativity," *Psychoanalytic Review* 70, 4 (1983):463–91. Similarly, Stephen Black observes that Walt Whitman had

envisioned himself writing for an ideal reader, who would stand in for the idealized nurturing mother of infancy—"an ideal reader who would love and accept him unconditionally, acknowledge his genius and omnipotence, and affirm that the bard had reestablished, through poetry, the psychologically archaic world of infantile security." The ideal reader would serve, also, to affirm Whitman's fragile, painfully constructed identity. And the ideal reader—ultimately a phantom reflecting only Whitman's own narcissistic preoccupation with self—would "relieve the loneliness inherent in the narcissistic world." Stephen A. Black, *Whitman's Journey into Chaos: A Psychoanalytic Study of the Poetic Process* (Princeton: Princeton University Press, 1975), 43, 85–86, 113, and 146.

15. Schuyler, *Urban Landscape*, 65.

16. CV to Edwin Lawrence Godkin, March 17, 1878, *FLOP*, reel 33.

17. FLO to JO, September 23, 1859, and February 6, 1860, ibid., reel 6.

18. FLO to the Board of Commissioners of Central Park, January 22, 1861, ibid., reel 31; McLaughlin, *Papers*, 3:297–323. See chapter 9, n. 41.

19. The emphasis on the phrase "at the present time" is Olmsted's; all other emphases in this passage have been added. For some reason, the latter half of Olmsted's "artist" argument was struck out in the manuscript, with a line drawn horizontally through it (see reel 31). The *Papers* editors, wisely, restored this material to their presentation of this crucial argument. McLaughlin, *Papers*, 3:304, the middle paragraphs. It may be that Olmsted remained ambivalent about exposing his "artist self" to the possible ridicule of the board.

20. FLO to CLB, December 8, 1860, *FLOP*, reel 6. FLO to JB, February 9, 1861, McLaughlin, *Papers*, 3:323–27.

21. FLO to the Board of Commissioners of Central Park, May 31, 1858, ibid., 191–92; FLO to James T. Fields, October 21, 1860, ibid., 269–70. Fields was a partner in Ticknor and Fields, which had acquired the *Atlantic Monthly*, of which he would soon become editor.

22. Emphases Olmsted's. In the two places where Olmsted used the word *imposter*, he had originally written *swindler*. Thus, his cry of protest formerly had read, "I am *not* a swindler." *FLOP*, reel 31.

23. In the psychology of Donald Winnicott, the task of a healthy false self is to protect the true self, to find a compromise (with the demands of society) by which the purposes of the true self may be achieved. Such a compromise, however, "ceases to be allowable when the issues become crucial," at which point "the True Self is able to override the compliant [False] self." In an unhealthy state of mind, the false self takes over and becomes a "truly split-off compliant [self]" that seeks accommodation with the environment at all costs, while the true self is isolated and repressed. Winnicott, *Maturational Process*, 148–50.

See also Ralph R. Greenson, "On Screen Defenses, Screen Hunger, and Screen Identity," *Journal of the American Psychoanalytic Association* 6 (1958):242–62. Greenson writes of individuals who construct "screen identities"—identities that are meant to deny or to contradict other more painful or conflictual identifications.

24. Phyllis Greenacre notes that the impostor "appears always to be striving

toward oedipal realization," searching for the identity, the "new character" that would fulfill his "ego hunger and a need for completion," that would provide "a satisfying identity in the world." Phyllis Greenacre, "The Relation of the Artist to the Impostor," *Psychoanalytic Study of the Child* 13 (1958):521 and 539–540. She makes a connection between the artist and the impostor, observing that the artist "is at least two people, the personal self [akin to the Winnicottian enabling false self of social accommodation] and the collectively stimulated and responsive creative self [the true self]."

25. FLO to JO, March 23, 1861, *FLOP*, reel 6; McLaughlin, *Papers*, 3:328–30.

26. FLO to the Board of Commissioners of the Central Park, March 28, 1861, *FLOP*, reel 31; McLaughlin, *Papers*, 3:334–38.

27. Copy of the resolutions of the Board of Commissioners transmitted to Olmsted by the clerk of the board, June 8, 1861, *FLOP*, reel 31. The wording of the resolution implies that this autonomy itself was subject to Green's discretion in the matter.

28. Daniel R. Goodloe to FLO, February 15, 1861, ibid., reel 6. See also McLaughlin, *Papers*, 3:329, n. 2.

29. HWB to FLO, April 29, 1861, *FLOP*, reel 6. McLaughlin, *Papers*, 4:120–121, n. 1, 128, n. 6.

30. MCO to JO, June 22, 1861, and FLO to MCO, June 9, 1861, *FLOP*, reel 6.

31. GEW Jr to FLO, June 23, 1861, ibid. Waring also wrote that Green "has the power to be mean now, but I shall pay him off someday."

32. FLO to JO, April 25, 1863, ibid., reel 7; McLaughlin, *Papers*, 4:613–15. John Olmsted's letter—apparently regretting that Frederick had given up without a fight a position that paid $5,000 per year—was occasioned by learning of Frederick's difficulties at the Sanitary Commission and of his inclination to now resign *that* position.

33. CV to FLO, October 19, 1863, *FLOP*, reel 8; CV to FLO, May 20, 1865, ibid., reel 32.

34. FLO to CLB, December 8, 1860; Alfred Field to FLO, September 21, 1859. Ibid., reel 6.

35. FLO to JB, February 9, 1861, McLaughlin, *Papers*, 3:323–27.

36. The *Herald* passage is cited in ibid., 267, n. 2. FLO to JTF, October 21, 1860, ibid., 269–70. See also ibid., 272, n. 14.

37. Nevins & Thomas, *Strong Diary*, 2:454–55. Strong's entry of June 11, 1859, celebrating both aspects of the park construction, was made within days of Olmsted's marriage to Mary, when Olmsted was at the zenith of his mastery of the park.

38. FLO to JTF, October 21, 1860, McLaughlin, *Papers*, 3:269–70; *Atlantic Monthly* article, April 1861, cited in ibid., 330, n. 9, and 273–74, n. 14.

39. HWB to FLO, April 29, 1861, *FLOP*, reel 6.

40. FLO to JO, March 22, 1861, ibid.; McLaughlin, *Papers*, 3:329–30. Olmsted was here coyly writing of himself in the third person.

41. George M. Frederickson, *The Inner Civil War: Northern Intellectuals and the Crisis of the Union* (New York: Harper, 1968), 98–112. See also introduction, n. 57.

42. Thomas Bender, *New York Intellect: A History of Intellectual Life in New York City, from 1750 to the Beginnings of Our Own Time* (Baltimore: Johns Hopkins University Press, 1987), 172.

43. FLO to JO, July 22, 1860, *FLOP*, reel 6; McLaughlin, *Papers*, 3:256–57.

44. See Schuyler's discussion in *Urban Landscape*, 169–174 (citation on 172); Jon C. Teaford, "Landscaping America," *Reviews in American History* 15, 4 (1988):661.

45. FLO to Henry H. Elliott [August 27, 1860], McLaughlin, *Papers*, 3:259–69. The editors identify Elliott as the older brother of Charles Wyllis Elliott, the Central Park Commissioner who had encouraged Olmsted, in 1857, to apply for the position of Superintendent. This offers a good example of the "networking" within patrician and gentry circles that benefited ambitious young men like Olmsted and his peers.

46. Ibid.

47. FLO to CHR, November 12, 1861, *FLOP*, reel 7.

11. The Sanitary Commission and Mariposa

1. This story is told most completely in four different works. The pioneering work is William Quentin Maxwell, *Lincoln's Fifth Wheel: The Political History of the U.S. Sanitary Commission* (New York: Longmans, Green, 1956), the most exhaustive as to the scope and detail of the Sanitary Commission's efforts during the Civil War. Roper, *FLO*, 168–232, and Stevenson, *Park-Maker*, 195–246, both deal with this subject extremely well. But the best single source on this subject is now Jane Turner Censer, "Introduction," in McLaughlin, *Papers*, 4:1–69. This essay is a model of its kind and can hardly be improved upon. Besides covering a very complex and diffuse subject with admirable clarity and conciseness, Censer's assessment of the characters and motivations of Olmsted, his associates, and his antagonists is both fair and convincing. The volume itself is exceptional: it is not only of extraordinary historical value, but presents (with its superb notation and editorial comments) a human drama of very high order.

See also Katharine Wormeley's introduction to her book, *Other Side of War*, 5–14. This is a useful, concise account of the Sanitary Commission from its origins as a spontaneous alliance of women's relief associations, covering both its organizational structure and functioning and the scope of its accomplishments.

2. Censer, "Introduction," in McLaughlin, *Papers*, 4:17–20; Maxwell, *Fifth Wheel*, 110–15. *The Cotton Kingdom* (1861) (New York: Modern Library, 1969), was the revised and augmented collection of his travel books. The published book showed much greater concern with the economics of slavery than was evident in Olmsted's individual works or, especially, in the original newspaper dispatches from which these earlier books were compiled. There are three reasons for this. First, as noted previously, Olmsted had long since begun to tailor his work to the

Free Soil sentiments he shared with his literary circle of the mid-1850s. Second, both Olmsted and the editor of the latter work, Daniel R. Goodloe, added a considerable amount of statistics, gathered from the 1860 census and other sources, as well as lengthy analysis of this data. Third, in cutting the earlier works' 185,765 words to 27,625 words in *The Cotton Kingdom*, an enormous amount of Olmsted's impressionistic material was omitted. This gave even greater emphasis to the augmented material dealing with the economics of slavery.

3. FLO to JO, April 19, 1862, *FLOP*, reel 7; McLaughlin, *Papers*, 4:309–13. Frederick's letter to his father is somewhat disingenuous, since it is clear from his papers that he had devoted an enormous amount of time to this effort and had made a deep psychic investment in it as well.

4. FLO to JO, February 24, 1862, *FLOP*, reel 7 (emphasis added).

5. John Stuart Mill, "On Liberty," in *The Utilitarians* (Garden City: Anchor, 1973), 590–93. See introduction, n. 33.

6. FLO to Abraham Lincoln, March 8, 1862, McLaughlin, *Papers*, 4:286–88; *FLOP*, reel 7 (emphasis Olmsted's).

7. FLO to JO, April 19, 1862, *FLOP*, reel 7; McLaughlin, *Papers*, 4:309–13.

8. Censer, "Introduction," in McLaughlin, *Papers*, 4:27–28; Maxwell, *Fifth Wheel*; FLO to John Foster Jenkins, May 25, 1862, and FLO to HWB, June 13 and 19, 1862, McLaughlin, *Papers*, 4:349–51, 369–74.

9. Olmsted first confronted the full horror of the war in the last days of May, as the seemingly endless trainloads of wounded and dying soldiers rolled into White House landing from Fair Oaks Station. The terrible experiences of Fair Oaks Station are told in Olmsted's letter to Bellows, June 3, 1862, ibid., 357–67, and Wormeley, *Other Side of War*, 59–64 and 101–8.

Roper, *FLO*, 194–201, offers a good description of the manner in which Olmsted organized the transport operation, aboard ship and ashore, and his beneficial impact upon the Medical Bureau's own preparations for dealing with the sick and wounded. See also Censer, "Introduction," in McLaughlin, *Papers*, 4:27–32.

10. Censer, "Introduction," in McLaughlin, *Papers*, 4:33; Maxwell, *Fifth Wheel*, 161–62.

11. As Censer notes, all of the Sanitary Commissioners were highly educated, some with postgraduate degrees. Olmsted was the only man among them who was not a college graduate. "Introduction," in McLaughlin, *Papers*, 4:5–6.

12. Entry of January 26, 1863, Nevins & Thomas, *Strong Diary*, 3:291 (emphasis Strong's).

13. FLO to OWG, November 5, 1862, McLaughlin, *Papers*, 4:466–71. The editors state that Olmsted's letters to Gibbs "illustrate his hatred both of aristocratic ideals of social organization and of the states' rights doctrines that he believed had helped to bring about the Civil War." The observation is certainly true, but Olmsted's hatred of "aristocratic ideals" can only refer to his fear that a vulgar moneyed class might create a "legal aristocracy" that a talented outsider from the bourgeoisie, such as himself, could never hope to penetrate.

14. Raymond Williams, *The Long Revolution* (New York: Harper, 1961), 85.

15. FLO to ELG, February 20, 1865, cited in Roper, *FLO*, 276–77.

16. Maxwell, *Fifth Wheel*, 14.

17. Nevins & Thomas, *Strong Diary*, 3:276.

18. Entry of January 26, 1863, ibid., 291.

19. Entries of March 5 and March 10, 1863, ibid., 303 and 304.

20. HWB to Rev. John H. Heywood (a functionary in the Western Sanitary Commission), March 10, 1863, cited in Roper, *FLO*, 218. Citing this letter and another by Bellows to the secretary of the Western Branch, John S. Newberry, Laura Wood Roper accuses the "weak, mixed, vacillating" President of the Sanitary Commission of "double-dealing," of cutting the ground out from under Olmsted just as the latter was attempting a rapprochement with the independence-minded western branch. She also writes: "Bellows was wrong about Olmsted's pride of opinion, Strong about his appetite for power" (219). However, the evidence suggests that Bellows and Strong held accurate views of Olmsted's strengths and weaknesses. Bellows' actions in undermining Olmsted were ill-advised, to say the least, but were prompted by his ambivalence toward this brilliant, obsessive man who had been furiously hectoring him, by letter and in person, for many months.

21. FLO to HWB, January 13, 1863, McLaughlin, *Papers*, 4:503; FLO to HWB, May 25, 1863, *FLOP*, reel 7; FLO to HWB, July 25, 1863, McLaughlin, *Papers*, 4:671. On one occasion, Roper notes, Olmsted "burst into tears in the office" following a rebuff by the Executive Committee. Roper, *FLO*, 211.

22. FLO to HWB, July 25, 1863, McLaughlin, *Papers*, 4:664 (emphasis Olmsted's). Olmsted felt so passionately about this that he repeated the passage cited very nearly word-for-word at the end of this very long letter. "I have hoisted a flood-gate and let run a pent up stream," Olmsted also noted at the end (673–74).

23. FLO to HWB, July 28, 1863, McLaughlin, *Papers*, 4:680–81 (emphasis added).

24. FLO to HWB, August 16, 1863, ibid., 698.

25. Censer, "Introduction," in McLaughlin, *Papers*, 4:6–7; ibid., 702 n. 7.

26. FLO to HWB, August 15, 1863, ibid., 693; FLO to HWB, August 16, 1863, ibid., 698.

27. In Raymond Williams' lexicon, the *exile* is a nonconformist and one who struggles for the authentic life, though he may not achieve it. "The exile is as absolute as the rebel in rejecting the way of life of his society," Williams writes, "but instead of fighting it he goes away." While the rebel fights for change in his society, a change that will allow him to lead an authentic life, the exile "is committed to waiting: when his society changes, then he can come home, but the process of change is one in which he is not involved." Some exiles can find another society, one in which they are able to lead an authentic life. Most do not: they remain in exile, unable to go back to the society that they have rejected or that has rejected them, "yet [they are] equally unable to form important relationships with the society to which [they] have gone." Williams, *Long Revolution*, 88–90. In mid-1863, Olmsted once again had the chance to be a rebel (just as he had

had at Central Park), by "going public" with his complaints about the way the Sanitary Commission was being run. Bellows recognized this and expressed the hope that Olmsted would not, that he would leave without a public quarrel. HWB to FLO, August 18, 1863, *FLOP*, reel 8. In the end, Olmsted chose not to be a rebel, and went into exile with a rather tame letter of resignation. September 1, 1863, McLaughlin, *Papers*, 4:704–10.

28. HWB to FLO, August 18, 1863, *FLOP*, reel 8.

29. Anthony Storr, *The Dynamics of Creation* (New York: Atheneum, 1985), 221–22.

30. Stevenson, *Park-Maker*, 234.

31. FLO to JO, August 10, 1863, *FLOP*, reel 8.

32. FLO to HWB, August 16, 1863, McLaughlin, *Papers*, 4:695–703.

33. HWB to FLO, August 13, 1863, *FLOP*, reel 8 (emphasis Bellows').

34. FLO to HWB, August 16, 1863, McLaughlin, *Papers*, 4:695–96.

35. FLO to HWB, August 15, 1863, ibid., 691–95.

36. "Prospectus for a Weekly Journal," [June 25, 1863], ibid., 628–36.

37. FLO to JO, April 18, 1863, ibid., 604–8; *FLOP*, reel 7.

38. In his letter to his father, he also asked for a copy of Horace Bushnell's sermon "Barbarism, the First Danger. A Discourse for Home Missions." Olmsted was to request a copy of it again while at Mariposa, working on the "Civilization" notes in 1864. McLaughlin, *Papers*, 4:608, n. 12.

39. FLO to MCO, June 26 and 29, 1863, *FLOP*, reel 8.

40. KPW to FLO, December 7, 1863, ibid. Olmsted's father also had his doubts, though he was as supportive as ever. "I still hope & think you will not regret your removal to [California]," John Olmsted later wrote, "notwithstanding your isolation from the busy world in which you have so long moved." JO to FLO, July 24, 1864, ibid.

41. FLO to MCO, October 12, 1863, ibid.

42. FLO to John Foster Jenkins, May 21, 1862, and FLO to HWB, July 7, 1862, McLaughlin, *Papers*, 4:343–49 and 394–96. FLO to JO, August 17, 1864, *FLOP*, reel 8.

43. FLO to MCO, October 14 and 17, 1863, ibid.

44. FLO to JO, October 30, 1863, ibid.

45. FLO to MCO, December 6, 1863, ibid. The situation was exacerbated by the return of the problem associated with his adolescence, and which would strike him again in 1873. "Between my head & eyes," he wrote two days later, "I can't write much." FLO to MCO, December 8, 1863, ibid.

46. FLO to JO, March 11, 1864, and JO to FLO, April 14, 1864, *FLOP*, reel 8. His father and his former medical associates at the Sanitary Commission doubted the diagnosis, and in time the "enlarged heart" was forgotten.

47. Roper has a fine description of the trip Olmsted and his family made that July and August. Roper, *FLO*, 265–70.

48. FLO to JO, August 17, 1864, *FLOP*, reel 8.

49. FLO to JO, September 14, 1864, ibid.

50. Entry of October 15, 1866, Nevins & Thomas, *Strong Diary*, 4:109–10.

51. Roper, *FLO*, 271–78; Stevenson, *Park-Maker*, 253.

52. FLO to FNK, September 28, 1864, *FLOP*, reel 8.

53. FLO to FNK, ibid.; F. F. Low to FLO, September 29, 1864, ibid. After a three-day pack trip to Yosemite in 1865, Olmsted wrote his father: "I am preparing a scheme of management for the Yo Semite, which is far the noblest public park, or pleasure ground in the world." FLO to JO, July 5, 1865, ibid., reel 9. In the report he later authored on behalf of the commission, Olmsted accurately predicted "the millions" who would, within "a century," wish to visit Yosemite, and he sketched out the need to prevent commercialization of the parkland and to provide adequate facilities without compromising the integrity of the valley itself. Harold Gilliam, "Designing with Nature: Olmsted's Legacy," *San Francisco Chronicle*, November 23, 1986; rpr. in *NAOP* Newsletter (Winter 1986):3–4.

54. Roper, *FLO*, 275–76; FLO to MCO, February 10 and March 2, 1865, *FLOP*, reel 9.

55. FLO to FNK, April 9 and 16, 1865, Knapp Manuscripts, Massachusetts Historical Society, Boston, Massachusetts. I first became aware of these important letters in a footnote to a biographical essay on Knapp in McLaughlin, *Papers*, 4:101–2, which aptly described these letters as "remarkably revealing." The editor of this volume, Jane Turner Censer, referred my inquiry to the editor of the forthcoming volume 5 of the *Papers*, which is to include these two letters, along with editorial notes. The editor of volume 5, Victoria Post Ranney, supplied me with transcripts of both letters. I am most grateful for the kindness of these scholars.

56. Robert Jay Lifton, *Life of the Self: Toward a New Psychology* (New York, Touchstone, 1976), 42–43. Lifton's thesis draws upon his work with survivors of Hiroshima and American Vietnam veterans.

57. Lifton observes that "survivor's guilt" is related to "death anxiety" and that this anxiety is defended against by striving for immortality—for example, through one's work or through one's children. Ibid., 31–37.

58. Charles Strozier, *Lincoln's Quest for Union: Public and Private Meanings* (New York: Basic Books, 1982), 202–3. Strozier also points out that, as Civil War had neared, Lincoln "became a passionate spokesman for a return to the wisdom of the [founding] fathers." But after the years of a dreadful war, "Lincoln had been lifted by history to look directly into the eyes of his heroes." Ibid., 64–65.

59. Olmsted's language here is remarkably similar to Winnicott's notion that when one allows false self needs to dominate one's thinking, the true self is hidden away, in isolation, with "a secret hope of rebirth" at a later time.

60. CV to FLO, April 13 and May 10 and 12, 1865, *FLOP*, reel 32. Aspects of this correspondence were previously dealt with in chapter 10, above; and it has been cited also in chapter 1.

61. CV to FLO, July 21 and 31, 1865, *FLOP*, reel 32.

62. FLO to CV, March 15, 1865, ibid., reel 9.

63. FLO to CV, August 1, 1865, ibid.

64. CEN to ELG, July 13, 1865, and ELG to FLO, July 23, 1865, ibid.
65. CV to FLO, July 6, 1865, ibid., reel 33.
66. CV to FLO, February 5, 1864, ibid., reel 8.
67. FLO to JO, August 31, 1865, ibid., reel 9.

12. "Civilization"

1. FLO to "Harding," October 10, 1864, *FLOP*, reel 8.
2. Ibid. (emphasis Olmsted's).
3. Ibid. (emphasis mine).
4. Olmsted's notes for his projected masterwork on "The History of Civilization in the United States during the Last Fifty Years," are to be found in reels 41–43, *FLOP*, and are principally in the form of random notes, fragments, and observations and short essays and hundreds of clippings from contemporary newspapers and journals of the United States and Great Britain. Some of these date as late as the 1880s, suggesting that Olmsted continued to think of completing this work even then, but the bulk of his writing and thinking seems to have been done between 1863 and 1866. The notes are frequently repetitive, and at times contradictory, as he, at different times, took opposite sides of an argument (arguing with himself, that is). Reel 42 also contains a lengthy, disjointed draft essay, which, according to Roper, was put together for an article on Mariposa that his friend, Charles Eliot Norton, had requested for the *North American Review*, an article never completed. Roper, *FLO*, 249–50. This material seems also to have been intended as chapters for his projected book, and some of it is derivative or repetitive of material that has gone before.
5. Roper has attempted to present the essence of the work Olmsted intended to create. Ibid., 248–56. She has done an excellent job of pulling together the scattered materials into a coherent and logical presentation of Olmsted's observations and thoughts—but perhaps *too* coherent. The main drawback of her essay, from my point of view, is that it tends to suppress Olmsted's worst doubts and darkest fears about mankind and himself, his sometimes Hobbesian point of view. Nevertheless, Roper's presentation has served well as a source for Olmsted's thinking on this subject, though it will surely be superseded by the material in the forthcoming volume 5 of the Olmsted papers, edited by Victoria Post Ranney and her colleagues, which will include a definitive draft of Olmsted's long, unfinished essay. As of this writing, its suggestive working title is: "The Pioneer Condition in American History: Notes Toward a Definition of the American National Character." VPR to MK, private communication, February 20, 1987.
6. See also the discussion by Robert Lewis in "Frontier and Civilization in the Thought of Frederick Law Olmsted," *American Quarterly* 29 (1977):385–403.
My reconstruction is, of course, based on Olmsted's often disconnected fragments of observations and argument that are found helter-skelter throughout his "Civilization" notes and (in a more organized form) his "Mariposa" essay. Thus, like Roper, I run the risk of making this reconstruction *too* coherent—a problem also presented in the cogent and valuable presentations by Lewis and by Charles

Beveridge in the final chapter of "Formative Years." "In Memory of the Summer Days: The Mind and Work of Frederick Law Olmsted," Ph. D. dissertation, New York University, 1988, part 3, ch. 9, discusses the "Civilization" notes in greater detail than I do here.

7. Frederick Law Olmsted, *A Journey Through Texas: Or, A Saddle-Trip on the Southwestern Frontier* (Austin: University of Texas, 1978), 382–85.

8. Roper, *FLO*, 253, and Beveridge, "Formative Years," 453–54, both call attention to this important passage. In fact, Roper makes the characteristic Olmsted defined here the leitmotif of the concluding pages of *her* essay. However, she gives the word as "communicativeness," while Beveridge has reproduced it as I show it in my text. Clearly, these variant readings suggest very different concepts. I am grateful to Victoria Post Ranney for affirming that "communitiveness" was the correct reading and supplying me with reproductions of the manuscript pages of the passage in which it occurs, as well as the microfilm references that permitted me to locate and study the entire section. VPR to MK, private communication, February 20, 1987. In my reproduction of the defining sentence, I have omitted words that Olmsted struck out.

9. FLO to "Harding," October 10, 1864, *FLOP*, reel 8.

10. FLO to CEN, December 27, 1876, ibid., reel 16. The comment was occasioned by a discussion of yet another of the stressful political squabbles Olmsted had become involved in, at the center of which was, once again, Andrew H. Green.

11. Olmsted has, with this observation, anticipated by nearly half a century Freud's own definition of the effects of repression—wherein unwelcome feelings, wishes, desires, and so on, which have been pushed deep into the unconscious, make their effects felt all the more strongly in later years for having been repressed.

12. Cited by Howard Feinstein in "The Use and Abuse of Illness in the James Family Circle: A View of Neurasthenia as a Social Phenomenon," in Robert J. Brugger, ed., *Our Selves/Our Past: Psychological Approaches to American History* (Baltimore: Johns Hopkins University Press, 1981), 230.

13. FLO to MCO, August 12, 1863, *FLOP*, reel 8; McLaughlin, *Papers*, 4:687–89.

14. The phrase quoted belongs to H. Dicks, *Marital Tensions: Clinical Studies Toward a Psychological Theory of Interaction* (Boston, Routledge and Kegan, 1984). Cited in Robert May, "Concerning a Psychoanalytic View of Maleness" *Psychoanalytic Review*, 73, 4 (1986):579–97.

15. Leo Marx, *The Machine in the Garden: Technology and the Pastoral Ideal in America* (New York: Oxford University Press, 1978), 239. See also Schuyler, *Urban Landscape*, 2–4 and 24–25.

16. Clarence C. Cook, *A Description of the New York Central Park* (1869) (New York: Benjamin Bloom, 1972) 9–12 and 23–30 (below).

17. FLO to MGVR, June 11, 1893, *FLOP*, reel 22. See also Roper, *FLO*, 291 and chapter 1, n. 33.

18. Even more might have been accomplished had Olmsted's later proposals

for Rockaway Point and Staten Island ever borne fruit, for these would have fulfilled the Olmsted-Vaux proposal of extending their landscape design all the way to the Narrows and the Atlantic Ocean itself. For a deeper appreciation of all that Olmsted and Vaux had achieved, and of what might have been achieved, for New York, it is essential to see Fein, *Cityscape;* Barlow and Alex, *Olmsted's New York;* and Jeffrey Simpson and Mary Ellen W. Hern, *Art of the Olmsted Landscape: His Works in New York City* (New York: New York City Landmarks Preservation Committee and The Arts Publisher, 1981), a companion volume to Kelly, Guillet, and Hearn, *Olmsted Landscape.*

19. Interestingly, the editors of the Olmsted Papers reveal that for the post of general secretary, Bellows had also considered none other than Edward Everett Hale—the man who had married Olmsted's quondam fiancée, Emily Perkins, and who had been an important part of Olmsted's literary and free soil activities during the mid-1850s. McLaughlin, *Papers,* 4:85.

20. LLS to FLO, August 26, 1863, and GWC to FLO, March 30, 1864, *FLOP,* reel 8. CEN to ELG, July 13, 1865, ibid., reel 9.

21. Cook, *Central Park,* 23–30. Roper, *FLO,* 340–41. Roper reports that Olmsted was embarrassed by the whole affair, hid from reporters who sought him out, and disassociated himself from the ticket—though some friends suggested the nomination "was not to be despised."

22. Neil Harris, "Four Stages of Cultural Growth: The American City," in Indiana Historical Society, *Lectures 1971–1972: History and the Role of the City in American Life* (Indianapolis: Indiana Historical Society, 1972), 25–49.

23. Thomas Bender, *New York Intellect: A History of Intellectual Life in New York City, from 1750 to the Beginnings of Our Own Time* (Baltimore: Johns Hopkins University Press, 1981), xx. Bender describes "Academic Culture" as the third phase of intellectual leadership of the city, ultimately succeeding the "Literary Culture" through which Olmsted and his peers in the "metropolitan gentry" had risen to prominence.

24. McLaughlin, *Papers,* 4:204, n. 5.

25. Ibid.

26. CV to FLO, June 3, 1865, *FLOP,* reel 32.

27. Lewis, "Frontier and Civilization," 393–400.

28. David D. Hall, "Victorian Connection," in Daniel Walker Howe, ed., *Victorian America* (Philadelphia: University of Pennsylvania Press, 1976), 86–87. See part 3, chapter 7.

29. Geoffrey Blodgett, "Frederick Law Olmsted: Landscape Architecture as Conservative Reform," *Journal of American History,* 62, 4 (March 1976):875.

30. Ibid., 877.

31. CV to ELG, March 17, 1878, *FLOP,* reel 33 (emphasis added). Vaux suggested that Olmsted prepare a paper to be read at Cooper Union, "throwing his whole personality into it, having no respect for dignitaries as he is not now bound to have being out of office, saying his uttermost, past, present and prophetic."

32. Roper, *FLO*, 383–89. His lowest point in this period was surely reached late in 1881. In November, his stepson, Owen, died; in December, Olmsted fell from a horse and broke his breastbone. Again, his recuperative powers were amazing—as if the accident had been an end in itself and its having happened had freed him from mental and physical decline. By February 1882, approaching sixty years of age, Olmsted was on the road again, back to his "long journeys."

33. CEN to FLO, October 23, 1881, Sara Norton and M. A. De Wolfe Howe, eds., *Letters of Charles Eliot Norton*, 2 vols. (Boston: Houghton Mifflin, 1931), 2:395. The two were then associated in the drive to restore and make a park of the grounds surrounding Niagara Falls.

34. CEN to J. B. Harrison, July 23, 1882, to Leslie Stephens, January 8, 1896, from a speech of 1898, to Leslie Stephens, July 8, 1895, all in ibid., 135, 237, 272, and 244. In an historiographic study of these gentry reformers, Blodgett observes: "Their staying power is remarkable, all things considered. But their morale changed along the way." Geoffrey Blodgett, "The Mugwump Reputation, 1870 to the Present," *Journal of American History* 66, 4 (1980):869.

35. Stow Persons, *The Decline of American Gentility*, (New York: Columbia University Press, 1973), vii.

36. As was noted in part 1, chapter 2, Katharine Wormeley would become quite upset at Olmsted's attitude in this quarrel with Godkin, writing: "I cannot help thinking that your life in NY where the democrats are rampant, odious, & corrupt, darkens your mind—& even narrows it." KPW to FLO, January 5, 1877, *FLOP*, reel 16.

37. E. L. Godkin, *Reflections and Comments* (New York: Scribner's, 1895), 202–3; cited in Persons, *American Gentility*, 153.

38. Bender, *New York Intellect*, 184–91.

39. FLO to CLB, March 15, 1887, *FLOP*, reel 21. See also introduction, n. 31. Olmsted was bemused by the fact that his injury in the railroad accident near Salt Lake City had been reported in the newspapers, commenting to Brace, "Can't I stub my toe without its being telegraphed [throughout] the country?"

40. Frederick Law Olmsted, "Trees in Streets and in Parks," *Sanitarian* 10, 14 (September 1882):518.

13. A Philosophy of Urban Landscape Design

1. FLO to CLB, December 1, 1853, *FLOP*, reel 4.

2. Frederick Law Olmsted, "Description of the Central Park," Central Park Commission, *Second Annual Report* [January 1859]. McLaughlin, *Papers*, 3:213.

3. FLO to HWB, October 30, 1860, McLaughlin, *Papers*, 3:273.

4. Sutton, *Civilizing*, p. 96.

5. Cited in Ian R. Stewart, "Politics and the Park," *New York Historical Society Quarterly* 59, 3/4 (July–October 1977).

6. [Andrew Jackson Downing], "A Talk About Public Parks and Gardens," *Horticulturist* 3, (1848), cited in Schuyler, *Urban Landscape*, 65. See also Schuyler's

discussion of the general belief in "parks as an instrument of moral improvement" during the two decades prior to the development of Central Park (64–67). Schuyler also notes the importance of the belief in parks as a benefit to public health in creating the climate of opinion that gave rise to Central Park. He cites Horace Greeley's wish (in an 1851 book) that the development of New York City had allowed for a great many public parks and gardens in what is now "midtown" (between Thirtieth Street and the upper Fifties). Greeley called for "all that can be . . . done immediately to secure breathing-space and grounds for healthful recreation to the Millions who will ultimately inhabit New York." See 63–65.

7. FLO to CV, November 26, 1863, *FLOP*, reel 2 (emphasis added).

8. See Roper, *FLO*, 293 and 299; Olmsted & Kimball, *Forty Years*, 15–17.

9. Ross L. Miller, "The Landscaper's Utopia Versus the City: A Mismatch," *New England Quarterly* 49, 2 (June 1976):179–93.

10. Fein, *Cityscape*, 100–1 (emphasis Olmsted and Vaux's).

11. The art of the landscape designer must be employed in assuring that neither purpose interferes with the other, Olmsted and Vaux wrote. We must be mindful, again, that Vaux undoubtedly contributed much of the writing for this report, issued January 24, 1866, only a few months after Olmsted's return. Vaux's significant contribution may explain the prominent references to "the art of landscape design," references not so prominent in the other reports issued under the firm's name.

12. Geoffrey Blodgett, "Frederick Law Olmsted: Landscape Architecture as Conservative Reform," *Journal of American History* 62, 4 (March 1976):880–81. Robert Lewis makes a similar point in "Frontier and Civilization in the Thought of Frederick Law Olmsted," *American Quarterly* 29 (1977):403.

13. David Cavitch, *My Soul and I: The Inner Life of Walt Whitman* (Boston: Beacon Press, 1985), 142 and 158.

14. Roper calls attention to the importance of Olmsted's various reports of these years, and to the difficulty in ascribing reports issued in the name of Olmsted, Vaux and Company to Olmsted's pen. Her first-rate discussion of Olmsted's purposes in some of the reports with which I will be dealing can be found in *FLO*, chs. 26 and 27, 303–31. In my own discussion of these reports, below, I will try to focus on passages that seem to be most typically in Olmsted's idiom, as well as the more visionary sections that are reflective of Olmsted's inner concerns. I will also be dealing mostly with the connections between Olmsted's personal experience and psychology and his public philosophy.

15. This fundamental premise of Olmsted's emerges clearly in Fein, *Cityscape*, through the broadly conceived and imaginative papers written by Olmsted and Vaux, or Olmsted alone, as well as through Fein's valuable editorial essays and notes. A similar theme runs through Sutton's compilation of Olmsted's papers in *Civilizing American Cities* and Thomas Bender's section on Olmsted in *Toward an Urban Vision: Ideas and Institutions in Nineteenth-Century America* (Lexington: University of Kentucky Press, 1975), 161–87. Olmsted's preoccupation with this notion is exemplified by his long disquisition on the history of cities, which he

was moved to include in the Olmsted and Vaux proposal for a Brooklyn parkway in 1868. See Fein, *Cityscape*, 146–47; Sutton, *Civilizing*, 35–36. Olmsted's historical survey of the growth of cities was probably originally conceived for his masterwork on civilization, though used imaginatively here to promote sound planning for the anticipated growth of both Brooklyn and metropolitan New York.

16. Fein, *Cityscape*, 129–64. The major portion of this paper is also presented in Sutton, *Civilizing*, 23–42, under the title "The Structure of Cities: A Historical View." This reprinting omits the interesting section on the proposed parkway, including the passages I will be citing.

17. In an earlier report (1866), Olmsted and Vaux visualized such a parkway as being connected to "New York island" via ferries or "high bridges," whereupon it would link up with a "system of somewhat sylvan roads" leading into and beyond Central Park, northward to the upper end of Manhattan. Such a design would permit a person, in a day's carriage ride, to view both the Atlantic seashore and the Palisades along the Hudson River. Fein, *Cityscape*, 126–27. Since this report was composed only a few months after Olmsted's return to the East, we must assume there is much of Calvert Vaux's thinking in it. And indeed, the grand vision here is in keeping with Vaux's assertion to Olmsted in May 1865: "Our right unquestionably is to control matters from Washington Heights to the other side of Brooklyn." CV to FLO, May 12, 1865, *FLOP*, reel 32.

18. Fein, *Cityscape*, 160–61.

19. As excerpted in Sutton, *Civilizing*, 104–29, under the title "San Francisco, 1866: A City in Search of Identity." The "Preliminary Report" was issued in the name of Olmsted and Vaux (March 31, 1866), but clearly was the result of Olmsted's years in California.

20. June 11, 1859, Nevins & Thomas, *Strong Diary*, 454–55. This tour of the lower park was made in Olmsted's heyday, while this area, "in ragged condition" was still seething with "Celts, caravans of dirt carts, derricks, steam engines." It was marked by "long lines of incomplete macadamization, 'lakes' without water, mounds of compost, piles of blasted stone, acres of what may be greensward hereafter but is now mere brown earth." Nevertheless, Strong judged that the park would be "a feature of the city within five years and a lovely place in A.D. 1900," while the Promenade, with its "quadruple row of elms," would look like Versailles "in A.D. 1950." A photograph of Vista Rock, probably looking much as Strong had seen it, is reproduced in McLaughlin, *Papers*, 3:422. Pp. 440–43 reproduce the views he might have seen from atop the observation tower.

21. Roper, *FLO*, reel 304–5.

22. The discussion of Olmsted's Berkeley proposal is based upon the version reproduced in Sutton, *Civilizing*, 264–91, under the title "Berkeley: A University Community." The original report was issued June 29, 1866, by Olmsted, Vaux and Company. Berkeley was, as Roper observes, Olmsted's "first effort to plan a community on an unoccupied site, to create a town where none had before existed." Roper, *FLO*, 305.

23. Olmsted's second requirement was that the plan should discourage "noisy and disturbing commerce" in the neighborhood, as well as anything else "which would destroy its general tranquility." The third requirement of his plan related to the buildings and grounds of the college itself. But, here, too, a key notion was applicable to his ideal suburb—the suitable arrangement of public buildings, exercise grounds, gardens, and so on, permitting adequate open space even with future development.

24. In Olmsted's time, an apartment was defined as "a portion of a house or building, consisting of a suite of rooms, allotted to the use of a particular person or party." OED, vol. 1, part 1, 381.

25. Howard Feinstein, "The Use and Abuse of Illness in the James Family Circle," in Robert J. Brugger, ed., *Our Selves/Our Past: Psychological Approaches to American History* (Baltimore: Johns Hopkins University Press, 1981), 333–34 and 336.

26. FLO to HHE, August 27, 1860, McLaughlin, *Papers*, 3:259–69. See part 3, chapter 10, n. 45.

27. Sutton, *Civilizing*, 292–305. According to Roper, Olmsted seemed to take on this project personally, with little involvement of Vaux, who was in Europe at the time. Roper, *FLO*, 322–23.

28. The latter passage is cited by Roper, *FLO*, 323, and is not included in the excerpts from the Riverside report reproduced by Sutton.

29. Jon C. Teaford carefully delineates what Olmsted had sensed—that it was the unprecedented migration to the urban centers that spurred the creation of increasing numbers of new municipalities clustered around these centers, a phenomenon that Teaford calls "the fragmentation of the metropolis." Jon C. Teaford, *City and Suburb: The Political Fragmentation of Metropolitan America, 1850–1970.* (Baltimore: Johns Hopkins University Press, 1979), 5–31. See also Edward K. Spann, *The New Metropolis: New York City, 1840–1857* (New York, Columbia University Press, 1981), 176–204.

30. FLO to MAO, March 20, 1841, *FLOP*, reel 3; McLaughlin, *Papers*, 1:127–29.

31. See Schuyler's discussion of the antebellum notion of a domesticated nature as an antidote to, and morally superior to, urban life. *Urban Landscape*, 24–36. Spann cites Walt Whitman ("perhaps the most urban of American poets") as writing, in *Specimen Days*, "Democracy most of all affiliates with the open air, is sunny and hardy and sane only with Nature." Spann, *New Metropolis*, 177. Olmsted did not sentimentalize rural life, and he continually pointed to the civilizing advantages of modern cities. But his work fed upon this shared romantic impulse, especially among the gentry and patrician classes for whom, as a public artist, he was a delegate.

32. Thomas Bender, "Spontaneity and Constraint in the City: The Genesis of Frederick Law Olmsted's Park Ideas," ms., 1975.

33. The phrases are from Olmsted's 1873 description of his father—the lines that I have suggested more truly refer to himself: "Yet the world was driving

along so fast that a man of any spirit could not but feel himself cruelly prodded up to take more upon himself than he was equal to." *FLOP*, reel 43; McLaughlin, *Papers*, 1:98.

34. The paper is "Public Parks and the Enlargement of Towns," which has been cited several times previously. S. B. Sutton notes that the paper was originally prepared "as a contribution to the popular discussion of the requirements of Boston in respect to a public park." It was later published as a pamphlet. Sutton, *Civilizing*, 52.

35. Frederick Law Olmsted, "Trees in Streets and in Parks," *Sanitarian* 10, 14 (September 1882):515–18.

36. Sutton, *Civilizing*, 65–66. See part 3, chapter 8, n. 18.

37. Ibid. (emphases added). In a letter to W. R. Martin, president of the New York Parks Department—concerning plans for restoring the Thompkins Square park—Olmsted would write with equal indignation of trees and shrubs that were "slowly mutilated, starved and murdered" by men "incompetent to earn their living honestly." FLO to WRM, August 9, 1876, *FLOP*, reel 15.

38. One must also note the psychosexual implications—the castration imagery—in "lower limbs" that are found to be "inconvenient" so that the body is "deformed by butcherly amputations." Among other things, it certainly expresses what small boys think about women's bodies and what they fear might happen to their own. Fetish symbols are meant to allay such castration fears. One can then understand the anxiety caused by a fetish symbol—like a tree—that has itself experienced an amputation.

39. In his 1882 essay, "Trees," Olmsted wrote that the public must be educated "not simply to admire verdant vistas and canopies, but to admit and respect the conditions of life and health in the trees of which they must be framed" (514).

40. Discussing this same passage, Thomas Bender observes that, while "surely overstating the pleasure and social unity that his park brought to the city," Olmsted had also "articulated a very complex notion of metropolitan culture." This notion, according to Bender, is that people sharing in a cultural activity such as a promenade in the park (or, one must assume, being part of the audience for a play or a concert) take on a dual identity. They retain their identity as a member of some more discrete community or social group (delimited by "class, gender, ethnicity, and geography") while taking on the identity and sharing in the experience of being "a public in a public place." Thomas Bender, *New York Intellect: A History of Intellectual Life in New York City, from 1750 to the Beginnings of Our Own Time* (Baltimore: Johns Hopkins University Press, 1987), 202. Such "gregariousness," I might add, is an experience they take back with them to their more discrete community and is one that Olmsted hoped would have a beneficial impact upon their lives and relationships within that smaller social circle.

41. *Manliness*, in Olmsted's time referred to "the virtues proper to a man as distinguished from a woman or a child; chiefly, courageous, independent in spirit, frank, upright." *OED*, vol. 1, part 1, 128.

42. The paradigm was, of course, his screen memory, his only memory, of his

mother: sitting under a tree in a meadow, sewing, while Frederick, a little child, played nearby.

14. Defending the Vision

1. FLO to CV, November 4, 1883, *FLOP*, reel 20 (the words in brackets were struck out by Olmsted). A few years earlier, Olmsted had used similar language in arguing that existing salt marshes should be retained in the Boston Fens. These marshes, he wrote, would be, "in the artistic sense of the word, natural, and possibly [would] suggest a modest poetic sentiment more grateful to town-weary minds than an elaborate and elegant garden-like work would have yielded." Cited in Zaitzevsky, *Boston Parks*, 57.

2. FLO to Henry K. Beekman, President of the Department of Parks, New York, June 10, 1886, *FLOP*, reel 20.

3. Sam B. Warner Jr., *Streetcar Suburbs: The Process of Growth in Boston, 1870–1900* (New York: Atheneum, 1976), 1–45.

4. Sutton, *Civilizing*, 259. This observation is contained in excerpts from Olmsted's "Notes on the Plan of Franklin Park and Related Matters," 1886, for the Boston Park Department.

5. Zaitzevsky, *Boston Parks*, 68–69.

6. Cranz dates the Reform Park stage from 1900–1930, followed by the Recreation Facility (1930–1965) and the Open-Space System (1965 and after). Galen Cranz, *The Politics of Park Design: A History of Urban Parks in America* (Cambridge: MIT Press, 1982), 14–22, 63–80, 101–17, and 236–37. Daniel M. Bluestone makes a criticism similar to mine in a review essay: "Olmsted's Boston and Other Park Places," *Reviews in American History* 11, 4 (1983):532. David Schuyler—one of the most knowledgeable of Olmstedian and urban landscape scholars—has expressed even stronger disagreement with Cranz's "static interpretation of park planning in the second half of the nineteenth century." *Urban Landscape*, 229.

7. Geoffrey Blodgett, "Frederick Law Olmsted: Landscape Architecture as Conservative Reform," *Journal of American History* 62, 4 (March 1976):884–85. See also Zaitzevsky, *Boston Parks*, 66–68.

8. Frederick Law Olmsted, "Trees in Streets and in Parks," *Sanitarian*, 10, 14 (September 1882):517–18. Olmsted's speculations as to the conscious and the unconscious influence of natural scenery and the superior restorative power of unconscious influence seems strongly founded in Emerson's idealism. See Emerson's essay on "Nature," in William H. Gillman, ed., *Selected Writings of Ralph Waldo Emerson* (New York: Signet, 1965), 200–2.

9. FLO to MGVR, June 17, 1893, *FLOP*, reel 22. I am reminded of the ambivalence revealed in Olmsted's passage on "Dame Nature" in *Walks and Talks*.

10. FLO to MGVR, June 11, 1893, *FLOP*, reel 22. (Word in brackets struck out by Olmsted; emphasis Olmsted's).

11. Williams, *The Long Revolution* (New York: Harper, 1966), 91.

12. Geoffrey Blodgett has touched on this in his study of the changing attitudes toward the Mugwumps in the last century. The "exaggerated sex differentiation and rigid role definitions" of Victorian society, he writes, seem to have given males "strong, ambivalent attitudes toward the cultural meaning of sex difference." Manliness was equated with "potency and animal aggression while the female symbolized not only virtue but fragile passivity." Men who proposed reforms for the aggressivized masculine spheres of life (such as politics) "ran the risk of acquiring a queer, desexed public reputation." Geoffrey Blodgett, "The Mugwump Reputation, 1870 to the Present," *Journal of American History* 66, 4 (1980):884. I might note again the frequent defensive use of the word *manly* by Olmsted and his gentry peers to describe their activities.

13. See Olmsted's letter to the developers of Mount Royal Park in Montreal (1881), cited in Sutton, *Civilizing*, 204–5. Among the great works of art that Olmsted referred to in this passage were "the psalms of David, the novels of Scott, the idylls of Tennyson." "You know also," he added, "that of the works of two men, given the same subject to draw, paint, or carve, one representing no more school-knowledge, industry, faithfulness, or hand-labor, only higher art, will sell at once for ten times as much as the other."

14. See Michael T. Gilmore, *American Romanticism and the Marketplace* (Chicago: University of Chicago Press, 1985).

15. Advertisement for Trump Park on Central Park South, *New York Times Sunday Magazine*, March 1987.

16. For Thomas Bender, Richard Watson Gilder was prototypical of the "modern literary intellectual," the final evolution of the literary culture in New York City which had first flourished at mid-century. Thomas Bender, *New York Intellect: A History of Intellectual Life in New York City, from 1750 to the Beginnings of Our Own Time* (Baltimore: Johns Hopkins University Press, 1987), xv and 213–16.

17. In dealing with the purposes and architecture of the Exposition, I have relied on Mario Manieri-Elia, "Toward an 'Imperial City': Daniel H. Burnham and the City Beautiful Movement," in Giorgio Ciuccio, Francesco Dal Co, Mario Manieri-Elia, and Manfredo Tafuri, *The American City: From the Civil War to the New Deal* (Cambridge: MIT Press, 1979), 8–50; Roper, *FLO* 425–33 and 447–49; Schuyler, *Urban Landscape*, 184–91; and Fabos, Milne, and Weinmayr, *Founder*, 90–98. For Lewis Mumford, the Exposition was a watershed cultural event, turning American architecture toward decadence and imitation—a retreat from the simplicity, stability, and dignity that had characterized the new skyscrapers and office buildings of the previous decade. Mumford believes that this retreat could have been prevented had H. H. Richardson and John W. Root not passed so early from the scene. For Mumford, Louis Sullivan was then the only architect left to struggle for originality in the design of new commercial and governmental structures in America. Lewis Mumford, *The Brown Decades: A Study of the Arts in America, 1865–1895* (New York: Dover, 1931, 1959), 141–42. Manieri-Elia and Fabos and his colleagues are far more positive about the fair and about the contributions of Burnham to American architecture (as in the landmark Flatiron

Building in New York City). And all agree that Olmsted's work needs little or no apology at all.

18. Roper, *FLO*, 425.

19. Olmsted, Vaux and Company, "Report Accompanying Plan for Laying Out the South Park" (1871), as excerpted in Sutton, *Civilizing*, 156–80.

20. FLO to JCO, November 12, 1890, *FLOP*, reel 41; FLO to Edouard André, February 1, 1891, ibid., reel 22. Olmsted also referred to the essential feature of "the grandeur of the adjoining Lake," as well as the availability of convenient rail transportation, in explaining his preference for the Jackson Park site to a writer from the *Century* who was preparing an article on the Exposition. See FLO to Henry Van Brunt, June 24, 1891, and the manuscript article following, ibid., reel 41.

21. FLO to Rudolph Ulrich, Superintendent of Landscaping, March 11, 1893, and October 7, 1892, ibid., reel 41. Olmsted's concern for providing visual relief extended to an obsessive concern with the nature and variety of boats that would carry visitors about the fair grounds. He continually hectored Burnham about the "poetic" effect the boats should make. See for example: FLO to DHB, January 26, 1891, and June 24, 1893, ibid.; FLO to DHB, December 23 and 28, 1891, and February 6, 1892, ibid., reel 22.

22. Frederick Law Olmsted, "A Report Upon the Landscape Architecture of the Columbian Exposition to the American Institute of Architects" (a paper read before the World's Congress of Architects at Chicago and published in *American Architect and Building News* in September 1893), excerpted in Sutton, *Civilizing*, 180–96. The complete draft of this report is located in *FLOP*, reel 41. The report itself borrows heavily (including the essence of this citation) from Olmsted's earlier draft report to the Board of Directors of the Exposition, October 17, 1892. Ibid.

23. FLO to HSC, November 4, 1891, *FLOP*, reel 22.

24. Olmsted, "Draft of AIA Report," 17–19.

25. FLO to DHB, June 20, 1893, *FLOP*, reel 41 (emphasis Olmsted's). Since little could be done architecturally as a corrective, Olmsted recommended to Burnham what today would be called "happenings"—pseudospontaneous "incidents of vital human gaiety," such as parties of "merry-making masqueraders" and singing children, fiddlers, wandering minstrels, small groups of musicians on the boats and on the Wooded Island.

26. FLO to DHB, October 2, 1893, ibid., reel 23.

27. FLO to WAS, November 4, 1893, ibid., reel 22. The critic was William Robinson, editor of the English publication, the *Garden*, with whom Olmsted had had a friendly visit in 1892. See FLO to MGVR, November 7, 1892, ibid. Robinson had apparently disapproved of the several bridges across the great Lagoon to the Wooded Island and of the number of boats that had plied the Lagoon, destroying the picturesque effect—criticisms Olmsted himself had raised to Burnham, Ulrich, and Codman during the design process. Now Olmsted responded that such criticisms were no more than the differences of opinion that might exist among "cultivated men" as to "what fashions should rule." But, he

noted, "artists, real artists, looking to ideals [work] independently of the influence of temporary fashions."

28. FLO to WAS, November 4, 1893, ibid.

29. Olmsted, "Draft of AIA Report," 20.

30. There is an interesting sidelight to this spirit of collegiality. At the beginning of the work on the Exposition, Olmsted and Burnham had established offices together in the "The Rookery," and the Exposition letterhead had the two listed together (Burnham as Chief of Construction and Olmsted's firm as landscape architects) in equal type size, much smaller than the "World's Columbian Exposition" heading. See circa 1891, ibid., reel 22. Later on, another letterhead appeared, with Burnham and his office given equal billing with the Exposition, while Olmsted's firm was listed lower down and in a much smaller type size. See October 1892, ibid.

31. FLO to Thomas L. Livermore, January 30, 1893, ibid. See also FLO to HKB, June 10, 1886, ibid., reel 20.

32. FLO to JCO, October 27, 1893, ibid., reel 23.

33. FLO to "Partners," July 9(?), 1892, ibid..

34. FLO to CV, undated (summer of 1894), ibid.

35. Schuyler, *Urban Landscape*, 190. Schuyler notes that several of Calvert Vaux's rustic buildings—designed to complement the naturalistic park landscape—were destroyed in this era, while a great many others were constructed "according to the principles of Beaux Arts classicism," transforming the park into "the associational and educational landscape Olmsted and Vaux had guarded against."

36. HWSC to FLO, February 23, 1892, *FLOP*, reel 22. Originally from the Boston area, Cleveland had been a one-time collaborator with Olmsted and Vaux on Prospect Park. During the 1870s and 1880s, he practiced landscape architecture in the Midwest. Roper, *FLO*, 334–35, 394.

Learning that Olmsted continued to travel thousands of miles in his business, the English editor William Robinson commented, "I am astonished at your energy." WR to FLO, December 7, 1892, ibid.

37. W. M. R. French to FLO, November 3, 1892, ibid.

38. WAS to FLO, April 20, 1892, and FLO to "Partners," July 9(?), 1892, ibid., reel 22; WAS to FLO, March 1, 1895, ibid., reel 23.

39. FLO to GP, January 19, 1893, ibid., reel 22; Stevenson, *Park-Maker*, 416. Codman died of appendicitis at the age of twenty-nine. Pinchot had been hired by Olmsted to direct the forestry work at Biltmore.

40. FLO to his "partners," November 1 (dated October 2), 1893; *FLOP*, reel 23.

41. Fabos, Milne, and Weinmayr, *Founder*, 86–89. See also Frederick Gutheim, "Olmsted at Biltmore," in White and Kramer, *Olmsted South*, 240–42; and FLO to "Messrs. Croux & Son," [January 7, 1893], *FLOP*, reel 22.

42. New York Department of Public Parks to FLO, February 28, 1895, ibid., reel 23.

43. FLO to WAS, March 10, 1895, ibid. Olmsted noted in this letter that he

had declined the invitation on Stiles' advice because he presumed that Stiles had counseled with Vaux. But, as it turned out, Stiles himself ended up serving on the committee.

44. Up until the passage cited above, the letter had been typewritten (by Rick, Olmsted noted). This observation, and the rest of the letter, is in Olmsted's own handwriting, obviously the result of considerable reflection. Olmsted commented that he had been dissatisfied with the earlier section and requested that Stiles translate "the metaphoric into plain language" for him. Clearly, Olmsted regretted the extremity of his language; and yet he sent it to Stiles, wanting it on record.

45. For Frederick Gutheim, Olmsted's great effort at Biltmore was "a tragic failure," and the seeds of failure lay in the "too pragmatic orientation" of Olmsted's later years, including an excessive concern with "accommodation of the client's view and the terms laid down by his architects." Gutheim, "Biltmore," 239 and 244.

46. FLO to FLO Jr., July 15, 1895, *FLOP*, reel 23.

47. FLO to CE, May 19, 1895, ibid.

48. FLO to JCO, May 10, 1895, ibid.

49. FLO to FLO Jr., undated (Summer 1895), ibid.

50. FLO to FLO Jr, October 14, 1895, ibid.

51. MCO to "Boys," March 2 and April 10, 1896, ibid.

52. Edward Cowles to FLO Jr, December 5, 1898, ibid., reel 52 (emphasis added).

53. These are the letters discussed in part 1, chapter 3.

Afterword

1. Olmsted & Ward, *Olmsted Family*, 109. Rick had graduated from Harvard in 1894, whereupon his father had apprenticed him at Biltmore.

2. John W. Reps, *Monumental Washington: The Planning and Development of the Capital Center* (Princeton: Princeton University Press, 1967). See also Mario Manieri-Elia, "Toward an 'Imperial City': Daniel H. Burnham and the City Beautiful Movement," in Giorgio Ciuccio, Francesco Dal Co, Mario Manieri-Elia, and Manfredo Tafuri, *The American City: From the Civil War to the New Deal* (Cambridge: MIT Press, 1979), 52–64. The theme for the 1901 AIA convention had its origins in the activities in the previous year of the Senate Committee for the District of Columbia under Senator James McMillan. The committee had originally projected the creation of a great Centennial Boulevard to run through the Mall between the Capitol and the Washington Monument. But the project quickly grew into the notion of both renovating and aggrandizing the entire central part of the city, surrounding the Mall.

3. Reps, *Monumental Washington*, 89 and 139.

4. Schuyler, *Urban Landscape*, 195.

5. The criticism is Werner Hegemann's. It is paraphrased by Francesco Dal

Co in his article "From Park to the Region: Progressive Ideology and the Reform of the American City," in Ciuccio *et al*, *The American City*, 143–291 (see 176).

6. Charles Moore, Rick's colleague on the commission, has described the way in which Burnham, McKim, and Rick worked together. "Olmsted being younger [than the other two] and possesssing a brain fertile in expedients, offered many variations on the themes," Moore writes. See Reps, *Monumental Washington*, 96.

7. Ibid., 91 and 134.

8. Carol A. Christensen, *The American Garden City Movement and the New Town Movement* (Ann Arbor: UMI Research Press, 1986), 33.

9. Cited in Reps, *Monumental Washington*, 50–53.

10. Dal Co, "From Parks to the Region," 160.

11. The report of the Senate Park Commission, submitted January 15, 1902, was coauthored by Rick and Charles Moore. In using it here, however, I will be dealing with the aspects of landscape design that seem to have been mostly Rick's responsibility. The entire section of the report dealing with central Washington is reproduced in Reps, *Monumental Washington*, 112–33.

12. McLaughlin, *Papers*, 3:125–26.

13. Reps, *Monumental Washington*, 137. We should also emphasize Reps's almost inevitable slighting of Calvert Vaux's role in the design of the sunken transverse roads at Central Park.

14. See FLO to General Francis A. Walker, Boston Park Commissioner, February 1895, *FLOP*, reel 23.

15. The description of Olmsted's intention was Calvert Vaux's—from a letter to E. L. Godkin, March 17, 1878, *FLOP*, reel 17.

16. Reps, *Monumental Washington*, 137–38.

17. Cited in ibid., 152.

18. Ibid., 194.

19. Christensen, *American Garden City*, 34–35.

20. Manieri-Elia, "City Beautiful," 108–11. The citations from speeches by Burnham and Matt Barbutt are Manieri-Elia's.

21. Cited in ibid., 102. See also Reps, *Monumental Washington*, xiv; and Christensen, *American Garden City*, 40–41. Mumford also attacked the imposing neo-classic temple of the Lincoln Memorial. "Who lives in that shrine?" he asked. "Lincoln or the men who made it"—that is, the "imperialists" who had made the Spanish-American War. The memorial, he charged, did not represent, as had Lincoln, "the homespun and humane and humorous America." Cited in Manieri-Elia, "City Beautiful," 119. Of course, Mumford was, in his own way, setting up one myth of Lincoln versus another.

22. Manieri-Elia, "City Beautiful," 119–21. Burnham's colleague, McKim, had died three years earlier. Richard Morris Hunt had died in 1895, and Stanford White was shot in 1906.

23. Robert H. Wiebe, *The Search for Order, 1877–1920* (New York: Hill and Wang, 1967), 196–97.

24. Sam Bass Warner, Jr., *The Private City: Philadelphia in Three Periods of its Growth* (Philadelphia: University of Pennsylvania Press, 1971), 219–20.

25. Ibid., 205.

26. Fein, *Cityscape*, 144.

27. Ibid., 352. This report was coauthored with J. James R. Croes.

28. Dal Co, "From Park to the Region," 251.

29. John M. Glenn, Lillian Brandt, and E. Emerson Andrews, *Russell Sage Foundation, 1907–1946*, 2 vols. (New York: Russell Sage Foundation, 1947), pp. 3, 22–23. Horace Coon, *Money to Burn: What the Great American Philanthropies Do With Their Money* (Freeport: Books for Libraries Press, 1938, 1972), pp. 74–75 and 84. The design of "garden cities" such as Forest Hills Gardens owed much to such precedents as the elder Olmsted's Riverside plan. And, as with the Riverside plan, they were usually meant for upper middle-class patronage. See also Joseph L. Arnold, *The New Deal in the Suburbs: A History of the Greenbelt Town Program, 1935–1964* (Columbus: Ohio State University Press, 1971), 7–8. Arnold points out that Rick Olmsted had worked for the U.S. Housing Authority, helping to design towns for defense factory workers during World War I (9).

30. Dal Co, "From Park to the Region," 231–32 and 251–58.

31. George E. Mowry, *The Progressive Era, 1900–20: The Reform Persuasion*. American Historical Association Pamphlets, no. 212, Washington, D.C., 1972), 36.

32. Arthur A. Ekirch, Jr., *Progressivism in America* (New York: New Viewpoints, 1974), 147–52. While directing the landscaping of the Biltmore estate, Olmsted hired Pinchot to manage the forest preserve being created on the thousands of acres at Asheville. Pinchot, born in 1865, was the contemporary of Rick, born in 1870, who worked with him at Biltmore. Pinchot organized a sophisticated information service at the Forestry Bureau that propagandized the cause of conservation and, not incidentally, fostered his own role as its champion. For the first three decades of the century, Pinchot also served as professor of forestry at Yale. Yet he achieved real public authority only through election to political office, as Governor of Pennsylvania in 1923–1927 and 1931–1935. Even in this role, Sam Bass Warner points out, he was unable to accomplish real economic and social reform—despite the urgency of the Great Depression during his second term—because he was unable to resolve the competing claims of the public needs with the private interests in the state. *CDAB*, 787–88; Wiebe, *Search for Order*, 202; Warner, *Private City*, 219–20.

33. Cranz, *Politics of Park Design*, 101, 121, and 125.

34. Robert A. Caro, *The Power Broker: Robert Moses and the Fall of New York* (New York: Vintage, 1975). Paul Goldberger, "Robert Moses: Patron Saint of Public Places," *New York Times*, December 18, 1988, 38H and 43H. Roger Starr, "Still Debating Robert Moses," *New York Times*, August 18, 1988, editorial page.

35. Zaitzevsky, *Boston Parks*, 78; Jeffrey Simpson and Mary Ellen W. Hern, *Art of the Olmsted Landscape: His Works in New York City* (New York City Landmarks Commission and the Arts Publisher, 1981), 23; Cranz, *Politics*, 101. The justifiable criticism of the Moses administration is by Bob Makla of the Friends of Central Park, and is reported in Peter Canby, "Friends of the Parks: A New York-based alliance fights to restore Olmsted's vision," reprinted from *Horticulture*

59, 10 (1983), and distributed by the Greensward Foundation. See also Barlow and Alex, *Olmsted's New York*, 49–51.

36. Stephen Rettig, "Influences Across the Water: Olmsted and England," in Kelly, Guillet, and Hern, *Olmsted Landscape*, 85.

37. Canby, "Friends of the Parks"; Thomas J. Lueck, "Battling Urban Development With Parks," *New York Times*, March 18, 1987, B1; Kate Simon, "Bringing New Life to the Parks," *New York Times Magazine*, April 26, 1987, 22–25, 39; Cranz, *Politics*, 135–46; Zaitzevsky, *Boston Parks*, 209–12. Among the features of this revival, as reported by Zaitzevsky and Cranz, are the massive public events and "happenings"—sponsored by the city and by private corporations—staged in Central Park. Cranz dates this phenomenon to the Lindsay administration. She cites Lindsay's commissioner of parks as saying that "electrified programming was . . . the only way to attract enough people to the parks to make them safe." To this thinking, Makla (in Canby's article) responds: "Ninety-five percent of the people who come to Central Park come for unstructured, unorganized activity, but the Parks Department persists in trying to draw crowds for special events. It's simple. If you advertise hoopla, you draw hoopla." We might add that such events are probably a good example of Olmsted's "gregarious" form of recreation, and more democratic than ever before, but are terribly destructive of the pastoral park, which offers the "neighborly" form of recreation that fosters communitiveness.

38. Canby, "Friends." The hospitality of the Koch administration is also revealed in the attempt to implement a Master Plan created by the Conservancy in partnership with the city, and in the activities of the current Parks Commissioner, Henry J. Stern. See Simon, "New Life." One happy example of the fruits of this attention is the recently completed restoration of the Terrace Bridge and Bethesda Fountain, that treasure of Central Park, created by Calvert Vaux with Jacob Wrey Mould. An editorial in the *New York Times*, October 25, 1987, celebrated the results of this partnership: "Central Park is back, a place of pleasure and beauty. A renaissance has taken place" (E22).

39. Ada Louise Huxtable, "Creeping Gigantism in Manhattan," *New York Times*, May 17, 1987, section 2, 1 and 36.

40. Paul Goldberger, "Fighting City Hall on the Size of a Huge Tower," *New York Times*, October 18, 1987, H1 and 41. The article is about opposition to a proposed enormous complex at Columbus Circle, which would cast "a shadow so huge that it is estimated to cut all the way across Central Park in late afternoon." See also Paul Goldberger, "Square Deal for Columbus Circle?" *New York Times*, October 18, 1987, 2:1 and 41.

41. Sutton, *Civilizing*, 81.

42. Brendan Gill, "The Sky Line: The Malady of Gigantism," *New Yorker*, January 9, 1989, 73–77.

43. Jan Morris, "The Future Looks Familiar," *New York Times Magazine*, part 2, April 26, 1987.

44. *FLOP*, reel 41.

Index